SAN XAVIER TO SAN AGUSTÍN

SAN XAVIER TO SAN AGUSTÍN

An Overview of Cultural Resources for the
Paseo de las Iglesias Feasibility Study, Pima County, Arizona

♦ **Scott O'Mack and Eric Eugene Klucas** ♦

with contributions by Pamela Asbury-Smith, Matt C. Bischoff,
S. Greg Johnson, Charles R. Riggs, and Matthew A. Sterner

Prepared for the
Pima County Administrator's Office
Archaeology and Historic Preservation
201 N. Stone Ave., 7th floor
Tucson, AZ 85701-1207

Contract No. 16-04-S-125897-0599, Work Order No. 4FPDLI
Contract No. 07-04-S-130897-0602, Work Order No. 4FPDLI
Contract No. 25-64-S-134069-0404, Work Order No. 4FPDLI

Technical Series 81
Statistical Research, Inc.
Tucson, Arizona

Statistical Research Technical Series

Series editor: Jeffrey H. Altschul
Production manager: Toni Tallman
Graphics manager: Cynthia Elsner Hayward
Production assistants: Karen Barber, Peg Robbins

Cover design: Lynne Yamaguchi and Cynthia Elsner Hayward
Front cover photograph: Mission San Xavier del Bac, view to the northwest.
Photograph by Leo Goldschmidt, 1887. Reproduced with the permission of
the Arizona Historical Society, Tucson.

This report was originally published as Technical Report 01-72.

Published by Statistical Research, Inc.
P.O. Box 31865
Tucson, AZ 85751-1865

ISBN 1-879442-80-9

First printing: July 2004
2 4 5 3 1

Typeset and printed in the United States of America.
Printed on acid-free paper.

CONTENTS

LIST OF FIGURES

LIST OF TABLES

ACKNOWLEDGMENTS

The authors extend their thanks to the many people who contributed to the Paseo de las Iglesias overview. We are especially grateful for the various contributions of our colleagues at Statistical Research, Inc. Chuck Riggs helped write the descriptions of prehistoric sites in the study area. Matt Bischoff wrote much of the section on transportation in Chapter 4. Matt Sterner wrote most of the section on mills, brick making, and entertainment in the same chapter. Pam Asbury-Smith helped pull together the General Land Office (GLO) information and prepared the first draft of the GLO map. She also helped with the archaeological site file research at the Arizona State Museum (ASM). Greg Johnson checked the ASM site locational and survey information against the available original survey reports and also helped edit the tables, the maps, and the references cited section. Cindy Elsner Hayward and Lois Kain prepared the numerous graphics. Teresita Majewski, principal investigator for the overview, oversaw the research and writing and provided frequent and timely encouragement. And Lynne Yamaguchi, Karen Barber, and Peg Robbins assembled the drafts and final of overall product, complex and difficult tasks made even more difficult by the time constraints we placed on them.

We would also like to thank the staff of the following Tucson institutions for their assistance in researching one or another aspect of the history of the Paseo de las Iglesias study area: the Arizona Historical Society, Southern Arizona Division; Special Collections at the University of Arizona Library; the Arizona State Museum; and the Tucson field office of the Bureau of Land Management.

Finally, our thanks go to Homer Thiel for various leads on historical-archaeological research in the study area, to Allen Dart for access to an in-press report on the Herreras Farmstead, and to Linda Mayro, Cultural Resources Coordinator for Pima County and our contact for the Paseo de las Iglesias project. Linda has been helpful and understanding throughout the preparation of the overview.

CHAPTER 1

Introduction

In April 1998, the Pima County (Arizona) Administrator's Office presented a plan for cultural and environmental restoration of a section of the Santa Cruz River valley near Tucson. The proposed project, called Paseo de las Iglesias, would restore and enhance the riparian environment of the Santa Cruz River along an approximately 8-mile stretch between Mission San Xavier del Bac and the archaeological site of its dependent settlement, Mission San Agustín del Tucson. In recognition of the important role of this area in the prehistory and history of the Tucson Basin, the project would include measures to protect and interpret cultural resources along the river, with an emphasis on how these resources reflected the movement of people along the river corridor—hence, the name Paseo de las Iglesias, "Walk of the Churches."

In 2000, Pima County designated Paseo de las Iglesias an element of its Sonoran Desert Conservation Plan, a major conservation planning effort designed to protect selected natural and cultural resources in eastern Pima County from future impacts caused from urban sprawl. In January 2001, following an expression of interest by the U.S. Army Corps of Engineers in assisting with Paseo de las Iglesias, Pima County entered into an agreement with the Corps to conduct a feasibility study for the project. Statistical Research, Inc. (SRI), was contracted by Pima County in June 2001 to prepare the current cultural resources overview of the Paseo de las Iglesias project area as part of the larger feasibility study. As the lead agency for the project, the Corps is responsible for compliance with Section 106 of the National Historic Preservation Act, which requires federal agencies to consider the impacts of their proposed undertakings on archaeological and historic properties eligible or potentially eligible for listing in the National Register of Historic Places (NRHP). Preparation of this overview is the first step in the compliance process, providing an account of previously identified archaeological and historical-period properties in the project area, a context for evaluating their significance, and recommendations for further field study.

Project Setting

The Santa Cruz River has its source on the southern slopes of the Canelo Hills in southeastern Arizona. For its first 20 miles or so, it flows south, entering Mexico, then almost immediately turns west and north to flow back into Arizona. It continues generally northward for about 60 miles to the Tucson Basin, where it runs south to north immediately west of downtown Tucson (Figure 1). Just beyond (north of) Tucson, the river continues northwest for another 75 miles to its confluence with the Gila River (Betancourt 1990:29–31).

Historically, the Santa Cruz River from its headwaters to a point near Tubac (about 40 miles south of Tucson) was a perennial stream, fed by runoff from the mountains that stand near it—the Patagonia, Tumacácori, and Santa Rita Mountains—and by valley springs. Just north of Tubac, at a point immediately east of Canoa Ranch, the flow in the Santa Cruz sank into the ground. Except for periods of heavy rain, the bed of the Santa Cruz north of Tubac was dry down to the point where it was fed water by

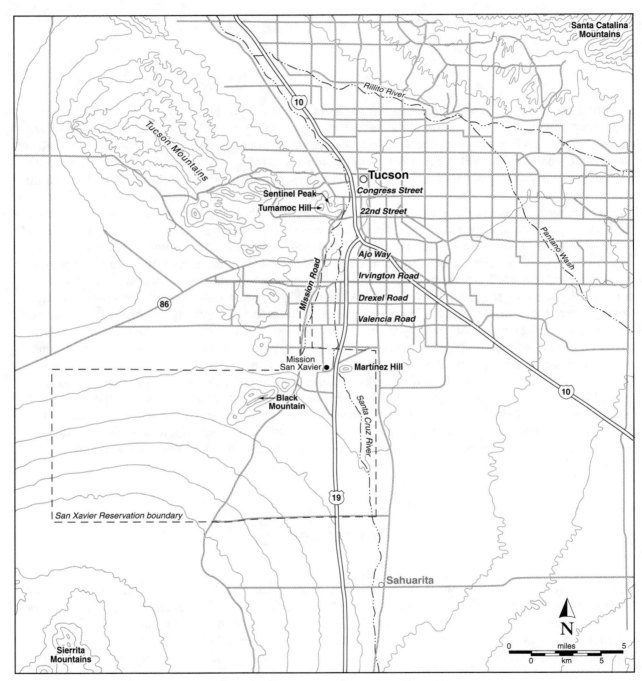

Figure 1. Map of Tucson, Arizona, and vicinity.

springs at Punta de Agua, a few miles south of Mission San Xavier del Bac. Near the mission, the water again sank into the ground, then reappeared a few miles to the north, only to sink again a mile farther down. From Tubac to Tucson, and for several miles downstream, the Santa Cruz followed a shallow, un-entrenched bed that frequently shifted its alignment depending on the intensity of precipitation. Between Punta de Agua and Tucson, the Santa Cruz created less a river valley than a *cienega*, or marsh, fed by the springs south of Mission San Xavier and other springs just south of Sentinel Peak, the prominent hill just west of modern Tucson (Betancourt 1990:42–58). Along the Paseo de las Iglesias, the Santa Cruz re-mained a shallow, marshy, meandering stream until the 1880s, when flooding and erosion, exacerbated by efforts to exploit the river's flow for irrigation and other purposes, led to the deep entrenchment of the river evident today.

Before the current entrenched channel was established, a second shallow streambed, also fed by springs south of Mission San Xavier, ran immediately west of what is now the Santa Cruz. On most early maps, this second stream is in fact labeled the Santa Cruz, reflecting the fact that not far south of the mission, the eastern stream was not often visible on the surface, so either stream might be viewed as the main branch of the river. The rapid erosion of both channels during the late nineteenth century and associated problems with flooding led to the construction of a ditch, flanked by dikes, that diverted the flow from the western channel into the eastern channel. This project, completed in 1915 and now known as the West Branch diversion channel, is located a few miles upstream of San Xavier in Township 16 South, Range 13 East, Sections 1 and 12 (Betancourt 1990:143–146). Since its completion, the eastern channel has been known as the Santa Cruz River proper, and the western channel has been called the West Branch of the Santa Cruz.

The Area of Potential Effects and the Study Area

The area of potential effects (APE) for the Paseo de las Iglesias project consists of an approximately 1,750-foot-wide corridor centered on the current entrenched channel of the Santa Cruz from a point due east of Mission San Xavier downstream to the Congress Street Bridge, just north of the Mission San Agustín archaeological site and immediately west of downtown Tucson (Figure 2). The APE also includes a 400-foot-wide corridor centered on a portion of the West Branch from Valencia Road down to the point where it now drains into the Santa Cruz. This section of the West Branch represents a recent truncation of its earlier channel, which still runs for another 3 miles downstream to a confluence with the Santa Cruz just south of Sentinel Peak. The APE also includes another corridor of the same width along a channelized portion of Julian Wash, from the east bank of the Santa Cruz to the Interstate 19 right-of-way (ROW).

The study area for this overview encompasses all of the Paseo de las Iglesias APE, plus an area to the east and west of it that corresponds roughly with the limits of the Santa Cruz Valley (see Figure 2). The study area is bounded on the north by Congress Street, on the east by Interstates 10 and 19, on the south by an imaginary line passing just south of Mission San Xavier del Bac, and on the west by Mission Road (except that where Mission Road meets the south side of Sentinel Peak, the boundary extends directly north to Congress Street). The study area boundary was established primarily to limit the scope of our archaeological site file search. We expand our discussion beyond the boundary many times in the over-view, as required by the subject matter.

3

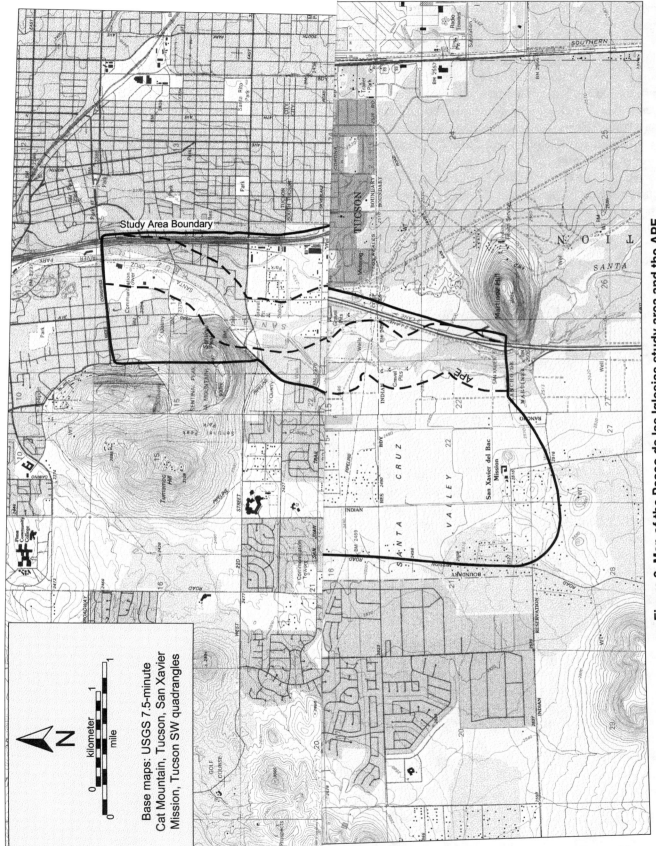

Figure 2. Map of the Paseo de las Iglesias study area and the APE.

4

Organization of the Overview

The overview consists of five chapters, including this introduction. Chapter 2 is a brief history of archaeological, historical, and ethnographic research on southern Arizona, outlining a context for future research in the study area. Chapter 3 is a survey of Native American culture history in southern Arizona, as documented both archaeologically and ethnographically, with an emphasis on the study area. Chapter 4 surveys Euroamerican culture history in the same region, with a similar emphasis on the study area. Chapter 5 presents our summary of information on previously recorded archaeological sites and archaeological survey coverage in the study area, including detailed descriptions of 11 archaeological sites (9 prehistoric and 2 historical-period sites).

The overview also has an appendix consisting of descriptions of sites previously recorded in the study area (excluding the 11 major sites described in Chapter 5). Note that throughout the overview, including the appendix, all archaeological site numbers are Arizona State Museum (ASM) designations.

As a final note, we generally avoid the term "Papago" when referring to the Tohono O'odham or any aspect of their culture, out of respect for their own decision, in 1981, to change the name of their tribe from the Papago Indian Tribe to the Tohono O'odham Nation. However, we do use Papago when referring to historical entities such as the Papago Indian Reservation or to the pottery made by the Tohono O'odham in the historical period, for which archaeologists have long used a number of type names that include the word.

CHAPTER 2

History of Research

This chapter outlines the history of research into the prehistory, history, and ethnography of the Paseo de las Iglesias study area. Our emphasis is on the place of the study area in the wider research context of southern Arizona culture history. As a part of the middle Santa Cruz River valley, the Paseo de las Iglesias study area has been a focus of human life in southern Arizona for at least 12,000 years and has witnessed virtually every aspect of human use of the wider region. Not surprisingly, the study area has played a significant role, occasionally a leading one, in the development of scholarly thinking about southern Arizona culture history. Our goal in this chapter is to outline the context within which future archaeological, historical, and ethnographic research along the Paseo de las Iglesias will unavoidably take place.

We mention individual cultural resources within the Paseo de las Iglesias study area many times in the discussion that follows, but we reserve discussion of the research carried out at individual sites in the study area for Chapter 5. In the same chapter, we provide an inventory of all previously identified cultural resources in the study area and a discussion of previous cultural resource survey coverage.

The Archaeology of Prehistory

The Paseo de las Iglesias study area encompasses, partially or wholly, several large, well-known prehistoric village sites, most notably the Valencia, Dakota Wash, Julian Wash, and West Branch sites. It also encompasses or is in close proximity to several other important, less intensively studied prehistoric sites, ranging from the Clearwater site, an extensive Late Archaic (Early Agricultural) settlement at the north end of the study area, to the Martínez Hill site, a large Classic period ruin just outside the southeastern corner of the study area. All of these sites have contributed in important ways to our understanding of the history of human settlement in southern Arizona, and all have the potential to make further contributions. At the same time, archaeological surveys of widely varying size and purpose have been conducted in much of the study area, recording a diverse set of prehistoric limited-activity and special-use sites. Identification and study of these smaller sites have also contributed in important ways to the study of southern Arizona prehistory, especially the study of changing patterns of settlement and land use. In this section, we consider how studies of the range of prehistoric sites in the study area fit into interpretations of southern Arizona prehistory as a whole, how archaeological research along the Paseo de las Iglesias has influenced, and has been influenced by, the study of archaeology in southern Arizona as a whole.

Early Reconnaissance and Excavation in the Tucson Area

It did not constitute archaeological research in the strictest sense, but one of the earliest observations of prehistoric ruins in the Tucson Basin was made by Adolph Bandelier when he passed through the area in the 1880s en route to the Sierra Madre. Bandelier noted the remains of a "few scattered houses of the detached dwelling type," located 16 miles east of Tucson at "Estanque Verde" (Bandelier 1890:470–471). He described the associated pottery as typical of southern Arizona.

Some 30 years after Bandelier's brief visit, Ellsworth Huntington, an associate of the Carnegie Desert Laboratory at Tumamoc Hill (see Chapter 4), visited several major sites along the Santa Cruz River, including the Martínez Hill, St. Mary's, Jaynes Village, and Hodges sites. His most important contribution during these informal visits was his conclusion that the alluvial deposits along the Santa Cruz River were geologically recent. Huntington argued that there was a high likelihood of cultural deposits buried beneath the alluvium and that sites along the course of the river may not be readily visible on the surface. This hypothesis has since been substantiated numerous times, perhaps most dramatically in recent excavations by Desert Archaeology, Inc., of Tucson, along the Interstate 10 corridor (Gregory 1999; Mabry, ed. 1998; Mabry et al. 1997).

By the mid-1920s, more-formal archaeological investigations within the Tucson Basin were beginning to take place. Much of this early work was directed by Byron Cummings, then-head of the Department of Archaeology at the University of Arizona. In part as a means of providing training for students, Cummings directed excavations at several sites in the Tucson Basin, as well as conducting reconnaissance surveys of the eastern portion of the basin. Sites investigated by Cummings and his students included Martínez Hill Ruin, the Tanque Verde Ruin, and the University Ruin. Work at the last site continued intermittently into the 1930s under the direction of Emil Haury. More-extensive excavations were carried out in 1940–1941 under the direction of Julian Hayden, with aid from the National Park Service (NPS) and the Civilian Conservation Corps (Hayden 1957).

The Era of Private Research Institutions

The early 1920s saw the establishment of three private research institutions that would have a profound impact on the course of archaeological research in the Southwest, including the Tucson Basin, for decades to come. The first was the Museum of Northern Arizona (MNA) in Flagstaff, founded by Harold S. Colton and Mary-Russell Colton in 1928. Established in part as a response to the archaeological activities of eastern institutions, which shipped most of their collections out of state, the MNA was dedicated to the art and science of northern Arizona with a focus on the interdisciplinary study of human-land relationships. Perhaps the most enduring aspect of the early research of the MNA was the work on ceramic typology conducted by Colton and his colleague Lyndon Hargrave (Colton and Hargrave 1937). This taxonomy, reflecting Colton's training as a biologist, remains the standard classificatory system for the ceramics of northern Arizona. Colton attempted to create a similar typology for the ceramic wares of southern Arizona, but poor health prevented him from completing this project.

The activities of the second private research institution had a more direct impact on southern Arizona. Gila Pueblo, founded in 1928 by Harold Gladwin and Winifred Macurdy (who later married Gladwin), focused much of its research efforts on the desert regions of the Southwest. Archaeologists from Gila Pueblo, led by E. B. Sayles, were the first to report on the Archaic cultures of southern Arizona. In their pursuit of the spatial boundaries of the "red-on-buff" culture, Gila Pueblo archaeologists scoured the greater Southwest, from Texas to California and from Utah to northern Mexico. In the Tucson Basin, much of this work was carried out by Frank Midvale, who first recorded many of the large sites known today. This reconnaissance work by Gila Pueblo, along with pioneering excavations at such sites as Snaketown (Gladwin et al. 1937) and Roosevelt 9:6 (Haury 1932), both directed by Emil Haury, served to define the Hohokam culture.

One of the most important projects directed by Gila Pueblo in the Tucson Basin was the excavation of the Hodges site (AZ AA:12:18), located at the confluence of the Santa Cruz and Rillito Rivers. Work at this large village, then referred to as the Gravel Pit Ruin, was begun in 1936 under the direction of

Carl Miller (Betancourt 1978a:7). Gila Pueblo began its work at the site in 1937, with Isabel Kelly directing the excavations. During the course of the project, Kelly noted the similarities and dissimilarities in the ceramic collection when compared with contemporaneous materials for the Phoenix Basin and, in response, developed a ceramic typology for the Tucson Basin that is still used today. Unfortunately, Kelly's tenure with Gila Pueblo ended in 1938, delaying the publication of her work. In the 1950s, James Officer, then a graduate student in the Department of Anthropology at the University of Arizona, began the work of compiling Kelly's document for publication, but he did not complete the task. The volume was finally edited by Gayle Hartmann and published as an Anthropological Paper of the University of Arizona in 1978 (Kelly 1978).

The same year that Gladwin and Macurdy established Gila Pueblo, William Shirley Fulton and Rose Hayden Fulton founded the last of the three privately funded institutions in the Southwest. The Amerind Foundation was established in Dragoon, Arizona, with the stated purpose "to increase the world's knowledge of ancient man by excavation and collection, by study and analysis, and to display and publish the resultant artifacts and data for public enlightenment" (Di Peso 1967). Fulton hired Carl Tuthill, then a student at the University of Arizona, to supervise the early field endeavors, including excavations at the Gleeson site (Fulton and Tuthill 1940). This work laid the foundation for the primary research focus of the Amerind Foundation—studying the cultural identity of the prehistoric inhabitants of southeastern Arizona.

The debate over the cultural identity of the prehistoric inhabitants of southeastern Arizona pitted the archaeologists of Gila Pueblo against their counterparts at the Amerind Foundation. The position of Gila Pueblo was that the early inhabitants of southeastern Arizona were Mogollon, a culture defined by Haury in 1936. Fulton, who had earlier proposed the term "Dragoon" to refer to archaeological materials observed in the vicinity of Texas Canyon, saw the prehistoric peoples of southeastern Arizona as "basically Hohokam with little Mogollon influence" (Fulton 1940:63). Later, Charles Di Peso, hired by Fulton to replace Tuthill at the Amerind Foundation, proposed a third alternative. Di Peso argued that rather than being a version of a previously identified archaeological culture, the prehistoric peoples of southeastern Arizona represented a discrete cultural tradition of their own, one he called O'otam. The O'otam, in Di Peso's view, occupied the nonriverine desert regions of southern Arizona. The Hohokam, he argued, were an immigrant group from Mexico that settled along the Salt and Gila Rivers, establishing large villages and extensive irrigation systems. The Hohokam culture "dominated" the O'otam until ca. A.D. 1300, when the Hohokam were forced back into Mexico and the O'otam reemerged during what became known as the Classic period (Di Peso 1956). Far from resolving the issue, Di Peso's proposal simply fueled the debate, with the competing positions becoming further entrenched.

Few excavations were conducted in the Tucson area during the 1940s, when archaeological investigations of the area were largely limited to surface reconnaissance. During this period, Emil Haury and his students surveyed much of the Empire Valley, the results of which were presented by Earl Swanson in a master's thesis (Swanson 1951). In 1941, Edward Danson conducted an archaeological survey along the Santa Cruz River from its headwaters north to the town of Tubac. These data also were presented in a master's thesis (Danson 1946). Nearly a decade later, Paul Frick extended the coverage of the Santa Cruz River valley through his survey of the middle reaches of the river from Tubac north to Sahuarita (Frick 1954).

The hiatus in excavations ended with work at a portion of the Zanardelli site in 1948 (Wright and Gerald 1950) and at Mission San Agustín in the early 1950s (Smiley et al. 1953; Wasley 1956). The late 1950s also saw the first archaeological investigations carried out at Mission San Xavier del Bac, with survey work on nearby Black Mountain (Fontana et al. 1959) and excavation adjacent to the extant mission buildings (Fontana et al. 1962; Robinson 1963). The survey on Black Mountain identified rock terraces (trincheras), enclosures, and petroglyphs similar to those observed on Martínez Hill and Tumamoc Hill. The excavations by Fontana et al. (1962) adjacent to the mission were geared toward refining the local ceramic sequence.

The New Archaeology and Cultural Resource Management

The archaeological investigations described above were focused largely on addressing questions of culture history—defining the spatial parameters of archaeological "cultures" and building regional chronologies. This characterized American archaeology until the early 1960s, when, prompted in part by Walter W. Taylor's polemical 1948 publication *A Study of Archaeology,* several scholars began to extend the focus of archaeological research to include investigation of the processes whereby cultures adapted to their physical surroundings and how these adaptations changed through time. Under the general rubric of the "new archaeology," the study of cultural processes came to dominate American archaeology, influencing both the direction of research and the kinds of data that were collected and analyzed. Projects emphasized interdisciplinary research, with environmental data taking a prominent role in archaeological interpretation.

Concurrent with the ascendence of processual archaeology among American archaeologists was an equally important transition in how archaeological projects were selected and funded. Beginning with the Interagency Salvage Program of the NPS and the Reservoir Salvage Act of 1960 (King et al. 1977), federal monies became available for archaeological research. In 1955, the Arizona Highway Salvage program was established at ASM. For the next 26 years, archaeologists surveyed more than 2,000 linear miles of ROW in advance of road construction and improvement, recording hundreds of cultural properties. Unfortunately, few of these sites were excavated, and reports on even fewer were fully published.

In 1965 and 1966, ASM engaged in salvage excavations at 10 sites in the southern portion of the Tucson Basin for the Arizona Highway Department under the auspices of the Arizona Highway Salvage program (Greenleaf 1975). All but two of these sites were within the San Xavier District of the Tohono O'odham Nation (then the Papago Indian Reservation), a few miles south of Mission San Xavier del Bac. Collectively referred to as Punta de Agua, the sites included both prehistoric and historical-period properties (Greenleaf 1975:11). Data recovery operations were conducted at six of the 10 sites. Excavations at the prehistoric sites produced data that allowed for the refinement of the Tucson Basin ceramic chronology first proposed by Kelly from her work at the Hodges site (Greenleaf 1975). These data reinforced Kelly's observation of a divergence in ceramic traditions from the sequence established for the Gila Basin beginning with the Colonial period, insofar as the Tucson Basin materials shared characteristics of both the Gila Basin and the Mogollon area (Greenleaf 1975:108; Kelly 1978:3).

With the passage of the National Historic Preservation Act in 1966, the National Environmental Policy Act of 1969, and the Archaeological Resource Protection Act of 1979, the pace of contract archaeology accelerated in the American Southwest, because of both rapid growth and the extent of public lands. In response, cultural resource management (CRM) divisions were established at ASM, Arizona State University, and MNA. Archaeologists were also added to the staffs of several federal agencies, including the Bureau of Land Management and the various national forests. With the enactment of CRM laws, archaeology in the United States became largely reactive in nature, with samples often dictated by management needs rather than research agendas. This being said, the increased pace of archaeological data collection and research prompted by the new legislation resulted in significant advances in our understanding of prehistory, especially in the traditionally overlooked areas of the desert Southwest.

The Tucson Basin was one of the areas that benefited greatly from the expanded attention mandated by the new cultural resource laws. Many of the early CRM projects in the basin were surveys, greatly expanding the inventory of known sites. In 1978, the City of Tucson contracted with ASM to survey a 22-km-long (13.6-mile) section of the Santa Cruz River prior to the establishment of the Santa Cruz Riverpark, part of a comprehensive plan of urban improvements (Betancourt 1978a, 1978b). At about the same time, the NPS undertook a survey in the eastern portion of the basin within Saguaro National Monument (Simpson and Wells 1983, 1984). In addition to surveys, ASM engaged in several excavation projects in the Tucson Basin, notably one at the San Xavier Bridge site (Ravesloot 1987a, 1987b) and a reinvestigation of the Hodges site (Layhe 1986). Private CRM firms also were active in the Tucson Basin during this period. During the mid-1980s, the Institute for American Research (the precursor of Desert Archaeology) conducted excavations at the West Branch site (Huntington 1986), the Tanque Verde Wash site (Elson 1986), the Dakota Wash site (Craig 1988), and the Valencia site (Doelle 1985). Three of these—West Branch, Dakota Wash, and Valencia—are located within the Paseo de las Iglesias study area, and so their research history is discussed in more detail here.

The West Branch site (AZ AA:16:3), a large Sedentary period village located along the West Branch of the Santa Cruz River, has a long history of research. Unfortunately, much of the early interest given to the site was in the form of areal surveys that, in part because of incomplete publication, resulted in the assignment of several separate site numbers to what was likely a single community. The earliest of these visits to the site was by Frank Midvale under the auspices of Gila Pueblo. In 1929, Midvale produced a sketch map and provided a brief description of the site, to which he gave the Gila Pueblo number Tucson:7:1. The site was given its first ASM designation in 1942, when M. A. Brown completed an ASM site card with the designation AZ AA:16:3 (Doelle and Huntington 1986:19). Brown described the site as having three mounds, located north of Irvington Road and west of Mission Road near the Tucson Mountains. In 1955, three students from the University of Arizona recorded a series of five discrete sites in the vicinity of the West Branch site, designated AZ AA:16:14, 18, 19, 20, and 21 (Doelle and Huntington 1986:19). In 1960, Bernard Fontana and John Ingmanson recorded a site described as a Hohokam village with a ball court at the northwest corner of the intersection of Irvington and Mission Roads (Doelle and Huntington 1986:19). They designated this site AZ AA:16:25.

The confusion created by the assignment of multiple site numbers to what is now believed to have been a single settlement was exacerbated in the mid-1970s with the assigning of site numbers AZ AA:16:45 and 46 to portions of the site recorded in the 1950s (Grady 1975). The final recording of the site was accomplished during the Santa Cruz Riverpark survey (Betancourt 1978b). During the first phase of the project, AZ AA:16:45 and 46 were revisited and their boundaries were redefined. An additional site, AZ AA:16:48, was recorded near the southern end of AZ AA:16:3. This small site encompassed a surface scatter of lithic artifacts and a number of bedrock mortars.

Private development and the widening of Mission Road in the early 1980s prompted the first excavations at the complex of sites now referred to as the West Branch community (Huntington 1986). Desert Archaeology conducted data recovery operations for both the Pima County Department of Transportation and the Estes Corporation at two loci of the site, referred to as the Wyoming Street and Irvington Road loci, as well as at the Dakota Wash site (see below). The excavations at the Wyoming Street and Irvington Road loci exposed deposits dating primarily to the early and middle Rincon phase.

The Dakota Wash site (AZ AA:16:49) was first identified during the Santa Cruz Riverpark survey as a large, multicomponent Hohokam village occupying the toe of an alluvial fan at the confluence of the fan and the West Branch of the Santa Cruz River (Betancourt 1978b; Craig 1988). The site was revisited by Pima Community College as part of their survey of Midvale Park (Stephen and Hewitt 1980). During this project, a preliminary map of the site was made, and two cremations were excavated. In 1983, Pima Community College returned to the site for limited testing, determining that the subsurface deposits were largely intact and recovering ceramic data confirming previous pronouncements that the site was occupied from the Pioneer through early Classic periods (Craig 1988). Later excavations at the site suggested that, contrary to the conclusion derived from the survey data, the occupation of the Dakota Wash site dated primarily to the Pioneer and Colonial periods (Craig 1988), temporal components that were largely lacking from the nearby West Branch site. This led to the hypothesis that, rather than representing separate villages, the West Branch and Dakota Wash sites may be better characterized as temporally distinct components of the same community (Doelle and Huntington 1986:21).

The Valencia site (AZ BB:13:15) is a large pre-Classic Hohokam village site located east of the current channel of the Santa Cruz River (Elson and Doelle 1986:1). As was the case with the West Branch site, several ASM site numbers have been assigned to different loci of what is now interpreted as a single settlement. The site was first recorded as AZ BB:13:15 by William Wasley, who was a member of the

ASM staff at the time. The area was surveyed again in 1976 by James Hewitt, who divided AZ BB:13:15 into two sites based on an apparent break in the surface artifact scatter (Elson and Doelle 1986:4). The southern portion of the site retained the AZ BB:13:15 designation, and the northern area was given the new number AZ BB:13:74. Test excavations were conducted in the northern locus in 1978 (Schott 1978). All of the temporally diagnostic sherds recovered during these excavations were Rincon phase in association. Similar testing was carried out in the southern locus in 1979 by Complete Archaeological Services Association (CASA) under contract to the City of Tucson (Hammack and Bradley 1979). Subsequent data recovery operations conducted by CASA documented a Late Archaic component, represented by a pair of pit houses, several Rincon phase houses, and two Tanque Verde phase cremations.

Further archaeological investigations were conducted at the Valencia site during the 1980s. In 1981, Henry Wallace identified what was probably a ball court at the western margin of the site (Doelle 1985: 19). In 1982 and 1983, the Institute for American Research conducted test excavations and data recovery for the City of Tucson in anticipation of the construction of Calle Santa Cruz, a four-lane road planned along the western margin of the site. During these investigations, several pit houses dating to the Rincon phase were excavated, as well features dating to the Late Archaic, Pioneer, and Colonial periods, attesting to the impressive time depth at the site.

With ASM's withdrawal from active CRM research in 1990, the burden for federal-, state-, and county-mandated archaeological work in southern Arizona fell largely to private firms. This work was accelerated through the enactment of new legislation at both the federal and state levels. In 1990, the Native American Graves Protection and Repatriation Act (NAGPRA) was enacted, mandating the reburial of human remains held in museum collections and the repatriation of sacred objects to federally recognized Indian tribes. The act also affected the direction of future research on human remains and burial goods, requiring tribal input throughout the process. Although NAGPRA applied only to projects on federal lands or funded with federal monies, similar laws were enacted by the State of Arizona, affecting state lands and state-funded projects. Tribal input in the NAGPRA process was also enhanced by the establishment of CRM programs administered by the tribes themselves.

The decade of the 1990s saw an explosion of archaeological activities in the Tucson Basin. Road improvement and development projects sponsored by the Arizona Department of Transportation (ADOT), Pima County, the U.S. Army Corps of Engineers, and others, resulted in expanded survey coverage and excavations at a diverse set of archaeological sites from small, seasonal settlements to large villages. Several areas that had not been intensively explored in the past, such as the heavily alluviated floodplain of the Santa Cruz River, became the focus of extensive investigation. Data generated during these projects have led to lively debate concerning the culture history of the Tucson Basin and the cultural affinity of its prehistoric inhabitants. The following summarizes the results of a sample of these projects.

One of the most extensive survey projects undertaken in the Tucson Basin was the Northern Tucson Basin Survey (Fish et al. 1992). This survey centered on the area between the Tortolita and Tucson Mountains and encompassed large areas of *bajada,* the floodplain of the Santa Cruz River, and areas around the Picacho and Silverbell Mountains. This project resulted in the delineation of the Marana Platform mound community and the investigation of Cerro Prieto, a large *trincheras* site in the Los Robles area (Downum 1993).

Pima County–sponsored improvements along Mission Road required additional excavation at the West Branch site. This work, carried out by SRI, expanded on the previous work by Desert Archaeology, testing its hypothesis that the site was an important locus of pottery manufacture for the Tucson Basin. SRI uncovered evidence of ceramic production and additional data demonstrating the importance of local clay sources in the production process (Altschul et al. 1996). The construction of the Desert Vista Campus of Pima Community College gave Desert Archaeology a similar opportunity to revisit a previously excavated site. This project affected a portion of the Valencia site, previously investigated by Desert Archaeology (Doelle 1985). The Desert Vista project afforded the opportunity to investigate the early ceramic period occupation of the site (Wallace 2003).

Two separate projects, one conducted under the auspices of Pima County and the other sponsored by ADOT, led to archaeological investigations of portions of the Julian Wash site, a large multicomponent village located near the intersection of Interstates 10 and 19. In 1992 and 1993, SRI conducted data recovery operations on a section of the site between 10th Avenue and Interstate 19, along the channelized portion of the wash (Whittlesey 1999). This work was carried out for Pima County and the U.S. Army Corps of Engineers in advance of the construction of a park along the wash. A larger section of the site closer to the Santa Cruz River was investigated by Desert Archaeology for ADOT in advance of improvements to Interstate 19. These two projects collected important data on the early Colonial period, a time period that had not been widely studied in the Tucson Basin.

Perhaps the most-extensive excavations conducted during the 1990s in the Tucson Basin were sponsored by ADOT as part of improvements to Interstate 10, along a stretch of the Santa Cruz River several miles downstream from the Paseo de las Iglesias study area. This work, carried out by Desert Archaeology, included the excavation of several substantial Archaic period settlements, most notably the Santa Cruz Bend and Los Pozos sites. Prior to this work, the Archaic period was known primarily from seasonal camps and limited-activity sites away from the river (Gregory 1999; Mabry 1998; Mabry et al. 1997). Evidence of maize agriculture and water-control features were found at several Archaic period sites by Desert Archaeology at about the same time that SRI was finding similar evidence at the Costello-King site, an Archaic period site in northwestern Tucson (Ezzo and Deaver 1998). Radiocarbon dates from Costello-King indicated maize production as early as 3,000 years ago, the earliest evidence so far of maize agriculture in the Southwest. These data supported Huckell's argument for an "Early Agricultural period" coterminous with the San Pedro phase of the Late Archaic (Huckell 1995). This proposed shift in terminology for the Late Archaic period is still controversial.

The discovery of evidence for irrigation and maize cultivation at several sites along the middle Santa Cruz River has prompted a reanalysis of the mechanisms whereby agriculture was adopted in the Southwest. Conventional wisdom had irrigation technology being introduced into the area by the Hohokam, replacing a system of farming dependent on rainfall and seasonal flooding. These data indicate the appearance of more sophisticated techniques much earlier than previously believed, suggesting the indigenous development of the technology.

Projects funded by private developers also contributed to the rapidly expanding archaeological database of the Tucson Basin. In 1993, SWCA, Inc., excavated part of the Gibbon Spring site, a Tanque Verde phase village in the northern Tucson Basin. Of special note was the recovery of charred beams of piñon pine that provided the first tree-ring dates from the desert Southwest (Ahlstrom and Slaughter 1996). Although dates were obtained only from a single feature, the data indicate that it may be possible to develop a dendrochronological sequence for the Tucson area, significantly enhancing the precision of local chronologies.

Research on the Historical Period

The historical period in southern Arizona began with the arrival of the first Europeans to the region in 1539. In that year, the Franciscan friar Marcos de Niza and a small Spanish expedition traveled north from Mexico to the pueblo of Zuni, following the San Pedro and Gila Rivers for part of their route. The expedition left no trace of its momentary presence in the region, but it did inaugurate a century and a half of intermittent Spanish exploration of what is now the state of Arizona (see Chapter 4). It was not until the explorations of the Jesuit father Eusebio Francisco Kino at the end of the seventeenth century that the Spanish presence in southern Arizona became substantial enough to produce a significant documentary record, but the impact of the Spanish presence farther south was probably felt along the middle Santa

Cruz River long before Kino arrived. We use "historical period" here in the conventional sense of the entire period from first Spanish contact to the end of the twentieth century, with the understanding that the first 150 years or more are sometimes better characterized as the "protohistoric period," a time when European impacts on native ways of life were real but not yet direct.

The historical period can be studied through both written documentation and the archaeological record, which has led to the development of the two independent disciplines of history and historical archaeology in the Southwest, as elsewhere in the United States. The overlap between the two is inevitable and frequent, nowhere more obviously than along the Paseo de las Iglesias, but their histories are distinct enough to warrant separate consideration here. As with the prehistoric archaeological sites in the study area, our discussions of the history of work at individual historical-period sites are reserved for Chapter 5.

Documentary Research

The history of southern Arizona, and thus of the Santa Cruz River valley, first became a subject of modern scholarly study in the work of the late-nineteenth-century American historian Hubert Howe Bancroft. In a monumental synthesis of western history that eventually swelled to more than 30 volumes, Bancroft was the first historian to dig systematically into the unpublished sources documenting the history of the Southwest, from the beginnings of Spanish exploration to the acquisition of the region by the United States. A Californian, Bancroft was interested primarily in the broad sweep of events that shaped California history, but he compiled a large amount of primary source material on the greater Southwest and dedicated a full volume of his work to the history of Arizona and New Mexico (Bancroft 1889). His work has the Anglocentric shortcomings of most historical work of his era—Weber (1992:341) called his treatment of the Hispanic *californios* "fictive, condescending . . . and profoundly racist"—but it is the practical predecessor of all subsequent historical work on the Southwest, including the history of the river that has figured so prominently in southern Arizona for the last three centuries.

After Bancroft, the next American historian to take the formerly Spanish and Mexican territories of the United States as his particular subject was Herbert Eugene Bolton, professor for most of his career at the University of California at Berkeley. During the first half of the twentieth century, Bolton invented, then dominated historical study of the region he dubbed the "Spanish Borderlands." Technically, the borderlands included a broad band of the United States extending from ocean to ocean, and Bolton's work occasionally addressed the entirety of that region, but his most important work focused on the Southwest, especially on the early years of Spanish exploration and settlement in Arizona, California, and New Mexico. An early essay on the importance of Spanish missions as frontier institutions (Bolton 1964 [1917]) was the start of a focus on Spanish-indigenous interactions that can still be seen today in the study of the Spanish Colonial period in the region. Bolton was particularly fascinated by the experiences of prominent individual explorers. His detailed studies of the Coronado expedition (Bolton 1990 [1949]) and Kino's many accomplishments (Bolton 1984 [1936]) remain standard works on their subjects. Apart from the work of compiling sources and writing syntheses, Bolton's single most important contribution to the field was to shift the emphasis in western history from a perception of the Spanish and Mexican presence as a minor hindrance to westward Anglo expansion to a perception that that presence was fundamental in determining the subsequent character of the region (on Bolton's contributions and those of his many students, see Bannon 1964, 1978; Weber 1988a, 1991).

Bolton had a prominent successor in borderlands history in John Francis Bannon, who in turn dominated the field from the 1950s into the 1970s. Like Bolton before him, Bannon emphasized the Spanish role in the history of the region, partly as a foil to the continuing Anglocentrism of mainstream American history. Also like Bolton, Bannon wrote important syntheses of borderlands history (e.g., Bannon 1955, 1970), trained many doctoral students in the field, and otherwise avidly promoted professional study of the region. One shortcoming of his work, as with the work of Bolton, was a kind of "overcorrection" inherent in its sometimes romanticized Hispanic emphasis. Bannon and Bolton—and many of the students of both historians—brought Spanish involvement in the history of the region to the fore but thus became apologists, if largely unintentional ones, for Spanish misdeeds. Subsequent historical work on the borderlands, including important work on southern Arizona, has helped to counteract this overcorrection, providing a more balanced view of the Spanish presence in the region, a view that does not neglect, for example, the Spanish role in the precipitous decline of native populations (Weber 1988b).

Since the emergence of the borderlands school, the history of southern Arizona has benefited from the work of numerous historians who have addressed the region in studies of the greater Southwest, of the state as a whole, and of specific places within southern Arizona. Because southern Arizona is one of the few regions in the United States with a lengthy Spanish Colonial occupation, an important Mexican period occupation, and a continuing, substantial Mexican-American population, many works dealing with southern Arizona history are devoted to one or another aspect of the Hispanic presence in the region. Weber, in a series of major works on Southwest history (1979, 1982, 1992), included southern Arizona as an important and, in many ways, unique region during the Spanish Colonial and Mexican periods. Officer (1987) provided a detailed synthesis of the Spanish Colonial and Mexican periods in what he calls Hispanic Arizona, basically the part of Arizona sold by Mexico to the United States in 1854. Kessell (1970) provided one of the few detailed studies ever made of a single mission in what was once northern New Spain, the Jesuit mission at Guevavi, on the upper Santa Cruz. Elsewhere, Kessell (1976) redressed the long-standing neglect of the Franciscan presence in southern Arizona, a neglect fostered by an enduring fascination (partly attributable to Bolton) with the earlier Jesuit presence in the region. Sheridan et al. (1991) compiled scattered scholarly articles on the Franciscan period to a similar end. Kessell (1976) is also a fundamental source on other aspects of the later Spanish Colonial and Mexican periods in southern Arizona.

Other important sources on the missions of northern New Spain include Burrus (1971), McCarty (1976, 1981, 1996), and Polzer (1976, 1998). Fontana (1996) assembled and considered widely scattered information on the mission at San Xavier del Bac, carrying the story to the present day. Dobyns (1976), taking Spanish Colonial Tucson as his focus, documented the role of the missions, and the Spanish presence more generally, in the decline of native populations in southern Arizona. The impact of Spanish colonialism on native demography in northern New Spain was also the focus of books by Jackson (1994) and Reff (1990). Dobyns (1959) was also responsible for a large, unpublished compilation of sources and writings on the presidio at Tubac, the center of Hispanic settlement in the region during two decades of the eighteenth century.

The study of the Spanish Colonial and Mexican periods in southern Arizona does not, of course, end at the current international border. Once a part of the vast colony of New Spain and subsequently of the Mexican state of Sonora, southern Arizona must ultimately be understood with reference to the greater history of those political entities. In this regard, it is important to note that a substantial body of relevant historical literature on northern New Spain and Sonora exists only in Spanish, produced primarily by Mexican scholars. An introduction to this literature, and an important resource to all historians of the region, is the six-volume *Historia general de Sonora*, recently released in a second edition (Gobierno del Estado de Sonora 1997).

An important institutional resource for the history of northern New Spain is the Documentary Relations of the Southwest (DRSW) section of ASM. Since the creation of DRSW in the 1970s, its staff has worked to collect, catalog, transcribe, translate, analyze, and publish primary source materials on northern New Spain preserved in Mexican, U.S., and European archives. This ongoing effort has resulted in the publication of major individual documents, collections of documents, and research guides, including Barnes et al. (1981), Naylor and Polzer (1986), Polzer (1976), Polzer and Sheridan (1997), and Hadley et al. (1997), as well as the production of indexes to document collections and microform copies of important documents and collections. Of related significance is a detailed study by Gerhard (1993) of territorial and administrative units in northern New Spain, based on a comprehensive review of sources in Mexican and Spanish archives. Gerhard's book is an important guide to the amount and kinds of primary source material available for specific areas in northern New Spain.

Tucson became the social and economic center of southern Arizona during the latter half of the nineteenth century, and historical research on the century following the Gadsden Purchase reflects this status. Two works on the history of Tucson bear particular mention. The first is Sonnichsen's *Tucson: The Life and Times of an American City* (Sonnichsen 1982); the second is Sheridan's *Los Tucsonenses: The Mexican Community in Tucson, 1854–1941* (Sheridan 1986). Together, the two works illustrate the diversity of subject matter presented by Tucson's history and the variety of research emphases that such diversity requires. Sonnichsen's *Tucson* is a highly original and entertaining history of political events and social change in the city, basically since the Gadsden Purchase. Mexican-Americans are an important part of his account, because they have always been a part of the city's population, but their presence is often overshadowed by the dominant roles played by white Tucsonans. Sheridan's *Los Tucsonenses* also begins with the Gadsden Purchase, but his deliberate focus is the "other Tucson," the Mexican-American community that formed the majority of the city's population until the first decade of the twentieth century. The Mexican-American community had deep roots in the pre-U.S. period, enduring connections with the Mexican state of Sonora, and an important but often undervalued role in the political and economic life of the city. Both Sonnichsen's and Sheridan's works are valuable in their own ways, but *Los Tucsonenses* is an important reminder of how much of southern Arizona's history would escape a purely Anglocentric approach.

Histories of the state of Arizona as a whole naturally devote considerable attention to southern Arizona, the portion of the state with the longest continuous historical-period occupation. Important syntheses of Arizona history include works by Farish (1915–1918), Lamar (1966), Wagoner (1970, 1975), and, most recently and most notably, Sheridan (1995). Sheridan's survey of Arizona history has quickly become the standard introduction to the subject and includes useful summaries of events and processes in southern Arizona, especially Tucson and the Santa Cruz Valley. Sheridan is also a contributor to an excellent collection of essays by various authors on the history of Tucson (Southwestern Mission Research Center 1986). The collection includes its own useful summary of works on Tucson history (Southwestern Mission Research Center 1986:149–152).

Use of the term "Borderlands" in Bolton's sense of the term has not died out entirely, but in recent years the historiography of the region has undergone a significant shift in perspective away from an emphasis on the status of the region as an outpost first of Spanish, then Anglo civilization. The shift corresponds with a major shift in Latin American and western history in the last few decades away from an elitist, event-oriented historiography and toward a "history from below" (Radding 1997:xvi), a focus on the broader implications of the often mundane aspects of everyday social and economic life, including the lives of previously neglected groups of people such as ethnic minorities and women. The "new western history" (Limerick 1987; Limerick et al. 1991), for example, eschews an earlier emphasis on the western American frontier as simply an instrument in the inevitable expansion of U.S. agriculture and industry and devotes itself to reconstructing the lives of all people living under, affected by, or simply bypassed by that expansion. Similar emphases are evident in recent Latin American history as a whole and in borderlands history more particularly. Work by Weber (1992) was a turning point in this regard for the history of the borderlands, a term he generally avoided (on other aspects of the evolving historiography of the borderlands, see the essays in Weber 1988c). A recent book by Cynthia Radding (1997) took up the typical borderlands topic of colonial society in northwestern Mexico, but instead of focusing on the successes and failures of the Spanish empire in the region, she looked at how the convergence of Spanish and Indian cultures, and of different classes of people within Spanish colonial society, shaped the history and environment of the region. Jackson (1998) gathered essays of a similar bent by several authors dealing with various parts of the borderlands. Another aspect of the shift is a greater emphasis on comparative studies. In a series of essays, a volume edited by Guy and Sheridan (1998) compared the impacts of Spanish colonialism on northern New Spain and northern Argentina, the two most peripheral portions of Spain's American colonies.

Spanish, Mexican, and Anglo-American occupation of the Santa Cruz River valley, particularly within the Paseo de las Iglesias study area, has centered on the manipulation of the river's water for agricultural and other purposes. All such manipulation has had an impact on the character of the river, but the impact increased dramatically with the arrival of the Anglo-American industrial economy in the second half of the nineteenth century. In addition to modifications of the river itself, wider processes of environmental change prompted or exacerbated by the spread of ranching, farming, and other landscape-modifying activities led eventually to the transformation of the river from a shallow, meandering, perennial stream to a deeply entrenched channel that carries water only during heavy rains. The transformation of the river in the decades after the Gadsden Purchase has been treated in several book-length works, some dealing specifically with the Santa Cruz River valley or the Tucson Basin more generally (Betancourt 1990; Kuper 1986; Logan 2002), others dealing with the general phenomenon of environmental degradation and arroyo formation in the Southwest (Bahre 1991; Cooke and Reeves 1976; Dobyns 1981; Hastings and Turner 1965; see also Sheridan 2000).

Despite scholarly attention to the major historical-period processes that have shaped the Paseo de las Iglesias study area—the development of the Spanish system of missions and presidios, the emergence of Tucson as first a Mexican and then an American city—there is no comprehensive historical study of precisely the study area or even of, less precisely, the middle Santa Cruz River valley. (Logan [2002] recently provided the closest thing so far.) Such a study would include detailed looks at the history of land ownership and land use in the area, the evolution of its built environment, and the changing role of the area in the wider economic system of southern Arizona. Partial treatments of such subjects do appear in reports of historical-archaeological investigations, thanks ultimately to the influence of the "history from below" paradigm discussed earlier. At least as early as the 1960s, historical archaeology began to focus less on major historical sites and events and more on the daily lives of ordinary people in ordinary times and places. Part of this shift can be attributed to the rise of compliance-driven CRM archaeology (see below), but the recognition of the potential importance of historical sites once dismissed as mundane and uninteresting—from abandoned rural shacks to urban tenements—is in great part an extension of "history from below." In turn, the great increase in the archaeological attention paid such sites in the last few decades has generated a great deal of locally focused historical research, such that today, in southern Arizona as elsewhere in the United States, much of the historical research on the typical subjects of "history from below"—ordinary people in ordinary times and places—is carried out by historical archaeologists or by historians working in conjunction with archaeologists. Major and minor instances of this pattern abound in southern Arizona; some noteworthy examples of work combining history and archaeology within or near the Paseo de las Iglesias study area are by Ciolek-Torello and Swanson (1997), Mabry et al. (1994), Thiel (1993, 1997), Thiel and Desruisseaux (1993), and Thiel et al. (1995).

Historical-Archaeological Research

As elsewhere in the United States, the archaeology of historical-period sites in southern Arizona got its start as a tool of historic preservation. In the early 1900s, as a response to national concern for the loss of major historical sites, a federal program to protect and preserve important ruins was established, and in 1908, the ruins of the Franciscan mission at Tumacácori, on the west bank of the Santa Cruz River about 40 miles south of Tucson, was designated a national monument. By 1920, Tumacácori was the focus of excavations aimed at identifying and reconstructing features that would help to stabilize the crumbling church (Pinkley 1936). Limited excavations of a similar nature in the 1920s and 1930s and then a major excavation in 1934 and 1935 by Paul Beaubien (1937) followed. Beaubien's purpose was to provide a detailed map of the mission by tracing wall lines through excavation. The results of his efforts, which

17

include a detailed map of the 79-plus rooms of the complex, served as a guide to subsequent reconstruction and landscaping at the monument. Unfortunately, his original site records have been lost, and most of the artifacts he recovered were from contexts disturbed by the extensive looting that plagued the site prior to its designation as a monument. Later archaeological work at Tumacácori in the 1950s and 1960s included further efforts at stabilization and reconstruction and also resulted in the identification of the earlier Jesuit mission at the site (see Shenk [1976] for a summary of work at Tumacácori, much of it unpublished).

No other historical-period site in southern Arizona has received the sustained attention paid to Tumacácori, although Tumacácori itself still awaits a comprehensive archaeological study (for summary comments on Spanish Colonial period archaeology in southern Arizona as a whole, see Majewski and Ayres [1997]). Three other Spanish Colonial period sites on the upper Santa Cruz—Guevavi, Calabazas, and Tubac, all associated with different parts of Tumacácori's history—did not see professional archaeological work until much later, when stabilization and interpretation were again the motives. The modest ruins of the mission church at Guevavi, several miles upstream from Tumacácori, were documented as part of a larger architectural study in 1917 and recorded as an archaeological site by Emil Haury in 1937, but the site was not formally excavated until 1964 (Robinson 1976). Further excavation took place at Guevavi in 1991 (Burton 1992a), and documentation of surface features at both Guevavi and Calabazas, a nearby *visita* (dependent mission settlement), took place in 1992 (Burton 1992b). The only other archaeological work at Calabazas was an evaluation of the ruins for a stabilization plan (Stone 1979). Fontana (1971) has looked at the history of Calabazas in detail, from the establishment of the *visita* through the abandonment of the site by later Anglo-American residents in the late nineteenth century. The site of the former presidio at Tubac, just downstream from Tumacácori, was not formally excavated until the 1970s (Shenk and Teague 1975). Later excavations at the site have still not been reported in full (Williams 1992). A number of small-scale excavations have also been carried out recently at Tubac (Barton et al. 1981; Fratt 1981; Huckell and Huckell 1982). To the east of the Santa Cruz River valley, along the San Pedro River, the ruins of the presidio at Terrenate were excavated in the 1950s by Charles Di Peso (Di Peso 1953), who assumed that the site also had a significant protohistoric Sobaipuri occupation (this component is in fact probably of prehistoric age). The Spanish occupation of the presidio lasted only four years (1776–1780; Williams 1986a), but Di Peso's excavations documented a substantial Spanish Colonial component. More recently, surface remains at the site have been studied by Sugnet and Reid (1994) and Waugh (1995).

Apart from the early work at these Santa Cruz River sites, historical archaeology in southern Arizona had a relatively late start, especially when compared with the development of the field in the eastern United States. As elsewhere in the West, the late start was due in large part to a relative scarcity of historical-period sites, at least of the kinds of sites that historical archaeology was initially interested in. In addition to its early role as a tool of preservation, historical archaeology began as an adjunct to history, a way of addressing questions posed by traditional historical research. This dual role as preservation tool and adjunct to history prompted an early emphasis on the major sites of traditional narrative history— colonial-period missions, townsites, forts, battlefields, and the like—the kinds of sites the East had in abundance but that were fewer and widely scattered in the West. In southern Arizona, the Spanish Colonial presence was especially ephemeral, limited to a handful of major sites, and two of these—the mission and the presidio at Tucson—were largely destroyed in the nineteenth and early twentieth centuries by the growth of the region's single urban center.

Mission San Xavier del Bac, the best-preserved Spanish Colonial site in southern Arizona, has been subject to surprisingly little archaeological work. The first excavations at the site took place in 1958, when a group of University of Arizona students led by Bernard Fontana and William Robinson dug in two areas near the extant mission church (Robinson 1963). The most important find was an architectural complex initially thought to be a series of workshops associated with construction of the 1797 church. Later excavations by Fontana in the 1970s showed that the architectural remains were in fact part of the

1757 church, which had been subdivided into rooms (Majewski and Ayres 1997:72). Other than later analyses of animal bone (Olsen 1974) and artifacts (Barnes 1972, 1980; Cheek 1974) recovered from the site and a few small-scale excavations (e.g., Ayres 1970a; Ciolek-Torrello and Brew 1976), San Xavier has not seen any further archaeological study. The lack of archaeological research is due in part to the status of the mission and its grounds as a sacred and actively used part of the San Xavier District of the Tohono O'odham Nation.

Within the city of Tucson, the first professional recognition that the archaeology of nonindigenous peoples not only was possible but could contribute significantly to the history of the region, came in 1954 (Barnes 1984:213), when Emil Haury and Edward Danson excavated a small area near the presumed northeast corner of the Tucson presidio (Chambers 1955; Olson 1985). The project was prompted by the demolition of a building to make way for a parking lot. In addition to apparent remnants of the presidio wall, Haury and Danson documented the remains of a U.S. period house that stood on the site and, below the level of the presidio, a Hohokam pit house. This brief episode set the pattern for much of the historical archaeology subsequently carried out in Tucson and its vicinity: it has usually been done in association with construction projects, and it has usually been done by archaeologists trained first as prehistorians, not historical archaeologists. To the credit of Haury the prehistorian, he recognized the importance of the presidio find and presented it with as much enthusiasm as he did the pit house (Haury and Fathauer 1974).

Despite its central role in the history of Tucson, the presidio has seen only limited archaeological work since Haury and Danson dug there, the primary reason being that it was largely destroyed or is obscured by modern downtown Tucson. Ayres (1979; see also Barnes 1983) excavated in the Tucson Museum of Art block and the presidial cemetery during the Tucson Urban Renewal Project of 1968–1974. Since then, Thiel (1998a, 1998b; Thiel et al. 1995) has made significant contributions in a series of small-scale projects, tentatively identifying further portions of the presidio wall and excavating associated and overlying features. Thiel will also lead excavations in the near future at the northeast corner of the presidio, near the site of Haury and Danson's 1954 excavations, as part of the City of Tucson's Río Nuevo development project.

The remains of Tucson's other major Spanish Colonial site, Mission San Agustín del Tucson, mark the northern limit of the Paseo de las Iglesias study area, across the river from downtown Tucson and at the eastern foot of Sentinel Peak. Like the presidio, Mission San Agustín has been heavily disturbed by later development, and until only recently it had seen even less archaeological work than the presidio. Summaries of the history of the site and of the limited (and unpublished) archaeological investigations there have been provided by Doelle (1997), Hard and Doelle (1978), Smiley et al. (1953), Wasley (1956), and Williams (1986b). In recent years, a series of surveys and test excavations has been carried out in the vicinity of the mission (Diehl 1997; A. Diehl and M. Diehl 1996; M. Diehl and A. Diehl 1996; Elson and Doelle 1987a; Freeman et al. 1996; Mabry and Thiel 1995; Thiel 1995a, 1995b, 1997, 1998c), confirming the generally disturbed nature of the area but also documenting features associated both with the mission and with later periods.

Large-scale excavations of Mission San Agustín were conducted between November 2000 and February 2001 by Desert Archaeology, as another part of the city's Río Nuevo project. The results have not yet been published, but the work has established that much of the site documented by Wasley in the 1950s has since been destroyed, including the foundations of the mission *convento* and church. The site was damaged significantly prior to 1940 by clay mining, then used as a landfill by the city in the late 1950s. The latter use apparently included bulldozing much of the site. Desert Archaeology did discover substantial sections of the stone foundation of the west wall of the mission compound, the stone foundation of the mission granary, a stone-lined canal that may have served as the mill race for nearby Warner's Mill (built after the mission was abandoned), a well used for trash disposal by Chinese gardeners living near the abandoned mission in the late nineteenth century, and numerous pit houses and other features associated with intensive prehistoric use of the same location (Bawaya 2001; Center for Desert

Archaeology [CDA] 2001). In yet another part of the Río Nuevo project, Desert Archaeology carried out excavations in 2001 in the area immediately north of Mission San Agustín and just south of Congress Street, where, in addition to abundant prehistoric features, segments of a historical-period canal were found that correspond to the Acequia Madre Primera, a canal depicted on an 1862 map of agricultural fields in the area. Portions of the Acequia Madre Tercia, part of the same system, were documented near the mission site in earlier work by Desert Archaeology (Thiel 1995b; see also the discussion of irrigation in Chapter 4).

More often than in most places in the United States, historical archaeology in southern Arizona has been practiced by archaeologists trained in prehistoric rather than historical archaeology (see especially Ayres [1991] on this tendency in the Southwest and its associated problems). One reason for this is the nature of the earliest historical-period sites in the region. The missions and presidios of the eighteenth and early nineteenth centuries were never exclusively nonindigenous settlements and, indeed, were intended as the places where the Spanish missionary and military enterprise would strive to incorporate indigenous people into greater Spanish society. Accordingly, prehistorically oriented archaeologists have always viewed Spanish Colonial sites and the documentary records associated with them as important sources of information on indigenous culture. This means that an interest in the most recent version of pre-Hispanic indigenous culture (or the least-adulterated historical-period version of indigenous culture) has been the motivation for a significant amount of historical and historical-archaeological (using historical-archaeological in a strict sense) research in southern Arizona. Much of this research is best characterized as protohistoric in focus (e.g., Di Peso 1948, 1951, 1953, 1956; Doelle 1984; Huckell 1984a; Riley 1975, 1976, 1985, 1987), given that indigenous peoples of limited or no direct experience with Europeans are often the primary subjects of interest, but the accompanying historical reconstructions of the earliest Hispanic presence and the nonindigenous material culture recovered at protohistoric sites can be important sources of information regarding the history and archaeology of unequivocally historical times.

In the 1960s, two changes affecting the professional archaeological community brought about both a great expansion in the amount of historical archaeology carried out in southern Arizona and a shift in the kinds of sites studied by historical archaeologists. The first change was a sudden expansion of historic preservation law at the federal, state, and local levels, as already noted in our consideration of the development of prehistoric archaeology. The second change was the growing influence of the loosely defined "history from below" paradigm discussed above. The impact of the new historic preservation laws was to set as the focus of archaeological research whatever site happens to be physically in the way of a development project. Working with a very liberal definition of historical significance (any site at least 50 years old is potentially significant), contract archaeologists since the 1960s have been busy recording and evaluating everything from urban outhouses to abandoned mine shafts to farmstead artifact scatters. Prompting further interest in these mundane historical-period sites was the growing perception that it is precisely such sites that can contribute to a fuller understanding of the social, cultural, and economic life of a period and place—in other words, historical archaeology from below (for example, see Berge [1968:2], who characterizes historical archaeology's proper focus as "the way of life of common, ordinary people of which the world is comprised in far greater numbers than the famous heroes of history").

The increasing recognition in historical archaeology that small, peripheral, nonelite, or rural sites were potentially important sources of historical or anthropological information was also partly the result of the rise of processual archaeology in the 1960s, an approach that, in the simplest terms, led archaeologists to consider not simply what their data told them about a specific time and place but what the broader implications were for other times and places—what the general anthropological implications of their data were. Processual archaeology never became the force in historical archaeology that it became (and remains) in prehistoric archaeology, but aspects of the processual approach made their way into the practice of historical archaeology throughout the United States at about the same time that a whole variety of previously ignored historical-period sites were being recorded by contract archaeologists. Historical archaeologists continued to search for and excavate the sites prominent in traditional historical narratives, but their research even at these sites became structured around processual concerns.

In southern Arizona, the first time that historic preservation law and the processual variety of historical archaeology converged in a significant way was in the excavations carried out in the Tucson Urban Renewal Project, which began in 1968 and continued intermittently until 1974 (Ayres 1968, 1970b). The project included historical research, architectural inventories, and archaeological excavations in anticipation of the complete razing of a large area in downtown Tucson. Although it was hindered by inconsistent funding and has never been completely reported, the project yielded a number of interesting studies of the Spanish Colonial, Mexican, and U.S. period occupations in downtown Tucson, most showing the influence of the processual concerns newly current in archaeology (Anderson 1968, 1970; Ayres 1969, 1971, 1978, 1979, 1980; Clonts 1983; Lister and Lister 1989; Olsen 1978, 1983; Renk 1969; Roubicek 1969). There have been numerous subsequent compliance-driven excavations of historical-period sites in downtown Tucson, with a continued emphasis on processual interpretations, but none has addressed as large an area as the Tucson Urban Renewal Project. The largest of subsequent projects have been devoted to individual city blocks or portions of blocks (Ayres 1990; Ciolek-Torrello and Swanson 1997; Eppley and Mabry 1991; Mabry 1991; Mabry et al. 1994; Thiel 1993, 1995c; Thiel et al. 1993, 1995). Smaller projects have addressed individual or multiple small parcels and linear utility corridors (Dutt and Thiel 1999; Fortier 1980; Gilman 1997; Gilman and Swartz 1998; Levi 1996; Mazany 1981; Noll and Euler 1996; Thiel 1995d, 1996, 1998b, 1998d; Thiel and Desruisseaux 1993).

Contract archaeology in southern Arizona during the past several decades has seen a similar explosion in the number of projects recording, testing, and excavating historical-period archaeological sites. In most cases, historical archaeology has been only a part (and often a small part) of the overall focus of such projects, in which prehistoric archaeology continues to be the chief concern. Nonetheless, there is a growing body of information on the historical archaeology of the Tucson Basin, in large part because of the efforts of contract archaeologists. Because many of these projects have been outside of the historical urban core of Tucson, most of the historical-archaeological sites they have recorded have been rural in nature, such as ranches, homesteads, mines, and dumps. The projects have ranged in size from relatively large survey projects (e.g., Ayres 1984a; Ayres and Stone 1983; Betancourt 1978a, 1978b; Dart 1989; Fontana 1965; Gregonis and Huckell 1979; Jones and Dart 1997; Seymour et al. 1997; Simpson and Wells 1983, 1984; Stein 1993; Wellman 1994; Wells and Reutter 1997) to a variety of smaller survey, testing, and excavation projects (e.g., Baar 1996; Chavarria 1996; Diehl et al. 1996; Doak et al. 1995; Faught 1995a, 1995b; Harry and Ciolek-Torrello 1992; Jones 1995a, 1995b, 1996, 1997, 1999; Kaldahl 1999; Mabry 1998; Slaughter et al. 1993; Slawson et al. 1987; Sterner 1996, 1999; Tucker 1997; Vanderpot et al. 1993; Wallace 1996, 1998; Yoder, Holloway, Myers, and Slaughter 1996; Yoder, Myers, and Slaughter 1996).

Individual ranch sites in the Tucson area that have been subject to significant archaeological study include two nineteenth-century ranches: Rancho Punta de Agua, an early Anglo-American (and later Mexican-American) ranch located a few miles south of San Xavier (McGuire 1979, 1983), and Romero Ranch, an early Mexican-American ranch forming part of the Romero Ruin archaeological site at Catalina State Park (Elson and Doelle 1987b; Roubicek et al. 1973; Swartz 1991, 1993). The first post-1900 homestead to be intensively studied in the Tucson area (and one of the few post-1900 sites of any kind to be studied intensively) is the Lewis-Weber Homestead, located on the site of the NPS's Western Archeological and Conservation Center in Tucson (Curriden 1981). Another notable ranch site that has recently received archaeological attention is Agua Caliente Ranch, located in the northeastern corner of the Tucson Basin (Slaughter et al. 1995; Wellman and Slaughter 2001). Elsewhere in the northern Tucson Basin, a number of ranch and homestead sites were the focus of historical research and archaeological survey by Stein (1993), and another nineteenth-century Mexican homestead, the Bojórquez Ranch, was recently excavated by Jones (2001). East of the Tucson Basin, at Fort Huachuca in Cochise County, Sterner and Majewski (1998) conducted historical-archaeological investigations of the Slash Z Ranch and three other early-twentieth-century sites. Not far from Fort Huachuca, along the San Pedro River in Santa Cruz County, an early Anglo-American ranch that eventually was home to Mexican- and Chinese-Americans has been intensively studied by Fontana and Greenleaf (1962).

Historical-archaeological studies of mining in southern Arizona include Ayres's survey of sites in the Rosemont area (1984a), Teague's study of mines on Tohono O'odham lands (Teague 1980), and surveys of other parts of the region by Slawson and Ayres (1992, 1993, 1994). Kentucky Camp, a small, early-twentieth-century gold-mining camp in the Santa Rita Mountains south of Tucson, has been the focus of historical investigations and an ongoing restoration project by the U.S. Forest Service. The project has included limited excavations associated with the restoration efforts (Farrell 1993, 1995). Fort Lowell, the single U.S. fort in the Tucson Basin, saw limited archaeological work 40 years ago (Johnson 1960) but has yet to see an in-depth study.

Ethnographic Research

The history of ethnographic research in southern Arizona is short and uncomplicated, at least in comparison to other parts of the Southwest, where some Native American groups—the Navajo, most notably—have seen the seemingly continuous presence of professional ethnographers for the last 75 years or more. The relative lack of attention the region has received is not because of any lack of Native Americans in the region or lack of Native Americans still living on their traditional lands. The largest Native American community in southern Arizona, the Tohono O'odham Nation (prior to 1981, known as the Papago Indian Tribe), is the fourteenth-largest federally recognized tribe in terms of population (the Cherokee and the Navajo are the largest and second largest, respectively) and occupies the second-largest reservation in the country (about 3,000,000 acres; the Navajo reservation is larger). The Tohono O'odham today also occupy much the same territory used by their ancestors since long before the arrival of Europeans in the region. The lack of attention is also not the result of any failure of traditional culture to survive intact to the era of modern ethnography. By the end of the nineteenth century, Tohono O'odham culture was changing rapidly and dramatically, and many traditional practices disappeared entirely in the first half of the twentieth century, but the ethnography that has been carried out among the Tohono O'odham indicates that there has never been a shortage of traditional culture to study, whatever kinds of changes it might be undergoing.

The principal reason for the limited ethnographic record in southern Arizona is ultimately environmental: the severity of the climate in the region long discouraged Euroamerican settlement outside of a few well-watered riparian strips like that along the Santa Cruz River. This meant that the Native Americans of the region, in particular the Tohono O'odham living in the vast desert region west of the Santa Cruz River, had only limited contact with Spanish, Mexican, and Anglo-American settlers. This in turn meant there were relatively few conflicts between Tohono O'odham and Euroamericans over land and other resources and a corresponding lack of Euroamerican interest in the nature of Tohono O'odham social and economic organization. This eventually translated into a relative lack of anthropological interest on the part of Anglo-American anthropologists, whose access to Native American subjects was typically made possible by the reduction of a once-recalcitrant tribe's range to a small reservation. The Tohono O'odham adaptation to their extreme environment demanded a simple material culture and an intermittently nomadic way of life. This also contributed to the aforementioned lack of interest, at a time when many anthropologists were attracted to the highly developed craft traditions or ceremonial complexities of southwestern communities like those of the Hopi and Zuni.

Nonetheless, a significant amount of ethnography exists for the Tohono O'odham, as it also does for the closely related Akimel O'odham (or Pima) of the Gila River and for the Yaqui, who first settled in

Tucson in the late nineteenth century to escape persecution in Mexico. The Apache, long the nemesis of Spaniards, Mexicans, Anglos, and O'odham in southern Arizona, also have been frequent subjects of formal ethnography, and their presence in the region, generally viewed by non-Apaches as predatory and destructive, has been an important one. Here we consider briefly the history of the ethnography of each of these Native American groups.

O'odham

Formal ethnographic research in southern Arizona began in the late nineteenth century with the work of W. J. McGee, an anthropologist with the Bureau of American Ethnology (BAE). McGee made an ethnographic foray into Mexico through Nogales in 1894, eventually preparing a monograph on the Seri but leaving unpublished his notes on the Tohono O'odham, especially those living south of the international border (Fontana 1989:86–89). McGee was among the first anthropologists to note the great *trincheras* constructions of Sonora and Arizona. Frank Russell, another BAE anthropologist, spent a year with the Akimel O'odham (or Pima) of the Gila River in 1901–1902, a period when the Akimel O'odham culture and economy were rapidly succumbing to Anglo-American impacts. His monograph on the Akimel O'odham (Russell 1975 [1908]) remains the primary source on Akimel O'odham culture.

Ruth Underhill, a student of pioneer anthropologist Franz Boas at Columbia University, conducted fieldwork among the Tohono O'odham from 1931 to 1935. Boas's students had already worked among most of the other major tribes of the Southwest prior to Underhill, and her work represented one of the last extensions of the Boasian program into the region. Her many subsequent publications on the Tohono O'odham (then still called the Papago), particularly two monographs (Underhill 1939, 1946), form the heart of the ethnographic record for the tribe. Underhill also collaborated with biologist Edward Castetter of the University of New Mexico on important ethnobiological work among the Tohono O'odham (Castetter and Underhill 1935). Castetter did additional ethnobiological work among the Tohono O'odham independent of Underhill (Castetter and Bell 1942). More recently, Rea (1997, 1998) has carried out major studies of O'odham ethnobotany and ethnozoology.

Not surprisingly, anthropologists at the University of Arizona in Tucson have been responsible for the bulk of the ethnographic work carried out among the Tohono O'odham since Underhill. When Emil Haury began his Papaguería project in 1938, he included ethnographic investigations as a complement to his studies of the archaeology and physical anthropology of the region, and soon other University of Arizona anthropologists took interest. Graduate students in the Department of Anthropology began turning out theses and dissertations on a variety of Tohono O'odham topics. Bernard Fontana, generally recognized as the leading authority on Tohono O'odham culture and history, completed a dissertation on cultural change among the Tohono O'odham in 1960 (Fontana 1960). This work was preceded by an important monograph on the modern Tohono O'odham pottery tradition by Fontana and other University of Arizona students (Fontana et al. 1962), prepared just before the tradition almost completely disappeared. Fontana has since published a wide variety of articles and monographs on the Tohono O'odham, including the only book-length survey of the Tohono O'odham since Underhill's monographs (Fontana 1989) and valuable essays on Tohono O'odham culture and history in the *Handbook of North American Indians* (Fontana 1983a, 1983b). Fontana, who has lived adjacent to the San Xavier District of the Tohono O'odham Nation since the 1950s, has also been actively involved in the extensive preservation work recently undertaken at Mission San Xavier del Bac (Fontana 1997). His history of the mission, originally published in 1961 but recently revised (Fontana 1996), remains a standard reference.

Because Tohono O'odham culture changed dramatically before the era of formal ethnography, students of the modern Tohono O'odham have almost always combined ethnographic observations with ethnohistorical research to reconstruct at least some aspects of the culture as it was prior to the major impacts of the twentieth century. In fact, it is safe to say that Tohono O'odham ethnography has always been at least as ethnohistorical as it has been ethnographic. Examples of such work are studies carried out under the auspices of the University of Arizona's Bureau of Ethnic Research (later the Bureau of Applied Research in Anthropology) as part of a Tohono O'odham federal land claims case (e.g., Hackenberg 1974). Many other projects by University of Arizona–trained anthropologists have had an applied-anthropology focus (e.g., Van Willigen 1971).

The form and function of the many small, O'odham-built Catholic churches on the Tohono O'odham reservation were the subject of another University of Arizona anthropology dissertation (Griffith 1973). This study initiated the career of the well-known University of Arizona folklorist, James "Big Jim" Griffith, whose many subsequent interests have included the "spiritual geography" of the Tohono O'odham, a subject he considered from various angles in a collection of essays (Griffith 1992). Another student at the University of Arizona, Gary Nabhan (1983), wrote a dissertation on Tohono O'odham agriculture, the first of several notable studies of Tohono O'odham ethnobotany by him (e.g., Nabhan 1982, 1985).

Outside the University of Arizona, Harvard-trained anthropologist Donald Bahr of Arizona State University has published several books and numerous articles on Tohono O'odham language and culture, based on his own ethnographic fieldwork and reanalysis of O'odham texts gathered by earlier investigators (Bahr 1975; Bahr et al. 1974, 1997). In addition, he has looked closely at the evidence for Hohokam-O'odham cultural continuity in O'odham oral tradition (Bahr 1971; Bahr et al. 1994). His student David Kozak also has worked closely with O'odham oral tradition (Kozak and Lopez 1999). All of this work recognizes the central role of oral tradition in Tohono O'odham culture, a role emphasized earlier by Underhill (1938; Underhill et al. 1979). The work of Bahr is notable also for its inclusion of individual Tohono O'odham in the process of gathering and analyzing texts and its explicit acknowledgment of their participation.

Also worth noting here is a valuable synthesis of Tohono O'odham culture and history by Erickson (1994), prepared on behalf of the Tohono O'odham Nation as a textbook for Tohono O'odham schools.

Apache

In 1793, the commander of the Spanish presidio at Tucson established a settlement for pacified Apaches *(apaches mansos)* on the east bank of the Santa Cruz River, immediately adjacent to the presidio. This settlement, never large but always important as an example of how the Apache of southern Arizona might be convinced to live in peace, endured until at least the 1870s. It is probably the only time prior to the twentieth century that Apaches ever stayed in the Santa Cruz River valley for longer than it took to raid an O'odham or Spanish village. But despite their usual absence from the valley, the Apache had a profound impact on its history through their persistent raids, beginning at least as early as the seventeenth century and continuing well into the second half of the nineteenth century. For this reason, we include a discussion of Apache culture and history in Chapter 3. Here, we summarize the history of ethnographic research on the Apache.

Of the seven generally recognized Apachean-speaking tribes, two lived in relative proximity to the Santa Cruz River valley and had a role in its history: the Chiricahua Apache and the Western Apache. The Chiricahua occupied a large area in southeastern Arizona and southwestern New Mexico, and the Western Apache—actually five distinct bands lumped together for convenience by anthropologists—occupied a comparably large area in eastern and central Arizona. The often violent interaction of both major groups with Euroamericans, especially Anglo-Americans in the second half of the nineteenth century, has been documented in countless histories (Spicer [1962:229–261] provides a concise history of Apache-Euroamerican interaction), but purely ethnographic research has been very limited. For the Chiricahua Apache, Opler (1937, 1941, 1942, 1983) has produced the most substantial works. For the Western Apache, important works are by Goodwin (1939, 1969), Kaut (1957), and Basso (1969, 1970, 1983, 1996).

Yaqui

For most of their history, the Yaqui lived exclusively in a region centered on the Río Yaqui in what is now southern Sonora, Mexico. Only in the late nineteenth century did groups of Yaqui come to settle in southern Arizona, forced to emigrate by a Mexican government eager to turn over their communal lands to large private landholders, or *hacendados*. In the Tucson area, small groups of Yaqui settled principally in two locations: Pascua Village on the near north side of Tucson and a smaller satellite community in Marana, northwest of Tucson. In 1982, the Pascua Yaqui acquired a parcel of land immediately west of the Paseo de las Iglesias study area, on the south side of Valencia Road, a site best known today as the location of the Yaqui-owned Casino of the Sun.

The foremost ethnographic works on the Yaqui, in both Mexico and Arizona, are those of Spicer (1940, 1954, 1983), a professor of anthropology at the University of Arizona for most of his career (now deceased). He was also author of a detailed overview of Yaqui culture and history (Spicer 1980). Other important ethnographic works dealing with the Yaqui, primarily in Mexico, are by Beals (1943, 1945). A valuable autobiographical account by a Yaqui has also been published (Moisés et al. 1971).

CHAPTER 3

Native American Culture History

This chapter provides an overview of Native American culture history in the Paseo de las Iglesias study area, from the earliest occupation by Paleoindians some 12,000 years ago to the present day (Figure 3). The discussion has two main sections: the first surveys the prehistoric era prior to the arrival of Europeans; the second considers the Native Americans who have lived in or near the study area since European contact. The focus in both sections is, of necessity, wider than the Paseo de las Iglesias study area, but we make direct connections to locations within the study area as appropriate.

Prehistory

The focus of human occupation in the Tucson Basin shifted numerous times in prehistory, but the focus always included at least a portion of the Santa Cruz River. The river was a constant source of water for mouths and crops and presumably of a sense of identity for the people living along its banks. The Paseo de las Iglesias study area encompasses much of the heart of the river and so much of its prehistory, including many of the largest and most-significant prehistoric settlements within the Tucson Basin.

Despite the importance of the Santa Cruz River in Tucson Basin prehistory, it is impossible to discuss the prehistory of the Paseo de las Iglesias study area without discussing other parts of the Tucson Basin, and southern Arizona more generally. The major tributary drainages of the Santa Cruz—the Rillito River, the Cañada del Oro, Pantano Wash—all had major prehistoric occupations with close connections to developments along the Santa Cruz. Often, the connections extended outside of the basin to the nearby valleys of the San Pedro and Gila Rivers and, occasionally, to more-distant regions. Also important in Tucson Basin prehistory were the intermittent and changing uses of the surrounding mountains and *bajada* slopes, including those immediately adjacent to the Paseo de las Iglesias study area.

In this section, we discuss the prehistory of the Paseo de las Iglesias study area and how it fits within the larger research domain of Tucson Basin prehistory. The discussion includes comments on the major prehistoric sites in the study area as well as many of the known smaller sites in an effort to provide an outline of prehistoric settlement along this important and relatively well-studied stretch of the Santa Cruz River.

Paleoindian Period

The earliest human occupation of the Americas is generally associated with the Paleoindian period (10,500–8500 B.C.). Paleoindian culture was characterized by a hunting-and-gathering economy and small, highly mobile bands adapted to a climate that was cooler and wetter than today. Paleoindian sites are often associated with the remains of extinct species of mammoths, camels, and giant ground sloths, leading many archaeologists to consider big-game hunting the focus of the Paleoindian economy.

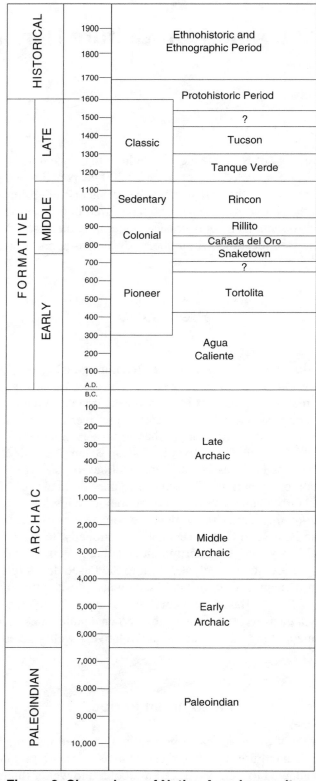

Figure 3. Chronology of Native American culture history in southern Arizona.

28

Despite a considerable number of buried Paleoindian sites in southeastern Arizona, most notably along the San Pedro River (Haury 1953; Haury et al. 1959), very little evidence of a Paleoindian presence in the Tucson Basin has been found. The sparse remains that do exist consist of isolated surface finds of Clovis projectile points (Huckell 1982). These isolates include points from the Avra Valley, the Valencia site (AZ BB:13:15) (Doelle 1985:181), the San Xavier District of the Tohono O'odham Nation, and the Tucson Mountains (Huckell 1982). The absence of buried Paleoindian sites in the Tucson Basin and along the Santa Cruz has been variously attributed to a lack of deep excavations in the heavily aggraded Santa Cruz River floodplain (Huckell 1982), a massive erosional event that removed these deposits (Haynes and Huckell 1986; Waters 1988), and sporadic, low-intensity use of the Tucson Basin by Paleoindians, resulting in an inherently sparse archaeological presence (Whittlesey et al. 1994:109).

Post-Clovis Paleoindian materials are all but nonexistent in the Tucson Basin. Huckell (1982) described two points from two sites just outside the Tucson Basin that resembled Plainview points. One point came from the Tortolita Mountains and the other from the lower San Pedro River valley.

Archaic Period

The Archaic period is relatively better known in southern Arizona than the preceding Paleoindian period. This is especially true of the later portion of the period and is largely the result of a recent explosion in contract archaeology related to development in and around the Santa Cruz River floodplain, especially in the area north of the Paseo de las Iglesias study area. Similar to the Paleoindian period, the Archaic period was characterized by an economy based on the gathering of wild plant and animal resources. The Archaic period differs from the Paleoindian period, however, in the greater diversity of plant and animal species that were exploited. This more diverse subsistence base undoubtedly lessened the need for a highly mobile way of life.

The Archaic period has traditionally been divided into three periods: the Early Archaic period (8500–4800 B.P.), the Middle Archaic period (4800–1500 B.P.), and the Late Archaic period (1500–200 B.P.) (Huckell 1984b:138). Whittlesey (1997:46) has discussed the recent confusion in terminology related to the expanding Archaic database and the terminological dilemmas resulting from the recognition that agriculture is considerably older in the southern Southwest than once believed.

Early Archaic Period

The Early Archaic period is poorly known in southern Arizona and is especially underrepresented in the archaeological record of the Tucson Basin. In fact, as Huckell (1984b:137) has reported, the Tucson Basin has yielded no direct evidence for an Early Archaic occupation. Once again, it is probably an investigative bias rather than a lack of occupation in the region that has created this gap in our knowledge. At present, the Early Archaic is known in detail only at sites in the Sulphur Springs Valley of southeastern Arizona. There, Sayles (1983) defined the Sulphur Spring and Cazador stages of the Cochise culture based on the presence or absence of projectile points at sites along Whitewater Draw. These Early Archaic deposits are characterized by frequent milling stones and flaked stone tools, excluding projectile points in the Sulphur Spring stage but including a variety of point types in the Cazador stage. More recently, Whalen (1971) challenged the validity of the Cazador stage, suggesting that it and the Sulphur Spring stage are simply variant expressions of the same cultural phenomenon.

Middle Archaic Period

In contrast to the Paleoindian and Early Archaic periods, the Middle Archaic period is relatively well known in southern Arizona and the Tucson Basin. In southern Arizona, the Middle Archaic period includes the Chiricahua stage of the Cochise culture, known from sites in the San Pedro River valley and Sulphur Springs Valley (Sayles and Antevs 1941), and the Amargosan I and II stages of the Amargosan tradition, known from sites in the Papaguería and the lower Colorado River valley (Rogers 1939).

The economy of the Middle Archaic period was based on the exploitation of a number of environmental zones. Small base camps and limited-activity sites associated with resource procurement and processing are common in upland and *bajada* environments (Huckell 1984b:139–140). The data are sparse, but Middle Archaic peoples probably practiced a seasonally organized procurement strategy that emphasized upland environments in the fall and lowland areas during the rest of the year (Whittlesey 1997:48). In contrast to the preceding Early Archaic period, projectile points are common at Middle Archaic sites, but the large floodplain villages of the Late Archaic period have not been documented for the Middle Archaic (Huckell 1984b:139), and only recently have excavations of a Middle Archaic site been undertaken on the Santa Cruz River floodplain (Gregory 1999).

Excavation of the Middle Archaic component at Los Pozos, a site on the Santa Cruz River floodplain several miles north of the Paseo de las Iglesias study area, has produced a single direct radiocarbon date on maize of 4050 B.P. (Gregory 1999:118). This date helps to push back the timing of the introduction of maize in the Southwest and is consistent with other material recovered from sites in and along the Santa Cruz River floodplain, suggesting that maize agriculture and irrigation had a long history of codevelopment in this environment (see also Ezzo and Deaver 1998). Although no irrigation features were recorded in the Middle Archaic component at Los Pozos, the presence of maize in an area of such intensive use of the floodplain suggests that the stage was set early on for the development of subsequent agricultural strategies.

Ongoing excavations by Desert Archaeology for the Río Nuevo project have recovered possible evidence of Middle Archaic houses arranged in a courtyardlike group at AZ BB:13:6, at the north end of the Paseo de las Iglesias study area. Analysis of radiocarbon dates and artifacts from these excavations will be necessary to verify this interpretation.

Late Archaic (Early Agricultural) Period

The beginning of the Late Archaic period, or the beginning of what is now often called the Early Agricultural period, is marked by an apparent intensification of human occupation of southern Arizona, including the Tucson Basin. Settlements became larger, and a movement toward dependence on agriculture is evident. Because of important recent discoveries along the Santa Cruz River floodplain (Ezzo and Deaver 1998; Mabry 1998) and in the Cienega Valley (Huckell 1995), we now know substantially more about this period than we did 10 years ago (see Huckell 1984b).

The Late Archaic period is now generally subdivided into two phases. The San Pedro phase, first defined by Sayles (1941), is estimated to date from 1500 to 500 B.C. and is characterized by large side- or corner-notched projectile points, shallow oval to egg-shaped structures with basin floor plans and often a single large bell-shaped pit, a ground stone assemblage reflecting seed milling, a limited assemblage of shell artifacts, and some anthropomorphic figurines of fired clay (Huckell 1995:118–119). The succeeding Cienega phase dates roughly from 500 B.C. to A.D. 200 and ends with the appearance of pottery. Houses of the Cienega phase are typically round in plan with vertical pit walls and level floors. Many houses contain postholes (Huckell 1995; Mabry 1998), and at the Santa Cruz Bend site, many houses had numerous bell-shaped and cylindrical pits, suggesting an increased concern with storage. The Cienega projectile point is a hallmark of the Cienega phase. Unlike San Pedro projectile points, Cienega points have a distinctive corner notch and are often manufactured from siliceous materials. There is also an elaboration of ground stone manufacture in the Cienega phase.

In general, the Late Archaic period was a time of decreasing mobility in which people came to rely more and more on agriculture. This is not to say that previous patterns of land use were abandoned entirely. There continues to be evidence for the use of seasonal camps in upland areas. These camps likely complemented the more intensively focused settlements of the Santa Cruz River floodplain at sites like Santa Cruz Bend and Stone Pipe, where hundreds of habitation structures have been uncovered (Mabry 1998). This duality of settlement is consistent with a seasonally based system in which upland areas were used in fall and winter for gathering wild resources, and large settlements like the Santa Cruz Bend site were used during the summer, when agriculture on the floodplain and the alluvial fans was most productive (Whittlesey 1997).

Several sites within the Paseo de las Iglesias study area have evidence of Late Archaic or Early Formative period occupations, and it is likely that many more contain as-yet-unrecognized components of similar age. This is especially true for sites located on or near the floodplain of the Santa Cruz. During investigations at the San Xavier Bridge site (AZ BB:13:14), radiocarbon samples obtained from a hearth exposed by the river returned a date of 820 ± 400 B.C. (Ravesloot 1987a:65). This feature, cut into the basal clays, probably represents the earliest preserved occupation of the site. Excavations by ASM on Tumamoc Hill have produced evidence of not only a Late Archaic period occupation but early maize cultivation as well (Fish et al. 1986). Radiocarbon dates from maize kernels recovered in levels below the better-known Classic period component returned dates with range midpoints of 520 B.C., A.D. 320, and A.D. 620 (Fish et al. 1986:569). Recent explorations by Desert Archaeology in Locus 2 of the Valencia site (AZ BB:13:15) exposed several Cienega phase houses arranged in a roughly circular pattern around an area devoid of architectural features. Farther north along the river, Desert Archaeology exposed a Cienega phase component at the Clearwater site, the name given to the prehistoric component of the Mission San Agustín site (AZ BB:13:6). Here, Cienega phase canals and several Early Formative period houses were investigated (CDA 2001). In addition to these newly acquired data, several houses at nearby AZ BB:13:74 have recently been reinterpreted as Cienega phase in age (Mabry 1998).

Formative Period

For the purposes of discussing Tucson Basin chronology, the Formative period is usefully divided into five discrete periods: the Early Formative period, the Pioneer period, the Colonial period, the Sedentary period, and the Classic period.

Early Formative Period

As with the Late Archaic period, our knowledge of the earliest portion of the Formative period in the Tucson Basin has been greatly enhanced by recent excavations. The Early Formative period began with the adoption of ceramic container technology, an extension of the growing dependence on agriculture noted in the Late Archaic period. Although some very early, crude ceramics were recovered from the Coffee Camp site dating from 200 B.C. to A.D. 1 (Halbirt and Henderson 1993), the earliest developed ceramic industry did not appear until around A.D. 200 (Whittlesey 1997). Recently, Deaver and Ciolek-Torrello (1995) developed a chronology for the Early Formative period that they saw as pansouthwestern in application. The chronology is based on subdivision into several broad horizons based on changes in material culture as a whole but named for changes in ceramic technology.

The earliest period is the Plain Ware horizon, which extended from A.D. 1 to 425. In the Tucson Basin, the Plain Ware horizon equates with the Agua Caliente phase and is characterized by a thin-walled, sand-tempered, coiled brown plain ware; an expedient lithic technology with remnant Archaic period biface technology; a Late Archaic period milling assemblage; and architectural forms similar to Early Pithouse period Mogollon houses (Ciolek-Torrello 1995, 1998). In addition, subsistence seems to have been a mix of agriculture and hunting and gathering, with a continued emphasis on upland resources. Several recently discovered archaeological sites have been assigned to the Agua Caliente phase, including the Houghton Road site (Ciolek-Torrello 1995, 1998), El Arbolito (Huckell 1987), and the Square Hearth site (Mabry and Clark 1994; Mabry et al. 1997).

The Plain Ware horizon was followed by the Red Ware horizon, which Deaver and Ciolek-Torrello (1995:512) have dated to A.D. 425–650. In the Tucson Basin, this horizon is expressed by the Tortolita phase. In the Tortolita phase, red-slipped pottery was added to the ceramic assemblage, and various changes in vessel forms occurred, including the introduction of flare-rimmed bowls. This vessel form may have its source in the Phoenix Basin (Whittlesey 1997), whereas other aspects of the Red Ware horizon technology appear more closely tied to San Francisco Red ware of the Mogollon ceramic tradition (Whittlesey 1995). The flaked stone assemblage continued to be generalized, and the Archaic period biface component disappeared from the tool kit (Deaver and Ciolek-Torrello 1995). Changes in architecture during this phase included a general increase in house size and the formality of construction, but both large communal structures and small residential houses continued to be constructed. Representative sites of this period include the Houghton Road site (Ciolek-Torrello 1995, 1998), Rabid Ruin (Slawson 1990), El Arbolito, and the Valencia Road site, Locus 2 (Huckell 1993).

The Early Broadline horizon began around A.D. 650 with the introduction of painted ceramics and lasted until around A.D. 700, when what is traditionally called the Snaketown phase of the Hohokam culture first appeared (Deaver and Ciolek-Torrello 1995:512). This horizon is poorly represented in the Tucson Basin, and no local phase has been associated with it. The similarity between traditional Mogollon ceramics like Dos Cabezas Red-on-brown and Hohokam Estrella Red-on-gray is the impetus for defining this period as a widespread cultural horizon (Whittlesey 1997:54). The only excavated site in the Tucson Basin to be associated with this horizon is the Dairy site (Altschul and Huber 1995).

Pioneer Period

The beginning of the Pioneer period in the Tucson Basin, dating to around A.D. 700, is signaled by the appearance of a widespread material culture thought to be intrusive from northern Mexico. According to Deaver and Ciolek-Torrello (1995), Snaketown ceramics are the horizon marker of this period. It is in this period that traditional Hohokam culture emerged throughout much of southern Arizona. Occupation of the Tucson Basin appears to have been fairly extensive, but few sites have been excavated that can contribute information on the Snaketown phase. In general, changes in technology suggest the complete adoption of a sedentary, agricultural way of life. The Pioneer period in the Tucson Basin ended around A.D. 800 with the adoption of a new ceramic tradition and with the construction of ball courts at large primary villages.

Colonial Period

In the Colonial period (A.D. 800–900), the initial Cañada del Oro phase was characterized by the appearance of ball courts as public ritual structures and possibly courtyard groups. Dual occupation of the uplands and lowlands continued as the dominant settlement pattern. It was during the Cañada del Oro phase that a distinct tradition of Tucson Basin ceramics first emerged (Kelly 1978; Whittlesey et al. 1994:142).

There was an increase in the number of sites recorded for the succeeding Rillito phase (A.D. 900–1000), which some have interpreted as a population expansion (Whittlesey et al. 1994:144). The intensity of use of alluvial fans and floodplain environments increased, but upland areas continued to be important for settlement. With the expansion came a new emphasis on large primary villages, which functioned as community centers fulfilling political and social requirements in highly localized social systems. Primary villages were large, exhibited a high diversity and density of associated material culture, and often had one or more public features, namely ball courts. The settlement system focused around the primary village often consisted of one or more hamlets and any number of small farmsteads or other temporary camps associated with resource procurement (Doelle et al. 1987:77).

Sedentary Period

The beginning of the Sedentary period, which in the Tucson Basin is equivalent to the Rincon phase (A.D. 1000–1150), saw the maximum expansion of population in the Tucson Basin. Primary villages continued to be important, but settlements were often located along secondary drainages, and a diversity of settlement types and uses of different environmental zones became the settlement norm. Although Rincon Red-on-brown ceramics were the hallmark, there was an apparent florescence of ceramic color schemes that began in the middle portion of the Sedentary period (Deaver 1989:80–81). This fluorescence was associated with a major settlement shift, which occurred throughout the Tucson Basin. Several large primary villages appear to have been abandoned at this time, and settlement generally became more dispersed (Craig and Wallace 1987; Doelle and Wallace 1986; Elson 1986). The causes for this sudden settlement shift are not entirely clear, and both environmental and social factors have been implicated. The diversification of settlement types in the middle and late Rincon phase, however, reflected a new emphasis on resource-procurement and -processing sites as part of the overall adaptation to the Tucson Basin. Despite the shift in settlement patterns, elaboration of village structure continued, and courtyard groups remained an important organizational form at many communities. At the same time, several Rincon phase sites exhibited a less formal site structure, with some communities lacking courtyard groups altogether (Whittlesey 1997:61).

Classic Period

The Classic period in the Tucson Basin is divided into two phases, which have traditionally been defined on the basis of associated ceramics. Adequate, independent chronological control for this time period is lacking. The Tanque Verde phase (A.D. 1150–1300) was characterized by the presence of Tanque Verde Red-on-brown ceramics (Greenleaf 1975; Kelley 1978). In the subsequent Tucson phase, Gila Polychrome was added to Tanque Verde Red-on-brown (Whittlesey 1997). This latter phase has been dated A.D. 1300–1450. In addition to the appearance of Tanque Verde Red-on-brown ceramics, the onset of the Classic period has traditionally been defined by widespread changes in material culture, settlement organization, and public architecture. With the Classic period came a new architectural style: rectangular, semisubterranean, adobe-walled rooms became the preferred house form, although pit houses continued to be used. As in preceding periods, dwellings were often stand-alone structures (Whittlesey et al. 1994: 155), although during the Classic period, many were constructed in contiguous groups sharing walled compound spaces (Fish et al. 1992:20). Platform mounds replaced ball courts as public structures in the Classic period, and there was a marked shift in burial practices from cremation to inhumation.

Initially, the Classic period was thought to have been brought about by the movement of Salado populations into the Phoenix Basin and points south (Haury 1945). More recently, several investigators have posited that these changes were a result of in situ cultural change with little external influence (Sires 1987; Wasley and Doyel 1980). As with the rest of the Hohokam area, the situation in the Tucson Basin is not entirely clear. Evidence for a gradual, in situ shift was found at some sites, such as at Punta de

Agua, where Greenleaf interpreted the transition between late Rincon and early Tanque Verde Red-on-brown ceramics as a continuum in which changes in vessel shapes and design elements represent a transformation of Rincon Red-on-brown into a new ceramic type (Greenleaf 1975:52). Architectural evidence suggests a similar type of experimentation at several communities. Several instances of houses-in-pits existing contemporaneously with aboveground or semisubterranean adobe-walled structures have been documented (Jones 1998; Slaughter 1996). By contrast, the sudden appearance of large settlements such as the Marana Community in the northern Tucson Basin is more in accord with population movement into the region (Fish et al. 1992). Clearly, further research that targets migration and the material correlates of ethnicity is necessary before the question can be put to rest. Unfortunately, the level of temporal control available for most sites in southern Arizona will seriously limit our ability to resolve such questions.

Native Americans of the Historical Period

In this section, we discuss the Native American cultures of southern Arizona after the arrival of Europeans to the region. First, we consider the difficulties of defining the end of prehistory and the beginning of history in southern Arizona and the usual solution of referring to a protohistoric period. Then, we provide brief overviews of the three major historical-period Native American cultures that have lived in the vicinity of the Paseo de las Iglesias study area: O'odham, Apache, and Yaqui (Figure 4).

Protohistory

Southern Arizona was the northernmost frontier of New Spain for nearly three centuries, from 1539 to the independence of Mexico in 1821, or for most of the Spanish colonial presence in the New World. The remoteness of the region from the center of New Spain meant that the period between initial exploration and actual settlement by Spaniards was unusually long, more than a century and a half (see Chapter 4). The conventional definition of the beginning of the historical period as the moment when Europeans first arrived applies less to southern Arizona than perhaps to any other part of New Spain, because the first substantial European presence, and thus the first substantial descriptions of the region and its inhabitants, did not come until the late 1600s. That is when the Jesuits, most notably Eusebio Francisco Kino, began a program of exploration and missionization in what are now Sonora and southern Arizona—the Pimería Alta, or the upper (i.e., northern) region of the Pima.

The protohistoric period in southern Arizona, linking the end of true prehistory and the beginning of tangible history, is inconsistently defined and poorly understood but a convenient way of referring to Native American cultural developments during a time when European influences—crops and livestock, material culture, and especially disease—were undoubtedly present but largely unaccompanied by Europeans. The first Spanish explorers to cross the Southwest, and presumably Arizona, were Fray Marcos de Niza in 1539 and Francisco Vásquez de Coronado in 1540. Both journeys were poorly documented, the actual routes they followed are uncertain, and neither prompted any further exploration of southern Arizona. The region continued essentially unvisited by Spaniards for the next century and a half. The documentary gap spanning the period between 1539 and the beginning of sustained contact with the Spanish, from approximately 1700, defines the protohistoric period for most archaeologists, although some extend the end date to the establishment of presidios in southern Arizona, beginning in the 1750s (Majewski and Ayres 1997; Ravesloot and Whittlesey 1987; Whittlesey et al. 1994).

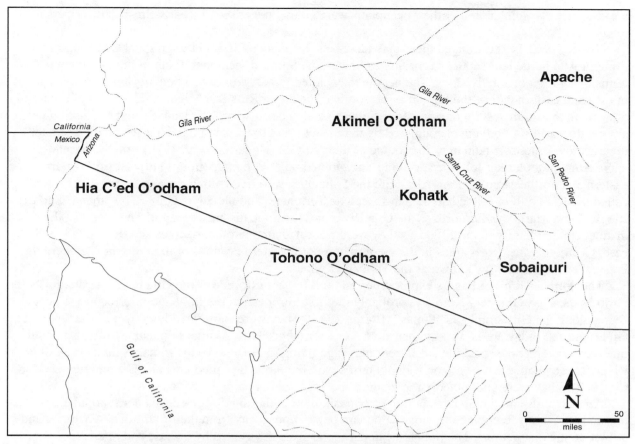

Figure 4. Distribution of Native American groups in southern Arizona during the early historical period.

There were two major groups of indigenous peoples living in the Pimería Alta at the earliest Spanish contact, distinguished by language and lifestyle. One group was the O'odham, Piman-speaking peoples who were agricultural to a greater or lesser degree, depending on the local environment. Several discrete groups of O'odham can be distinguished on the basis of linguistic and cultural differences. The O'odham as a whole were sometimes referred to by the Spanish as *pimas altos*, the upper Pima, and were recognized as the linguistic brethren of the *pimas bajos*, Piman speakers of the lower Pimería, living farther south in Sonora. The other major group was the Apache, Athapaskan speakers who were primarily hunter-gatherer-raiders living a highly mobile way of life and farming very little. The Apache lived primarily in the regions bordering the Pimería on the north and east, making frequent forays into the Pimería to raid. South of the Pimería Alta and living adjacent to *pimas bajos* were the Opata of the Sonora River valley and the nearby Sierra Madre. Still farther south were the Yaqui, centered on the Yaqui River valley. Sometimes traveling through the Pimería Alta, either to reach sacred places or to trade, were the Zuni, who lived on the high, arid Colorado Plateau of present-day New Mexico. There were also two areas adjacent to the Pimería Alta that were apparently uninhabited, described as *despoblados* in the records of the Coronado expedition. One extended north from the headwaters of the Río Sonora to the headwaters of the San Pedro River, and a second lay north of the Gila River, encompassing much of the central mountains of Arizona (Di Peso 1953; Reid and Whittlesey 1997). Whether these

35

areas were truly uninhabited or their occupants were simply never seen by early Spanish observers is unknown.

Spicer (1962:119) estimated there may have been as many as 30,000 Piman speakers living in the Pimería Alta in the late 1600s. According to Spicer, the Spanish seemed to think of the O'odham in terms of four major subdivisions. The people they called Pimas, without any qualifying adjectives, lived in the southeastern part of the region, as far south as the upper Ríos San Miguel and Sonora of modern Sonora. In the southwestern area were the Soba, so called because of their leader's name. The Soba were among the earliest O'odham encountered by the Spanish and lived along the Altar River, a place later regarded by Tohono O'odham as the source of their culture (Underhill et al. 1979). As disease and encroachment took their toll, the surviving Soba joined other O'odham groups (Erickson 1994). In the eastern and northeastern Pimería Alta were the Sobaipuri, who lived along the San Pedro River (then called the Río Quiburi or the Río de San Joseph de Terrenate) and the Santa Cruz River (then called the Río de Santa María), as far north as the Gila River and for some distance along it. They too lost their distinct ethnic identity in the 1700s, as they were relocated among other peoples and devastated by disease. Occupying the desert areas in the western and northwestern portions of the Pimería Alta were the Papago, or Papabota, now known as the Tohono O'odham.

The northern limit of Kino's explorations and missionary efforts was the Gila River. Traveling as far north as the Casa Grande—Kino was probably the first European to see it—Kino referred to the people living along the Gila simply as "Pimas" (Bolton 1948). They were subsequently known as the Gileño or Gila Pima and today are known by their own name for themselves, Akimel O'odham. Kino also noted that there were people speaking a different language living to the west of the Pima, as far as the Colorado River. These people, who were on friendly terms with the Pima, he called Opa and Cocomaricopa (Bolton 1948). They were undoubtedly the Yuman-speaking Maricopa.

Apache raids and the Spanish policy of *reducción*, or gathering dispersed *ranchería* populations into missionary centers, combined to move O'odham populations away from their traditional territories and to blur ethnic distinctions. The Sobaipuri in particular were devastated by disease and relocation. By the late eighteenth century, they had ceased to exist except as scattered anonymous elements of other O'odham populations. At the same time, many of the desert-dwelling Tohono O'odham relocated to the Santa Cruz River valley, encouraged by Spanish missionaries who hoped to find replacements for the disappearing Sobaipuri.

By the time professional ethnographers came to record their ways of life, the O'odham people themselves recognized three major divisions based largely on economy and residential patterns, which may approximate much more closely the subdivisions of the protohistoric period than the labels applied to them by the Spanish. These were the Hia C'ed O'odham, or Sand People, the most mobile and least agricultural of the O'odham, living in the western deserts as far south as the Gulf of California; the Tohono O'odham, or Desert People (the Papago to the Spanish, although this term was sometimes also used for the Hia C'ed O'odham), who shifted between summer farming villages and winter hunting-gathering encampments; and the Akimel O'odham, or River People, who stayed year-round in permanent villages along the Gila River. In the terminology of Fontana (1983b), these groups are, respectively, the No Villagers, the Two Villagers, and the One Villagers. O'odham lifeways are discussed in more detail below.

The Apache also were given many different labels by the Spanish. Unfortunately, the tendency was to call any nomadic people "Apache" whether they were Athapaskan speakers or not. The Jocome and Suma occupied what was later Chiricahua Apache territory in southeastern Arizona and southwestern New Mexico (Spicer 1962:237). Farther to the east were the Jano, Manso, and Jumano, who occupied Chihuahua as far east as the Río Grande. Although the Jocome were probably Apache, Spicer did not think that the Suma were Athapaskan speakers. They more likely were related to the Jumano, semisedentary people who ranged into the Great Plains. Spicer suggested that the Jano were a band of Chiricahua or Mimbreño Apache. Schroeder (1974a, 1974b) thought that the Jano and Jocome were not Apache and that no Apache peoples occupied the region south of the Gila River before the 1680s. Almost nothing is known of the Manso, because they were missionized in the vicinity of El Paso in the 1700s and abandoned their former nonagricultural way of life (Spicer 1962:231).

To the north of the Pimería Alta, beyond the Gila River, were simply the "Apache." Apachería was the term Kino applied to the land lying between the lands of the Pima and those of the Hopi and Zuni to the north (Opler 1983:402). Basso (1983:465) believed the people living in this area later became the Western Apache, who by 1700 had successfully claimed an extensive territory that stretched south from the Mogollon Rim across the Natanes Plateau to the Gila River—essentially the country called *despoblado* by a chronicler of the Coronado expedition.

Other Spanish names for Apache were Querecho, applied to the nomadic people encountered by Coronado and later applied to Apache groups living near Acoma in New Mexico, and Apaches de Gila (or Xila), a vague term for Apache living in southeastern Arizona and southwestern New Mexico. Opler (1983:402) thought that some of the Querechos might have belonged to the Eastern Chiricahua Apache band.

It is difficult to identify protohistoric archaeological sites in southern Arizona, for a number of reasons. First, the documentary sources provide little information about lifeways and material culture. The best descriptions of O'odham culture were written after it had been dramatically transformed by European contact. Similarly, the misinterpretation of some early historical-period sites has created confusion about the material remains that might correspond to actual protohistoric settlements. Second, it is difficult to date protohistoric sites. No archaeomagnetic chronology has been developed for this period, and radiocarbon dates are typically returned with ranges too wide to be useful. Third, the way of life of at least one of the peoples to occupy the region, the Apache, was not likely to leave easily recognizable remains.

We do know that the Akimel O'odham (Gila Pima) and Sobaipuri at the time of European contact were agricultural and lived in brush houses covered with mats, similar to Hohokam pit houses. Juan Mateo Manje, Kino's military escort on many of his travels, provided the following description of San Agustín de Oiaur, one of the largest settlements in the vicinity of modern Tucson:

> Here the river runs a full flow of water, though the horses forded it without difficulty. There are good pasture and agricultural lands with a canal for irrigation. The Indians harvest corn, beans, and cotton from which they make cloth to dress themselves. Squash, melons and watermelons were also raised. We counted 800 souls in 186 houses (Manje 1954:92).

It is difficult to reconcile this view of early Sobaipuri life with the picture painted by archaeology. Sites that have been attributed to the Sobaipuri in southern Arizona are ephemeral, with little refuse deposition and few artifacts, indicating short-term occupation. They are characterized by oval or subrectangular houses marked by single courses of cobbles presumably used to foot or brace the brush superstructure. Moreover, virtually nothing is known of the lifeways of early Apache peoples in southern Arizona, and no unequivocal early Apache sites have been located.

O'odham

The O'odham were the most populous group of Native Americans living in southern Arizona at the time of European contact. As already noted, the Spanish made a variety of distinctions among groups of O'odham, but these distinctions probably reflect the circumstances of Spanish encounters with the O'odham as much as any distinctions recognized by the O'odham themselves. The most enduring distinctions are those of Akimel, Tohono, and Hia C'ed O'odham, which are based on differing economic emphases and degrees of residential mobility. Here we discuss these three groups individually, plus two others that had disappeared by the late eighteenth century, the Kohatk and the Sobaipuri. The first three groups have survived into the twenty-first century and are known through a combination of historical and ethnographic documentation. The last two groups are known only through Spanish documentary sources.

Akimel O'odham

Kino first encountered the Akimel O'odham when he reached Casa Grande in 1694. He returned several times over the next eight years, but following his death in 1711, the Akimel O'odham had little if any contact with Europeans until 1736, when another Jesuit, Ignacio Javier Keller, visited the Gila River. By this time, the *rancherías* that Kino had encountered had dispersed. From the mid-eighteenth century to the 1840s, contact with Europeans remained limited, with only sporadic trading by Akimel O'odham at the presidio in Tucson and occasional visits by Spanish traders traveling to the Gila River (Russell 1908).

In the 1840s, most notably during the California gold rush of 1849, the Akimel O'odham proved to be friendly and helpful to Anglo-Americans and others traveling along the Gila Trail, a major route to California. The Akimel O'odham became an invaluable source of supplies, feed for stock, and even protection. Following the Gadsden Purchase, the U.S. Army also found the Akimel O'odham to be helpful, both as a source of supplies and as scouts against the Apache. In the early 1860s, Mormon towns were established at Tempe and Lehi by settlers from Utah. Often at the mercy of the Apache, the Mormons requested assistance from the Akimel O'odham and Maricopa, some of whom moved to Lehi to provide security for the settlers. Later in the nineteenth century, European settlement began to displace the Akimel O'odham, just as it had other peoples in the Pimería Alta. By the start of the twentieth century, the Akimel O'odham were reduced to eight villages along the Gila, most on the south bank (Russell 1908). It is ironic that the Akimel O'odham villages, which for several decades served as the breadbasket of southern Arizona, were deprived of water and reduced to poverty as non-Indian farmers in the Phoenix area diverted the water of the Gila River to their own fields (DeJong 1992).

Prior to Spanish contact, the Akimel O'odham lived in villages or smaller settlements called *rancherías* by the Spanish. Their pole-and-thatch houses were positioned generally within sight but not sound of each other. They raised corn, beans, melons, squash, cotton, and gourds. Whether they practiced irrigated agriculture before the eighteenth century, diverting water from the Gila River by means of ditches, is a topic of controversy. There is no mention of irrigation in the accounts of Kino and Manje, who did mention the use of irrigation by the Sobaipuri; the first mention occurs in Spanish accounts of the mid-1700s. It does seem likely that the Akimel O'odham used the Gila River as a source of water for their crops (see discussion in Whittlesey [1998]).

Akimel O'odham men cleared, planted, and irrigated the fields that were harvested later by the women. The diet was mixed but predominantly plant based, with saguaro fruit and mesquite pods being the most abundant and available native foods. During water shortages, the Akimel O'odham were forced to rely more on wild foods, even seeking plants and animals in Apache territory. Around the turn of the nineteenth century, floods occasionally would destroy the irrigation canals and crops, forcing the Akimel O'odham to rely entirely on wild resources (Rea 1997; Russell 1908).

Russell (1908) identified 65 native food plants that provided edible stems, leaves, flowers, seeds, roots, bulbs, nuts, fruits, and berries. Food plants included saltbush *(â'nûk i'avak)*, cottonwood *(a'opa hi'âsik)*, agave *(aot)*, ironwood *(hait''kam)*, mesquite mistletoe *(hâ'kowat)*, pumpkin *(halt)*, tree cholla *(ha'nûm)*, saguaro *(ha'rsany)*, mesquite *(koi)*, palo verde *(ko'kitc uhûtaki)*, screwbean *(ko'ûtcilt)*, watermelon *(me'la)*, prickly pear *(naf')*, catclaw *(o'-opat)*, beans *(pavf(I))*, wild onion *(rsat)*, muskmelon *(si'etcu)*, cotton *(tâki)*, squash *(tapkalt)*, pepper *(tcil'tipin)*, and acorns *(to'a)*. The Akimel O'odham also used many of these food plants—particularly several shrubs, trees, gourds—for medicinal needs, and used willow shoots, cattails, and devil's claw for basket weaving (see also Rea 1997).

The Akimel O'odham used many wildlife species from the *bajada*, river, and mountains to supplement their plant diet. Animals hunted, fished, and trapped included fish *(vatop)*, peccary *(kâ'-âtci)*, badger *(kaf)*, antelope *(ki'-ovik)*, mountain lion *(ma'vit)*, ground squirrel *(rsu'lik)*, deer *(si'-ik* and *wh'ai)*, a variety of birds *(ta'matâlt)*, rabbit *(tâpi, tcok tcof,* and *to'a tcof)*, mountain sheep *(tcirsâny)*, and raccoon *(va'owok)*. Eagles and hawks were kept for their feathers, which were used by the medicine men. The villagers caught lizards and other small animals to feed these birds (Russell 1908; see also Rea 1998). As did other indigenous groups, the Akimel O'odham adopted many plants and animals introduced by the Spanish. Wheat and sorghum were added to their indigenous crops. Winter wheat enabled them to grow two crops in a single season. Cattle, horses, burros, mules, and poultry greatly increased their domestic animal population, which had previously been limited to dogs (Russell 1908).

Tohono O'odham

The Tohono O'odham occupied a large area in the north-central Pimería Alta, also known as the Papaguería to the Spanish, after the Spanish name for the Tohono O'odham, *papagos*. Their intermittently transhumant way of life, a combination of agriculture, hunting, and gathering, was an adaptation to the seasonal extremes of their desert environment. They spent the hot summers in lowland villages, farming the alluvial fans extending from the bases of the mountains, and the mild winters at camps near wells or springs in the mountains, hunting and gathering. This is the typical "Two Villager" way of life discussed by Fontana (1983b). Tohono O'odham farming was most often of the *ak chin* variety, which involved placing brush dams across washes to better distribute mountain runoff across the cultivated portions of alluvial fans (Nabhan 1983).

Castetter and Bell (1942:57) estimated that collected plant foods and game constituted 75 percent of the Tohono O'odham diet. Saguaro, mesquite, prickly pear, and cholla were the most important plants. Each spring, the Tohono O'odham set up cactus camps to gather saguaro fruit, from which they made a variety of dried foods and wine. The saguaro wine ceremony was performed each year to ensure the arrival of the summer rains. Old men who knew the traditional procedures fermented syrup from the saguaro fruit while villagers gathered nightly to dance and sing. When it was ready, the wine was served as a symbol of renewal of life, and participants would drink to the point of intoxication (Underhill et al. 1979).

The Tohono O'odham lived in pole-and-brush houses, slept on grass mats, and carried out many of their daily activities outdoors under *ramadas*. The house, or *ki*, was a dome-shaped structure similar to Hohokam pit houses. Although best known for their beautifully detailed baskets made of devil's claw and grass, the Tohono O'odham were also excellent potters. In the late nineteenth and early twentieth centuries, their manure-tempered ollas were used in virtually every household in Tucson, regardless of ethnicity. Several painted pottery types were made, including red-on-brown, white-on-red, and black-on-red (Fontana et al. 1962; Whittlesey 1986). Saguaro syrup in narrow-necked jars was consistently traded to the Akimel O'odham in exchange for wheat and other goods (Russell 1908).

Tohono O'odham villages consisted of extended patrilineal families. Marriages were arranged with people from other villages, and the wife would usually move into her husband's home, helping her mother-in-law with daily tasks (Underhill 1939). Sometimes the husband would move in with the wife's family, however, if they needed help. Although polygamy was allowed, close relatives could not marry (Erickson 1994). When villages became too large, daughter settlements would split off, retaining close social and ceremonial ties to the mother village.

Although the Tohono O'odham were not aggressive, they were accomplished warriors and generally successful at defending themselves from Apache and other attacks. The Tohono O'odham maintained amicable relations with most of their neighbors, including the Seri to the south, the Lower Pima and Opata to the southeast, the Akimel O'odham to the north, and the Cocopa and Yuma peoples living along the lower Gila and Colorado Rivers to the west. The Tohono O'odham traded with most of their neighbors, exchanging food items, hides, sleeping mats, pottery, and baskets. Songs, ceremonies, and labor also were traded on occasion for food and goods (Erickson 1994).

Because the Tohono O'odham were closely related to the Akimel O'odham in language, culture, and economy, there was much trading, sharing, and intermarriage between the two groups, and especially between the northern Tohono O'odham villages and the Akimel O'odham. The Akimel O'odham, distinguished by permanent houses and large, irrigated fields, were wealthy in comparison to the Tohono O'odham. Tohono O'odham sometimes worked in Akimel O'odham fields during times of shortage, and food was often shared freely between the two groups.

The history of contact between other O'odham groups and Europeans was repeated with the Tohono O'odham. Kino greatly influenced religious and subsistence changes among the Tohono O'odham, just as he had among the Sobaipuri and Akimel O'odham, although the raising of cattle and rituals regarded as curing techniques spread more rapidly than formal Christianity (Spicer 1962). Kino's mission program took approximately 50 years to spread from Sonora to San Xavier del Bac. Following the Gadsden Purchase, the Tohono O'odham developed strong relationships with Mexican and Anglo-Americans based on their shared need to defend against raiding Apache. The raids were frequent and fierce into the 1860s but decreased significantly following a tragic episode at Camp Grant in 1871, discussed below in the section on the Apache.

In 1874, a reservation was established by executive order for the Tohono O'odham, consisting of 69,200 acres surrounding Mission San Xavier. Eight years later, a second, much smaller reservation was established at Gila Bend for Tohono O'odham who had resettled on the Gila River to the west of the Akimel O'odham villages. Only about 10 percent of the Tohono O'odham population lived on the two reservations in the early years, but the formal designation of reservations eventually provided the Tohono O'odham, particularly those living at San Xavier, with a certain amount of political clout. Squatting on reservation lands by non–Tohono O'odham, especially Mexican-Americans, was at first common near San Xavier, and the lack of a government agency on the reservation (it was at first administered from Sacaton on the Gila River) meant squatting could happen freely. But by 1882, with the help of their federal Indian agent, the Tohono O'odham managed to expel all squatters from the reservation (Erickson 1994:78, 87). A single Mexican-American, José María Martínez, retained his pre-Gadsden Mexican land grant near the mission, under special circumstances (see Chapter 4).

The late nineteenth century brought another important Anglo-American-imposed change to the Tohono O'odham living at San Xavier. The Dawes Severalty Act of 1887 provided for the allotment of small parcels of reservation land, typically 160 acres, to individual O'odham. The purpose of the act was to encourage O'odham to abandon their previously communal approach to land use, in which families used whatever land they needed, and fixed ownership was unknown. After 25 years, allotted land could be sold like any privately held land, and any reservation land not yet allotted to individual O'odham would be made available to non-O'odham settlers. The federal government considered individual land ownership a necessary step in making reservations throughout the West less dependent on federal aid and administration, but the concept of private ownership was alien to the O'odham, as it was to many other Native Americans, and they adapted slowly to the new system. The act ultimately did have the effect of converting many traditional O'odham into organized growers, commercial stock raisers, and even individual wage earners, and it pushed the O'odham toward a cash-based economy (Erickson 1994:91–94).

In 1916, the federal government granted the Tohono O'odham a much larger reservation to the west of San Xavier, extending from the Baboquivari Mountains westward almost to Ajo and from the border with Mexico northward almost to Gila Bend, encompassing some 2.75 million acres. With a number of minor additions and subtractions during its early years, this huge area has survived largely intact as the current Tohono O'odham reservation. In 1934, the federal Indian Reorganization Act, intended as an impetus to Indian self-government, led to the establishment of a centralized Tohono O'odham tribal government and 11 constituent districts. Each district elected a council, two members of which served as representatives on the tribal council, which itself was headed by a chairman, vice chairman, secretary, and treasurer. The districts also elected their own officers to head the district councils. The U.S. Constitution was the model for the tribal constitution, but the tribal bylaws also reflected O'odham traditions, which encouraged the communal use of land. The tribal council continued the practice of going to villages to discuss problems and issues before they made decisions (Blaine 1981; Erickson 1994:104–107).

Hia C'ed O'odham

The traditional lands of the Hia C'ed O'odham extended from the Gila and Colorado Rivers in the north through the Sierra Pinacate region of Sonora to the Gulf of California and southward to Seri country. The Hia C'ed O'odham have also been called Sand Papago, Areneros, Areneños, and Pinacateños. Other O'odham have called them *Hiá Tatk Kuá'adam,* sand-root eaters, and *Otomkal Kuá'adam,* desert iguana eaters. Although this O'odham group was declared extinct in the early 1900s and consequently denied rights to their traditional lands, approximately 1,300 individuals today identify themselves as Hia C'ed O'odham (Rea 1998).

The Hia C'ed O'odham were divided into northern and southern groups, the latter sharing land and cultural similarities with the Seri in Mexico. The northern group interacted with Yuman-speaking peoples and shared similarities with them. The Hia C'ed O'odham were the most linguistically distinct among the O'odham, speaking faster and having exclusive terms, but were still easily understood by all other O'odham (Erickson 1994).

The Hia C'ed O'odham lands were the driest and hottest of the Pimería Alta and the least densely settled. With only a few places suitable for farming, which they carried out using the *ak chin* system (Rea 1998), most of the Hia C'ed O'odham lived as hunters and gatherers ranging over a large area in small family groups. The Hia C'ed O'odham were distinctive for their heavy use of native fish that could be harvested from tidal pools along the Gulf of California. As a consequence of the lack of arable lands and sparse settlement, the Hia C'ed O'odham remained generally isolated from the influences of Spanish culture, as other areas were explored for ranching, farming, and mining. These same characteristics also kept Apache raiding to a minimum (Erickson 1994).

The Hia C'ed O'odham suffered greatly during the 1850s and 1860s, when disease devastated the population. Miners at Ajo and ranchers at Quitobaquito encroached on some of their most desirable lands during this time, but the people managed to survive and found employment constructing the railroad through the Gila River basin. Today, they remain scattered. Most live among Tohono O'odham but have never completely assimilated into the main body of O'odham people. In Mexico, the southern Hia C'ed O'odham met a similar fate, having been relocated by the government from the western end of O'odham lands to Quitovac and other inland areas. They too have merged with other O'odham people (Erickson 1994).

Another detrimental impact to the Hia C'ed O'odham of Arizona came when what is now known as the Barry M. Goldwater Air Force Range was established in the 1940s. The Hia C'ed O'odham were prohibited from using that enormous part of their traditional area. The establishment of Organ Pipe Cactus National Monument and the Cabeza Prieta Game Range left virtually no traditional lands in the United States for Hia C'ed O'odham use (Erickson 1994).

Kohatk

The Kohatk, also spelled Koahadk and Kwahatdk, were distinguished among Tohono O'odham as a dialect group (Erickson 1994), although they were closely related to the Akimel O'odham through intermarriage and trade (Erickson 1994; Rea 1998). Kohatk settlements extended as far south as an imaginary line

41

extending between modern Santa Rosa and Tucson (Erickson 1994). They lived mostly in villages located between the Picacho Mountains and the Gila River villages of the Akimel O'odham, in an area today known as the Santa Cruz Flats. Important villages were Kohatk, near the Slate Mountains; Ak Chin, near Picacho; and Santa Ana de Cuiquiburitac, east of the Santa Rosa Mountains (Fontana 1987; Russell 1908; Whittlesey et al. 1994:250). The Kohatk moved between *ak chin* fields on the lower Santa Cruz River and adjacent washes to fields along the Gila River as opportunities allowed (Dobyns 1974; Rea 1998). They seem to have been neither "desert people" nor "river people," but O'odham who regularly moved between and used both environments (Whittlesey et al. 1994:252).

The documentary history of the Kohatk is confusing, including references to village locations (Whittlesey et al. 1994:249–251). What little is known of their cultural ecology parallels the practices of the other O'odham groups (Rea 1998), although they were noted for bringing cattle to the area in the 1820s (Ezell 1961; Rea 1998; Russell 1908; Whittemore 1893). Some desert settlements were sustained by artificial reservoirs, and Dobyns (1974:325) has pointed out that the Kohatk also dug ditches as necessary to water their fields. Their ethnobiology, however, remains speculative. Little is known about Kohatk social organization. If, as documentary sources suggest, the Kohatk were intermediate between Akimel and Tohono O'odham in economic organization and settlement practices, it may be appropriate to view them as socially intermediate as well (Whittlesey et al. 1994:255).

Kohatk material culture was generally similar to that of other O'odham. Historically, they were known as excellent potters (Russell 1908:124). The Akimel O'odham obtained many painted vessels from the Kohatk in exchange for Pima wheat and other foodstuffs. Apparently, Kohatk pottery was highly polished and more often decorated than other O'odham pottery (Fontana et al. 1962:107–109).

The Kohatk experienced little influence from the Spanish, although there were early attempts at missionization (Fontana 1987). Increased pressure from Apache raiding after Mexican independence forced the Kohatk to abandon their villages along the lower Santa Cruz River and take refuge among the villages of neighboring O'odham. Fontana (1987) indicated that the remaining Kohatk people settled across the Gila River from the Sacaton community, a village that eventually became known as Santan. Other members moved to the Salt River reservation. By the early 1900s, the Kohatk had lost identity as an independent group and had been assimilated into Akimel O'odham and Tohono O'odham communities (Rea 1998).

Sobaipuri

Unfortunately, we know little about the Sobaipuri, who were once the most populous O'odham group in the vicinity of the Santa Cruz River. Although it was the Sobaipuri who were described in Kino and Manje's accounts of the late 1600s, there is little if any overlap between the documentary and archaeological evidence for the Sobaipuri occupation of southern Arizona. There are several reasons for this. Most important, the Sobaipuri intermixed early on with Tohono O'odham and other Piman-speaking peoples, such that by the 1800s they had lost their social and ethnic identity. The documentary evidence itself is difficult to interpret and understand. Sobaipuri *rancherías* were easily moved, and because the Spanish names for villages, including saints' appellations, moved along with the villages, maps made at different times may show several places with the same names. It is difficult, therefore, to match an archaeological site with the location of a named Sobaipuri village.

With this caution, what we know of the Sobaipuri is that they once lived in the well-watered valleys of the Santa Cruz and San Pedro Rivers, farming and producing "plentiful crops" of "calabashes, frijoles, maize, and cotton" (Bolton 1948:I:170–171). Chroniclers of the Coronado expedition noted the Sobaipuri's use of turquoise and body painting or tattooing of their faces and bodies. They came to be known, consequently, as Rsársavinâ, meaning "spotted." The Sobaipuri had few interactions with the Spanish until the latter part of the seventeenth century. They maintained trade relations, however, with the Spanish in the Río Grande Valley and presumably also with the Spanish of the Pimería Baja. In the early eighteenth century, the Spanish enlisted the Sobaipuri for military purposes; they provided an armed buffer against raiding Apache (Di Peso 1953). The Sobaipuri were fierce warriors, aggressive and accustomed to war because of their proximity to and frequent encounters with the Apache (Erickson 1994).

From the late 1600s to approximately 1762, the landscape of the Santa Cruz and San Pedro River valleys was characterized by *rancherías,* larger villages, irrigation canals, wells, and cultivated fields (Griffith 1992). Sobaipuri villages appear to have been occupied briefly, and settlement locations shifted rapidly. Seymour (1989:215) suggested that the suitability of the floodplain for farming was the major determinant in locating villages. Inferred Sobaipuri sites in the San Pedro River valley were located on ridges and terraces above the river. There were at least 14 *rancherías* along the San Pedro River when Kino and Manje visited there in the late 1600s (Whittlesey et al. 1994:237). Approximately 100–500 people lived in each of these villages. South of Santa Cruz de Gaybanipitea (Di Peso 1953), more than 2,000 people lived in numerous small villages. Although villages had existed between the *rancherías* of Quiburi and Cusac, they were abandoned by the 1700s.

The Tucson Basin was densely settled, apparently because of intensive agriculture (Doelle 1984). The stretch of the Santa Cruz River between San Xavier del Bac and San Clemente (thought to be located near Point of the Mountain, at the northern end of the Tucson Mountains) was the center of Upper Pima culture at the time of Spanish contact, with an estimated 2,000 residents (Doelle 1984:207). Other important villages were San Agustín de Oaiur (also spelled Oyaur and Oyaut), San Cosme del Tucson, and Valle de Correa in the north, and Guevavi, Tumacácori, and Calabazas in the south (Whittlesey et al. 1994:234–236).

Sobaipuri lifeways and material culture were evidently similar to those of other O'odham groups in southern Arizona. They lived in oval or round structures built of brush, poles, and mats. Whether they built adobe structures as suggested in some documents (Burrus 1971; Pfefferkorn 1989) is controversial. Some authors (e.g., Masse 1981) think this was the product of Spanish influence. It is probable that the earliest Sobaipuri pottery was the thin, wiped brown ware called Whetstone Plain. Whetstone Plain is very different from known historical-period ceramics of O'odham manufacture, which are thick, well polished, and often red slipped, and which often have black cores resulting from the use of manure temper. Sobaipuri pottery is puzzling for other reasons. Whetstone Plain pottery exhibits similarities to other protohistoric and early-historical-period pottery over a vast region, including Patayan or Yuman ceramics, Apache pottery, Yavapai pottery, and the pottery made by Numic-speaking people, such as Shoshone and Paiute (Ravesloot and Whittlesey 1987). Differentiating among native peoples on the basis of their ceramics is a time-honored practice in archaeology but is notoriously difficult for the early historical period.

A particular type of projectile point with a deeply concave, indented base and serrated edges is attributed to the Sobaipuri (Masse 1981; Ravesloot and Whittlesey 1987). Points like this have also been attributed to the Yavapai (Pilles 1981). Other stone artifacts were relatively undiagnostic, although the raw materials are typically thought to be of better quality than those used in Hohokam stone tools (Brew and Huckell 1987:171).

Little is known of Sobaipuri farming techniques. Documentary evidence suggests use of simple, gravity-fed irrigation channels to divert water from rivers and swampy areas to fields, but no archaeological evidence of these has yet been found. The archaeological data indicate a low frequency of ground stone tools, plant remains, storage facilities, and other materials usually associated with an intensive reliance on agriculture. We do not know whether this reflects factors of preservation or other factors. Prior to Spanish contact, the Sobaipuri raised maize, beans, squash, cotton, melons, and three kinds of gourds. Cotton was spun and woven into clothing. Following the arrival of the Spanish, they added wheat, barley, chili, sugar cane, sweet potatoes, and watermelons to their fields. The Sobaipuri used a wide variety of native wild plants for food, construction purposes, and medicine. Mescal, or agave, was used for food and drink and in crafts; mesquite wood was used for construction, and mesquite beans were eaten; and the fruit of cacti such as prickly pear and saguaro was used for food. Many plants provided treatments for a variety of ailments (Di Peso 1953). The Sobaipuri also added stock raising to their subsistence activities when the Spanish introduced cattle, sheep, goats, horses, donkeys, and mules. The introduction of these new foods brought changes to the allocation of labor and the value system, in addition to changes in subsistence.

Interactions among the Sobaipuri and their neighbors ran the gamut from hostilities to intermarriage. Spanish sources from the late 1600s indicate that, although Apache peoples lived east of the San Pedro River and along the banks of the Gila River, they had been raiding O'odham settlements for many years. Language was a common bond among the natives of the Pimería Alta, and the Sobaipuri maintained frequent communications with the Akimel O'odham and the Tohono O'odham. Their relations with the Akimel O'odham in particular included frequent trade and intermarriage. During the 1600s, the Sobaipuri evidently maintained friendly communication and commerce with their Hopi and Zuni neighbors to the north. Although Wyllys (1931, cited in Di Peso 1953) characterized the Sobaipuri as haughty and arrogant, they were looked up to by the other natives of the Pimería Alta, presumably because of their lack of malice. Citing Bolton (1948), Di Peso (1953) wrote that Kino also noted these temperament differences, adding that the Sobaipuri were generous in their poverty, sharing necessities with visitors as they were able. Opposition and rivalry between the Sobaipuri and other indigenous groups was expressed through fighting, and later in races and contests.

Sobaipuri living along the Santa Cruz and San Pedro Rivers had a long history of intermarriage and cooperative action when the need arose. When Kino arrived, the Apache were already pushing hard against the eastern boundary of Pimería Alta. Recognizing the warlike reputation of the Sobaipuri, the Spanish sought to organize the villages of the San Pedro Valley into a military alliance to defend the northern frontier of New Spain. This attempted militarization eventually had disastrous consequences (Fontana 1983a:137). The *reducción* policy and missionization actually increased Apache raiding, as the concentrated livestock, weapons, and stored food provided an additional lure (Ezell 1983:149).

Problems with Apache raiding became so great that in 1762 the San Pedro Sobaipuri joined the Santa Cruz Sobaipuri at Santa María de Suamca, San Xavier del Bac, and San Agustín del Tucson, significantly changing the ethnic composition of the valley. This also left the San Pedro Valley—once a Sobaipuri barrier against the Apache—essentially defenseless and unprotected. There is controversy over the reasons that the Sobaipuri abandoned the San Pedro River valley. Some authors think that the Sobaipuri simply fled in the face of the hostile Apache (Kessell 1976), whereas others believe that Sobaipuri resettlement was by order of Spanish *reducción* policy and carried out by military officers (Dobyns 1976). Both processes were probably at work.

The densely settled villages of the Santa Cruz River valley quickly succumbed to epidemics against which the residents had little inherited resistance. By 1773, the population of San Xavier del Bac was greatly reduced as a result of epidemics and Apache raids. Tohono O'odham, encouraged to settle at the mission beginning around 1800 to replace the Sobaipuri population lost to disease and war, intermarried with the remaining Sobaipuri, and the loss of Sobaipuri ethnic identity was inevitable. In 1776, the Tubac presidio was relocated to Tucson. Within the next quarter century, the Spanish population increased as ranchers and miners moved into the Santa Cruz Valley, contact between Spanish and O'odham peoples increased, and the native population decreased (Bronitsky and Merritt 1986; Erickson 1994; Ezell 1983; Whittlesey at al. 1994). No Sobaipuri remain today.

Major sites that have been attributed to Sobaipuri occupation include England Ranch Ruin, located along the Santa Cruz River south of Tucson (Doyel 1977); Santa Cruz de Gaybanipitea, excavated by Di Peso (1953); three sites in the Santa Rita Mountains excavated during the ANAMAX-Rosemont project (Huckell 1984c); and Alder Wash Ruin, on the San Pedro River (Masse 1985). Some of these sites have objects of European manufacture, such as glass beads and metal tools, but others do not. There are other isolated finds and components at sites that have been attributed to the Sobaipuri, including a late occupation at the San Xavier Bridge site (see review in Ravesloot and Whittlesey [1987]). Several flexed inhumations with Sobaipuri-style projectile points and unusual accompaniments, including a shell trumpet, a golden eagle skeleton, and arrow-making kits, were found at the site (Ravesloot 1987b). Excavated sites that Di Peso attributed to the Sobaipuri—the supposed village of Quiburi in the San Pedro Valley (Di Peso 1953) and San Cayetano in the Santa Cruz Valley (Di Peso 1956)—probably were not the native Sobaipuri settlements their excavator claimed them to be. The former is the site of the Spanish presidio of Santa Cruz de Terrenate, and although some Sobaipuri may have lived at or near the presidio, the structures that Di Peso excavated and attributed to them probably were not Sobaipuri but Spanish (Masse 1981; Seymour 1989; Whittlesey 1994; Whittlesey et al. 1994:239–241); the latter site is a Classic period Hohokam site with evidence for some later (probably middle or late 1800s) O'odham occupation (Whittlesey 1994; Whittlesey et al. 1994:241; Wilcox 1987). It is unfortunate that, although there have been excavations at the locations of several Sobaipuri villages in the Santa Cruz Valley, including San Xavier del Bac, Guevavi, and Tumacácori, few traces of the late-1600s to early-1700s occupation have been found.

Apache

In sharp contrast to sedentary farmers such as the Akimel O'odham, the Apache were the most mobile of southwestern peoples. Instead of defining their lives with reference to a particular river valley, the Apache centered their lives on the mountains of southern and central Arizona. The mountains defined their traditional territories, provided them with food and shelter, and embodied their sacred places. In times of conflict, the mountains were their refuge. Because of their uniquely close familiarity with the mountains, the Apache were able to pursue their way of life long after many other Native Americans had resigned themselves to reservations.

The Apache were relatively recent migrants to the Southwest, although the timing of their entry has been widely debated. Most scholars agree that the Apache, who are classified linguistically as Southern Athapaskan speakers, moved southward from an original home in Alaska or southern Canada sometime around A.D. 1500, if not earlier. Their language, culture, and lifeways reflect this distinctive origin and comparatively recent history. All Apache peoples were highly mobile and made their living by a combination of hunting, collecting wild plant foods, raiding, and some farming. This way of life brought them into frequent and often violent contact with sedentary, farming Native Americans and the Euroamericans who came later.

Ethnographers subdivide the Apache into several hierarchical groupings on the basis of territorial, linguistic, and cultural differences. The largest grouping was the tribe or division, traditionally subdivided into smaller groups and bands. Two groupings whose traditional territories overlapped are most important in southern Arizona history. These are the Aravaipa band, part of the San Carlos group of the Western Apache, and the Central Chiricahua band of the Chiricahua Apache.

The Aravaipa band was called *tcéjìné* ("dark rocks people") for a region in the Galiuro Mountains near to where they lived. As their name suggests, the Aravaipa band made Aravaipa Canyon their home base. Their territory included the lower San Pedro River valley as far north as the Gila River and the mountains bordering the valley—the Santa Catalina, Rincon, Santa Teresa, and Galiuro Mountains. Their seasonal round followed the cycle of the year and the ripening of wild crops. Family groups separated from the main band in search of wild foods, usually bringing back the prepared crop for consumption and storage. In late spring, they planted corn at Aravaipa Canyon. In summer, they lived in the mountains overlooking Tucson and the Santa Cruz River valley. The fruit of the saguaro brought them to the San Pedro Valley in July, and they gathered acorns near Oracle in the fall. Fall was harvest time, and after the crop was brought in, they lived in secure winter camps located in the Galiuro and Santa Teresa Mountains, from which their men mounted raids into Mexico. One of the most important traditional foods was mescal, or agave. The hearts of the plants were roasted in huge pits near the sites where they grew, and the prepared mescal was brought back to camp. In addition to food, mescal provided a fermented drink, fibers for sewing, and a fibrous stalk for lance shafts and musical instruments.

Bands were composed of 3–12 local groups, which were the fundamental unit of Western Apache and Chiricahua Apache society. Chiricahua bands were smaller, consisting of 3–5 local groups, and the local group was named after some prominent natural landmark in its range or labeled by the name of its chief. Each local group consisted of 2–10 family clusters, or *gota,* usually totaling 10–30 households, who returned each year to the group's farming site. Clans, or large kinship groupings, were nonterritorial and served to regulate marriage, extend kinship beyond the family, and provide economic and social support. Cutting across group and other boundaries, clans served to create an expansive web of kinship bonds. The minimal residential unit was the *gowa,* or camp, a term referring to the house, its occupants, and the camp itself. Dwellings were dome-shaped or conical pole-and-brush structures often referred to as wickiups. The largest and most permanent structures were called *nesdango'wa* (ripe fruits wickiup) and were located at the farm sites. Archaeologically, a *gowa* can often be recognized only by the rock rings that once formed the wickiup foundation. The Chiricahua Apache occasionally built tepees or hide-covered structures.

The Central Chiricahua band ranged around the present-day towns of Duncan, Willcox, Benson, and Elgin in southern Arizona, and they held mountain strongholds in the Dos Cabezas, Chiricahua, Dragoon, Mule, and Huachuca Mountains. Each local group had a "chief" or "leader" who gained prominence because of his bravery, wisdom, eloquence, and ceremonial knowledge. The local group was important in regulating social and economic institutions, including marriage, raiding parties, and ceremonial events. The Chiricahua depended more heavily on wild plant foods, hunting, and raiding, and less on farming, than the Western Apache, who probably were the most farming dependent of the Apache tribes. Mescal was also the Chiricahua band's most important food plant. The tender stalk was roasted and the crown was dug up, trimmed, and baked in an underground pit oven. The baked mescal was sun dried and stored, supplying food for many months.

Apache ceremonialism was based on the acquisition and manipulation of supernatural power and complicated rituals for curing and protecting against illness, success in hunting and warfare, and marking life-cycle events. The most important of the latter were puberty ceremonies for girls, which lasted four days and involved ritual songs and dances, dancing by masked impersonators of the mountain spirits, social dancing, and food redistribution.

Raiding was an integral part of Apache culture and was considered lawful and just. The principal ethnographer of the Western Apache wrote that "The size of the territory in Sonora over which the Western Apache raided is extraordinary. The Apache knew it like their own country, and every mountain, town, or spring of consequence had its Apache name" (Goodwin 1969:93). Raiding parties ventured as far as the Gulf of California. Raids brought the Apache horses, mules, cattle, hides, blankets, clothing, metal to fashion knives and arrow points, saddles and bridles, and firearms. O'odham, Mexican, and American farms in southern Arizona and northern Sonora, with their livestock and rich stores of grain, were frequent targets of Apache raids. Horses and mules were often killed and eaten during raids, providing a highly transportable food source as well as transportation and enabling the Apache to extend their raiding activities across considerable distances—as far as the Seri country along the Gulf of California.

As would be expected for such a mobile people, basketry, wood, and fiber products were used for most containers and most domestic purposes, and pottery was little emphasized. Pitch-coated baskets served as water containers. Cradleboards were made of wood, and these lightweight carriers enabled infants to accompany their mothers on resource-collecting parties. Beautifully fashioned carrying baskets were used in the harvest. Ceramics were typically dark gray or brown pots with conical bases, often with wiped surfaces and incised or finger-indented rims. During the historical period, bottle glass was often flaked to fashion arrow points, although metal was preferred. The Western Apache in particular were inveterate collectors and recyclers, often reusing grinding stones and other items collected from prehistoric sites (Whittlesey and Benaron 1998). This propensity, combined with the emphasis on perishable material culture, makes Apache sites difficult to identify archaeologically.

When the Spanish first arrived in Arizona, Apache predations on the O'odham were well established. Apache raiding crippled Spanish attempts to establish missions in Pimería Alta in the 1700s and was one reason for the abandonment of the San Pedro River valley by the Sobaipuri (Kessell 1976). The Spanish presidio of Santa Cruz de Terrenate along the San Pedro River was occupied for only four eventful years, beginning in 1775, before Apache raiding forced its abandonment (Sugnet and Reid 1994; Williams 1986c). The presidio at Tubac was relocated to Tucson in 1776, and as the Spanish population began to grow, the pace of Apache raiding accelerated. Following an unprecedented Apache attack on the presidio in 1782, commander Don Pedro Allande began a vigorous campaign against them. Four years later, the Spanish viceroy Bernardo de Gálvez instituted a pacification policy combined with aggressive military action. A key point of this policy was the resettlement of friendly Apache, called *apaches mansos* or *apaches de paz* (Dobyns 1976; Officer 1987), at the royal presidios. A contingent of more than 100 Apaches, primarily Western Apache of the Aravaipa band, was settled at Tucson in 1793 (Dobyns 1976:98). Members of the Pinal band settled there in 1819 (Dobyns 1976:102). Few if any traces of this occupation remain today.

As Anglo-American miners and settlers spread into Arizona, the Apache found it increasingly difficult to live by their traditional, mobile ways. No reservations had been established for them, and conflict was rampant. Soldiers and settlers kept the Aravaipa band on the move for many years, destroying their farms and camps. Beginning in 1866, several stations were set up to provide the Apache with rations, clothing, and protection from lawless settlers in exchange for their promise of peaceful behavior. Camp Grant was one such site, and the locale of one of the most shameful chapters in the history of Apache-American relations. The camp was established on the San Pedro River at its junction with Aravaipa Creek in the late 1850s and abandoned and reopened in response to federal policy after the Civil War. In 1871, the Aravaipa band under the leadership of Eskiminzin and a number of Pinal band members settled near Camp Grant, then commanded by Lt. Royal Whitman.

Mistakenly believing that the Aravaipa Apache at Camp Grant were responsible for raids on Tucson, Tubac, and Sonoita, and angered by what they perceived as the government's slow response to their requests for help and Whitman's supposed coddling of the "murderers," the people of Tucson decided to punish the Aravaipa on their own. In April 1871, 6 Anglos, 48 Mexicans, and 94 Tohono O'odham from San Xavier attacked the Aravaipa and Pinal Apache at Camp Grant, mutilating and killing more than 100, mostly women and children, and capturing 27 children. "It was slaughter pure and simple," wrote Sheridan (1995:80), "because most of the Apache men were off hunting in the mountains or carrying out surreptitious raids." President Grant insisted that the perpetrators be brought to trial. The sham deliberation lasted 19 minutes and ended with acquittal. Whitman was court-martialed three times after the massacre.

The Camp Grant massacre left all Apache people wary of Anglo-American claims of peace. It was also a stunning indictment of federal Indian policy. Following the massacre, Gen. George Crook was installed as the head of the Department of Arizona. His campaign against the Apache and Yavapai was based on a sweeping offensive assisted by Indian scouts, coupled with destruction of winter food supplies. Relationships between Western and Chiricahua Apache were always somewhat strained, and they worsened after some of the Western Apache allied with the U.S. Army in its campaign against the Chiricahua.

Starvation and weakness took their toll, and by 1872, Crook's campaign began to succeed. The remaining Apache leaders were ready to discuss peace. Many Apache were forced to move to a newly established reservation at San Carlos in 1875. After several unsuccessful attempts to relocate the Chiricahua, including a particularly sad sojourn at San Carlos and a failed attempt to establish a reservation for them in southeastern Arizona, the Chiricahua continued to raid in Arizona, New Mexico, and Sonora. Peace was not established until Geronimo surrendered in Skeleton Canyon in southeastern Arizona in

1886, and the Chiricahua were deported to Florida (Faulk 1969; Schmitt 1960; Sonnichsen 1986; Thrapp 1967).

Four Apache reservations were hurriedly established between 1871 and 1872 as part of the federal government's "peace policy" (Basso 1983:480). The White Mountain Reservation was established in 1871, and an executive order in 1872 added the San Carlos Division to the reservation (Kelly 1953:23). The White Mountain and San Carlos Apache Reservations were formally partitioned in 1897 (Majewski 1998:323). Many Aravaipa Apache also settled at Bylas on the Gila River in the late 1800s. The exiled Chiricahua Apache in Florida were transferred to a reservation at Fort Sill, Oklahoma, in 1894. In 1913, they were given full freedom, and some moved to New Mexico to share a reservation with the Mescalero Apache (Opler 1983:409). Today, most Western Apache in Arizona live on the White Mountain and San Carlos Apache Reservations; the Chiricahua Apache have intermarried and relocated, dispersing the once distinct band.

Yaqui

The Yaqui are members of the diverse Uto-Aztecan language family, which includes, at some remove from the Yaqui, the various Piman-speaking O'odham peoples. The Yaqui speak a dialect of Cahita, a language once spoken in a large area in what are now the Mexican states of Sonora and Sinaloa. The traditional home of the Yaqui is in Sonora, along both banks of the Río Yaqui and in the portions of the Sierra Madre drained by its tributaries. Because of persecution by the Mexican government in the late nineteenth century, groups of Yaqui abandoned their traditional territory for locations elsewhere in northern Mexico and southern Arizona. In the Tucson area, the Yaqui settled in two locations: Pascua Village on the near north side and a smaller satellite community in Marana, northwest of Tucson (Spicer 1983).

Traditional Yaqui territory included rich agricultural lands in the Río Yaqui valley and equally important gathering areas in the adjacent Sierra Madre. The lower elevations of the Río Yaqui valley were vegetated with subtropical, thorn-thicket vegetation and dense cane brakes. The valley's upper reaches, and the lands bordering the lower valley on the north, had typical Sonoran Desert vegetation: mesquite varyingly interspersed with cacti, cottonwood, palo verde, and other trees and shrubs (Moisés et al. 1971). At Spanish contact, the Yaqui were primarily horticulturalists and lived in scattered *rancherías* in the Río Yaqui valley. Initial contact came in 1533, but the interaction was brief and of little consequence to the Yaqui. The conquest of Sonora did not begin in earnest until the early seventeenth century, when Diego Martínez de Hurdaide headed three campaigns against the Yaqui. Although the Yaqui were successful in fending off all three attempts at conquest, Jesuits soon entered Yaqui territory and introduced the Yaqui to Christianity (Moisés et al. 1971).

The Yaqui had a social and political system that combined bilateral kinship with a strong sense of community. They lacked clans and had little in the way of hierarchical social structure. Family groups lived in scattered clearings along perennial watercourses, the typical *ranchería* settlement pattern noted by the Spanish in much of northern New Spain. The clearings were surrounded by tall, dense vegetation that gave a distinctly nonurban appearance to Yaqui settlements (Spicer 1980). Yaqui agriculture was tied to the natural flooding cycle of the river. The Yaqui hunted various wildlife species, with a special emphasis on deer. Deer also had a particular religious significance. Wild plants, including cane and native trees such as mesquite, supplied foods and construction materials (Moisés et al. 1971; Spicer 1980).

When Jesuits came to Yaqui country in the seventeenth century, they established churches in eight locations and in typical Spanish fashion consolidated the scattered *rancherías* around the missions (Moisés et al. 1971). Relations between the Jesuits and the Yaqui were generally good, and many Yaquis were quickly converted, at least nominally, to Christianity. Although most converts relocated near the missions, they insisted on retaining their scattered *ranchería* style of settlement, refusing to accept the

Spanish grid as a village plan. With a new focus on the missions as the center of their communities, the Yaqui developed highly productive and successful agricultural villages, as they continued to work and farm for community benefit. Their acceptance of Christianity resulted in a blending of traditional culture with a belief in Christ, the Virgin Mary, the saints, and the efficacy of Catholic ritual, particularly the rituals of Lent and Easter (Spicer 1980).

The Yaqui were incorporated into the Spanish colonial economy when they began using the lands at the missions to produce crops for market. The Yaqui were soon engaged in wage labor for mining and ranching interests that took them away from their home bases. They were generally recognized as hard workers and skilled miners, but most Yaqui never abandoned their traditional way of life, even when pressured to do so by Spanish colonial policies that threatened their traditional livelihood. Following the expulsion of the Jesuits from New Spain in 1767, encroaching Spanish settlement served only to strengthen the resolve of the Yaqui to protect their land and identity. Their intimate knowledge of the Sierra Madre and their ability to exploit a variety of environments made it difficult for the Spanish colonial government to impose its will on the Yaqui (Spicer 1980).

The Franciscans who replaced the Jesuits were not as successful with the Yaqui as their predecessors, and relations between the Yaqui and the Spanish became strained. Things grew worse following Mexican independence in 1821. In 1825, the Mexican government tried to collect taxes from the Yaqui, but joining forces with the Mayo, Lower Pima, and Opata, the Yaqui ran the Mexican government out of the region. The show of force, as in earlier events, was not sustained beyond that particular confrontation, and Mexican forces gradually returned. In 1853, a period of intermittent warfare began that would continue into the twentieth century (Moisés et al. 1971; Spicer 1980).

As the struggle for control over land and resources continued, factionalism developed among the Yaqui. Some fought against the Mexicans; others fought for them. By the late 1800s, decades of violence and the devastation of smallpox epidemics had taken their toll. The population of the Yaqui living under Mexican control in the eight Yaqui mission villages was approximately 4,000, although many more lived outside the Yaqui valley. The skirmishes continued, but peace treaties and settlement programs gradually brought more and more Yaqui under Mexican control (Moisés et al. 1971; Spicer 1980).

Massacres of the Yaqui by the Mexican army at the turn of the nineteenth century led to the emigration of many survivors, including to Arizona. Political turmoil continued into the 1920s, when another wave of Yaqui refugees fled to Arizona. Since 1927, the Yaqui have continued their struggle to hold on to their lands in Sonora, mostly without success, although a reservation of a sort was established by the Mexican government that included land north of the Río Yaqui and the Bacatete Mountains (Moisés et al. 1971). The Yaqui who sought refuge in southern Arizona brought with them a strong sense of community, many elements of their traditional culture, and their folk Catholicism. They also maintain ties to and communications with the Sonoran Yaqui (Griffith 1992; Moisés et al. 1971; Spicer 1980).

The Yaqui of southern Arizona, best exemplified by the residents of Pascua, retain many traditional cultural features, but they have undergone much social change in Arizona. In Arizona, they are not the dominant indigenous group they were in their Sonoran homeland, and they do not retain the cohesiveness of their Sonoran kin. They have an unstructured village authority, weak social control, and an economy based on wage labor and welfare. Their ceremonial lives are more individually based and are not coordinated with work as they are in Sonora. Despite these changes, such traditional Yaqui institutions as ritual coparenthood (compadrazgo) and ceremonial societies (cofradías) are still important in Pascua life (Spicer 1940). As a group, the Yaqui are deeply religious. Modern Yaqui religion is a fusion of aboriginal beliefs with Spanish and Mexican Catholic systems. The annual religious cycle functions through the cofradías, of which five are men's and two are women's. Although ceremonial cycles, feast days, and local patron saints differ from village to village, Easter is the major religious holiday for the Yaqui. The rituals and ceremonial events surrounding this religious season are complex (Moisés et al. 1971).

For the Arizona Yaqui, ethnic status takes precedence over nationality, entitling them to build a house, to farm, or to graze cattle on Yaqui territory, and to use the natural resources found in Yaqui territory, whether in Arizona or Sonora. They are also able to participate in Yaqui farming and fishing societies and cattle cooperatives. McGuire (1986) pointed to four characteristics of Yaqui polity and ethnicity that support the persistence of the ethnic Yaqui: (1) the Yaqui are a corporate ethnic group rather than an ethnic population; (2) recognition of being Yaqui is ascribed through genealogy rather than achieved; (3) ethnic identity is understated; and (4) the three dimensions of status—wealth, power, and prestige—are not connected.

Today, the Pascua Yaqui number more than 9,000 people. Many live in Pascua Village, which was annexed by the City of Tucson in 1952. Others reside on the recently established New Pascua reservation southwest of Tucson. Following a long and difficult battle, the Pascua Yaqui gained federal recognition from the U.S. government in 1982 and ratified their first constitution in 1988.

CHAPTER 4

Euroamerican Culture History

Europeans first set foot in what is now southern Arizona around 1539, thus inaugurating the historical period in the region. With the arrival of a society that would leave a written record of events, prehistory became history in southern Arizona, a transition that has long served as the basis for a division of labor between archaeologists and historians. Traditionally, archaeologists have studied the objects left behind by nonliterate Native Americans, and historians have studied the texts left behind by literate Europeans. The discussion of Euroamerican culture presented here, which begins with the arrival of Europeans in southern Arizona, makes the traditional assumption that what happened after that event is in some sense fundamentally different from what happened before it, at least in terms of the kinds of information left behind, and perhaps also in the way each side of the watershed must be understood.

In reality, however, a neat watershed has never separated the original Native American world of southern Arizona from the drastically transformed world that arose after the arrival of Europeans. European plants, animals, and diseases arrived in the region well ahead of European explorers, and Native American societies retained a major presence in the region long after European society came to dominate it. It is also a simplification, albeit an unavoidable one, to describe the non–Native Americans who have lived in southern Arizona as Europeans or even Euroamericans. By the latter term, we mean people of primarily European extraction who made their permanent homes in southern Arizona, but this glosses over a wide variety of non–Native Americans, including a fair number whose ancestors were not Europeans. We use *Euroamerican* in the most general sense and not very often; instead, we try to distinguish non–Native American ethnicity as narrowly as possible in each instance: Spanish, Mexican, Mexican-American, Anglo-American, or Chinese-American. The history of the Paseo de las Iglesias study area was affected to a greater or lesser extent by people of each of these ethnicities.

The discussion that follows is organized by broadly defined themes that have influenced the history of the Paseo de las Iglesias study area: Native American–Spanish interaction; the decline of the colonial system after Mexican independence; mining, farming, and ranching; land tenure; transportation; Anglo-American water-control projects; other early Anglo-American enterprises; and scientific research. Rather than a strictly chronological discussion, we consider change through time as it relates to these themes, although we make regular links to the conventional major periods of southern Arizona history: the Spanish Colonial period (1539–1821), the Mexican period (1821–1854), and the U.S. period (1854–present). We also make finer chronological distinctions as necessary.

Native American–Spanish Interaction

For its first 280 years, southern Arizona history was largely defined by the interaction that took place between the Native Americans living in the region and the Spanish explorers, missionaries, and settlers who entered it and sometimes stayed. This is not to say that Native American lives were defined by this interaction—Native Americans had their own worlds of interest and significance and did not sit waiting for the Spanish to initiate things—but what we know of the nearly three centuries of Spanish presence in the region originates in documents produced by the Spanish in their efforts to understand and control what they found in the region, especially its native inhabitants. The history of the Spanish presence in southern Arizona is the history of how two ways of life confronted each other and responded to the demands imposed by the confrontation.

Early Spanish Exploration

The Spanish conquest of southern Arizona began as it had begun in so many other places in the New World following the arrival of Columbus—with exploratory journeys, or *entradas,* into the region by small groups of Spanish explorers accompanied by Native American guides (Figure 5). The earliest *entradas* into southern Arizona had little or no immediate impact on the region—no settlements were established, no resources were extracted, and interactions with the indigenous peoples were fleeting— but these journeys of exploration were nonetheless of great consequence to the subsequent history of the region. The information, accurate or otherwise, that was gathered in each *entrada* was inevitably the impetus for further *entradas,* then for religious missions, and eventually for attempts at settlement. Just as important, each successful *entrada* confirmed the feasibility and validity of the Spanish colonial enterprise and the greater purposes of spreading the Catholic faith, expanding the wealth of the crown, and bringing Spanish civilization to uncivilized places. An understanding of the Spanish presence in southern Arizona begins with an appreciation of this remarkable impulse to explore and expand, an impulse pursued at a scale without precedent in human history. The sources used in this section are summaries of the early period of Spanish exploration by Fontana (1994:19–31), Hartmann (1989:16–35), Officer 1987: 25–28), Sheridan (1995:24–28), Weber (1992:35–49), and Whittlesey et al. (1994:228–230).

The first directly documented Spanish *entrada* into what would become southern Arizona came in 1539, when a Franciscan friar named Marcos de Niza led a small expedition northward from the town of Culiacán, in what was then northernmost New Spain, to the vicinity of the pueblo of Zuni, in what is now western New Mexico. It is uncertain whether Niza himself made it as far north as Zuni, but he likely did pass through southeastern Arizona, traveling along a stretch of the San Pedro River and reaching the Gila River before returning to Culiacán. His only non–Native American companion for most of the northward journey was a North African called Esteban. Esteban did reach Zuni, where he was shot full of arrows by suspicious Zuni.

Niza's expedition was commissioned by the newly appointed viceroy of New Spain, Antonio de Mendoza, in an effort to gather knowledge of the northwestern frontier of the colony. Mendoza was especially interested in confirming reports that somewhere to the north lay the Seven Cities of Antilia, legendary places of high culture and fabulous wealth believed to rival Tenochtitlan, the Aztec capital in central Mexico conquered by Fernando Cortés in 1521. Interest in the Seven Cities had recently been piqued by the arrival at Culiacán of Alvar Núñez Cabeza de Vaca and his companions, who had spent the preceding eight years wandering the northern deserts after being shipwrecked on the coast of Texas. The doomed Esteban had been among Cabeza de Vaca's party, which might have passed through southern Arizona at some point, although their route is impossible to reconstruct precisely. Esteban was chosen for Niza's expedition based on his knowledge of the northern deserts and his presumed skills in dealing with the indigenous peoples, skills that failed him in the end.

The most important product of the first *entrada* into Arizona was Niza's subsequent report to Antonio de Mendoza, which, for many people, confirmed the existence of the Seven Cities (thenceforth the Seven Cities of Cíbola, the name for Zuni heard by Niza). Because of Niza's glowing descriptions of Cíbola, Mendoza, in 1540, commissioned a much more substantial *entrada,* led by Francisco Vásquez de Coronado and consisting of some 300 Spaniards, 1,000 Native American guides and porters, and 1,500 head of cattle, horses, and mules. Niza, one of five friars who accompanied Coronado, served as

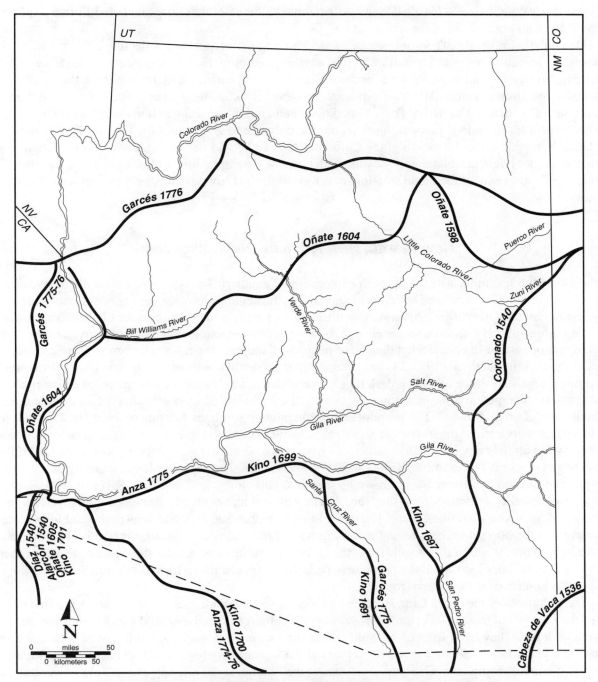

Figure 5. Routes of early Spanish explorers in southern Arizona.

53

Coronado's principal guide as far as Cíbola, where the hopes of Coronado and his companions were bitterly disappointed. Much of Coronado's route, which eventually led him as far as the Great Plains, is difficult to reconstruct, but he, too, passed through southeastern Arizona, probably also traveling along a portion of the San Pedro River. Over the next two years, Coronado's lieutenants made numerous exploratory side trips, including at least a dozen into Arizona, but none of these trips included further exploration of the southern portion of the state.

Despite the Coronado expedition's success in exploring a vast area and collecting a great deal of potentially useful information, its failure to find anything remotely like the legendary Seven Cities led to a near hiatus in exploration of Arizona for the next century and a half. During this period, the occasional Spanish expedition did enter Arizona from northern New Mexico, where a permanent Spanish settlement was founded at Santa Fe by 1610. These expeditions gathered information and made contacts with indigenous peoples in various parts of the state, but the only one to go south of the Gila River was Juan de Oñate's expedition to the mouth of the Colorado River in 1604. Intensive exploration of southern Arizona did not begin until late in the seventeenth century, corresponding with the efforts of Eusebio Francisco Kino to extend the Jesuit missionary effort northward from established bases in what is now Sonora.

New Plants, New Animals, New Diseases

If the most obvious impacts of the Spanish exploration of southern Arizona were not on the peoples and places encountered by explorers but on other Spaniards thus enticed to enter the region, a more subtle process initiated by the earliest *entradas* was ultimately of even greater significance. This was the process of biological and technological exchange that began the moment Europeans first arrived in the New World, a process that likely affected the native peoples of southern Arizona even before Spaniards set foot in the region. Sheridan (1995:23) has characterized the earliest *entradas* into Arizona as "little more than ripples on the surface of a deep dark lake," as compared with events of less immediate historical interest but much greater long-term impact, such as "the exchange of seeds, the theft of a horse herd, the introduction of an iron plow." The introduction of the plow to southern Arizona probably had to wait until Jesuits actually carried one there and showed the locals how to use it, but Spanish crops and domestic animals were already a part of Native American lives when Kino first visited the region at the end of the seventeenth century. For example, Kino's military escort, Capt. Juan Mateo Manje, reported that watermelons and muskmelons were being grown by the Sobaipuri along the Santa Cruz River in 1697. Both crops were Spanish introductions to the New World, but they had evidently entered the area well in advance of Spanish expeditions (Ezell 1961:32). In a more dramatic fashion, the Apache had long since incorporated the horse into their nomadic, raiding way of life. Ironically, Spaniards first brought horses to the New World to aid in its conquest, but the early acquisition of horses by the Apache, either by theft or by happenstance, soon turned the previously pedestrian Apache into a formidable and enduring threat to Spanish control of the northern frontier.

The Sobaipuri of the Santa Cruz River valley were long-accomplished farmers when Kino first entered the region, but they also depended heavily on the resources that they could extract from the surrounding desert. They lived lives of variable sedentism, settling in villages along the river to farm for part of the year, then dispersing to scattered parts of the surrounding region to hunt and gather a wide variety of animals and plants. One important reason the Sobaipuri did not rely exclusively on agriculture for their food was climatic: the elevation of the Santa Cruz Valley meant that for several months each winter, the possibility of frost made planting a winter crop an unacceptable gamble. Corn, beans, and squash, the three major native cultivars, all lacked the tolerance to frost necessary to survive a typical winter. Because of this vacant niche in the agricultural cycle, the Sobaipuri were especially receptive to the introduction of the principal Spanish cultivar, wheat, which was highly frost tolerant and made living and farming year-round on the Santa Cruz feasible. The increased yields from agriculture that resulted from adding wheat to the cycle also made larger settlements possible, which became a defensive consideration as Apache raiding intensified in conjunction with the influx of Spaniards into the region. Wheat was first introduced to the Santa Cruz Valley by Kino in the 1690s, but it probably did not become a major part of the Sobaipuri diet until the 1730s, when permanent missions were finally established at Guevavi and San Xavier del Bac. Nonetheless, by the middle of the eighteenth century, wheat was a major crop for the Sobaipuri along the Santa Cruz, and by the 1770s, it had become a major crop even for the Akimel O'odham along the Gila River, beyond the sphere of direct missionary influence (Sheridan 1988).

As much as any other factor, it was the Sobaipuri's own recognition of the potential role of wheat in their diet that led to its enthusiastic adoption, but the increased sedentism that growing wheat allowed for played perfectly into the Jesuits' plans to transform the Sobaipuri way of life from one of "pagan intransigence" (Sheridan 1988:156) to one of Christian stability. The Jesuits viewed the flexibility in the settlement pattern that the Sobaipuri required in their seasonal reliance on hunting and gathering as a major obstacle to be overcome by the missions, and the introduction of European crops was a logical first step in making a sedentary lifestyle both feasible and desirable. At least in this one aspect of the missionizing process, the motivations of the Sobaipuri and the Jesuits seem to have to coincided. In addition to wheat, the Sobaipuri benefited from the introduction of a vast array of Spanish cultivars, including legumes such as garbanzos and lentils; vegetables such as cabbage, onions, garlic, and leeks; herbs such as mustard, mint, anise, and pepper; and fruits such as grapes, apples, peaches, quinces, plums, pomegranates, apricots, and figs. As Sheridan (1988:157) put it, "Thousands of years of Old World experience and experimentation were suddenly placed in Piman hands." Of course, by the time the Jesuits arrived in southern Arizona, Europe as a whole was already benefiting from thousands of years of New World agricultural experimentation, as the many cultivars native to the Americas (most notably, corn and potatoes) had quickly become integral parts of many Old World diets and economies.

In southern Arizona, the Apache were the native people perhaps most transformed by the introduction of a Spanish domestic animal, but Spanish livestock had a significant impact on the Sobaipuri as well. In 1699, Captain Manje reported that horses were being kept by the Sobaipuri of the San Pedro Valley, and by the early 1700s, herds of horses, cattle, sheep, and goats had been started by the Jesuits at a number of other Sobaipuri settlements (Sheridan 1988:159–160). Horses were the first introduction to play a significant role among the Sobaipuri, serving both as beasts of burden and as weapons in their perpetual struggles with the Apache. Cattle, goats, and sheep spread more slowly and generally under missionary supervision, but their impact on the Sobaipuri economy was greater. Sheridan (1988:161) noted that these three domestics were especially important because they "converted grasses and other plants which humans could not eat into meat, cheese, and milk" and so provided a reliable source of animal protein. If the Sobaipuri were obliged by the adoption of year-round agriculture to give up much of their earlier hunting-and-gathering use of the desert, they partially recovered such use indirectly through the adoption of animal grazing.

Whatever benefits the native peoples of southern Arizona enjoyed as a result of the introduction of Old World plants and animals were greatly overshadowed by the effects of another, largely one-sided, biological exchange that spread deadly Old World diseases throughout the Americas beginning with Columbus's first landing in 1492. Prior to that first landing, the native peoples of the Americas had developed for at least 12,000 years in isolation from Old World diseases such as measles, influenza, and smallpox. Consequently, the rates of resistance to these diseases were extremely low among Native Americans at the time of contact, and the effects of the many epidemics that soon raced through the Spanish colonies, especially the epidemics of smallpox, were devastating. Native American populations throughout the hemisphere declined by 66–95 percent during the Spanish Colonial period, and entire societies simply disintegrated under the pressures of depopulation (Crosby 1972; Sheridan 1995:23–24).

There has been considerable debate about the effects and timing of epidemics among the native peoples of southern Arizona. Certainly, the first effects were felt before permanent Spanish settlements arose in the region, and at least a few archaeologists speculate that the demise of the prehistoric Hohokam people is attributable to the arrival of European diseases. The usual end date given for the Hohokam occupation of southern Arizona is A.D. 1450, but the archaeological chronology has enough room for error to make a close correspondence between the end of the Hohokam and the arrival of European diseases a possibility worth considering. Reff (1990:279–280) attempted to reconstruct the origin and course of epidemics in northwestern New Spain during the early colonial period and concluded that the region experienced the same rapid and devastating depopulations in the sixteenth century as the core areas of the Spanish colony—namely, central Mexico and Peru—had. Reff stopped short of attributing the Hohokam collapse primarily to the effects of disease, but he did see processes of change that began in late prehistoric times as likely exacerbated by epidemics during the first century or more of the colonial era.

Perhaps more significant is Reff's conclusion that what enabled the early missionizing efforts of the Jesuits in northwestern New Spain to succeed was the demoralization of Native American communities caused by epidemics and severe depopulation. Having suffered repeatedly from the effects of epidemics, the Native Americans of the region often responded favorably to Jesuit programs of conversion, resettlement, and agricultural change, because they were desperate for a solution to what they themselves perceived to be disintegrating social, cultural, and economic systems (Reff 1990:277–278, 1998). But Jesuit (and, later, Franciscan) attempts to restructure Native American society in northwestern New Spain ultimately failed, because Native American populations never stopped declining. And if an acceptance of social change was at first a response to increased mortality, increased mortality itself was soon the price of that acceptance. Jackson (1994) has stressed that epidemic disease, although a major factor in Native American population decline, was never the sole factor. The missionary institutions that were brought to the frontier and imposed on the local people, ostensibly for their benefit, were themselves devastating to Native American ways of life, often intentionally so. The physical and psychological stresses suffered by Native Americans under the missionary system contributed substantially, if not always measurably, to the decline of Native American populations throughout New Spain, and the Piman-speaking peoples of what is now southern Arizona were not exempt from these effects.

The Jesuit Expansion into Southern Arizona

The Spanish missionary effort in northwestern New Spain began in 1591, when two Jesuit fathers were sent from Mexico City to a small Spanish settlement along the Río Sinaloa, in what is now the Mexican state of the same name, to begin the conversion of the indigenous people of the region. From this modest start, the Jesuit order soon expanded northward, founding missions in the succession of river valleys that drain the western slopes of the Sierra Madre. Occasionally, the people they encountered staunchly resisted their efforts to introduce Catholicism and a Spanish way of life, but more often, the presence of the Jesuits was accepted or at least tolerated. By the 1620s, Jesuit missions extended well into the Pimería Baja, the "lower," or southern, portion of the territory belonging to the Piman-speaking peoples, in what is now northern Sinaloa and southern Sonora. The proselytization of the Pimería Baja would occupy the Jesuits for the next 65 years, after which the Jesuit order finally expanded into the northern portion of Piman-speaking territory, the Pimería Alta, an expansion made possible largely by the efforts of Kino (Bannon 1955; Ortega Noriega 1985a).

Born and educated in northern Italy, Kino arrived in Mexico as a Jesuit in 1681. His first assignment was to accompany a military expedition to Baja California, where he served both as cartographer and as minister to the Native Americans subdued by the expedition. The attempt to establish a Spanish settlement in Baja California was ultimately unsuccessful, and Kino was eventually selected to direct the expansion of the mainland Jesuit frontier into the Pimería Alta. He began by establishing a series of missions that extended up the principal rivers of the region—most notably, Mission Nuestra Señora de los Dolores at the headwaters of the Río San Miguel, near the present-day city of Magdalena, Sonora. Founded in 1687, Mission Nuestra Señora de los Dolores served for the next 24 years as Kino's base of operations, the starting point of his famous expeditions into the northern Pimería Alta that led to the founding of missions along the Santa Cruz River (Ortega Noriega 1985b).

Kino's first entry into what is now Arizona was in 1691, when he reached the Sobaipuri settlement at Tumacácori on the Santa Cruz River. Over the next 10 years, he made numerous trips up the same river—which he called Santa María—as far north as the ruins of Casa Grande, and he eventually traveled down the Gila River to its confluence with the Colorado. Kino was interested in finding both new territory to missionize, which he found in abundance in the Sobaipuri villages along the fertile Santa Cruz, and a land route to Baja California, which would ease the transport of supplies and livestock to fledgling missions there. After a series of arduous trips into the deserts south of the Gila, Kino eventually convinced himself that there was a land route to Baja California, but his claimed discovery was viewed with skepticism until years after his death in 1711. It was the opening of a vast new area to Jesuit missionizing and his subsequent direction of that missionizing effort that became Kino's most enduring contributions (Bolton 1984; Hartmann 1989:36–56; Ortega Noriega 1985b).

In 1731, 20 years after Kino's death, the first permanent Jesuit missions were established at the Sobaipuri villages of Guevavi and Bac along the Santa Cruz (Figure 6). Each of the two missions was intended to be a *misión cabecera,* a primary mission with a resident Jesuit priest who would minister to the natives both at the *cabecera* and at two or three nearby dependent *visitas,* smaller settlements without resident priests. Earlier attempts to establish missions at both Guevavi and Bac during Kino's lifetime had failed, but now the Jesuits succeeded in instituting essentially the same missionary program that was already in place at the many Jesuit missions to the south. The basic goal of the Jesuit mission was the conversion of the natives to Catholicism, but the pursuit of that goal along the Santa Cruz River, like its earlier pursuit elsewhere in northwestern New Spain, involved fundamentally changing the lives of the natives, convincing them not only to abandon their religious beliefs but to alter the nature of their association with the landscape around them.

The keystone of the Jesuit effort to convert Native Americans was the *reducción,* literally "reduction," the gathering of Native Americans into permanent communities "for more efficient and effective administration, both spiritual and temporal" (Polzer 1976:7). In the communities formed by *reducción,* Native Americans were instructed in the faith, encouraged to abandon practices incompatible with Catholicism, monitored as to their genuine acceptance of Catholic doctrine, and put to work in projects for the communal good—most notably, the construction and maintenance of irrigation systems. The success the Jesuits had in convincing the natives of northwestern New Spain to participate in *reducción* varied widely, from violent rejection to peaceful acquiescence, but the Sobaipuri of the Santa Cruz Valley were generally amenable to the process. The precise reasons for their apparent acceptance of this most basic of Jesuit demands were complicated. The constant threat of Apache raids undoubtedly made the Jesuits and their Spanish military escorts appealing as potential allies. The agricultural regime introduced to the region by the Jesuits, with its livestock, wide variety of cultivars, and dependable winter crops, also must have appealed to people living in a demanding and inconsistently productive environment. And there is the real possibility, already noted, that the Sobaipuri way of life at the end of the seventeenth century was already so devastated by the impact of European diseases that the Sobaipuri would accept any change that would bring stability to their lives.

Whatever factors influenced the original decisions of the Sobaipuri, the Jesuit mission settlements at Guevavi and San Xavier del Bac became permanent homes for many of them for much of the remainder of the eighteenth century. They were baptized there, participated in the religious life of the mission (to the degree that the resident Jesuit saw fit), and farmed mission lands using both indigenous and Spanish crops and methods. But beyond the adoption of Spanish agriculture and the rudiments of Catholicism, it

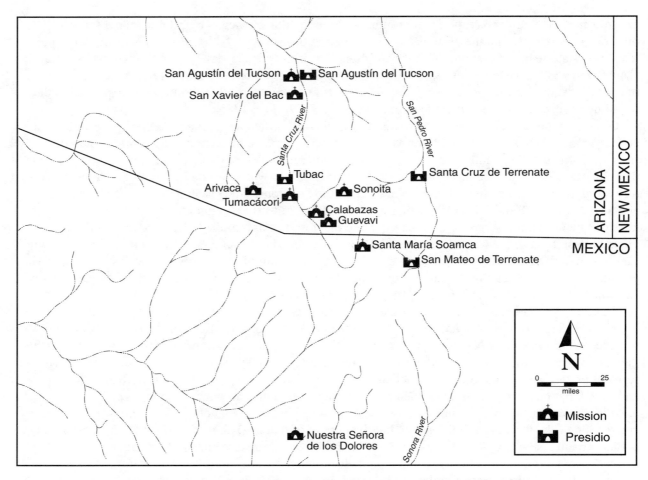

Figure 6. Selected Spanish Colonial period sites in the Pimería Alta.

is impossible to say how much their new lives actually reflected a conversion to a Spanish way of life, and this is even more the case for the Sobaipuri settled in or near dependent *visitas* such as Tucson and Arivaca. In addition, almost nothing is known about the impact of the missions on the Sobaipuri's use of areas away from the main rivers, the areas once frequented in the Sobaipuri seasonal round. The enthusiasm with which the Sobaipuri adopted wheat farming and livestock raising at the missions suggests that they quickly abandoned the nomadic dimension of their way of life, but Sobaipuri culture consisted of more than the routines of subsistence. According to Reff (1990:268–271), native acceptance of Jesuit teachings—religious, social, and economic—throughout northwestern New Spain was at best superficial, and even a century or more after initial contact, Jesuits would complain about the continuing difficulties in transforming native lives. In the northernmost Pimería Alta, where the Jesuit presence was more tenuous than anywhere else in the northern borderlands, the veneer of Catholicism and Spanish culture must have been especially thin.

The Jesuit missionary effort in northwestern New Spain differed in a number of significant ways from earlier missionary efforts by other orders elsewhere in the colony, and these differences had their effects in the northern Pimería Alta. One major difference can be found in the character of the Jesuit order itself. Founded in 1536, the Society of Jesus was the youngest of the major orders to proselytize in New Spain, and it had attracted an especially devoted and well-educated group of young men to its ranks. Jesuit devotion included a genuine concern for the well-being of the native people placed in their charge, which frequently led them to shield the natives from the abuses of ordinary Spaniards eager to exploit their labor. "The Jesuits," wrote Reff (1990:7), "largely were free of the vices that characterized their countrymen." A basically humane approach to their dealings with the natives (there were exceptions, of course), combined with an emphasis on learning native languages and understanding native customs, was an important factor in the success of the Jesuits in expanding their missions over such a vast area in a relatively short period of time.

Another important difference between the Jesuit enterprise and earlier missionary efforts was the nearly exclusive access to native populations that the Jesuits enjoyed, especially in the northern reaches of the Pimería Alta. In central Mexico, by contrast, the first Spanish institution that many native people were exposed to was the *encomienda,* which placed the Native American population of a given region at the disposal of a private Spaniard (usually a former conquistador). In theory, the Native Americans would simply pay tribute to the Spaniard, but in practice, the tribute took the form of labor in the Spaniard's mining or agricultural ventures. The *encomienda* was responsible for the early deaths of tens of thousands of Native Americans in central Mexico and elsewhere in the New World and had largely ceased to be royal policy by the time the Jesuits began their efforts in northwestern New Spain (Weber 1992:124–125). Elsewhere in New Spain, including much of northern Mexico, missionization occurred simultaneously with the expansion of secular Spanish enterprises, most notably mining. Missionary orders such as the Franciscans often had to recruit natives in competition with mining operations and to negotiate for the rights to native labor. But in the Pimería Alta, the Jesuits were almost always the vanguard of Spanish exploration and settlement. Private Spanish interests would eventually arrive to compete with a Jesuit mission for land and labor but usually arrived after the mission had chosen lands for itself, established relations with the local Native Americans, and generally made itself the principal Spanish presence in the region (Atondo Rodríguez and Ortega Soto 1985).

Following the expulsion of the Jesuits from all Spanish colonies in 1767, the Franciscan order inherited the Jesuit system of missions in the Pimería Alta and pursued largely the same policies of *reducción* and conversion, except that severely dwindling native populations forced the Franciscans to look elsewhere for new converts. The Franciscans working at the Santa Cruz River missions found them primarily among the Tohono O'odham, the Piman speakers of the vast desert region to the west of the river. Coaxed into becoming sedentary river farmers, the Tohono O'odham became the largest component of the native populations at Guevavi and Bac beginning in the late eighteenth century. Life at the Franciscan missions was relatively benign for them, especially compared with the fate of Native Americans living in the Franciscan missions soon established in Alta California. Jackson (1998:78) noted how the Franciscans placed much heavier demands for labor on the natives in the Alta California missions than they ever placed on the natives in southern Arizona, and the California natives suffered accordingly. The difference in the Santa Cruz Valley was the result of less ambitious Franciscan architectural projects, a more intermittent Franciscan presence at the missions, and less reliance on mission production by the local Spanish military.

Presidios and *Gente de Razón* in Southern Arizona

In addition to the task of converting the Sobaipuri to Catholicism, the Jesuits in the Santa Cruz Valley, like their brethren elsewhere in the Pimería Alta, were charged with transforming the local way of life into a Spanish one, based in permanent, year-round villages and the raising of Spanish crops and livestock. As discussed above, their efforts met with only limited success. However, from the perspective of ordinary Spanish people on the northern frontier—*gente de razón,* as they called themselves, "people of reason"—the presence of the missions and the military protection afforded them suddenly made settlement of the region seem feasible. Spanish settlers in search of irrigable fields, grazing lands, and minerals began to drift into the region, often establishing operations near the missions. In the vicinity of the

Santa Cruz Valley, this pattern of settlement received a boost in 1736 when silver was discovered a few miles southwest of modern Nogales, at a place called Arizonac (the place-name, slightly modified, now refers to an American state). By the end of the 1730s, a fair number of Spanish families had settled in the immediate vicinity of Guevavi and Tubac, and there were likely other Spanish families farther north along the Santa Cruz (Kessell 1970:51–52; Officer 1987:32).

The discovery at Arizonac quickly played out, but the modest influx of Spanish population prompted by the discovery created an increased demand for Spanish military protection of the region. It was clear even prior to the Arizonac discovery that the most persistent and vexing problem faced by the Jesuit missions, by the Sobaipuri settled at the Santa Cruz missions, and by the few Spaniards bold enough to settle along the far northern frontier was unrelenting harassment by the Apache, who roamed unrestricted over a vast area to the north and east of the Pimería Alta. Each new Spanish arrival in the Santa Cruz Valley and its vicinity represented another tempting target for Apache raids. The Spanish military responded in 1741 by establishing a presidio at San Mateo de Terrenate on the headwaters of the San Pedro River, at what was presumed to be the front line of the Apache problem, although still some 50 miles southeast of Guevavi (Kessell 1970:76–78; Officer 1987:33). The new presidio did extend the Spanish military presence to the north and west of the presidio at Fronteras, but the Santa Cruz River missions remained isolated and poorly protected from Apache predations. Nonetheless, the number of Spanish settlers in the vicinity of the missions gradually increased.

As Spanish settlement of the Pimería Alta slowly expanded northward, the Upper Pima were increasingly obliged to share or relinquish entirely the limited arable lands available along the region's major rivers. By the middle of the eighteenth century, following a variety of abuses by both settlers and Jesuits around the Pimería Alta, the Upper Pima, including the Sobaipuri of the Santa Cruz Valley, had had enough. In 1751, under the direction of an Upper Pima leader who had earlier assisted the Spanish military in pacifying the Seri, they revolted, killing more than 100 settlers and badly damaging missions throughout the region, including those at Guevavi and San Xavier del Bac, and their outlying *visitas*. The Spanish settlers living along the Santa Cruz retreated as a group to the presidio at Terrenate, abandoning their fields, herds, and belongings to the enraged Sobaipuri. The wider uprising, now known as the Pima revolt, was quelled within four months of the initial violence, but sporadic attacks by groups of disaffected Sobaipuri continued to occur for several years afterward.

In 1752, as a direct response to the Pima revolt, the Spanish military established a presidio at Tubac, about halfway between Guevavi and Bac, in an effort to better protect the Santa Cruz missions. San Ignacio del Tubac thus became the first permanent, officially sanctioned Spanish settlement in what is now Arizona. By 1760, Juan Bautista de Anza's (the younger) first year as *comandante* of Tubac, the problems with the Sobaipuri had largely subsided, partly because of Anza's charismatic presence but also in great part because of a steady decline in the Sobaipuri population caused by disease, relocation to avoid the missions, and flight from Apache depredations (Dobyns 1976:10–17; Ewing 1945; Kessell 1970:102–109, 154–156; Officer 1987:35–39).

The Apache threat grew steadily from 1760 onward, abetted early on by the Spanish military in two unintentional ways. In 1762, in an effort to repopulate the dwindling Santa Cruz missions, the colonial government ordered the military to relocate the entire Sobaipuri population of the San Pedro Valley to the settlements of their congeners along the Santa Cruz River. This action removed the last buffer between the Santa Cruz missions and the Apache, whose nearest targets for raids were simply moved one more valley to the west. Also in the 1760s, the attentions of the military force garrisoned at Tubac were diverted from the Santa Cruz missions by several extended expeditions to the south to help fight the resurgent Seri. With a weakened military force at Tubac, raids by Apaches in the Santa Cruz Valley escalated in frequency and ferocity (Dobyns 1976:19–23; Kessell 1970:161–162; Officer 1987:44–45).

The Jesuit tenure in southern Arizona came to an abrupt end in 1767, when the Jesuit order in its entirety was expelled from all Spanish territories by royal decree. Control of the northern missions transferred to the Franciscans, who soon sent friars to the Pimería Alta, that "unsolicited inheritance from the

Jesuits" (Kessell 1976:3). The Franciscan order, founded in 1226, was much older than the Society of Jesus (founded in 1534) and also preceded the Jesuits in the New World by 67 years. The Franciscans were the first and most active order in the missionization of central Mexico, beginning their work in 1524, just three years after the fall of the Aztec capital of Tenochtitlan. The Franciscan friars assigned to the existing missions of the Pimería Alta would build on the work of conversion and resettlement begun by the Jesuits, but they would also bring with them two and a half centuries of experience missionizing elsewhere in Mexico. They would leave their own distinctive mark on the people and places of the northern frontier, a mark they would eventually leave on the many Franciscan missions of Alta California (McCarty 1996).

The expulsion of the Jesuits brought chaos to the already unstable missions along the Santa Cruz River. In the interim year preceding the arrival of the Franciscans, the chaos deepened, as the mission Sobaipuri, recently decimated by disease, abandoned many of the river homes and fields they had maintained under the Jesuits. When the Franciscans arrived, only a few dozen Sobaipuri were still in residence at Guevavi and Bac, and the *visitas* were in comparable decline. Almost all of the Spanish living in the region, a total of about 500 people, were settled at the Tubac presidio, largely as a defense against continuing Apache raids. Shortly after the first Franciscan friar settled at San Xavier, the mission suffered a devastating Apache attack, the first of countless Apache raids witnessed by the Franciscans during the 70-odd years of their presence along the Santa Cruz (Kessell 1976:11–25; Officer 1987:45–48).

Apache aggression made all lives difficult in the later eighteenth century and was the chief influence on the pattern of native as well as Spanish settlement in the Santa Cruz Valley. In 1768, the *misión cabecera* at Soamca was completely destroyed in an Apache attack, never to be reoccupied. In 1770, the Sobaipuri who had resettled at Tucson were threatening to abandon the area for the Gila River because of Apache attacks. Fearing that their departure would mean a badly weakened Spanish presence on the middle Santa Cruz, Anza persuaded them to stay by promising them help in building fortifications and a church. A large earthen breastwork and a church, presumably of adobe and soon dedicated to San Agustín, were completed by 1773, marking the first Spanish attempts at architecture in the immediate vicinity of Tucson (Kessell 1976:56; McCarty 1976:16–18; Officer 1987:48).

Around the same time, farther up the Santa Cruz River, the Franciscans installed at Guevavi decided that life at the original *misión cabecera* had become too dangerous. Prompted by devastating Apache attacks on the *visitas* of Calabazas and Sonoita, the Franciscans transferred the *cabecera* downstream to Tumacácori, which was considerably closer to the presidio at Tubac (Kessell 1976:57). The Franciscans at Tumacácori and San Xavier, the two remaining *cabeceras* on the Santa Cruz, spent the next few years suffering further Apache raids, watching their already badly thinned Sobaipuri population continue to dwindle from disease and desertion, and making largely unsuccessful attempts to coax the Tohono O'odham into converting and settling along the river (Kessell 1976:78–80; Officer 1987:48–50).

In 1775, the military organization of the entire northern frontier of New Spain underwent a transformation at the hands of Hugo O'Conor, an Irish expatriate and officer in the Spanish army who had been assigned the task of modernizing and improving the presidial system of frontier defense, from the gulf coast of Texas to the Pimería Alta (Moorhead 1975:47–74). For the presidio at Tubac, this meant transfer downstream to a site just across the river from the Sobaipuri *ranchería* at Tucson, a site marked out by O'Conor on August 20, 1775. Like the Native American village that became a *visita,* the new presidio was christened San Agustín del Tucson. By 1776, the garrison formerly stationed at Tubac was in residence at Tucson, and in 1777, the first fortification of the new site was erected: a wooden palisade with a surrounding ditch. The palisade was eventually replaced by a massive wall of adobe that stood 10–12 feet high, measured 3 feet wide at the base, and enclosed an area 300 yards square. The layout of the fortification followed (at least loosely) the specifications of a royal order for presidio construction (Dobyns 1976:56–61; Officer 1987:50–51; Williams 1988). Also in 1775, just a few days after O'Conor chose the site for the Tucson presidio, he chose a new site for the presidio at San Mateo de Terrenate, a location farther down the San Pedro River, not far from modern Tombstone. This second new presidio, named Santa Cruz de Terrenate, suffered unrelenting Apache attacks and crippling problems with supplies for a little more than four years before being abandoned in early 1780 in favor of its previous location (Whittlesey et al. 1994; Williams 1986c).

From the establishment of the presidio to the early 1790s, the Spanish garrison at Tucson devoted almost all of its time and energy to fighting the Apache. The other Tucson, the *visita* and Sobaipuri village across the river, quickly became socially and economically linked with the presidio settlement and, of course, relied on it for its own defense from Apache attacks. A change in policy following the presidial reforms led the Spanish army to attempt to pacify the Apache through a combination of continuous military harassment and enticements to settle and live peacefully in the vicinity of the presidios. By 1793, the strategy had paid off, and pacified bands of Apaches *(apaches mansos)* began to settle just downstream from the presidio, ostensibly to take up the settled Spanish way of life. But the Apache never became the agriculturists that the Sobaipuri villagers across the river were, and their primary associations were always with the presidio. They depended heavily on the rations of grain, beef, and tobacco that the garrison supplied to them, provisions that, in the garrison's view, were well spent. The Spanish army continued its policy of alternating harassment and enticement of hostile Apache until the end of the colonial era (Dobyns 1976:82–105).

The period of relative peace that followed Apache pacification saw a continued decline in the Sobaipuri population, the intermittent settling of Tohono O'odham in Akimel O'odham villages, and a modest but steady influx of *gente de razón* into the region. By the start of the nineteenth century, the Sobaipuri who had been the original impetus for Spanish missionizing in the Santa Cruz Valley had become scarce, largely supplanted by Tohono O'odham. A minor effort to bring the faith directly to the Tohono O'odham was made by the Franciscans in 1802, when the friar Juan Bautista Llorens paid a visit to the village of Cuiquiburitac in the Santa Rosa Valley, some 50 miles west and somewhat north of San Xavier. Llorens's visit led to the construction of a *visita* church at Cuiquiburitac sometime after 1805, but it was abandoned before the end of the colonial period (Fontana and Matson 1987). The mission settlements at Tumacácori and San Xavier del Bac remained predominantly Native American, but the Spanish were now a conspicuous presence at Tumacácori, the Tucson presidio, and Tubac, which in 1787 had once again become a presidio. The total Spanish population was nonetheless very low: an official census taken of the Tucson presidio and the surrounding area (including San Xavier) in 1804 counted 1,015 *gente de razón*. The same census listed 88 soldiers and their families, plus 8 civilian households, at Tubac and 88 *gente de razón* at Tumacácori (Dobyns 1976:133–141; Kessell 1976:245–246; Officer 1987:77–82). With the gradual increase in the Spanish population and the relative security afforded by Apache pacification, the occasional Spanish family attempted farming, ranching, or mining in outlying areas such as Arivaca and the San Pedro Valley, but most Spaniards continued to congregate in or near the three Santa Cruz Valley settlements (Officer 1987:82–83; Sheridan 1995:37–38).

Late in the Spanish Colonial period, despite the decline of the Sobaipuri population and a consequently tenuous labor force, the Franciscan missions at Tumacácori and San Xavier del Bac managed to replace their modest old churches with new ones. Recent Tohono O'odham converts contributed much of the labor. Construction of the church at San Xavier, the same church that survives today, began around 1781 and was completed by 1797. At San Agustín del Tucson, San Xavier's dependent settlement located 8 miles downstream and across the river from the Tucson presidio, a new church and a large, two-story mission residence (or *convento*) were constructed sometime between 1797 and 1810 (see Chapter 5 for details on the buildings constructed at both mission sites). Together, San Xavier and San Agustín defined a sphere of interaction that survived the Spanish Colonial period and is now reflected in the Paseo de las Iglesias study area. At Tumacácori, a new church was begun in 1802, but because of financial difficulties and a shortage of labor, it was not completed until 1828, and only then in a much reduced version of the original plan. The remains of the church are now the primary attraction at Tumacacori National Monument (Schuetz-Miller and Fontana 1996:86–88, 90–94). Apart from these architectural accomplishments—of which the church at San Xavier was by far the most striking—the centers of the

Spanish presence in southern Arizona at the end of the colonial era were visually unimpressive. Tucson and Tubac were little more than "flat-roofed adobe buildings clustered beside a ragged patchwork of fields" (Sheridan 1995:38). But whatever its appearance, a Spanish way of life, albeit a way of life adapted to the harsh conditions of the Santa Cruz Valley—isolation, Apache predation, and limited water—was now well established on the northern frontier.

Decline of the Colonial System under Mexico

The Spanish Colonial period ended in 1821, when Mexico won its independence from Spain. The impact of independence on the far northern frontier was not immediate—the presidios accepted the transfer of power to the new Mexican government largely without issue—but it was decisive in determining the future of the region. Because of the inability of the Mexican government to continue providing support, financial or otherwise, to the northern frontier, independence from Spain brought with it the collapse of "just about every institution that had held the Spanish frontier together" (Sheridan 1995:45). The presidio at Tucson, soon weakened by lack of supplies, arms, and reinforcements, saw its most important weapon for Apache pacification—rations for the *apaches mansos*—withdrawn because of a lack of funds. Apache raiding throughout southern Arizona once again became a major threat and continued unabated throughout the Mexican era.

The missions, although they escaped the secularization mandated for the rest of Mexico shortly after independence, were dealt a serious blow when all Spaniards were officially expelled from Mexico in 1828. The Spanish-born Franciscans at San Xavier and Tumacácori were ordered to leave, and no priest was ever again in residence at either mission during the Mexican era. Officially, the missions remained intact and were generally viewed as useful to the government's purpose of securing the frontier, but through a combination of official neglect and local coveting of mission property, the influence of the missions in the Santa Cruz Valley steadily declined. As the missions declined and Hispanics put more pressure on mission lands, the Tohono O'odham who had come to depend on those lands suddenly became a problem themselves, although never to the same degree as the Apache (Kessell 1976:275–319; Officer 1987:100–104, 130–133; Sheridan 1995:44–47; Weber 1982:50–53).

During the turbulent decades of the Mexican period, the Hispanic population of southern Arizona actually declined somewhat. Despite the decline, the period saw a great increase in the number of land grants petitioned for and granted to Hispanic settlers in the region (the earliest large land grants were actually petitioned for under the Spanish government and eventually granted under Mexican law). Major land grants along the Santa Cruz River and in adjacent areas included San Ignacio de la Canoa (along the Santa Cruz, north of Tubac), San Rafael de la Zanja (along the headwaters of the Santa Cruz), Tumacácori and Calabazas (former lands of the Tumacácori mission), San Ignacio del Babocómari (in the San Pedro Valley), and San José de Sonoita (along Sonoita Creek, a tributary of the upper Santa Cruz) (Figure 7). In some cases, these grants included lands "abandoned" by the missions (the official status of such lands was often not clear) yet still farmed by Tohono O'odham associated with the missions. The granting of land to a Hispanic rancher usually meant an end to its use by mission dependents; this was an important source of unrest among the Tohono O'odham. Although the land grants consisted of many thousands of acres, the constant threat of Apache raids meant that they often did not actually get used for ranching. Sheridan (1995:49) has called them "little more than adobe islands in a desert sea—isolated, vulnerable, easily destroyed." By the end of the Mexican era, most either had been abandoned or were barely hanging on. The most substantial impact of the granting of these large tracts of land occurred after the tracts were bought by Anglo-American interests later in the century (Mattison 1946; Officer 1987: 106–110; Sheridan 1995:127–129; Wagoner 1975:159–239).

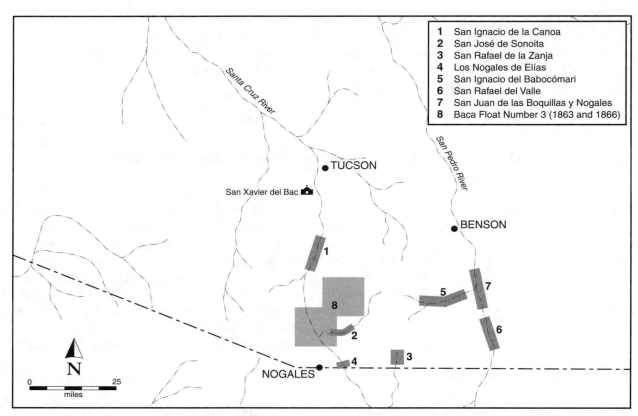

Figure 7. Selected Mexican land grants in southern Arizona.

The settlements along the Santa Cruz River saw little direct evidence of the war waged between the United States and Mexico from 1846 to 1848. The sole visit to the Santa Cruz Valley by U.S. troops was a brief stop in December 1846 by the Mormon Battalion, which was en route to the Pacific coast. The battalion entered Tucson unopposed by the presidio troops, who had withdrawn to San Xavier to avoid a battle. The loss of a huge portion of Mexican territory in 1848 due to the Treaty of Guadalupe also had no immediate impact on the people living along the Santa Cruz, whose status as the northernmost outpost of Sonora remained unchanged and whose hard lives fighting the Apache and farming the desert continued as before. The only substantial change in the last years of the Mexican era was the increasing number of Anglo-Americans passing through the area, most notably the sudden wave of Anglo-Americans headed to California during the 1849 gold rush. Even after the Gadsden Purchase was ratified in 1854, making all of what is now Arizona south of the Gila River a part of the United States, it was two years before the presidio at Tucson was abandoned by its Mexican garrison (Officer 1987:262–283; Sheridan 1995:49–57; Wagoner 1975:259–297).

Following the incorporation of southern Arizona into the United States, the Mexican presence in the region became increasingly centered in Tucson, at the same time that the city was becoming the hub of Anglo-American settlement and enterprise. The most significant aspect of the Mexican presence after the Gadsden Purchase was its essential continuity with pre-Gadsden days. Most of the families who had established themselves along the Santa Cruz River and in outlying areas chose to remain there, and even many of the presidio troops, after first abandoning Tucson and Tubac for Sonora, came back to lead civilian lives in U.S. territory. For most Mexicans, Tucson remained an extension of Sonoran culture and society. The Anglo-American population grew slowly but steadily in the first few decades after the

Gadsden Purchase, knitting itself, to a degree, into the existing Mexican social structure (intermarriage among Mexicans and Anglo-Americans was fairly common) and sharing the dangers of life in a region still under Apache threat. But despite their minority status, the Anglo-Americans quickly dominated the regional economy, in large part because of the capital they brought with them into an area that, prior to their arrival, had been decidedly poor. Although the culture of the city remained predominantly Mexican, as did its population, Anglo-American traditions grew steadily stronger as Anglo-American money entered the region. In 1880, the year the railroad arrived, Anglo-Americans truly began to dominate life in Tucson, politically, economically, and culturally. Nonetheless, people of Mexican descent and culture remained in the majority in Tucson until shortly after the turn of the century. Mexicans, or more properly, Mexican-Americans, remain a viable and distinctive presence in Tucson today, despite a century and a half of imposed secondary status.

Mining, Farming, and Ranching

Of the three major economic pursuits that characterized southern Arizona through much of the historical period—mining, farming, and ranching—only ranching was introduced by Europeans. The Native Americans of the region, using their own repertoire of crops and techniques, had farmed competently for many centuries before Europeans arrived, and the extraction of precious metals from the earth, although never pursued on a large scale, had a similarly long history in the Americas. Native American farming in the Pimería Alta was transformed by the introduction of Spanish crops in the seventeenth and eighteenth centuries (see above). Native Americans also were among the freelance prospectors at placer deposits in early Spanish mining camps on the northern frontier, although many more Native Americans ended up laboring in Spanish vein-mining operations, often against their will, particularly in the major mining settlements of what are now Sonora and Chihuahua (Radding 1997:32–40). As for ranching, the people of the Pimería Alta began raising cattle, sheep, and goats shortly after Jesuits introduced the practice in the late seventeenth century, and small-scale ranching remains a part of rural Native American life in the region today.

Spanish mining, farming, and ranching in the Pimería Alta also benefited from the encounter with Native Americans, but far more from the land and labor that the encounter yielded than from any exchange of knowledge and technology. Spanish settlers spread through the Pimería Alta on the heels of the Jesuits with little interest in the subsistence strategies of Native Americans—the New World crops that Spaniards used had been adopted many years earlier—and every interest in establishing Spanish-style mining operations, farms, and herds. On the northernmost frontier of New Spain, where isolation and Apache raids limited Spanish settlement largely to the Santa Cruz Valley, the scope of these three pursuits never approached that of other parts of the Pimería Alta, much less that of the wealthiest places in New Spain. Nonetheless, it was the attempt to recreate a traditionally Spanish economy on the far northern frontier that caused the first major transformation of the southern Arizona landscape.

The second major transformation came in the late nineteenth century, following the arrival to the region of the "industrializing world economy" (Sheridan 1992:168). Anglo-Americans began settling in southern Arizona immediately after the Gadsden Purchase of 1854, bringing with them their own interest in mines, farms, and ranches, and both the technology they used and the scale of their operations were at first similar to those of their Hispanic counterparts. Not until 1880, the year the railroad reached southern Arizona, did mining, farming, and ranching become large, heavily capitalized businesses, closely linked to the greater financial world of the United States. Almost overnight, the three mainstays of the southern Arizona economy saw sweeping changes in scale and complexity, and the landscape that supported them was altered forever.

The following paragraphs outline the history of mining, farming, and ranching in southern Arizona and note how each mode of production was pursued through time in and near the Paseo de las Iglesias study area.

Mining

The first Spanish settlements along the Santa Cruz River might have been the Jesuit missions at Guevavi and San Xavier del Bac, but the search for gold and silver was as responsible for bringing Spaniards to the region as a desire to spread Catholicism. The very name *Arizona* derives from a place called Arizonac, just southwest of modern Nogales, where silver was discovered in 1736. The discovery occurred just five years after the Santa Cruz missions were officially established, and the strike led to the first wave of Spanish prospectors to the region, many of whom stayed after the strike at Arizonac petered out (Officer 1987:4). Sheridan (1992:160), noting the central role of mining camps in opening new areas to settlement in northern New Spain, has called the Spanish mining frontier "the cutting edge of empire," where ordinary Spaniards first mingled regularly with Native Americans and where Native Americans were first exposed to the novelties of Spanish economy and society. In southern Arizona, mining never played the dominant economic role that it did in the major mining centers of Sonora and Chihuahua, but the hope that it might kept a steady flow of Spaniards coming to the region throughout the colonial period.

Officer (1991), sifting through a variety of confusing and ambiguous documentary data regarding Spanish mines in southern Arizona, concluded that the actual extent of mining in the region during the Spanish Colonial and Mexican periods was very limited. Locations where mining likely did take place were limited to silver deposits in the Santa Rita Mountains, in the Arivaca area, and at the south end of the Huachuca Mountains, and gold deposits in the Sierrita Mountains, in the Arivaca area, and on Mount Benedict, west of Guevavi. The precise locations where most of this mining took place are unknown. Despite a great number of optimistic legends to the contrary, there is no good evidence that Spanish and Mexican mining ever took place in the Tucson Mountains, the Patagonia Mountains, the Ajo region, or a variety of other places that would later claim the interest of Anglo-American miners. Factors that limited every Spanish enterprise in southern Arizona—remoteness from Mexico City and the constant threat of Apache raids—were especially limiting to mining. The remoteness of southern Arizona from Mexico City made the procurement of tools and supplies (such as mercury for processing silver) prohibitively expensive, and the limited range of presidio protection made miners who worked the isolated deposits easy targets for the Apache. "Even in the most favorable locations," Officer (1991:8) wrote, "Arizona mining could not have amounted to much in Hispanic times."

Two features of Hispanic mining in southern Arizona survived the Gadsden Purchase to become incorporated into the Anglo-American approach to mining. The first was an acceptance of the mythical abundance of Arizona's mineral resources, an abundance first postulated by Spaniards at Arizonac, accepted hopefully by Hispanic miners for the next 120 years, and seized on enthusiastically by Anglo-Americans from the 1850s onward. Polzer (1968) suggested that much of the mythology of Arizona's buried wealth was in fact Anglo-American in origin, either the optimistic yearnings of small-time prospectors or the propaganda of commercial mining interests looking for financial backing, but as Officer (1991) noted, there were plenty of Hispanic antecedents for the Anglo-Americans to build on.

The second feature of Hispanic mining that Anglo-Americans borrowed was its technology. Hispanic miners exploited the two basic varieties of deposit—placer and vein (or lode). Placer deposits (literally, "pleasure" deposits), the most common source of gold, consisted of gold-bearing gravels exposed on the ground surface, often in or adjacent to a streambed. The typical method used to isolate gold from a placer deposit was panning, using a *batea,* a large, conical-bottomed vessel of hardwood or sheet metal. This method was supplemented by dry washing, or winnowing the ore from heavier gravels by throwing the ore-bearing gravel in the air over a blanket, and by amalgamation, the use of mercury to draw small particles of gold together in the *batea.* Anglo-Americans entering the Spanish frontier adopted these simple methods early on (Coggin 1987; Fansett 1952; Sheridan 1995:147–148; Wilson 1952).

Silver was more commonly mined from veins than from placer deposits. Silver was also much more abundant than gold in northern New Spain, and the Spaniards entering southern Arizona brought with them a variety of methods for extracting and processing silver ore. Nonetheless, the technology was still relatively simple, and the more-involved processes used in the major mining centers of Mexico were generally not used on the northern frontier. Mining along a vein usually began with shallow, open-pit diggings, then progressed to vertical shafts 2–4 m deep, sometimes augmented with small horizontal drifts. Deeper shafts might prompt measures to control flooding and the use of wooden beams as reinforcements, but given the limited nature of mining in southern Arizona, it is doubtful that even these simple steps were commonly taken. An important tool for processing silver ore, also adopted by early Anglo-American miners, was the *arrastre,* a large, circular, stone-floored depression, with a central post and a horizontal beam suspending two large boulders. The boulders were dragged by mules in a circle around the post, pulverizing the coarse ore dumped on the stone floor (Keane and Rogge 1992:26; Sheridan 1995:147–148; West 1993:50–53). Officer (1987:16–17) noted that knowledge of these and other methods, first developed in the Spanish Colonial period, was brought by Mexican immigrants to Tubac after 1856, as mines abandoned many years earlier because of the Apache threat were reopened. "From this point on," he wrote, "Hispanic miners would play an indispensable role in the development of Arizona's mineral industry."

Although a great deal of placer and vein mining (including the beginnings of mechanized hard-rock mining) took place elsewhere in Arizona during the 1860s and 1870s, the first major strike in southern Arizona did not come until after the Apache threat in the region had been significantly curtailed by the U.S. Army. In 1878, silver was discovered in the hills near Tombstone in Cochise County, and by 1880, the discovery had created a town of 10,000 people or more where two years earlier there had been none. Mining at Tombstone during its short boom—the mines were largely abandoned by the end of the 1880s—underwent all of the changes seen in mining throughout the West during the same period. Powerful business interests bought up the major claims, the extraction and processing of ore became increasingly large scale and mechanized, and hired workers replaced individual prospectors in performing the manual labor of mining (Schillingberg 1999; Sheridan 1995:152–160). The railroad, which crossed southern Arizona two years after the Tombstone discovery, was a major factor in the early development of industrial mining in the region, linking the mines to the markets and technological innovations of the East. By the 1880s, large mining interests in Arizona were buying and building their own railroads to service their mining operations (Irvin 1987; Sheridan 1995:167–168).

Anglo-Americans began entering southern Arizona in search of mining opportunities immediately after the Gadsden Purchase. Although the number of miners in the region grew slowly, by the 1860s, the competition for claims, combined with a lack of clarity about how U.S. mining laws should apply in the newly acquired region, led to the establishment of mining districts modeled after those formed by groups of independent miners in California and Nevada. A mining district corresponded to a recognized mining area, such as a valley or group of hills. Its official boundaries and a set of regulations to govern mining within the district were established by agreement among the miners who were active there. The regulations addressed matters such as how claims must be filed, what the limits of individual claims were, and how disputes would be settled. Every district had its own set of regulations, but the regulations were generally very similar from district to district. Even after federal laws governing mining were passed in the late 1860s, mining districts continued to be an important regulatory mechanism at the local level, and districts continue to serve a regulatory function today (Lacy 1987:7–9).

The first mining district established in the vicinity of the Santa Cruz River was the Cerro Colorado District near Arivaca, the regulations of which were published in 1864 (Lacy 1987:9). Other districts soon followed, and by the 1970s, there were more than 30 recognized districts in Pima County (Keith

1974). The names and delimitations of districts have changed often since the 1860s, but the areas occupied by the districts have remained the same; most are situated in the islandlike clusters of mountains scattered around the county, typical locations of major mineral outcrops (Wilson 1995). Many of these districts have seen repeated episodes of mining since the nineteenth century, particularly copper mining, which began as early as 1865 in the Silver Bell District west of Tucson (Tuck 1963:31). In some districts, communities sprang up near ongoing mining operations. In the Rosemont District, another copper-producing area in the Santa Rita Mountains southeast of Tucson, for example, the town of Rosemont had two different incarnations, 1894–1910 and 1915–1921 (Ayres 1984a). In the Greaterville District, located on the eastern slopes of the Santa Ritas, the discovery of gold placers in 1874 gave rise to the community of Greaterville in the late 1870s, although the town was already dwindling by the early 1880s. Kentucky Camp, a complex of buildings erected as headquarters for a hydraulic mining operation at the Greaterville deposit in the early twentieth century, has since become a National Register Historic District (Mc-Donald et al. 1995; Orrell 1998).

Copper became the focus of the mining industry in southern Arizona not long after the collapse of the silver market in the late 1880s, a collapse largely responsible for the demise of Tombstone. The most important copper-mining operation in the region, by far, was centered at Bisbee in southeastern Arizona. By the end of the century, the Copper Queen mine at Bisbee had a large, modern smelter; many miles of underground rail; and a huge labor force. It was also one of the richest copper mines in the world (Graeme 1987; Sheridan 1995:165). Improved metal prices in the late 1890s also led to an increase in production in the Helvetia, Rosemont, Silver Bell, Twin Buttes, and Mineral Hill Districts of Pima County, districts that subsequently enjoyed a heyday during World War I), when the demand for copper rose sharply in response to weapons manufacturing. The Ajo District, about 110 miles west of Tucson, also began large-scale copper production at the start of the war. In all of these districts, production declined after the end of World War I, nearly disappeared during the Great Depression, and then rose again during World War II (Wilson 1949:5–6).

The most recent stage in the development of mining in southern Arizona has been the nearly complete conversion from underground mining to large, open-pit extraction, a change implemented throughout the industry after World War II. The conversion has involved a great increase in mechanization, which has in turn allowed both for increased exploitation of lower-grade ores and much less reliance on human labor. Yet despite the increased production created by open-pit extraction, the general trend for copper throughout the United States since World War II has been one of decline, largely because of the expansion of copper-mining operations overseas (Hyde 1998:189–190). Nonetheless, the copper industry continues to be a major force in the southern Arizona economy, and the enormous open excavations and mountains of tailings and slag left on the landscape by copper mining since World War II are inescapable reminders of the industry's importance.

Because the Paseo de las Iglesias study area consists largely of floodplain, it has never been affected directly by mineral mining. The Tucson Mountains, immediately west of the study area, constitute the nearest early focus of mining: they were probably mined as early as the Spanish Colonial and Mexican periods, although documentation of actual mining sites from these periods is lacking (Stein 1993:90). On the other hand, Ayres (1984b:130) has estimated that the Tucson Mountains hold some 300 mining-related sites from the U.S. period, none of which have been studied in any depth. More recently, Clemensen (1987) discussed mining activities in the Tucson Mountains in the U.S. period, and recent surveys in the area by Wellman (1994) and Wells and Reutters (1997) have documented a number of small mining-related sites (see also Wilson 1949:8–9).

The Sierrita Mountains, a small range located just south of the study area, was another early focus of mining, also probably as early as Spanish Colonial times. By the second half of the nineteenth century, several silver and lead mines were intermittently active and included substantial smelting operations. Small-scale copper mining efforts began in the 1890s but soon gave way to more-heavily capitalized operations, culminating in the 1940s with the emergence of huge open-pit mines and processing plants

(Wilson 1949:12–14). Large-scale open-pit mining of copper, zinc, and lead continues today in the Sierritas.

We searched the General Land Office (GLO) records kept by the Tucson field office of the Bureau of Land Management for mining claims filed in the two townships encompassing the study area (Township 14 South, Range 13 East, and Township 15 South, Range 13 East). Only a handful of successful claims have ever been filed in the two townships, and all fall within Sections 18, 19, 20, and 21 of Township 14 South, Range 13 East. The area of the claims is a group of small hills forming part of the eastern foothills of the Tucson Mountains, about a mile and a half southwest of Tumamoc Hill. We have been unable to find any other information about the individuals who identified or exploited these claims. The claim names are Arizona Sun Shine Nos. 1–4, Battle Axe, Little Betsey, Marion, Quien Sabe, and Quien Sabe No. 2 (Mineral Survey Nos. 2951 and 4080).

Within the Paseo de las Iglesias study area, archaeological evidence of mining-related activities is limited to the discovery of assaying crucibles and small amounts of silver-ore slag at AZ AA:16:61. This site, occupied in the second half of the nineteenth century, is the remains of a probable Hispanic residence, believed by the excavators to be the former residence of Jesús María Elías (Cohen-Williams and Williams 1982; Williams 1982; we note in our description of AZ AA:16:61 in the appendix that this specific claim is difficult to evaluate). The presence of assaying equipment and slag suggests that the residents were involved to some degree in mining operations, although similar artifacts are frequently found in residential contexts of the same period elsewhere in Tucson (Homer Thiel, personal communication 2001), reflecting a widespread interest in evaluating potential mining claims but not necessarily an active involvement in mining.

It is also worth noting that shortly after Solomon Warner built his grist mill at the eastern foot of Sentinel Peak (the ruins of which are recorded as AZ BB:13:57), he added a small, three-stamp ore mill to his operation (see the section on Solomon Warner and his mill later in the chapter).

Farming

The Spanish settlers of southern Arizona practiced agriculture largely for the sake of subsistence, much like the Native Americans who preceded them in the region. Somewhat ironically, the largest producers of both native and introduced crops in southern Arizona throughout the Spanish Colonial and Mexican periods were not the Spaniards, who had made so many additions to the Sobaipuri way of farming, but the Sobaipuri themselves and, later, the Tohono O'odham (Officer 1987:15). On the mission lands along the Santa Cruz River, Sobaipuri and Tohono O'odham farming never yielded the kinds of surplus that would make the trading of produce a major enterprise, but by the end of the Mexican period, the Akimel O'odham living along the Gila River had become prolific wheat farmers with abundant surpluses. When the California gold rush of the late 1840s started funneling people across Arizona along the Gila Trail, the Akimel O'odham became "the first agricultural entrepreneurs in Arizona" (Sheridan 1995:97), trading surplus wheat to supply-seeking travelers. By 1870, they were producing and selling a surplus of more than three million pounds of wheat per year. Unfortunately, the Akimel O'odham soon lost the key to their agricultural success when Anglo-American farmers upstream began diverting the water of the Gila River for their own irrigation projects (Sheridan 1995:97–98).

Two major factors limited the scale of Hispanic agricultural endeavors in southern Arizona. The first was the constant problem of distance: the Santa Cruz Valley was too far from central Mexico either to make the export of agricultural produce profitable or to encourage enough settlement to create a local market. Officer (1987:15) wrote, "The isolation of the Pimería Alta and its limited population provided little inspiration for major agricultural development." The second limiting factor was the obvious environmental one: in a region of generally high aridity, the land suited to agriculture was restricted to narrow swaths of the major river valleys, and for virtually the entire Hispanic era, the only valley sufficiently protected from the Apache by the presidios was the Santa Cruz. For Hispanic farming, as for Sobaipuri farming, irrigation was the key to maximizing productivity in an arid, circumscribed environment.

Irrigation had been used by Native Americans in southern Arizona for many centuries before Spaniards arrived in the region, but the Spaniards were also heirs to an ancient tradition of irrigation—one that ultimately had Roman and Arabic antecedents—that they brought with them from Europe (Meyer 1996).

On the northern frontier of New Spain, where labor was scarce and engineers were nonexistent, only the simplest techniques of the tradition came into common use; this made the physical side of Hispanic irrigation not substantially different from its Native American counterpart. The basic element was the acequia (canal), a hand-excavated earthen ditch, leading from a simple diversion dam in a stream to an agricultural plot. Acequias typically ranged in depth from 2 to 9 feet and in width from 1 foot to 7 feet. Depending on topographical circumstances, they might be straight or winding, single or multiple (Meyer 1996:41–42; Sheridan 1995:189).

The social side of Spanish irrigation was as important to the success of the system as the physical side. The amount of water available for farming along the Santa Cruz was limited and unpredictable, and even the small Spanish population living there had to be conservative in its use of the resource. The traditional Spanish institutions that helped ensure equitable distribution of irrigation water during times of scarcity were the común de agua (water users' association) and the juez de agua (water judge) or zanjero (canal overseer). The juez de agua, elected by the común de agua, was assisted by a mayordomo (ditch boss), who helped him implement a strict rotation of water usage when a shortage occurred. Indian settlements under Spanish control also were supposed to have jueces de agua or functionaries serving a similar role (Meyer 1996:64–66; Sheridan 1986:14–15, 1995:189). There is direct evidence of these institutions in the Mexican-American settlement along the Santa Cruz River as late as the 1880s (Sheridan 1986:64–65), and their pervasiveness throughout the northern frontier in the Spanish Colonial period makes it likely that they existed in southern Arizona from the start of Spanish settlement.

Despite the burdens of isolation and aridity, Spanish farming was largely a success along the Santa Cruz. Clustered at the Tubac and Tucson presidios, Hispanic farmers planted corn, wheat, barley, garbanzos, lentils, and a variety of vegetables, as well as fruit trees and grape vines. The most important crop was wheat, not entirely because of a Spanish preference for wheat over corn but because wheat, which was frost tolerant and matured in winter, could take advantage of the most dependable irrigation season. The occasional surplus raised by Hispanic settlers would be sold to the commander of the presidio. Soldiers at the presidio also sometimes cultivated gardens, and in the latter part of the Mexican period, they were expected to plant crops to feed their horses and other livestock. At different times during both the Spanish and Mexican periods, settlers from Tucson visited the San Pedro Valley to plant and harvest crops, protected from Apache attack by escorts of presidio soldiers (Jones 1979:194; Officer 1987:15; Sheridan 1986:15).

The essential characteristics of Hispanic agriculture along the Santa Cruz were, according to Sheridan (1986:15), "scarcity and cooperation," and the successful balancing of the two by Hispanic farmers continued well into the U.S. period. Officer (1987:290) noted that by 1862, eight years after the Gadsden Purchase, Anglo-American immigrants to Tucson had already acquired considerable property in and around the town, but they found it difficult to purchase agricultural lands along the river. A map of Tucson's fields prepared in 1862 shows that most of the irrigated land adjacent to the Santa Cruz, in an area at the base of Sentinel Peak and corresponding to the northernmost mile or so of the Paseo de las Iglesias study area, was still owned and farmed by Mexicans (Figure 8). This situation changed soon enough, as both Anglo-Americans and newly arrived Mexicans began to acquire land both by purchase and by claims made under the Homestead Act. The newcomers were often more interested in acquiring land for speculative purposes than for agriculture and, in either case, were altogether uninterested in conforming to the traditional Hispanic practice of irrigation conservation. Disputes soon arose along the Santa Cruz between new landholders who wanted to divert the flow of the Santa Cruz to some private purpose, such

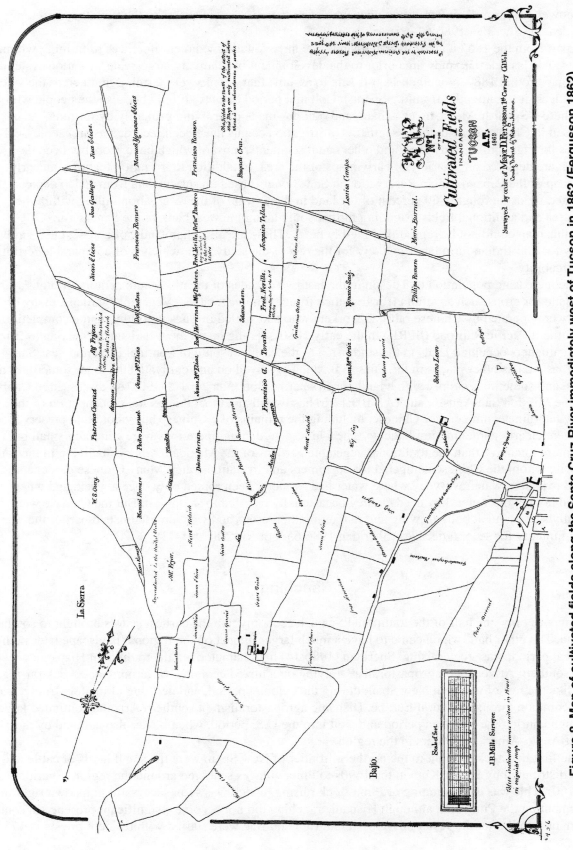

Figure 8. Map of cultivated fields along the Santa Cruz River immediately west of Tucson in 1862 (Fergusson 1862).

as to power a flour mill, and traditionalists who were thereby denied access to the flow they had long depended on (Sheridan 1986:63–65).

Apart from the 1862 map of irrigated lands, we have found few direct references to farming within the Paseo de las Iglesias study area prior to the development of relatively large-scale irrigation systems that began around 1880. Nonetheless, it is safe to assume that people were farming in much of the study area, at least intermittently, from the Spanish Colonial period onward, if only because the people who lived there—Spanish, Mexican, O'odham, and others—made their living primarily by farming. As is discussed in Chapter 5, abandoned segments of irrigation canals have been recorded as archaeological features throughout the study area, and other canal segments, most of which have probably been destroyed, are depicted on a variety of early maps of the area. In addition to irrigation features, an early GLO map of the Papago Indian Reservation at San Xavier (based on survey data from 1915) depicts cultivated fields on roughly 60 percent of the land in the portion of the reservation falling within the study area and additional fields extending farther south along the west bank of the Santa Cruz (GLO 1921; this map could not be reproduced legibly here). These are all Indian lands, of course, but a similar density for non-Indian farm lands is likely for the rest of the study area, which is of comparable fertility and irrigability.

The increasing population of Tucson in the last two decades of the nineteenth century brought a rise in demand for crops such as alfalfa (for livestock forage) and vegetables. Vegetable gardens, many of which were operated by Chinese railroad workers who had settled in Tucson following the completion of the Southern Pacific Railroad (SPRR) in the early 1880s, sprang up on the west bank of the Santa Cruz. These gardeners occupied lands in the study area to the east and south of Sentinel Peak and near San Xavier, as well as other places in the Tucson Basin. They lived on and cultivated the land, sometimes as renters, and sometimes simply with a landowner's permission (Xia 2001:84–90). As discussed in Chapter 5, the Mission San Agustín site (AZ BB:13:6) has two distinct loci that relate to occupation of the area by late-nineteenth-century Chinese, including the remains of a Chinese household that preserved what were clearly gardening implements. The Chinese gardening operations were generally small but much more intensive than the traditional vegetable gardens of the Mexican-Americans living in the same area, with whom the Chinese competed for customers and irrigation water. Many Chinese gardeners wanted irrigation water everyday where water had formerly been routed only once a week, and when they did not get the water they needed, they occasionally resorted to stealing it. But the Chinese were generally successful at both growing and marketing their crops and were an established part of the Tucson community for several decades (Sheridan 1986:65–66; Xia 2001:90–93).

Ranching

Farming was only one half of the traditional Spanish economy that the earliest setters brought to southern Arizona. The other half, which came to have a much larger impact on the regional landscape later in the historical period, was stock raising. Sheridan (1986:14) has characterized the traditional Hispanic way of life in southern Arizona as "agropastoralist," relying on a mixed economy of farming and stock raising, much like the rest of northern New Spain during the colonial period, and deriving ultimately from a way of life common throughout rural Europe. Hispanic agropastoralism in southern Arizona continued largely unchanged during the Mexican period and well into the U.S. period, when it was also adopted by the earliest Anglo-American settlers in the region.

The first livestock brought to the northern frontier of New Spain were the small herds of cattle and horses distributed by Father Kino in the 1690s to Pima villages scattered around the region (Sheridan 1988:160). This was the beginning of Pima stock raising, which was soon successful in its own right in supplementing the Pima diet, although Hispanic ranching did not become a significant presence in southern Arizona until after the Jesuit missions at Guevavi and Bac were staffed with resident priests in 1731.

The Spaniards drawn north by the discovery of silver at Arizonac in 1736 were soon settling along the upper reaches of the Santa Cruz River, grazing cattle on the lush grasslands of the valley, just as Spaniards had so often done farther south in New Spain during the previous two centuries. By 1752, when the presidio at Tubac was established in response to the Pima revolt of 1751, Spaniards were grazing cattle along much of the Santa Cruz south of Tucson and had expanded westward into the Arivaca region. By the end of the Spanish Colonial period, the numbers of cattle in the region reflected a successful but circumscribed enterprise. In 1804, 3,500 head of cattle were reported for the Tucson vicinity, with another 1,000 around Tubac; in 1818, the mission at Tumacácori reportedly had 5,000 cattle, and San Xavier had around 8,800 (Dobyns 1976:51; Officer 1987:15, 31; Sheridan 1995:127–129).

Except for the limited activity in the Arivaca region, stock raising in southern Arizona during the Spanish Colonial period was generally confined to the Santa Cruz Valley, for the perennial reason that the risk of Apache raid was too high at any distance from the presidios at Tucson and Tubac. Following Mexican independence, the effectiveness of the Santa Cruz presidios declined as the connections to central Mexico became even more tenuous, but despite the decline, Hispanic ranchers were determined to take advantage of the large grasslands that lay well outside of presidio control, such as along the San Pedro River. The result of their determination was the era of large land grants discussed above, when individual Hispanic settlers petitioned for and received vast tracts of land from the Mexican government. These grants soon supported large herds of cattle, but by the 1830s, the Apache had killed or chased away most of the ranch owners and run off their cattle (Wagoner 1952:24–36). These cattle were apparently the origin of the large herds of wild cattle reported by the earliest Anglo-American visitors to southern Arizona, although the numbers of cattle in the region, both before and after the ranches were abandoned, have often been exaggerated. Sheridan (1995:129) has suggested that the total population of cattle in southern Arizona during the Mexican era never exceeded 20,000–30,000 animals, because, in addition to the predations of Apache, ranching in the region before the 1840s was limited by the lack of a dependable market for beef.

The problems with the Apache continued for another 40 years, and by the time Anglo-Americans started passing through southern Arizona on their way to California in the late 1840s, Hispanic ranching in the region was a shadow of its earlier self. During the years following the gold rush, large herds of cattle were driven by Anglo-American ranchers across southern Arizona from Texas to be sold as beef in the mining communities of California (a pattern that actually continued until about 1870), but not until the Gadsden Purchase in 1854 did Anglo-Americans make some initial attempts to raise cattle in the region. Their successes were limited by the same factors that plagued Hispanic ranching: Apache raids and distance from markets. One of the first Anglo-Americans to run cattle in the Tucson area was Bill Kirkland, who in 1857 brought 200 head of cattle to the San Ignacio de la Canoa Ranch, located along both banks of the Santa Cruz just south of the study area. By 1860, the cattle had been stolen and Kirkland had moved on to a different location (Wagoner 1952:33). Also along the Santa Cruz just south of the study area, a German immigrant named Fritz Contzen started Rancho Punta de Agua in 1855 with about 500 head of cattle. He, too, suffered repeated Apache raids and had given up on ranching by the 1860s (McGuire 1979). Other ranchers in the Tucson Basin during the same period suffered similar fates. For example, in 1844, Francisco Romero established a ranch near the Cañada del Oro on the western slopes of the Santa Catalina Mountains north of Tucson. In 1870, after two and a half decades of intermittent Apache violence, the hardy Romero and his family were finally driven from the ranch for good (Mabry 1991:62–69).

The Civil War, which made southern Arizona an area of Union-Confederate contention for a brief time, put a stop to Anglo-American ranching at the start of the 1860s. The Apache extended the hiatus for another decade and a half. In 1870, the year U.S. Army Gen. George Crook arrived in southern Arizona to begin his long campaign to subdue the Apache, the territorial census reported only 1,800 cattle in all of Pima County, which at that time encompassed almost all of Arizona south of the Gila River (Wagoner 1952:36). The situation changed rapidly as the Apache frontier was pushed eastward from the

Tucson Basin during the 1870s. By 1873, both Mexican- and Anglo-American ranchers had successful small operations along the Santa Cruz River, and similar operations were soon springing up in the Arivaca region to the west of the Santa Cruz, along Sonoita Creek to the east of the river, and along the Cañada del Oro. There were also a number of successful Mexican ranches along Tanque Verde Wash to the east of Tucson (Mabry 1991; Wagoner 1952:39–41). The spread of ranches along the principal streams of the region was soon accompanied by the gobbling up of all available sources of water, including streams and springs, by ranchers claiming parcels under the Homestead Act and the Desert Land Act. By patenting a claim on a parcel with a water source, ranchers could have de facto control over surrounding parcels without water, and some ranchers built major land holdings by having other people (such as employees) file claims that the rancher would then buy up cheaply when they were patented (Mayro 1999:40).

The arrival of the railroad in 1880 was a major boost to the cattle industry in southern Arizona, which from then on was dominated by large business interests. An important example of the shift was the 1883 purchase of the San Rafael land grant along the headwaters of the Santa Cruz River by a consortium of eastern investors organized by Colin Cameron, who was not a cattleman by training or inclination, but a businessman. By combining shrewd legal maneuvering with ruthlessness, Cameron developed the San Rafael into a major enterprise. For years, he vigorously contested the original 17,000-acre allotment of the grant, claiming that it should have been 152,000 acres, and although he never won a larger allotment, he was able to graze a large herd on many times the official acreage for the remainder of the century. He was also one of the few large ranchers in the region to recognize and act against the problems of overgrazing that soon plagued the industry. In 1903, well after the boom of the 1880s was over and most of southern Arizona had been grazed to destruction, he was still able to sell the San Rafael for $1,500,000 (Hadley and Sheridan 1995:97–107; Sheridan 1995:125–126).

Most ranchers in the 1880s, however, kept grazing as many cattle as they could, both on their own acreage and on the abundant acreage still in the public domain. By the start of the 1890s, it was apparent to many ranchers that overgrazing had quickly become a serious problem. To compound the problem, the early 1890s saw several years of severe drought. The grass soon disappeared, having been pulled from the ground by its roots by starving cattle. "It was a disaster of biblical proportions," Sheridan (1995:141) wrote, "one in which nature and greed conspired to magnify their individual effects." From 50 to 75 percent of all of the cattle in southern Arizona died, most surviving animals were shipped out of the region to avoid complete losses, and numerous ranching operations of every size folded (Sheridan 1995:140–141; Wagoner 1952:53–54).

A key to the disaster of the 1890s was the nature of ownership and control over the range lands of southern Arizona. Cattle-raising operations were almost always based on private land holdings, but use of the large surrounding tracts of public lands for grazing was unavoidable, both from the standpoint of the acreage required to support a herd of profitable size and because the federal government could never practically prevent cattlemen from using the land. Since the 1890s, cattlemen and the federal agencies responsible for public lands have struggled, sometimes in cooperation, sometimes in conflict, to adapt the raising of cattle to the limitations of the southern Arizona environment and to address the dilemma posed by an industry that both requires access to large areas of public land to be profitable and constitutes a threat to the health of those public lands when multiple individuals use it for the same purpose. Mayro (1999:47–55) has reviewed the history of federal policies regarding the access to federal lands allowed to private ranchers. These policies have included grazing districts, leases, and fees administered by federal agencies such as the Forest Service and the Bureau of Land Management (see also Collins 2001). Although ranching in southern Arizona during the twentieth century saw periods of relative success and decline, it has survived into the twenty-first century as a viable industry in large part because of the conservation of public lands made possible by the combination of federal management and the responsible practices of many private ranchers.

As in the case of farming, there is little direct evidence of ranching in the Paseo de las Iglesias study area, but it is likely that many people who lived or owned land in the area did raise cattle. Large herds probably never grazed in such close vicinity to Tucson, but at least one major cattle operation did have a presence in the area. In 1912, Levi Manning, a former mayor of Tucson and one of its wealthiest entrepreneurs, purchased the San Ignacio de la Canoa Ranch, the 17,000-acre Mexican land grant situated on both banks of the Santa Cruz River, with headquarters about 20 miles south of San Xavier. By 1924, the Canoa was a flourishing enterprise, and Manning had established a breeding operation for Hereford bulls (known as Scotch Farms) just outside Tucson. Scotch Farms was "a five hundred acre tract of rich agricultural land on both sides of the Santa Cruz River, between Tucson and the famous San Xavier Mission" (MacTavish 1924:n.p.). We have been unable to determine the precise location of Scotch Farms, but it undoubtedly fell within the Paseo de las Iglesias study area, at least partially within the recent Midvale Park development north of Valencia Road. According to promotional literature published by Manning, in 1924 Scotch Farms was home to a herd of about 160 registered Herefords and had a substantial physical plant:

> The appointments at Scotch Farms are of the most modern type. There are two units, one of three hundred and forty acres, the other of one hundred and sixty acres, on different sides of the river, each with its corrals, breeding pens, silos and barns. The silos, in fours and sixes, are concrete cylinders without gates, sunk two-thirds of their forty-foot length into the ground. They are both filled and unloaded by huge buckets operated by cranes and cables run by electricity [MacTavish 1924:n.p.].

The silos held a mixture of grains that served as forage in the winter and early spring. The rest of the year, the cattle were fed alfalfa, grain, hay, and Sudan grass. All of these crops were grown at Scotch Farms: "The farmed land, irrigated by a stream from the Santa Cruz River, raises all the feed that is needed by the animals" (MacTavish 1924:n.p.).

During the early years of the twentieth century, Manning bought and sold land a number of times in the Paseo de las Iglesias study area, either on his own or in conjunction with other investors, as part of his involvement in a variety of irrigation projects (see below). His ownership of the Scotch Farms parcels probably reflects this activity, but we have not made any connection between a particular land deal and the land occupied by Scotch Farms.

Land Tenure

Hispanic encroachment on Native American lands was a constant of the Spanish Colonial and Mexican periods in the Santa Cruz Valley, just as Anglo-American designs on Native American lands were a constant of the U.S. period. The source of the conflict in all three periods lay in the fundamentally different conceptions of the human relationship to the landscape held by Europeans and Native Americans. For both Hispanics and Anglo-Americans, that relationship was defined by the principle of private property, the exclusive right of an individual to occupy and use land for his personal benefit and to dispose of that land as he saw fit. This relationship was guaranteed, at least in theory, by the highest sovereign authority, either the crown or the federal government. For the Native Americans of the Santa Cruz Valley, in contrast, the relationship of people to land had no formal definition, did not involve individual rights, and centered instead on the traditional association of a group of people with a loosely defined territory. In this section, we briefly consider how Hispanic, and then Anglo-American, concepts of land tenure came to be applied in a region where people had lived for millennia without a formal system of private property.

Spanish and Mexican Land Grants

The legal authority under which initial Spanish settlement along the Santa Cruz River took place is poorly understood. Spanish concepts of land tenure were, of course, meaningless to the Sobaipuri living in the area, but Spanish law, at least in theory, required that occupation of any part of the Spanish empire (or of any region not yet claimed by the empire) by a Spanish subject first be authorized by the crown (Radding 1997:175–182). The settlement of Spaniards along the Santa Cruz should have been preceded by some form of legal sanction, but in the first half of the eighteenth century and in this most remote portion of the empire, such was rarely the case. Even the Jesuit establishment of missions and the assumption of jurisdiction over surrounding areas was authorized only in the vaguest terms. When Spanish "civilians" began arriving in the area, they generally settled on mission lands, usually near the mission proper but occasionally well removed from it, with the informal permission of the mission priest. Elsewhere in the northern territories, Jesuits and civilians were already at odds over rights to lands and settlement, but in the Santa Cruz Valley, as Kessell (1970:99) put it, "Common defense and isolation drew Padre and settlers together."

Gradually, the Spanish occupation of lands near the missions and in outlying areas was regularized, often with legal sanctions adapted to local circumstances or official rewards for the continued efforts of Spaniards to colonize the region. For example, when the presidio at Tubac was reestablished in 1787, the new commander hoped to encourage Spanish settlement at the presidio by invoking a provision of the Royal Regulations of 1772, "whereby those who wished to engage in agriculture could receive title to presidio lands in return for keeping arms and horses available for defense of the country" (Officer 1987: 66). Such grants were made within the bounds of the four square leagues designated for each presidio (Jones 1979:194; Mattison 1946:281–282). Along the Santa Cruz River, these grants frequently conflicted with earlier assignments of mission lands to Native Americans. Under Spanish law, Native American communities also were legal holders of land, although Native American lands were considered to be held in common by a group and the right to ownership was based on historical association with a given parcel. Although Native Americans could and did resort to the colonial legal system to protect their Spanish-given rights, they were invariably at a disadvantage when tangling with private Spanish interests (Radding 1997:171–207). The remoteness of southern Arizona, which generally limited the Native Americans' recourse to either the mission priest or the presidio commander, only exacerbated that disadvantage.

The largest of the land grants to Hispanic settlers, and the ones that became significant as the bases of major Anglo-American cattle-raising operations in the late nineteenth and early twentieth centuries, were distributed at the start of the Mexican period, as mentioned earlier in this chapter. The grants were made, much like the grants of the Spanish Colonial era, to encourage permanent settlement in an area that the central government knew was only a tenuous part of its territory. Almost all of the petitions for large grants were submitted in the 1820s; by the 1830s, most of southern Arizona that was outside of the immediate area of the presidios was too plagued by Apache raids to allow for further settlement. The grants petitioned for were often vast (see Figure 7). San Ignacio de la Canoa, the earliest grant (approved in 1821), was typical in size, covering four *sitios* (four square leagues, or about 17,000 acres) along a prime segment of the Santa Cruz River, from the presidio at Tubac to modern Sahuarita (about 15 miles south of San Xavier). Other grants were as small as 5,100 acres, the final confirmed size of San José de Sonoita, which extended along Sonoita Creek, a tributary of the upper Santa Cruz, just west of modern Patagonia. The largest confirmed grant of the era falling wholly within Arizona was San Ignacio del Babocómari, which extended over some 35,000 acres along Babocomari Creek, a tributary of the San Pedro River (Mattison 1946; Officer 1987:106–110; Sheridan 1995:127–129; Wagoner 1975:159–241).

Another major land grant in the Santa Cruz Valley deserves particular mention, because of its unique origin and late confirmation date. This was the Luis María Baca Float No. 3, one of five vast parcels granted to the Baca family as compensation for an enormous grant they had won but were forced to abandon in New Mexico. The original grant was made in 1821 by the Spanish crown, but the Baca family did not win a settlement of the grant until 1860, after New Mexico had become part of the United States. The U.S. government, obliged to honor Spanish and Mexican land grants by the conditions of the treaty signed with Mexico at the end of the Mexican War, compensated the Baca family by allowing them to chose five 100,000-acre "floats" on any nonmineral lands within New Mexico Territory, which at the time included what is now Arizona. Luis María Baca Float No. 3 was first laid out in 1863 directly over the richest portion of the Santa Cruz River valley but was soon moved north and east to center on the Santa Rita Mountains. The validity and location of the grant were the focus of extended litigation that continued until 1908, when the original location was finally confirmed in federal court. Since the 1920s, the lands of the original grant have been subdivided and sold numerous times (Wagoner 1975:200–208).

José María Martínez Land Grant

Although none of the major land grants fell within or immediately adjacent to the Paseo de las Iglesias study area, the Spanish and Mexican policy of granting smaller parcels of land to individuals willing to settle near the presidios did eventually have a direct effect on the area. In 1838, José María Martínez, originally a soldier at the Tubac presidio, filed a petition for a parcel of land near Tubac along both sides of the Santa Cruz River. The petition was granted, under the usual condition that Martínez be ready to provide military assistance to the presidio as needed. In 1848, an Apache attack caused the abandonment of the settlements at Tubac and Tumacácori, and the former residents moved downstream to live within the protection of the Tucson presidio. Martínez and others took up residence in the O'odham village at San Xavier. In 1851, a new Mexican law provided that each of the former residents of Tubac should be given a parcel of vacant land to cultivate at Tucson or San Xavier. Martínez petitioned under the new law for a parcel adjacent to the mission. After the justice of the Tucson presidio consulted with the resident O'odham, he was granted the parcel, along with grazing rights on a portion of the mission lands (Mattison 1946:283–284).

Martínez was awarded his grant just a few years before the Gadsden Purchase. Under the provisions of Gadsden, the United States agreed to honor any land grants made by the Mexican government, which was the basis for the protracted court cases involving the large grants already discussed. The provision also meant that Martínez (who would die in 1868) and his heirs could retain possession of their land at San Xavier, even after the establishment of the original Papago Indian Reservation in 1874, which wholly encompassed their land. However, in 1884, two years after Mexican squatters were expelled from the reservation by the federal government (see Chapter 3), the Indian agent for the reservation decided to evict Martínez's daughter, María, and her husband, J. M. Berger, a German jeweler from Tucson. The Bergers were evicted, but they sued for and eventually won their original rights to the property and returned to the reservation in 1887. They received official title to about 70 acres of land (Figure 9), 30 of which were later sold to the government to be included as part of the reservation. The remaining 40 acres remained in the family. Shortly after returning to the reservation, J. M. Berger became its farmer-in-charge and, later, its Indian agent, a capacity in which he served until 1910 (Arizona Historical Society [AHS] n.d.a; Erickson 1994:87–88). Martínez's connection to the reservation survives in the name Rancho de Martínez, which still applies to the parcel of land that his daughter won back, and in the name Martínez Hill, which still applies to the large hill on the east bank of the Santa Cruz, immediately east of the land claim (also known, less commonly, as Sahuarita Butte).

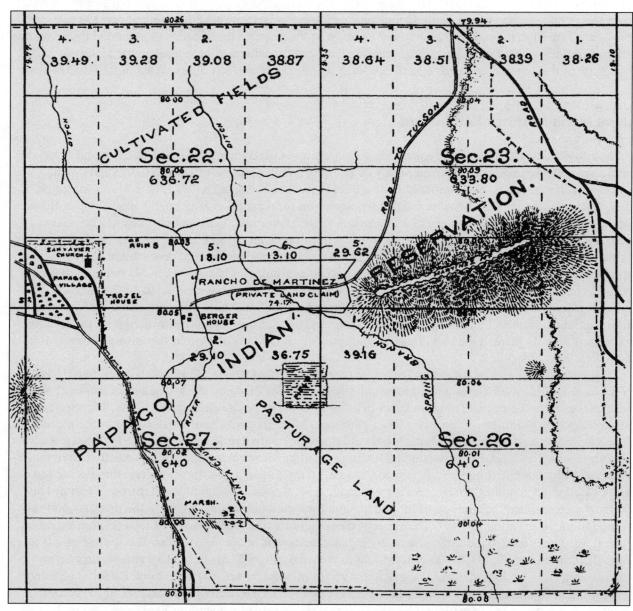

Figure 9. 1891 GLO survey plat of Rancho de Martínez land claim, Township 15 South, Range 13 East, Sections 22, 23, 26, and 27.

78

Land Ownership after the Gadsden Purchase

The Spanish Colonial policy of granting land to settlers, a policy that continued basically unchanged in the Mexican era, had a practical successor in the land-granting policies of the U.S. government, which instituted a more egalitarian (theoretically, at least) and systematic land-distribution program throughout the American West. The main objective of the program was to transform the public lands that had been recently acquired by purchase or treaty into private lands, allowing for the healthy spread of American agriculture and boosting the national economy. An important tool in instituting the program was the rectangular land survey, which divided the West (as it had previously divided the East) into a vast checkerboard of 1-by-1-mile sections. Following the passage of the Homestead Act of 1862, these parcels, further subdivided into four 160-acre quarter sections, were provided at a nominal cost to anyone who would live on the land and farm it for five years (Stein 1990:3–9; White 1991:137–142).

The concept of a 160-acre self-sufficient farm, a concept that had originated in the temperate East, failed in much of the arid West. Alternative acts were eventually passed in an attempt to accommodate the needs of farmers in arid regions. The Desert Land Act of 1876 expanded the amount of land an individual could claim to 640 acres (a full section), provided that the land was brought into irrigation within three years. This act was in some ways as inappropriate for arid lands as the original Homestead Act had been—640 acres into irrigation in three years was a feat few individual farmers could manage. Modifications to the act prolonged its life into the 1880s, but the desired effect of making the small individual farmer the dominant economic force in the West was never realized (White 1991:150–151).

Despite all the difficulties inherent in federal homesteading policies, homestead patents were the origin of much of the private land in Arizona. Statewide, almost 5,000,000 acres passed from federal to private hands through homesteading, and more than 3,000,000 of those acres are still privately held. The rate of failure of homesteads greatly exceeded the rate of success, but successful homesteads are found throughout the state, including in the Santa Cruz Valley (Stein 1990:8–9). In the Paseo de las Iglesias study area, the Homestead Act had a significant impact, but settlement in the area had begun well before its passage in 1862, which meant that much of the land that became U.S. territory following the Gadsden Purchase was already owned by former Mexican citizens. When Mexican troops abandoned the presidio at Tucson in 1856, they took with them any official record of land ownership around the presidio, and for the next six years, although the U.S. presence in Tucson remained limited and intermittent, formal titles to land were nonexistent. As Sonnichsen (1982:66) put it, "possession was the only proof of ownership."

In 1862, the same year, coincidentally, that the Homestead Act was passed, Maj. David Fergusson of the U.S. Army found himself in charge of Tucson while his fellow Union soldiers pressed eastward against the retreating Confederacy. One of his first acts as commander was to require everyone occupying land within 3 miles of town to register his property. A list of landowners was compiled by William S. Oury, an Anglo-American settler designated registrar by Fergusson. Shortly afterward, Fergusson commissioned surveyor J. B. Mills to make a map of Tucson and the fields surrounding it (following convention, we refer to it as the Fergusson map; see Figure 8). The Oury list and the Fergusson map contradict each other in many details (Byars 1966), but it is clear from both that land ownership in the vicinity of the abandoned Mission San Agustín and north along the Santa Cruz was dominated by Hispanic settlers who came to the area before the Gadsden Purchase. In contrast to the neat square and rectangular parcels that would characterize most of southern Arizona once the GLO began dividing up the land in the 1870s, the parcels on the Fergusson map have irregular shapes, conforming to the alignments of irrigation canals that pass through the area. This pattern of settlement continued well into the 1870s, as reflected on the earliest GLO maps of the area (Figure 10).

South of the abandoned Mission San Agustín and beyond the limits of the Fergusson map, the history of ownership prior to the GLO is poorly known. In the 1870s, the GLO began distributing previously unclaimed land in what is now the Paseo de las Iglesias study area through cash sales, Homestead Act and Desert Land Act patents, and the acceptance of scrip. The results of our search of the GLO on-line

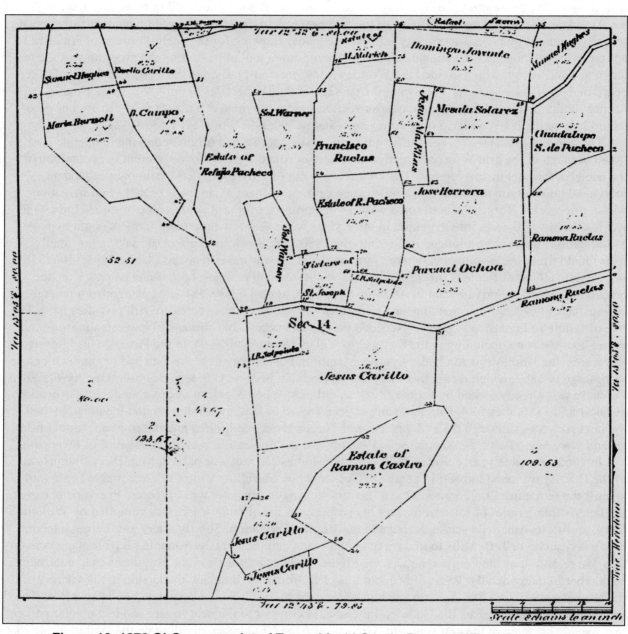

Figure 10. 1876 GLO survey plat of Township 14 South, Range 13 East, Section 14. Abandoned Mission San Agustín was located at the approximate center of the section, on the parcel labeled "J. B. Salpointe."

database (http://www.glorecords.blm.gov/) for early GLO transactions are summarized in Table 1. The distribution of the parcels covered by these transactions is depicted in Figure 11. Table 1 includes only claims by private individuals and not the occasional corporate claim (e.g., by the SPRR) or claims by public entities (e.g., the State of Arizona). It also does not include claims made on any part of the Papago Indian Reservation. Only the earliest claimant for a parcel is indicated; the few claims allowed on previously claimed land are not included. Figure 11 depicts the earliest claim by an individual for an indicated parcel. If a later claim included part of an earlier claim, that part is labeled only with the name of the first claimant.

The 60 transactions in Table 1 cover the years 1874–1938, with a fairly even distribution across that period. Of the 60 transactions, 36 were cash sales, 21 were Homestead Act patents, 1 was a Desert Land Act patent, and 2 were scrip transfers. The earliest transactions, 5 cash sales of 160-acre parcels in 1874, undoubtedly reflect the establishment of the Papago Indian Reservation that same year, which required that all non-O'odham living on the reservation leave and settle elsewhere. As discussed in Chapter 3, most of the people who were required to leave the reservation simply moved outside its newly established boundaries, and most were of Mexican descent. This is consistent with the names of the five claimants from 1874: Jesús María Elías, Guillermo Telles, José Herreras, Gabino Ortega, and Ramón Urías. Of the five, only Jesús María Elías is definitely known to have lived on what became reservation land, having built a house near his brother, Juan Elías, at Punta de Agua, a few miles south of San Xavier (McGuire 1979, 1983). As we note in the appendix, the remains of an adobe building at AZ AA:16:61 may represent a residence built by Elías on his new land after 1874.

Figure 11 depicts a composite of land ownership in the Paseo de las Iglesias study area over a period of 64 years and, thus, is not a meaningful picture of settlement for any particular moment, but the relatively large number of Mexican settlers it shows for the southern half of the study area during the last quarter of the nineteenth century can also be seen in two early maps. The first is an 1874 map of the Papago Indian Reservation, which shows that the area east of the reservation panhandle is settled almost exclusively by Mexicans. (Sketches of portions of this map were included by McGuire [1983:Figure 5] and by Cohen-Williams and Williams [1982], but we have been unable to examine the original, which is currently missing from the ASM archive.) The second is the 1893 Roskruge map of Pima County, which also shows heavy Mexican ownership in the same area (Figure 12 and Table 2), although many of the early claims had changed hands by 1893.

Tables 1 and 2 include many names that are prominent in the history of nineteenth-century Tucson: Aldrich, Allison, Berger, Buckalew, Elías, Goldschmidt, Hughes, Maish, Oury, Pacheco, and Warner, among others. The names reflect both the proximity of the Paseo de las Iglesias study area to the core of settlement in Tucson and the desirability of its land, which benefited, most notably, from the water in the Santa Cruz River.

Transportation

The Santa Cruz Valley, in addition to being a focus of human settlement in southern Arizona for many millennia, has long served as a transportation corridor through the region, providing a relatively hospitable route through an otherwise harsh landscape and connecting the region with the people, goods, and ideas of adjacent regions. In this section, we consider how transportation has helped to shape the history of the Paseo de las Iglesias study area and how events in the study area have in turn affected the development of transportation in southern Arizona.

Table 1. GLO Transactions within and adjacent to the Paseo de las Iglesias Study Area

Claimant	Year	Entry Type	Acres	Township	Range	Section	Aliquot
Angulo, Gabriel V.	1879	C	160	15 S	13 E	10	NW $\frac{1}{4}$
Banduraga, Gregorio	1882	C	161.71	15 S	13 E	3	NE $\frac{1}{4}$
Banks, Hiram	1922	C	160	14 S	13 E	21	NE $\frac{1}{4}$ of the SE $\frac{1}{4}$
						22	N $\frac{1}{2}$ of the SW $\frac{1}{4}$, NW $\frac{1}{4}$ of the SE $\frac{1}{4}$
Beck, Leoance C.	1924	H	162.95	15 S	13 E	3	W $\frac{1}{2}$ of the NW $\frac{1}{4}$
						4	N $\frac{1}{2}$ of the NE $\frac{1}{4}$
Bedoya, Elijio	1882	C	160	15 S	13 E	15	SW $\frac{1}{4}$
Brichta, Augustus	1881	C	161.59	15 S	13 E	2	NW $\frac{1}{4}$
Brothers, William G.	1928	H	120	14 S	13 E	33	SE $\frac{1}{4}$ of the SE $\frac{1}{4}$
						34	W $\frac{1}{2}$ of the SW $\frac{1}{4}$
Brunel, Charles	1898	H	160	14 S	13 E	35	SE $\frac{1}{4}$
Burruel, Martin	1886	H	160	15 S	13 E	14	NW $\frac{1}{4}$
Castro, Jesus	1881	C	160	14 S	13 E	35	W $\frac{1}{2}$ of the NE $\frac{1}{4}$, E $\frac{1}{2}$ of the NW $\frac{1}{4}$
Castro, Francisco	1883	C	160	14 S	13 E	26	E $\frac{1}{2}$ of the SE $\frac{1}{4}$
						35	E $\frac{1}{2}$ of the NE $\frac{1}{4}$
Contzen, Lizette S.	1938	H	160	15 S	13 E	4	SW $\frac{1}{4}$
Corbett, J. Knox	1901	C	100	14 S	13 E	15	NE $\frac{1}{4}$ of the NE $\frac{1}{4}$, SW $\frac{1}{4}$ of the NE $\frac{1}{4}$, E $\frac{1}{2}$ of the NW $\frac{1}{4}$ of the NE $\frac{1}{4}$
Crane, Carter O.	1931	H	160	15 S	13 E	9	NW $\frac{1}{4}$
Davidson, Alexander J.	1921	H	160	14 S	13 E	27	S $\frac{1}{2}$ of the NW $\frac{1}{4}$, NE $\frac{1}{4}$ of the SW $\frac{1}{4}$
						28	SE $\frac{1}{4}$ of the NE $\frac{1}{4}$
Davidson, Alexander J.	1927	H	160	14 S	13 E	22	S $\frac{1}{2}$ of the SW $\frac{1}{4}$
						27	N $\frac{1}{2}$ of the NW $\frac{1}{4}$
Drumm, Peter A.	1914	H	160	14 S	13 E	21	SE $\frac{1}{4}$ of the NE $\frac{1}{4}$
						22	SW $\frac{1}{4}$ of the NE $\frac{1}{4}$, S $\frac{1}{2}$ of the NW $\frac{1}{4}$
Elias, Jesus M.	1874	C	160	15 S	13 E	10	SW $\frac{1}{4}$
Elias, Thomas	1882	C	160	15 S	13 E	10	NE $\frac{1}{4}$
Espinoza, Roman	1888	C	80	14 S	13 E	35	E $\frac{1}{2}$ of the SW $\frac{1}{4}$
Flin, Julius	1892	H	161.47	15 S	13 E	2	NE $\frac{1}{4}$
Franco, Jose	1885	C	160	15 S	13 E	14	SW $\frac{1}{4}$
Gallego, Jose	1880	S	160	15 S	13 E	15	NE $\frac{1}{4}$
Gay, Murvin G.	1881	C	160	15 S	13 E	2	SW $\frac{1}{4}$
Godfrey, Charles	1910	H	160	15 S	13 E	11	NE $\frac{1}{4}$
Grant, Forman M.	1919	H	160	15 S	13 E	21	SW $\frac{1}{4}$
Grijalba, Antonio	1881	C	160	15 S	13 E	15	SE $\frac{1}{4}$
Herreras, Jose	1874	C	160	15 S	13 E	15	NW $\frac{1}{4}$
Hoyt, Celia V.	1938	H	80	15 S	13 E	4	SE $\frac{1}{4}$ of the NE $\frac{1}{4}$

Claimant	Year	Entry Type	Acres	Township	Range	Section	Aliquot
Lee, James	1884	C	160	14 S	13 E	23	SW ¼
Lefebose, Antonio	1890	H	160	15 S	13 E	2	SE ¼
Lonergan, Peter J.	1891	C	160	14 S	13 E	25	W ½ of the NW ¼
						26	E ½ of the NE ¼
Maldonado, Dolores	1885	C	160	15 S	13 E	11	SW ¼
Maldonado, Francisco	1884	C	160	15 S	13 E	11	NW ¼
Markham, William B.	1884	H	160	14 S	13 E	26	W ½ of the NW ¼
						27	E ½ of the NE ¼
McAnear, Alonzo Alpha	1935	H	241.17	14 S	13 E	33	SW ¼
				15 S	13 E	4	SW ¼ of the NW ¼, NW ¼ of the NW ¼
Merz, Henry	1918	H	160	15 S	13 E	14	NE ¼
Mundelius, Conrad	1885	C	160	14 S	13 E	22	S ½ of the SE ¼, SE ¼ of the NE ¼, NE ¼ of the SE ¼
Ortega, Gabino	1874	C	160	15 S	13 E	10	SE ¼
Ortiz, Felix	1901	H	160	15 S	13 E	11	SE ¼
Oury, William S.	1877	C	160	14 S	13 E	26	W ½ of the NE ¼, E ½ of the NW ¼
Pacheco, Guadalupe S.	1876	C	160	14 S	13 E	26	W ½ of the SW ¼
						27	E ½ of the SE ¼
Pacheco, Guadalupe S.	1895	H	160	14 S	13 E	27	W ½ of the E ½
Pacheco, Ramon	1882	C	160	15 S	13 E	3	SW ¼
Ramirez, Concepcion	1877	C	160	14 S	13 E	34	NE ¼
Ramirez, Marcial E.	1882	C	160.9	14 S	13 E	34	E ½ of the SW ¼
				15 S		3	E ½ of the NW ¼
Reason, Walter A.	1934	H	160	15 S	13 E	9	SW ¼
Rodgers, Mark A.	1901	C	40	14 S	13 E	15	SE ¼ of the NE ¼
Rodriguez, Francisco	1875	C	80	14 S	13 E	35	W ½ of the SW ¼
Sampson, Edward	1877	S	160	14 S	13 E	23	NE ¼
Shacklett, Thomas R.	1914	H	160	14 S	13 E	34	NW ¼
Telles, Guillermo	1874	C	160	14 S	13 E	26	E ½ of the SW ¼, W ½ of the SE ¼
Tome, Agustin M.	1915	C	160	15 S	13 E	14	SE ¼
Urias, Ramon	1874	C	160	14 S	13 E	34	SE ¼
Urias, Antonio	1877	C	80	14 S	13 E	35	W ½ of the NW ¼
Walters, Daniel	1883	C	160	15 S	13 E	3	SE ¼
Warner, Solomon	1876	C	160	14 S	13 E	23	NW ¼
West, Simon	1911	C	80	14 S	13 E	22	N ½ of the NE ¼
Wharton, Ford J.	1919	D	160	15 S	13 E	21	NW ¼
Wood, John S.	1882	C	160	14 S	13 E	23	SE ¼

Note: With the exception of a few obvious errors (e.g., "Ourz" for Oury, "Gelles" for Telles), the spellings of claimant names provided by the on-line GLO database are not corrected here.

Key: C = cash sale; D = Desert Land Act patent; H = Homestead Act patent; S = scrip transfer

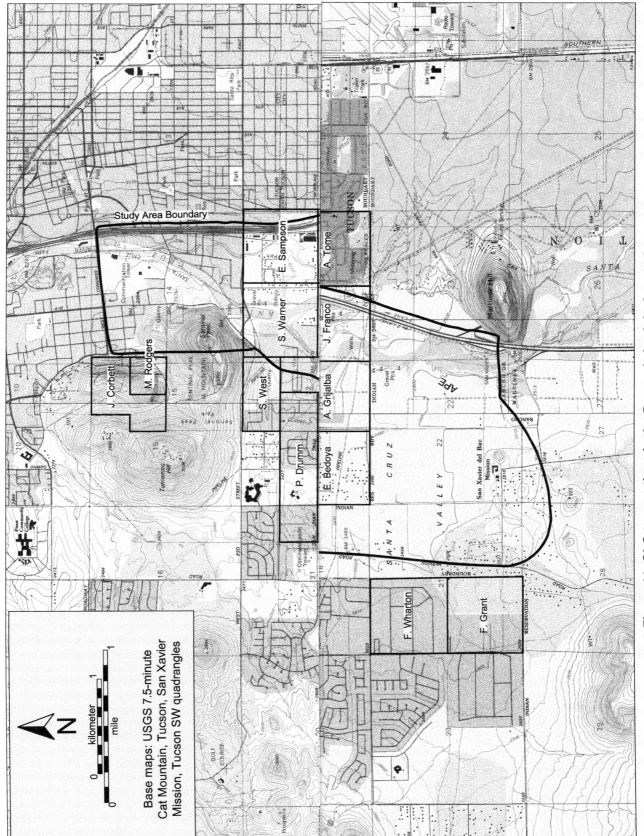

Figure 11. GLO transactions in the Paseo de las Iglesias study area.

84

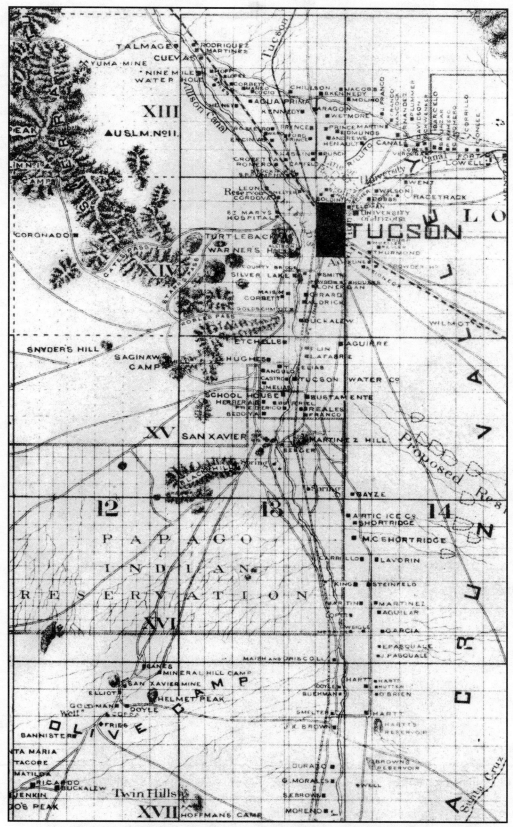

Figure 12. Portion of 1893 map of Pima County (Roskruge 1893).

Table 2. Individual Landholders in the Paseo de las Iglesias Study Area, 1893 (based on Roskruge 1893)

Name	Township	Range	Section	Aliquot	Notes	GLO
Aguirre	15 S	13 E	1	NE $\frac{1}{4}$		
Aldrich	14 S	13 E	26	SE $\frac{1}{4}$		
Allison	14 S	13 E	14	SW $\frac{1}{4}$		
Angulo	15 S	13 E	10	NW $\frac{1}{4}$		yes
Bedoya	15 S	13 E	15	SW $\frac{1}{4}$		yes
Berger	15 S	13 E	22	SE $\frac{1}{4}$	on section line	
			27	NW $\frac{1}{4}$		
Buckalew	14 S	13 E	35	N $\frac{1}{2}$	on east-west midline	
Burrel	15 S	13 E	15	C	center of section; probably same as GLO claimant Burruel	yes
Bustamente	15 S	13 E	14	NE $\frac{1}{4}$		
Castro	15 S	13 E	10	E $\frac{1}{2}$	on north-south midline	
Corbett	14 S	13 E	27	E $\frac{1}{2}$	on north-south midline	
Elias, J. M.	15 S	13 E	10	SW $\frac{1}{4}$		yes
Elias, T.	15 S	13 E	10	NE $\frac{1}{4}$		
Etchells	15 S	13 E	3	NE $\frac{1}{4}$		
Flin	15 S	13 E	2	NE $\frac{1}{4}$		yes
Franco	15 S	13 E	14	SE $\frac{1}{4}$	probably same as GLO claimant of same name in SW $\frac{1}{4}$ of same section	yes
Frederico	15 S	13 E	15	SE $\frac{1}{4}$		
Girard	14 S	13 E	26	NE $\frac{1}{4}$		
Goldschmidt	14 S	13 E	26	SW $\frac{1}{4}$		
Herreras	15 S	13 E	15	NW $\frac{1}{4}$		yes
Hughes	15 S	13 E	3	SW $\frac{1}{4}$		
Lafabrie	15 S	13 E	2	SE $\frac{1}{4}$	possibly same as GLO claimant Lefebose	yes
Lonergan	14 S	13 E	26	NE $\frac{1}{4}$		yes
Maish	14 S	13 E	27	NE $\frac{1}{4}$		
Smith	14 S	13 E	24	SW $\frac{1}{4}$		

Note: The 1893 map is sometimes hard to interpret because of the crowding of details. The locational information provided here constitutes our best reading of the map. All spellings on the map are preserved here. A "yes" in the GLO column indicates a probable correspondence with a GLO transaction (see text).

Early Spanish Routes

The precise routes of the Spanish explorers who traversed southern Arizona in the sixteenth and seventeenth centuries are largely unknown, but they likely followed existing Native American trails. Although chroniclers of the early expeditions rarely bother to mention the Native Americans who accompanied the Spanish, it is unlikely that any *entrada* ever set out without at least one Native American guide, and major expeditions like that of Coronado included many. The Native Americans who accompanied an expedition might not have been directly familiar with the territory they were entering, but it is safe to assume that they sought advice from their local counterparts as to where trails were and where they led. Spanish explorers might have been daring, but they would not have chosen to blaze a new trail rather than use an existing one. And Native American trails were followed by travelers long after the early *entradas* had come and gone. As Stein (1994:3) put it, "In Arizona, historic routes almost always have prehistoric roots."

Earlier in this chapter, we noted that Kino's interest in exploring the Pimería Alta was not limited to finding new places where he might extend his missionary enterprise. He also hoped to find a land route to Baja California, which, among other things, would make it easier to move supplies and livestock to the Jesuit missions there. During the period 1687–1711, Kino made numerous trips into almost every part of the Pimería Alta, with repeated trips down the Santa Cruz to its confluence with the Gila, then down the Gila to its confluence with the Colorado. In addition to these natural corridors, Kino also crossed the formidable western desert of the Pimería Alta many times and by several different routes, using ancient trails that would later serve miners, trappers, and the occasional military expedition (Bolton 1948:end map).

Following the establishment of missions and *visitas* along the Santa Cruz, the river valley quickly became the principal Spanish route—often the only Spanish route—of commerce, communication, and settlement in southern Arizona, maintaining the region's ties with Spanish settlements in Sonora and Sinaloa. In this sense, the road along the Santa Cruz was the *camino real*, or "royal road," as any official route between colonial administrative centers was known, although the use of this term for the Santa Cruz road was less consistent than it was for the better-known *caminos reales* of New Mexico and Alta California. Transportation into and through southern Arizona during most of the Spanish Colonial period varied little from this north-south orientation, and the missions of the middle Santa Cruz served both as the northern terminus of the Spanish colony and as the starting point for further exploration. Expeditions heading west to California followed the route established by Kino (down the Santa Cruz to the Gila, then down the Gila to the Colorado). The most famous and consequential of these after Kino's day were the California expeditions of the Tubac presidio commander, Juan Bautista de Anza, in the last quarter of the eighteenth century.

The Anza Trail

By the 1770s, the Spanish had established missions and presidios on the California coast, but their hold on the region was tenuous at best. The small outposts (consisting of roughly 70 people each) relied on supplies brought in from more-established settlements in Mexico. The two principal supply routes—one for ships and one on land—followed the California coast, and both routes were treacherous and unreliable. An overland route through Sonora that avoided the perils of the coast was sorely needed. To complicate matters, Russia was encroaching on the northern Pacific frontier, and French and English vessels were cruising the coast, threatening to take advantage of Spanish vulnerability. In 1772, Juan Bautista de Anza, stationed at the northern limit of the Spanish overland trail, requested permission to extend the route across the western desert to California. That request was soon granted.

Anza's first expedition to California, which departed from Tubac on January 8, 1774, consisted of 21 soldiers, five muleteers, an interpreter, a carpenter, a courier, two Franciscan friars, an Indian guide from Baja California (named Sebastián Tarabal), and two personal assistants. One of the Franciscans was Francisco Garcés, the priest in residence at San Xavier del Bac, who a few years earlier had explored as far west as the San Jacinto Mountains. He would provide valuable geographical knowledge of the region to be crossed. The first day, the party reached and camped at the northern end of the Tumacácori Mountains. From there, the party headed southwest toward the presidio at Altar, in what is now Sonora. Anza had planned to follow the usual route to the Colorado River, heading down the Santa Cruz, then down the Gila, but this plan was abandoned in favor of the route to the southwest. The party spent a month crossing the western desert, following what would later be known as the Camino del Diablo, before reaching the Colorado. Eventually, the party reached Monterey, the principal California presidio, then returned along the same route in April 1774 (Weber 1992:251–252).

It was the first continuous overland journey from northern New Spain to the coast of California Alta. In recognition of his success, Anza was promoted to the rank of lieutenant colonel by the king of Spain. Soon thereafter, he began organizing a second expedition to colonize the San Francisco Bay area. In March 1775, Anza began recruiting colonists in Sinaloa and Sonora. He and his recruits traveled to Tubac in mid-October of the same year and prepared for their journey. On October 23, 1775, the expedition departed.

The second Anza expedition consisted of 245 people (155 of whom were women and children), 340 horses, 165 pack mules, and 302 cattle. Accompanying the expedition was Pedro Font, a Franciscan who kept a detailed diary of the trip. On October 25, the expedition reached San Xavier del Bac, where Garcés was still in residence and where they camped for the night. The next morning, they left the mission and headed north, passing through the *visita* of San Agustín del Tucson. The expedition camped a league to the north of Tucson, where scouts sent ahead by Anza returned to the main party. The scouts reported water between that point and the Gila, much to the relief of Anza. The following day (October 27), the party camped at what they called Puerta del Azotado, near what is now known as the prehistoric archaeological site of Los Morteros. They probably camped near the future site of the Rillito railroad siding, about 12 miles north of San Agustín. This was near the hills that the Sobaipuri called Tututac, in the area where the Santa Cruz River runs closest to the Tucson Mountains (Bolton 1930:29–30).

Anza reached Monterey in March 1776, then proceeded on to San Francisco Bay, arriving in June. Having brought the first colonists and livestock to what is now San Francisco, Anza established a presidio and mission there. Eventually, Anza headed home with Font, 10 soldiers, the commissary, 14 muleteers, and 2 settlers who had decided to return to Sonora. For the most part, they followed the route they had taken on their way out. Anza was rewarded for this second successful trip by being appointed governor of New Mexico in 1777 (Weber 1992:248–258). The Anza Trail was open for only a short time. In 1781, it was abandoned when the Quechan living along the lower Colorado River massacred Spanish settlers sent there to secure the road (Santiago 1998). After just a few years as an entrepôt, southern Arizona resumed its status as the last outpost of New Spain.

Nineteenth-Century Routes

The road to California remained closed for more than 40 years. In 1823, two years after Mexican independence, the new emperor of Mexico, Agustín de Iturbide, ordered that the road be reopened. The task fell to Capt. José Romero, commander of the Tucson presidio, who left Tucson in June 1823, accompanied by Felix Caballero, the priest in charge of the California mission at Santa Catalina. The preceding month, Caballero had traveled from Santa Catalina to Arispe, Sonora, which made him valuable to Romero's purpose. Romero's expedition was a success and reestablished the connection between southern Arizona and the Pacific coast (Bean and Mason 1962; Officer 1987:101–102).

Apart from the reopening of the road to California, the influence of the centralized authority in Mexico City waned quickly in southern Arizona following Mexican independence. This was partly by design—there were far more-urgent demands on its resources—and partly because of a simple inability to exercise its authority at such a distance. An important consequence of the increased independence of the frontier was its de facto opening to foreign trade. As the economic system of the United States grew exponentially in the first half of the nineteenth century and expanded westward, the Mexican citizens residing in frontier settlements from Texas to California increasingly found Anglo-American buyers for their beef, hides, and grain. Mexican laws were passed to discourage such interaction, but there was little chance of enforcement. Ironically, as the economy of central Mexico suffered the aftermath of the extended war for independence, the humble settlements on the northern frontier enjoyed an occasional degree of prosperity (Weber 1982:147–157). Southern Arizona, the most isolated region in terms of access to transportation routes, benefited less than the rest of the frontier, but by the end of the Mexican period, the inhabitants of the region were well acquainted with the advantages of the U.S. economy.

Despite the shift in focus toward the north, Tucson's connections to the south remained intact. Prior to the Mexican-American War, the main road south ran along the west bank of the Santa Cruz River, eventually reaching Arispe in the Mexican state of Sonora. From there, the road continued south, connecting with larger Mexican settlements (Figure 13). This route was important to the economic survival of Tucson, as goods were carried by pack mule from towns in Sonora such as Hermosillo and Guaymas. It was also the way European goods were transported to Tucson from their first landing at distant Veracruz. During the Mexican period, the residents of Tucson were sometimes unable to produce sufficient food for themselves and relied heavily on products from Sonora. This was usually the direct result of Apache raiding (McGuire 1979:83). The route from Tucson to Sonora remained important throughout the pre-railroad years, even following the Gadsden Purchase. The arrival of American troops in southern Arizona in the 1850s made this trade with Sonora even more important, as foodstuffs were in higher demand. Items such as flour, mescal, ground corn, beans, dried fruit, chile, and other products were brought to southern Arizona via the same route. These goods were carried primarily by two-wheeled carts, or *carretas*.

Despite its relative proximity to the long-established Spanish colony in northern New Mexico, no permanent route between Arizona and New Mexico was established until Anglo-Americans established one late in the Mexican period, shortly after the U.S. government declared war on Mexico. In 1846, Col. Stephen Watts Kearney, after assembling his new Army of the West at Fort Leavenworth, Kansas, headed to Santa Fe with a company of 1,700 men. He met with little resistance from the Mexican force resident in Santa Fe and soon started southward again, intent on blazing a wagon trail to the Pacific coast. Kearney and his company turned westward at the head of the Gila River, then followed close along the river through rugged and desolate country all the way to its confluence with the Colorado. From there, Kearney continued west, finally reaching San Diego (Wagoner 1975:260–268).

The Mormon Battalion

Kearney's decision not to travel south of the Gila was made to avoid what he thought to be a significant Mexican force at the Tucson presidio, but the route he chose proved too rugged for wagon travel. The first practical wagon route across southern Arizona was not blazed until several months later, when the Mormon Battalion, assembled in Missouri and led by Capt. Philip St. George Cooke, traveled from Santa Fe to San Diego, crossing Arizona well south of the Gila. The Mormon Battalion was a volunteer company of 500 Latter-Day Saints assembled in the Midwest by church leaders in an effort to demonstrate the patriotism of the church and thus defuse growing anti-Mormon sentiments in the region. The U.S. Army, responding to its recently declared war with Mexico, welcomed what would prove to be a

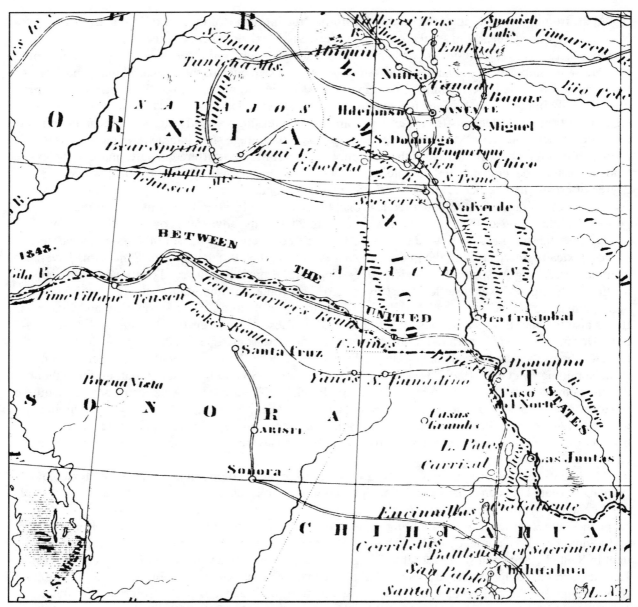

Figure 13. Portion of map of southern Arizona and northern Mexico, 1850 (Hughes 1850). Note road from "Santa Cruz" south into Sonora and Chihuahua.

dedicated and well-disciplined company. Cooke and his Mormon Battalion were ordered to find and build a wagon road to California.

The trek of the Mormon Battalion, combined with the Gadsden Purchase, would forever change the focus of travel through southern Arizona. Instead of following Kearney's route along the Gila River, Cooke and the Mormon Battalion departed from the former route in southwestern New Mexico and headed southwest. The party entered Arizona at Guadalupe Pass in the Peloncillo Mountains and, from there, headed west until they reached the San Pedro River. From the San Pedro, Cooke decided to press overland to Tucson. His guides assured him that any other route would be unnecessarily circuitous.

Other, older routes that the battalion might have taken were rejected in favor of the more direct line, as seen in Order Number 19 issued by Cooke on December 13:

> Thus far on our course to California we have followed the guides furnished by the general [i.e., Kearney]. These guides now point to Tucson, a garrisoned town, as our road and they assert that any other course is a hundred miles out of the way, and over a trackless wilderness of mountains and river hills. We will march then to Tucson. We came not to make war against Sonora, and less still to destroy an unimportant outpost of defense against Indians. But we will take the straight course before us and overcome all resistance. But shall I remind you that the American soldier ever shows justice and kindness to the unarmed and unresisting? The property of individuals you will hold sacred. The people of Sonora are not our enemies.
> By order of Lieutenant-colonel Cooke,
> (Signed) P. C. Merrill, Adjutant [quoted in Bieber 1938:147]

The Mormon Battalion passed through Tucson in December 1846, unopposed by the presidio troops, which had withdrawn to San Xavier to avoid a battle. Cooke and his men could see the mission from Tucson, which prompted Cooke to describe it briefly: "We saw, as we marched over the plains, far to the left, a very large stone church built by Jesuits; it is at a large Indian pueblo about ten miles above [i.e., upstream from Tucson]" (quoted in Bieber 1938:153). (The church was actually built during the Franciscan tenure at San Xavier.) Tucson was largely abandoned, and Cooke thought it similar to Santa Fe:

> Approached from the same direction, the southwest, like Santa Fe, Tucson is not seen until very close by. Of course, its adobe houses are the same in appearance, but inferior. There is a wall with abutments and battlements in bad repair, which surrounds the barracks; it is on the highest ground. The town is not on the bottom. It is a more populous village than I had supposed, containing about five hundred [quoted in Bieber 1938: 157–158].

From Tucson, the battalion traveled down the Santa Cruz River until it rejoined Kearney's route along the Gila. Overall, the route taken by the battalion showed that wagons could be brought into and through southern Arizona from the east, an important discovery for the years ahead. Beginning in 1848, the year the Mexican-American War ended and most of Arizona became part of the United States, the principal route of entry into the region changed from the south to the east. From then on, transportation into Tucson would no longer focus on the Santa Cruz River but would follow the general route taken by the Mormon Battalion, which became known as Cooke's Wagon Road. Several alternate routes emerged along this general route, but the new focus of travel was firmly established. The Southern Emigrant Trail, the Butterfield Overland Mail, and the SPRR would all follow the general route blazed by the Mormon Battalion (Wagoner 1975:268–272).

The Southern Emigrant Trail

The Southern Emigrant Trail was the most important alternative to Cooke's original wagon route. Following the end of the Mexican-American War, an American cavalry battalion under the command of Maj. Lawrence Pike Graham was sent west from Chihuahua, Mexico, to California. Graham entered what is now Arizona near San Bernardino Springs (in the southeast corner of the state) and headed west to the San Pedro River. He and his men then continued west and southwest until they reached the upper Santa Cruz River. They followed the river downstream to Tucson and, from there, to the Gila River.

Graham's route, eventually known as the Southern Emigrant Trail, was used by many people headed to California during the gold rush of the late 1840s.

The discovery of gold in the foothills of the Sierra Nevada in California in 1848 brought a rush of settlers from all over the world, a large number of whom passed through southern Arizona along the routes blazed by Kearney, Cooke, and Graham. The Southern Emigrant Trail alone saw more than 15,000 travelers between 1849 and 1850 (Etter 1995). Many of these travelers were drawn to the southern route by a journal of the Graham expedition written by Cave Couts. Newspaper accounts of the trail, which occasionally included maps, were based largely on Couts's report and were used by many of the emigrants heading west. Unfortunately, many of the maps were inaccurate, which often made the journey hazardous or even lethal.

A substantial portion of the Southern Emigrant Trail passed through Mexico on its way to Arizona. One emigrant, John E. Durivage, upon reaching Graham's trail in Mexico, commented on its appearance: "Major Graham's trail was visible everywhere, and chips, broken wagons, and harness showed that they had suffered some" (quoted in Bieber 1937:206). Durivage and his party eventually reached the Santa Cruz River in Sonora, following it north into what is now Arizona. They passed Tumacácori on May 27 and reached San Xavier del Bac on the following day. Durivage described his experience there:

> This morning, after traveling till nearly noon, Doctor Brent and myself pushed on ahead
> for the old Spanish mission of San Xavier, now inhabited by the Pima Indians and a few
> Apache touters. It is about thirty miles from our last night's camp. There stands the old
> cathedral, a splendid edifice erected at an enormous cost, in a very fair state of preserva-
> tion externally and internally. Its walls inside are covered with many splendid paintings
> by old Spanish masters. The solemn mass is no longer heard within its walls, and a smell
> of mold has displaced the fragrant fumes from the burning censer. No priest now treads
> its paved floors, and rarely the footfall of man awakes an echo there. As a contrast to the
> solemn grandeur of the cathedral and its buildings are the hovels of the present inhabi-
> tants—mud hovels, scarcely big enough for a sow and her litter, and little better than a
> sty or a dog kennel. The Indians here are mostly a bright and intelligent people. The
> lands in the vicinity are rich and fertile in the extreme, and well timbered with mesquite.
> A few cattle, horses, and mules are raised by the aborigines, and just corn enough for
> their own consumption [quoted in Bieber 1937:210].

From San Xavier, Durivage continued north to Tucson, which he also described, including a note on the abandoned Mission San Agustín:

> [Tucson] is eight miles from San Xavier and a miserable old place garrisoned by about
> one hundred men. Flour and a small quantity of corn were all that could be procured.
> The Santa Cruz river flows within half a mile of the town and then takes a southerly
> bend. Near the town are the remains of an old mission, the gardens of which are well
> stocked with fruit [quoted in Bieber 1937:211].

In 1854, several years after the start of the gold rush, an enterprising Texan by the name of Michael Erskine drove a head of more than 800 cattle along the Southern Emigrant Trail to California. Erskine was attempting to take advantage of the high demand for beef in California caused by the gold rush. He followed the Santa Cruz to the Gila River, which he then followed to its mouth at the Colorado, eventually continuing on to Los Angeles and arriving in July 1859 (Erskine 1859).

Government Surveys

Once the Mexican-American War had ended, the U.S. government was curious to know exactly what kind of land it had just acquired. Government surveyors were sent out to explore the Southwest. One of the first surveys was carried out in 1851 by John Bartlett, who was ordered to survey the new boundary between Mexico and the United States. Bartlett followed the Southern Emigrant Trail up the Santa Cruz River to San Xavier del Bac and Tucson. He reached San Xavier on July 19, 1852, noting that the mission was

> truly a miserable place, consisting of from eighty to one hundred huts, or wigwams, made of mud or straw, the sole occupants of which are Pimo [*sic*] Indians, though generally called Papagos. In the midst of these hovels stands the largest and most beautiful church in the State of Sonora. It is built of brick on the summit of a low hill, and has two towers and a dome. In square, around and directly connected with the church, are some adobe houses, which were occupied when the Mission was in a flourishing state. All save one are now tenantless, and this, which adjoins the church, is occupied by the only Mexican family in the place [quoted in Bieber 1937:210].

The "only Mexican family" was probably that of José María Martínez (see the section above on land grants). From San Xavier, Bartlett traveled to Tucson and was similarly disappointed in its condition: "The houses of Tucson are all of adobe, and the majority are in a state of ruin. No attention seems to be given to repair; but as soon as a dwelling becomes uninhabitable, it is deserted, the miserable tenants creeping into some other hovel where they may eke out their existence" (quoted in Bieber 1937:211).

To solidify its hold on its newly acquired territory, the U.S. government attempted to ease travel to the Pacific coast. This included appropriating money for the survey, development, and marking of wagon roads across Arizona. Many of these roads emerged during the late 1850s, as interest in a transcontinental railroad grew. In 1854, Andrew B. Gray was hired by the Texas Pacific Railroad to survey for a potential rail line across what was then still Mexican territory, south of the Gila River. Gray entered southern Arizona and headed generally southwest until he reached the Santa Cruz River near what is now the international boundary. From there, he headed up the river until he reached the Gila. The following year, Lt. John G. Parke surveyed from the Gila upstream along the Santa Cruz, which he followed to Tucson. From there, Parke headed east, eventually crossing Apache Pass in the Chiricahua Mountains before intersecting with Cooke's Wagon Road in New Mexico. The following year, Parke surveyed the route again and found a pass between the base of Mount Graham and the Chiricahua Mountains that shortened the route. This route was eventually followed by stage lines, the SPRR, the first automobile highway, and even Interstate 10.

Routes from Tucson south to Sonora also remained important during the 1850s and 1860s. During this period, a great deal of goods came to Tucson by way of Guaymas. Goods were brought by sailing ship to Guaymas and then overland to southern Arizona. The cost of carrying goods along this route was actually cheaper than using other routes, such as those from Yuma, Arizona, or New Mexico. The trade via Guaymas finally ended with the completion of the railroad across Arizona in the 1880s.

Stage Lines

By the late 1850s, with a growing population in California, there was an increasing demand for improved communication with points to the east. In June 1857, James Birch was given a contract by the federal government to carry mail from San Antonio, Texas, to San Diego, California. This first mail route was largely carried on mules and became known as the "Jackass Mail," until Birch's death later that year.

The contract was then given to George Giddings and R. E. Doyle, who operated the line for about one year, until October 1858. Meanwhile, John Butterfield had signed another contract for mail service between St. Louis and San Francisco, providing that it got underway by September 1858. The Butterfield Overland Mail, as the line became known, soon began operation and quickly supplanted the earlier lines. The Butterfield operated successfully until the start of the Civil War, carrying mail, as well as passengers, between St. Louis and San Francisco. Unlike Birch's San Antonio–San Diego line, the Butterfield had many more stations, and the stations themselves were greatly improved over their predecessors.

The Butterfield ran east from Tucson, through Apache Pass to Mesilla, New Mexico, following the route surveyed by Parke. It was an improvement over the main Southern Emigrant Trail, which dipped well to the south to follow the Santa Cruz River in Mexico. Parke's route was also used by the SPRR mail line, the National Mail and Transportation Company. This stage line became the primary commercial route to southern Arizona for many years. A few stage lines continued to follow the Santa Cruz River into Tucson from the south, but they were relatively minor operations by this time. The road from Tucson to Guaymas remained important, however, as a connection between the overland stage and Mexican routes (*Weekly Arizonian,* 4 April 1859).

The Butterfield stages, carrying both mail and passengers, were drawn by horses or mules. The route of the Butterfield through southern Arizona contained stations at regular intervals, including those at San Pedro River, Cienega Springs, Tucson, Point of Mountain (at the north end of the Tucson Mountains), and Picacho. Generally, the stations were spaced less than 20 miles apart, as horses or mules had to be replaced at that distance to keep the stage running. The stations themselves were constructed of adobe and generally contained four rooms, including a bar room, stable, and forage room (Figueroa 1938). The Tucson station was located downtown near the intersection of Alameda and Main, just outside the former gate of the presidio. Other stations were added later along the line, and some stations changed locations. Because the stations were always located near sources of water and were often the only trace of occupation in an area, many served as the start of settlements, either as small communities or clusters of ranches. The Point of Mountain station is a good example of the latter. By 1861, the Butterfield line in southern Arizona was an evident success, but that same year, the company shifted the line northward to pass through Salt Lake City, fearing that tensions surrounding the start of the Civil War might cause a disruption of service in Arizona (Conkling and Conkling 1947; Stein 1993:96, 1994:14–17; Wagoner 1975:351–359).

After the Gadsden Purchase, heavy wagons became the principal freight connection between southern Arizona and the East. Almost everything required by the growing settlements of the region had to be brought in from elsewhere, and wagons were the most efficient means of hauling freight. Freighters typically consisted of two or three wagons hitched in tandem to a team of 12–20 mules, carrying up to 18,000 pounds of cargo; some tandems were even bigger. The wagons themselves were often huge, with rear wheels as high as 8 feet (Sherman and Ronstadt 1975; Walker 1973). The large freighting outfits could generally travel 15 miles per day. Freighting was the biggest business in southern Arizona prior to the railroad, and the men who ran freight lines were often the only people with significant capital in the region. As was the case for the cattlemen of the 1860s and 1870s, one of the biggest customers for the freighting business was the U.S. Army (Sheridan 1995:104–105).

Departing in caravans from Texas, Arkansas, Missouri, and other points to the east, most freighters would follow Cooke's route across southern Arizona to the San Pedro River near present-day Bisbee. From there, many would head due west to the Santa Cruz River rather then heading down the San Pedro for a distance, as Cooke had done. The caravans would then turn north down the Santa Cruz and pick up Cooke's trail once again in Tucson (Wagoner 1975:299–300). This use of wagons—specifically, four-wheeled wagons with steel-rimmed wheels—to haul cargo in southern Arizona was largely an Anglo-American innovation. In the Spanish Colonial and Mexican periods, pack animals (horses and mules) carried the bulk of the cargo moving from settlement to settlement, which was comparatively inefficient but did not require much in the way of road maintenance (Dobyns 1981:117; Walker 1973). For 35 years following Cooke's opening of the road to California, wagons dominated the transportation of goods in southern Arizona.

After the Civil War, portions of the Butterfield line in southern Arizona were bought up and re-opened as smaller operations. One of the first such lines was the Tucson, Arizona City, and San Diego Stage Line, which operated from 1869 to 1870. Later, James A. Moore owned that portion of the line from Yuma to Tucson, operating and supplying the stations in between. This line was known in 1877 as the SPRR mail stage line but soon thereafter was called the Kerens and Griffen line.

A related development in the same period was the emergence of privately built toll roads. Because the territorial government was largely unable to fund the construction of new roads, private toll roads were encouraged. Liberal franchises were extended to several toll road companies. The companies were allowed to charge tolls on their roads for up to 10 years, often at extremely high rates. One such firm operating in southern Arizona was the Tucson, Pozo Verde and Libertad Road Company, which built several roads in southeastern Arizona (Janus Associates 1993).

Railroads

Plans to build a railroad across southern Arizona took shape as early as the 1840s, as part of the wider interest of the U.S. government and private business in creating a transcontinental railroad. In the years just prior to the Gadsden Purchase, spurred by the mineral strikes in California and Nevada, the federal government commissioned a series of surveys of the West in search of the most suitable route for a transcontinental line. Surveys along the southernmost of the proposed lines established the feasibility of a railroad across southern Arizona, and the Gadsden Purchase soon made the necessary land available. But the Civil War dampened federal enthusiasm for a transcontinental line that would best service the South. As a result, the first transcontinental line, completed in 1869, passed far to the north of Arizona (Cowdery 1948; Sheridan 1995:112–114).

Southern Pacific Railroad

The first transcontinental railroad became a reality when the Central Pacific and Union Pacific lines met in Utah. The owners of the Central Pacific, which had been constructed eastward from California, wanted to control rail traffic into and out of the Golden State. As it became clear that competing lines into California would eventually be constructed, the owners of the Central Pacific established another company to thwart these attempts. The result was the founding of the SPRR. Construction of the SPRR line began soon thereafter, and by 1876, the new line had connected San Francisco with Los Angeles and a line was being built eastward toward Yuma. The original intent of the line to Yuma was to meet the transcontinental Texas and Pacific Railroad at the California-Arizona border. The SPRR, in fact, did not have authority to build east of the California state line. With their incredible clout and money, however, the SPRR was able to convince the territories of Arizona and New Mexico to permit them to build eastward from Yuma. The SPRR, moving east from San Diego on track laid primarily by Chinese laborers, crossed the Colorado River into Arizona at Yuma in 1877 and in the following year started up the Gila River valley. Reaching the lower Santa Cruz River in early 1879, the railroad turned south toward Tucson, stopping at Casa Grande in May 1879. After a delay of several months, track was laid once again up the Santa Cruz River valley, and on March 20, 1880, the city of Tucson welcomed the railroad with a large celebration (Janus Associates 1989; Myrick 1975:19–55). Tucson soon became the largest rail center in the state.

In the spring of 1880, the SPRR line was pushed eastward from Tucson, and by May, it extended 28 miles to Pantano. From Tucson, the original SPRR line extended southeast, avoiding the Santa Cruz River and generally following the overland stage route. By September of the same year, the line was completed into New Mexico. The transcontinental connection was completed when the SPRR line reached the Texas and Pacific line east of El Paso in December 1881. During the next 40 years, the SPRR became the backbone of a series of branch railroads extending throughout southern Arizona, servicing towns, mining districts, and the Mexican border. Meanwhile, the Santa Fe Railroad had built a line south from Albuquerque, which connected with the SPRR line at Deming, New Mexico, providing another transcontinental link.

The arrival of the railroad in southern Arizona transformed the region, pushing it headlong into what Sheridan (2000:112) has called the "Era of Extraction." The regional economy quickly changed from a locally focused, low-capital, preindustrial system to an outwardly focused, heavily capitalized, fully industrial one. The change was swift and dramatic and, in many ways, devastating to the regional landscape. The railroad economy dominated southern Arizona until World War II, when trains began to decline in importance and the next great transformative modes of transportation, the automobile and the airplane, exerted their influence.

Following the arrival of the railroad, local stage lines actually proliferated for a time, serving a wide variety of routes that connected towns to the rail lines (Stein 1994:22). The arrival of the railroad was less kind to the long-distance freighters in southern Arizona, many of whom were put out of business overnight by the drastically cheaper hauling rates offered by the railroad. But local wagon lines often benefited, connecting mining camps and ranches to the rail lines (Sheridan 1995:104; Walker 1973:202).

Twin Buttes Railroad

Subsequent railroad construction in Arizona was primarily to provide transportation for large mining operations, and the construction of branch lines to service mines continued into the early twentieth century. Beginning in the late nineteenth century, mining began in the Twin Buttes area (Sierrita Mountains) just south of the study area. By the early 1900s, plans were made to complete a railroad from Tucson. The Twin Buttes Railroad Company was formed in 1904 by David Stuart Rose, who recognized the potential of this rich copper area. A year earlier, Rose had established the Twin Buttes Mining and Smelting Company. Survey of the route of the Twin Buttes Railroad began in late 1904. The line intersected with the SPRR line in Tucson at 16th Street, following 1st Avenue south out of town. A depot was built on 21st Street. The line was finally completed in the summer of 1906. It headed almost due south from Tucson along the east side of the Santa Cruz, crossing the river at Sahuarita. The mine, however, closed the following year as a result of lower copper prices. Although the mine reopened the following year, the railroad was having financial difficulties. In 1910, that portion of the line between Sahuarita and Tucson was purchased by the Tucson and Nogales Railroad (a company formed in 1909), a subsidiary of the SPRR. Mining picked up again in the 1910s, and the railroad continued to run. By the early 1920s, however, the railroad ran only infrequently. By 1934, the Twin Buttes Railroad had been discontinued, and the rails were pulled up (Myrick 1975:303–312).

Tucson and Nogales Railroad

Beginning in the early 1900s, Tucson businessmen sought a rail link with Nogales. The SPRR was eventually convinced to extend a line south from Tucson to Nogales in 1909. The next year, the Twin Buttes Railroad was purchased by the newly formed Tucson and Nogales Railroad, also known as the Nogales Branch of the SPRR (see above). As such, a line had to be constructed between Sahuarita and Calabasas (another line existed from there to Nogales). Meanwhile, construction had begun in the summer of 1909. The first train ran along the route in June 1910. The start of the Mexican Revolution that same year limited the importance of this line for the next decade. The line provided a connection to several cities in Mexico as other lines were completed. Copper mining in the area southwest of Tucson kept rail traffic flowing on the northern part of the Nogales Branch over the next several decades (Myrick 1975:313–326). The line continued in operation until 1951, when truck traffic completely supplanted it.

Roads, Highways, and Automobiles

By the end of the 1920s, railroad trackage in southern Arizona began to decline. The ascendancy of the automobile was the primary reason. Cheaper transportation became available by truck, and many rail lines became unfeasible. Mining in the region also declined during this period, leading to a decreased need for mining-focused rail transportation.

Conversely, with larger numbers of settlers, along with a growing number of tourists, a demand for better roads developed in Arizona beginning in the 1910s. As a result, one of the first pieces of road legislation in Arizona was passed in 1912. The so-called State Road Law proposed a statewide road system, including a network of approximately 1,500 miles that would connect all county seats and nearly all principal towns (ADOT 1977:1). Attention was focused on roads leading into and out of the state, as well as on those connecting major communities, such as Tucson and Phoenix.

In 1916, the Federal Aid Road Act was passed. This act appropriated funds for individual states to spend on roads, under the direction of the Bureau of Public Roads (BPR). The money was designed to be used on rural routes, particularly roads over which the U.S. mail was carried. Federal dollars had to be matched by the states or counties to which they were appropriated (Arizona State Engineer 1920:21). The act was designed to create a system of primary highways extending across a given state, and secondary highways extending across the counties (ADOT 1977:13). It was a landmark in federal road legislation, as it provided substantial resources to states to improve their transportation networks. Many states took advantage of the act, constructing many miles of new highway.

Before the Federal Aid Road Act, road conditions in southern Arizona were often poor. Many sections were frequently washed out and impassable in wet weather. The roads between Tucson and San Xavier were notoriously bad. A description of a harrowing trip through the study area appeared in the *Tucson Citizen* in 1914:

> In trying to avoid a four foot chuck hole, the driver steered too close to the side and the two outer wheels went over and the car nearly toppled over, but the inside wheels sank into the mud and held the car. By a lucky chance several Papagoes happened along with wagons loaded with cord wood and they were hired to pull the automobile back on the road. A lot of cord wood was thrown into the hole, and the party continued to Tucson without further incident [*Tucson Citizen* 1959 (1914)].

Mission Road

In the latter half of the nineteenth century, the main route of travel heading south from Tucson to Nogales was along the east side of what is now the main branch of the Santa Cruz River. It was along this route that the Tucson-Nogales Road would eventually run and the Tucson and Nogales Railroad would eventually be built. Late in the nineteenth century, the road was described as beginning at the corner of Congress and Meyer Streets, then running south to a point "a few hundred spaces west of Mr. Brown's Station" (*Arizona Daily Star,* 14 September 1892).

But there was also a well-traveled road on the west side of the river, leading from Tucson south to San Xavier del Bac and points beyond. This road was in existence at least as early as 1871, the year the original GLO survey plats of the area were prepared (Figures 14 and 15), and it probably corresponded to the Spanish Colonial route sometimes called the *Camino Real*. South from San Xavier, the road paralleled the river at least as far as Tubac. Lesser routes later extended west from this road to connect with mining operations in the Sierrita Mountains. The general alignment of this route between Tucson and San Xavier, which eventually became Mission Road (Figure 16), was first proposed in the 1890s as part of the main county road between Tucson and Nogales (*Arizona Daily Star,* 13 August 1892). There were

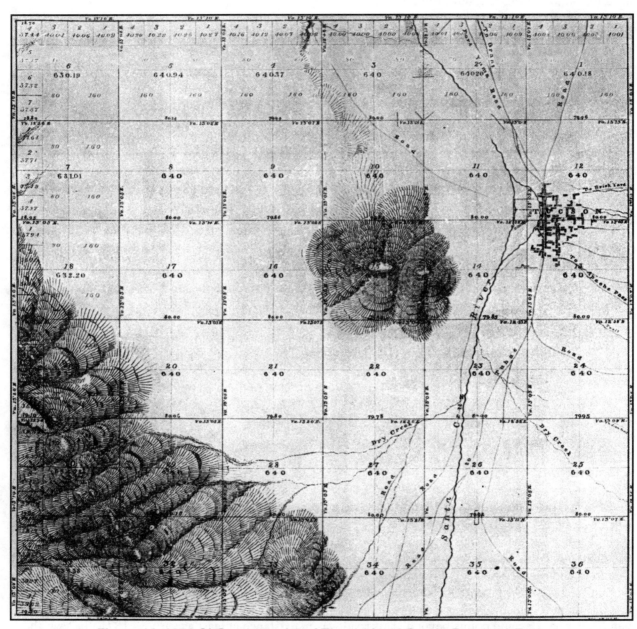

Figure 14. 1871 GLO survey plat of Township 14 South, Range 13 East.

98

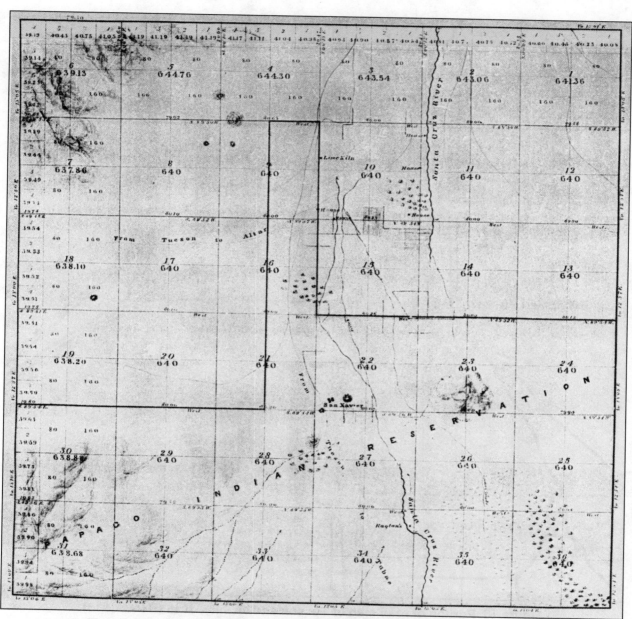

Figure 15. 1871 GLO survey plat of Township 15 South, Range 13 East.

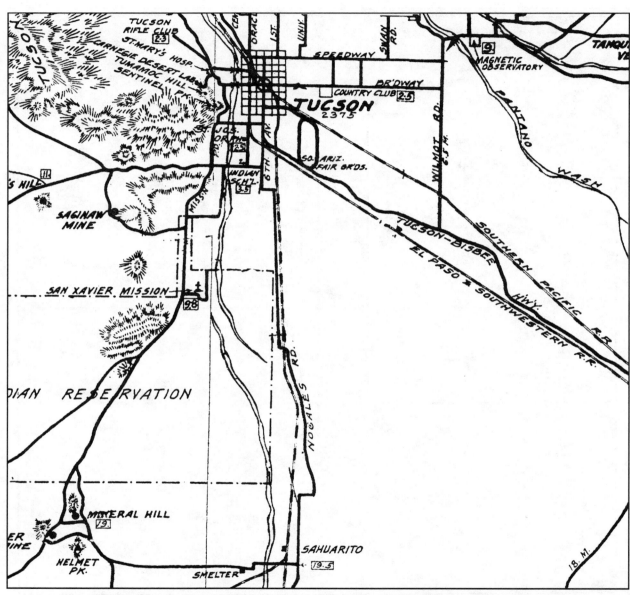

Figure 16. Portion of road map of Tucson and vicinity, 1918 (Goetz 1918).
Note Mission Road.

arguments regarding the relative merits of the east- and west-side roads. One of the most vocal proponents of the west-side road was John B. Allen. Allen and others claimed that the west-side road was a much less circuitous route and required fewer crossings of washes and the river itself. At that time, the stage running south to Nogales followed the east-side road, because the owner of the stage line owned a stock ranch along that route, at least according to Allen. Allen also claimed that far more freight traffic followed the west-side road and would continue to do so after the building of a railroad in the valley (*Arizona Daily Star,* 14 September 1892).

In the 1910s, the two routes were still vying for preeminence. For a time, it appeared that the western route would win out. Civil engineers seemed to favor the route, and some citizens urged its adoption as the primary route. A newspaper article from 1917 spoke out strongly against the alternative: "The east side route has not only been condemned by practical citizens whose knowledge of flood conditions in the section traversed by the east side route survey extends over a quarter of a century, but is condemned by engineers. The east side route is wrong in practice and in theory" (*Arizona Daily Star,* 11 May 1917).

During the 1920s, a fair amount of traffic followed Mission Road, and highway-related services emerged. Several major streets intersected with Mission Road, and businesses tended to be built at these locations. At the southwest corner of the intersection of Mission and Ajo Roads, for example, a gas station, tourist court, and grocery store were opened by Roy Probasco and his family in the early 1920s. The business was sold in 1936, and the property was subdivided. The store was remodeled into the Wagon Wheel Bar, which burned down in the early 1940s. In the early 1950s, the Mission Club was opened on the site of the Wagon Wheel Bar. This establishment became a favorite hangout for locals. Another grocery store, the Hilltop, was later opened on the same corner. On the southeast corner of the same intersection was the Mission Swimming Pool, where Opha Probasco, one of Roy's sons, became a talented diver, eventually winning the Southern Arizona Diving Championship. These businesses were all demolished during widening of Ajo Road during the 1960s (AHS n.d.b). The Mission Swimming Pool is depicted on maps dating as early as 1922 (Figure 17) and as late as 1936 (Figure 18).

Tucson-Nogales Highway

The road along the east side of the river eventually won out over Mission Road and became a part of the state highway system in 1917 and was officially named the Tucson-Nogales Highway. It was one of the few roads in the state to be in relatively modern condition at that time (Arizona State Engineer 1918:71). The road was designated State Highway 10 soon thereafter (by 1920) and was paved sometime in the early 1920s (*Tucson Citizen,* 15 January 1922) (see Figure 17).

Passage of the Federal Aid Road Act in 1916 led to the construction of roads in areas where states could afford the match. Many states, however, lacked concerted highway plans. As a result, the Federal Highway Act was passed in 1921, requiring that each state designate a road system on which federal appropriations could be spent. Because the law specified federal aid for 7 percent of a state's highways, it became known as the "seven percent system." Arizona's road mileage at the time was 21,400, making 1,498 miles eligible for federal aid (Hatcher 1931:7). The routes included in most state highway plans were generally those connecting larger communities, as well as interstate routes.

Included in Arizona's seven percent system was the Tucson-Nogales Highway, labeled Federal Aid Road Number 29. By 1917, the road's surface ranged from graded dirt to macadam. The road largely followed the railroad south of Tucson (Bryan 1922:351). Work on the Tucson-Nogales Highway under the seven percent system was completed by 1922 and included a total expenditure of $128,103 (Arizona State Engineer 1922:43). The highway was later included as part of U.S. Highway 89.

Mission Road continued to be used while the more prominent Tucson-Nogales Highway was being upgraded. The older road continued to run south from the mission to Twin Buttes, then intersected with the highway at Canoa Ranch. In the 1930s, it was a well-traveled road from Tucson to the mission, but

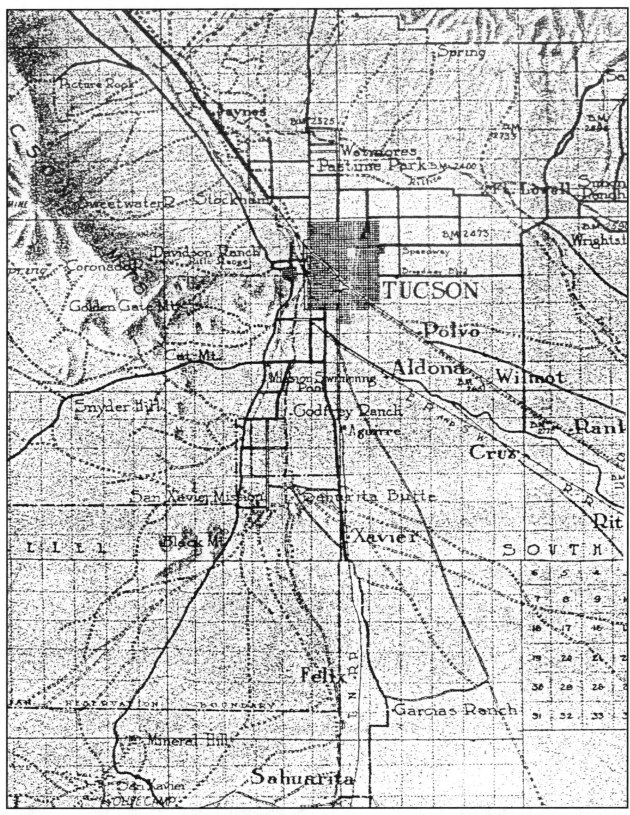

Figure 17. Portion of map of Pima County, 1922 (Pima County 1922).
Note the Tucson-Nogales Railroad and Mission Road to San Xavier.

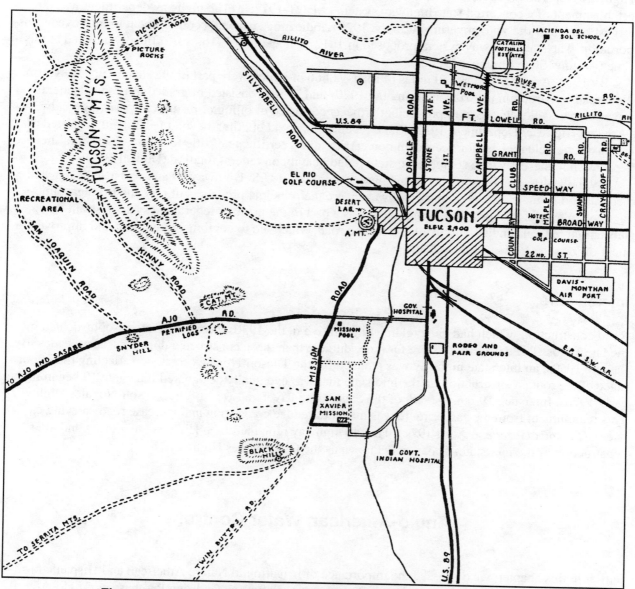

Figure 18. Portion of 1936 map of points of interest around Tucson (Chamber of Commerce 1936).

south of the mission, it was less used and unimproved. All of Mission Road remained unpaved during this period, whereas the Tucson-Nogales Highway was paved from Tucson south to a point near San Xavier (Figure 19).

Arizona's population exploded from roughly 40,000 in the 1880s to 400,000 in 1927. Roadways in the state expanded from 2,000 to 22,000 miles during the same period (ADOT 1977:1). The Arizona Highway Department and the Arizona State Highway Commission were created in 1927, leading to the establishment of a concerted state highway system (ADOT 1977:1). The highway department was the largest branch of the state government in the 1920s, indicating Arizona's commitment to improved transportation. The state highway system proposed in 1912, and again in 1916, was officially adopted at this time (Arizona State Engineer 1924:9).

By 1933, Arizona had 23,270 miles of roads, 2,866 of which were part of the state highway system. New road construction in Arizona during the 1920s and 1930s consisted of graded dirt roads, generally covered in gravel. Most road improvement projects consisted of oiling or resurfacing existing roadways (Arizona Highway Department 1952). State revenues for road building beyond federal aid consisted of gas taxes, vehicle registration fees, common carrier taxes, certificate of title fees, and chauffeurs' license fees. Despite these revenue sources, the state relied heavily on federal funding (Dowell 1933:4).

By the 1940s, the Tucson-Nogales Highway was part of U.S. Highway 89 and was also designated Federal Aid Route 5. These primary highways were the principal producers of revenue from gasoline-tax-paying traffic. The fact that the highway was a part of the primary federal aid system meant that substantial federal funding was available for the road, which led to continual upgrading and improvement of it.

Interstate 19

Road construction, which had been relatively primitive in the 1930s, became far more sophisticated by the late 1940s. The newer roads were far more durable than those constructed during earlier decades. By the late 1950s, an interstate highway was planned for the Tucson-Nogales corridor, reflecting the importance of the route. Construction on the interstate that was eventually designated Interstate 19 began in the early 1970s. Interstate 19 ran just east of the Santa Cruz River and west of the Tucson-Nogales Highway. This realignment from the earlier route was meant to reduce congestion and increase road carrying capacity (*Phoenix Gazette,* 6 April 1971). The old highway remained U.S. Highway 89 during and after construction of the interstate. Today, it is known as the Old Nogales Highway.

Anglo-American Water Control

Earlier in this chapter, we discussed the importance of irrigation to Native American and Hispanic farming in the study area. We also noted the conflicts that arose after the Gadsden Purchase as Anglo-Americans began to settle in Tucson and use the water in the Santa Cruz for their own purposes. Anglo-American settlers brought with them a distinctive view of the natural world shaped by a century or more of life in the East, where water was generally abundant, intensive agriculture was viewed as the best use of land, and lush gardens and landscaping were the requirements of civilized daily life. Soon after the West opened to Anglo-American settlement, earlier images of the region as a forbidding, arid wilderness were supplanted by a belief in its inherent agricultural potential, a belief promoted by railroad companies and land speculators eager to attract settlers to the region. Anglo-Americans came only slowly to Tucson in the first few decades after the Gadsden Purchase, but most of them saw themselves as part of the great

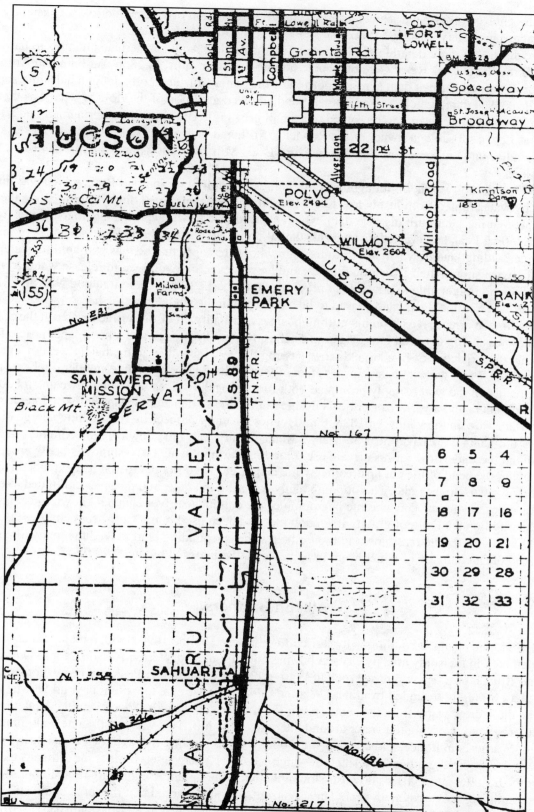

Figure 19. Portion of map of Pima County, 1932 (Pima County 1932).
Note Mission Road to San Xavier.

105

nineteenth-century Anglo-American enterprise, "the transformation of virgin land into a constantly growing agrarian society" (Kuperl 1986:34).

As we discuss in more detail later in this chapter, the earliest Anglo-American attempts to harness the flow of the Santa Cruz River were by people hoping to power mills. In 1856, William and Alfred Rowlett built a small earthen dam across a portion of the Santa Cruz at a point about a half mile south of Sentinel Peak. The dam, which created a small pond, allowed a portion of the flow of what was then essentially a marsh, or *cienega,* to be routed to a small grist mill. The pond was later named Lee's Pond after James Lee, a subsequent owner of the Rowletts' Mill, and then Silver Lake when Lee leased a portion of the adjacent land to be developed as a resort. Lee's Mill ceased to operate as early as 1884, the year he died.

In 1875, Solomon Warner built another mill, at the eastern foot of Sentinel Peak, which was initially powered by water routed from just below Lee's Pond through a stone-lined ditch running along the base of the peak. Warner later built his own dam, which captured the flow of springs in a marshy area just south of Sentinel Peak and created its own substantial pond. He was soon involved in a series of disputes with people holding land downstream from his dam who were angry that he was withholding water that would otherwise supply their irrigation ditches, and he was eventually obliged to release water from his dam. In 1886, no longer able to power his mill on a regular basis, Warner sold it, along with all of his property around Sentinel Peak, and ceased to be a presence in the study area (see below).

By the time Warner gave up on his milling business, virtually all of the surface water in the Santa Cruz Valley was being diverted into irrigation ditches. Kuper (1986:56) cited a newspaper article from 1886 noting the existence of five large ditches passing through the valley immediately west of Tucson, each measuring 7 feet wide and carrying $1\frac{1}{2}$ feet of water (there were also three smaller ditches). The heavy demands on the water supply prompted both further legal disputes between upstream and downstream landholders and a variety of projects designed to increase the supply, especially by intersecting the subsurface flow in the valley. In 1888, Sam Hughes, an early pioneer in Tucson, dug a large ditch in the bed of the Santa Cruz River near St. Mary's Road, about a half mile downstream from the study area, hoping to tap the underflow for his private use. Flooding during the next two summers badly eroded the ditch, moving the head of the cut upstream. By the end of the 1890 flood, erosion had extended Hughes's ditch all the way to Silver Lake. The flooding badly damaged the lake, and the river continued to entrench for miles upstream. This was the beginning of the entrenched river channel known today and the end of the traditional system of gravity irrigation that had been used in the valley for centuries (Betancourt 1990:106–110). The river now ran too far below the surrounding land to feed the many ditches that once served the area, many of which were in any case badly damaged by the 1890 flood.

Allison Brothers

In response to the changed conditions for agriculture imposed by the 1890 flood, a major canal project was undertaken in the study area by Tucson businessmen Frank and Warren Allison. Not long after the flood, the Allison brothers purchased the old Warner property at Sentinel Peak and began construction of a ditch that eventually extended from near Warner's Pond downstream to a point beyond St. Mary's Hospital. The ditch drew water from the same spring-fed marsh on the south side of Sentinel Peak that had fed Warner's Pond, carrying the water around the base of the hill. This was mostly a new alignment, not a reuse of Warner's mill race, and creating the ditch involved blasting through rock at the base of the hill to achieve the required gradient. By 1892, the ditch led to a 10-acre reservoir that the Allisons had dug north of the hospital and to fields downstream on the wide floodplain (Betancourt 1990:121–122). In personal reminiscences written 46 years later, Warren Allison remarked that the ditch could still be seen where it passed around Sentinel Peak, "on the east side of the highway [i.e., Mission Road]" (Allison

1938:14). Presumably, the ditch has since been largely destroyed or obscured by improvements to Mission Road.

The Allisons also built a flume across the Santa Cruz to carry water to fields along its east bank, downstream from Tucson (Betancourt 1990:126; Kuper 1986:70). The canal fed by the flume, completed by 1895, was known as the East Side Canal, with the original canal becoming the West Side Canal. The East Side Canal led to a large area soon to be known as Flowing Wells, several miles north of Tucson, where the Allisons cleared fields, planted crops, and, for a short time, operated a grist mill powered by the water from their canal. These holdings became especially important after the Allisons discovered that the land they were irrigating on the west bank of the river was too alkaline to farm. They sold the Flowing Wells property to Levi Manning and two other investors in 1900 (Allison 1938:14; Betancourt 1990: 126).

The alignments of the two canals and the location of a small dam where both begin are depicted on an oversized map of Tucson from 1900 (Helen 1900). This map, on file at the AHS, is too large and fragile to photocopy, so we simply describe its depiction of the three features. The dam is located just below the confluence of the two branches of the Santa Cruz, in the approximate center of the SE ¼ of the SW ¼ of Section 14 (Township 14 South, Range 13 East). The current confluence of the two branches is about a half mile south of this location; the dam on the map is depicted at approximately the point where the main branch of the Santa Cruz now meets the southeastern corner of Sentinel Peak and turns northeast. The West Side Canal is shown extending from the west side of the dam and immediately skirting the base of Sentinel Peak, along the west side of Mission Road (cf. Warren Allison's note that it was later visible east of the road). The canal continues north along the base of the Tucson Mountains to the northern edge of the map, or just south of present-day Speedway Boulevard. The East Side Canal also extends from the west side of the dam and at first runs adjacent to the west bank of the main branch of the river. It then crosses the river in the approximate center of the NE ¼ of Section 14, just above the point where a wash enters the river's east bank. This would have been the location of the flume that carried the canal across the river, but the map does not depict it. Today, this location falls approximately on the west bank of the main branch of the Santa Cruz about a quarter mile south of Congress Street. On the east side of the river, the East Side Canal soon meets Congress Street (labeled Stevens Avenue on the map), then heads north to the Flowing Wells area, where the map depicts a "water power flour mill" and a "copper smelter." The mill is the one built by the Allisons; we do not know if they owned the smelter. Any remains of either feature must have been destroyed by construction of Interstate 10 through the Flowing Wells area in the 1960s.

Among the Allison family's papers that are preserved at the AHS is an undated, hand-drawn sketch map showing a number of features in the same area (Township 14 South, Range 13 East, Section 14) (Figure 20). The map is not accompanied by an explanation, but we suspect that it records the locations of features present on the old Warner property at the time that the Allisons purchased it (1890). The map shows a small dam, presumably Warner's old dam, in the same location as it is on the 1900 map, and two canals extending from its west side. One canal, presumably Warner's original mill race, skirts Sentinel Peak (labeled "Tucson Mountain"), passing just east of Warner's Mill (labeled "old mill"). As noted above, the Allisons' West Side Canal apparently followed a new alignment, but it could not have differed much from the one depicted here. The other canal, labeled "old ditch" and presumably the forerunner of the Allisons' East Side Canal, runs along the west bank of what is labeled the "West Branch Santa Cruz" (this should instead be labeled the Santa Cruz). This canal ends just south of the point where the East Side Canal is depicted as crossing the Santa Cruz on the 1900 map (the wash that enters the Santa Cruz near the same point on the 1900 map is here mislabeled "Santa Cruz River"). The road crossed by the canal, labeled "old Mission Road," is present-day Mission Lane.

The sketch map likely depicts only those features that the Allisons purchased or that were otherwise relevant to their plans. It does not depict other features that would have been conspicuous at the time, such as the ruins of Mission San Agustín and the many other old ditches that were probably still evident

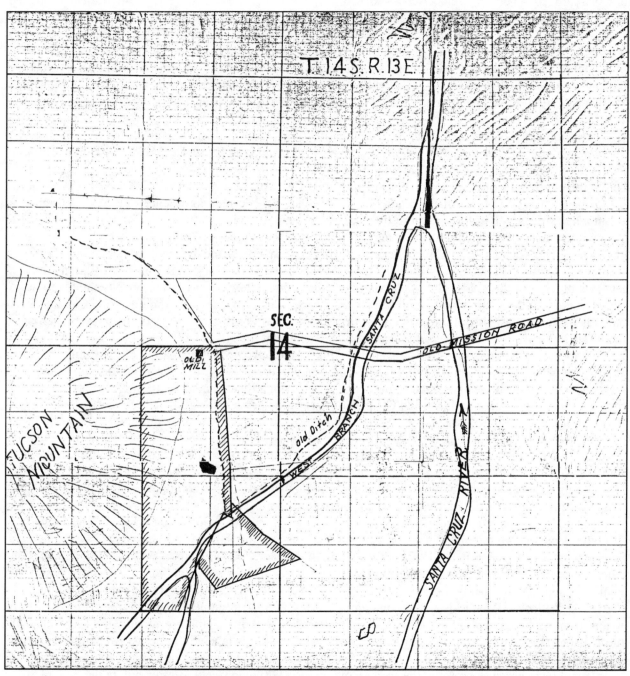

Figure 20. Undated sketch map of features in Township 14 South, Range 13 East, Section 14 (AHS n.d.c).

108

in the area. It is difficult to gauge the relative locations of features depicted here and on the 1862 Fergusson map (see Figure 8)—especially since the alignments of the river channels on the sketch map may reflect changes wrought by the flood of 1890—but the "old ditch," at least the portion north of Mission Lane, seems to be approximately in line with the Acequia Madre Primera as depicted on the Fergusson map. Whichever old ditch it represents, the fact that it served the area north of Mission Lane and was fed by Warner's dam is consistent with accounts of Warner's conflict with the downstream landholders who accused him of diverting water to which they had prior rights (see below).

Also visible on the sketch map is an apparent property boundary, enclosing the dam, the mill race, the old mill, and the land between the race and Sentinel Peak. This presumably corresponds to the parcel of land purchased by the Allisons and represents Warner's former holdings. There is also a solid line extending southwestward from the west side of the dam, apparently to the southern parcel boundary. This line is not a canal alignment, which would be a dotted line like the others on the map. It must represent the dike or levee marking the front of the pond built by Warner, which would make this the only precise depiction that we have seen of the location of that feature. The Allisons also maintained a reservoir on the south side of Sentinel Peak, described by Kuper (1986:70) as being "near the old Warner dam site." We have not found any clear indication of how much the Allisons relied on Warner's earlier reservoir for their own, but the correspondence of the features on the sketch map with the features known to be theirs on the 1900 map suggests that their project was, in many ways, simply an expansion and renovation of features first built by Warner and that Warner's Pond was still at least partially intact when they took over his property.

When the Allison brothers sold their Flowing Wells property to Manning and his partners in 1900, the sale included the dam and reservoir that fed it and the East and West Side Canals (the East Side Canal was redubbed the Manning Ditch). The Allisons had once experimented with increasing the water supply of their reservoir by drilling wells nearby to tap the underground flow. Manning and his partners greatly expanded these efforts and were soon routing more than 1.5 million gallons per day to farmland they held on both sides of the river (Kuper 1986:87–89). The Allisons began another irrigation project, running a ditch from Black Mountain on the Papago Indian Reservation to newly cleared land 14 miles downstream. They eventually sold the land after farming it successfully for several years (Allison 1938: 14). We do not have any information about the precise route of this ditch, which passed through the study area, or about the location of the land it served.

Tucson Farms Company

The arrival of the railroad in southern Arizona in 1880 had a major impact on every kind of business in the region, including the business of extracting water from the Santa Cruz Valley. Kuper (1986:52) summarized the contribution of the railroad to the development of irrigation systems in Tucson: "Pipes, well-drilling apparatus, and pumping machinery could now be delivered to Tucson with speed and ease." The Allisons were among the first to benefit from the technology imported by the railroad, and their successors in the study area, Manning and his associates, made even greater use of recent technological innovations, especially well-drilling equipment.

The entrenchment of the Santa Cruz after 1890, and the increasing availability of motorized drilling and pumping equipment, led during the next few decades to a proliferation of projects designed to intercept the subsurface flow of the Santa Cruz and its tributaries. One of the most ambitious projects along the Santa Cruz, and by far the most ambitious project within the study area, was a project carried out by a group of businessmen organized in 1910 as the Tucson Farms Company. The group included investors from London and the Midwest and a range of specialists in agronomy and engineering. The group began by buying Manning's interests in the area around Sentinel Peak in 1911 and soon bought farms and other land along the Santa Cruz north and south of Tucson. The group's ultimate goal was to control some

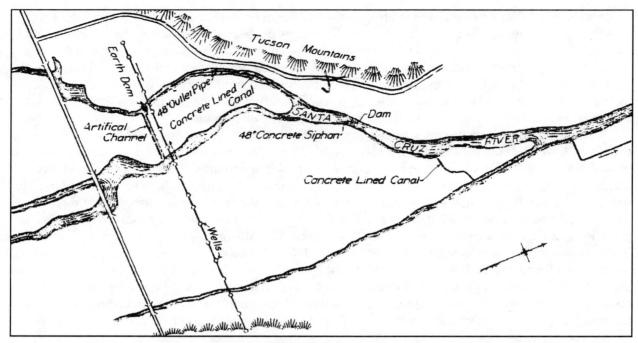

Figure 21. Plan of features associated with the Tucson Farms Company Crosscut (from Hinderlider 1913:200).

35,000 acres of land, all of it supplied with water pumped from the Santa Cruz Valley (Kuper 1986: 102–103).

To obtain the necessary water, the company's engineers designed a system of interconnected wells, arranged in an east-west line across the valley, at a point downstream of the old Silver Lake dam (Figure 21). Completed in 1912 and referred to locally as the Crosscut, the system was later described in detail by the chief engineer, M. C. Hinderlider, in a professional engineering journal (Hinderlider 1913; note that he refers to the company sponsoring the project as the Pima Land and Water Company, apparently an earlier name for the Tucson Farms Company). The design of the system took advantage of the natural basalt dike that passes underground across the valley at this point, forcing the underflow in the valley to rise near the surface. The presence of the dike was the reason for the natural springs that created the marshy areas, or *cienegas,* to the south of Sentinel Peak, but these areas had largely dried up with the entrenchment of the river in the 1890s. The line of wells would tap the subsided underflow and pump it to the level of a large, buried concrete conduit connecting the wells. The conduit would in turn route the water via a series of other features to the old Manning Ditch on the east side of the river (Hinderlider 1913:200).

Construction of the system was a complicated, expensive undertaking. The 19 wells, spaced from 100 to 300 feet apart, were dug to depths ranging from 45 to 150 feet. Each had mounted on it a large electric pump, housed in a pump house. The gravity conduit that connected the wells ran from 5 to 12 feet below the ground, emptying into a 48-inch concrete outlet pipe where the conduit crossed the West Branch (Figure 22). The outlet pipe ran for 1,500 feet down the bed of the West Branch, then emptied into a large, concrete-lined canal that ran for another 1,700 feet down the same channel, to below the confluence of the West Branch with the Santa Cruz. The water in the ditch then passed through a 48-inch concrete siphon below the Santa Cruz and into a second section of concrete-lined canal that ran inside the east bank of the Santa Cruz until it met the old Manning Ditch. The concrete outlet pipe and the section

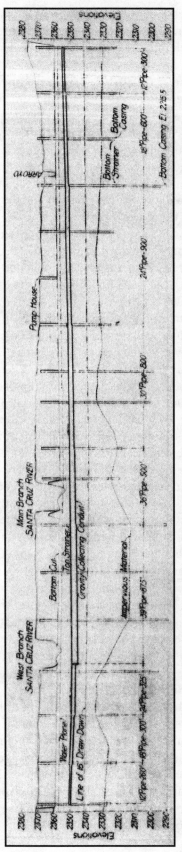

Figure 22. Section drawing of the Tucson Farms Company Crosscut (from Hinderlider 1913:201).

111

of concrete-lined canal running in the channel of the West Branch just below the Crosscut were protected from flooding in the West Branch by an earthen dam constructed immediately above the Crosscut. The dam routed the flow of the West Branch into the Santa Cruz via a channel excavated for that purpose (see Figure 21).

Betancourt (1990:130–134) and Kuper (1986:102–104) have provided further details on the construction of the Crosscut, which required unprecedented amounts of money, labor, and engineering expertise. Betancourt (1990:Figures 41–46) has reproduced photographs of the project that are on file at the University of Arizona Library's Special Collections. In addition, we found a previously unidentified shot of the Crosscut in the Buehman Collection at the AHS (Figure 23). This photograph was taken from near the east end of the Crosscut as it neared completion. It shows the line of wells and pump houses extending west toward the area south of Sentinel Peak. It is unclear what portion of each pump house was meant to remain aboveground. The ditch that the pump houses occupy is perhaps 8–9 feet deep, which suggests that at least some backfilling was planned.

The Crosscut was initially a success, and by 1915, it was supplying 28.25 million gallons of water per day to the fields of the Tucson Farms Company (Kuper 1986:105). On a map of the company's holdings from the same year (Figure 24), the Crosscut is clearly indicated crossing east-west across the north half of Section 23 (Township 14 South, Range 13 East). Within the Paseo de las Iglesias study area, the company held some 3,200 acres of land, a small portion of it watered by the Crosscut, but most of it watered by other wells dug farther upstream in the study area.

By 1920, the Tucson Farms Company was struggling to make a profit, in part because of a weakened economy following the end of World War I. The company began selling parcels of land to individual farmers, with much of the land eventually passing to the Flowing Wells Irrigation District and the Midvale Farms Company (Kuper 1986:105). The latter sale is probably represented in a 1920 map of the Tucson Irrigation Company's Midvale Farm Tract, an area falling in Sections 3, 10, and 15 of Township 15 South, Range 13 East, and corresponding closely with the Midvale Park development of the 1980s (Figure 25).

The alignment of the Tucson Farms Company Crosscut is still evident on recent maps, including the most recent Tucson 7.5-minute U.S. Geological Survey (USGS) quadrangle, where it is depicted as a perfectly straight ditch or wash running east-west across the northern half of Section 23 (Township 14 South, Range 13 East). It is also obvious in the field, as we discovered when we recently visited that location (Figure 26). It consists of a shallow, overgrown, linear depression, extending from the Interstate 10 ROW west to Santa Cruz Lane. The alignment parallels 26th Street, which between Santa Cruz Lane and Interstate 10 is still labeled on some maps Flowing Wells Crosscut Road. As we note in Chapter 5, features associated with the Crosscut have been found west of Santa Cruz Lane on either bank of the Santa Cruz River and recorded as archaeological site AZ BB:13:109.

A comparison of the Allison brothers' sketch map of water-control features on the old Warner property (see Figure 20) with the 1913 plan of the Crosscut (see Figure 21) emphasizes the continuities that existed between the two systems. Both systems exploited the fact that the subsurface flow of the Santa Cruz Valley was forced near the surface south and east of Sentinel Peak, and thus, both systems relied on features built in the same general location, near the confluence of the West Branch and the Santa Cruz. On the Crosscut plan, a small dam is depicted on the Santa Cruz immediately below the point where the system's concrete siphon passed west to east under the river. The function of this dam, if it had one by that time, was not explained by Hinderlider, although he did seem to include it as part of the system (it was apparently made of timbers; see his comment on a second dam [Hinderlider 1913:200]). This dam was apparently located right where Warner's old dam was depicted on the sketch map, suggesting that Warner's dam, or a version of it maintained first by the Allison brothers and then by Manning and his associates, was a functioning part of the Crosscut system. Similarly, the main canal in the Crosscut, which served the Tucson Farms Company's holdings downstream from the study area on the east bank of the river, was the Manning Ditch, first known as the Allison brothers' East Side Canal and supplied with water diverted by the same small dam.

Figure 23. Construction of the Tucson Farms Company Crosscut, view to the west, probably 1912 (photograph courtesy of the Arizona Historical Society, Accession No. B38488).

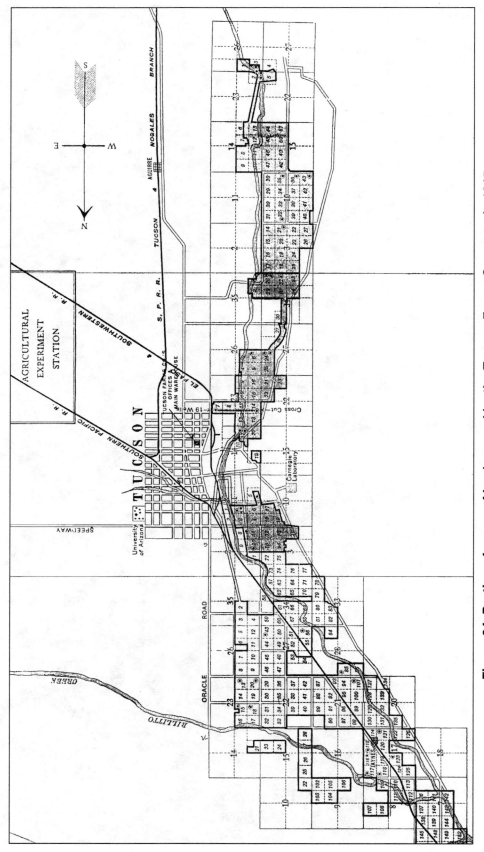

Figure 24. Portion of a map of lands owned by the Tucson Farms Company in 1915 (Tucson Farms Company 1915).

114

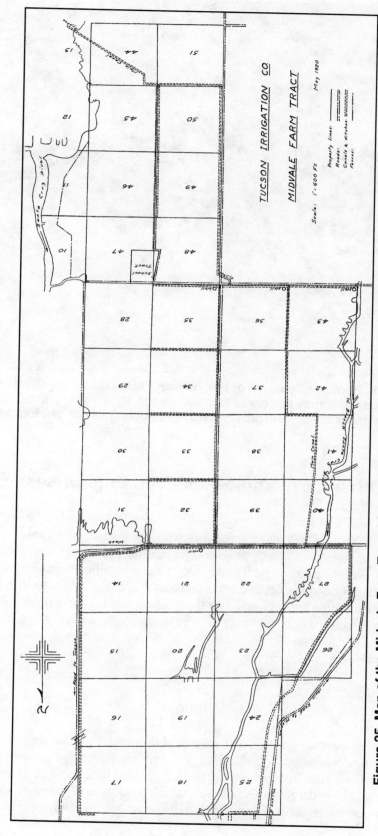

Figure 25. Map of the Midvale Farm Tract of the Tucson Irrigation Company in 1920 (Tucson Irrigation Company 1920).

115

**Figure 26. Former alignment of the Tucson Farms Company Crosscut,
viewed from approximately the same location as the 1912 photograph in Figure 23.
The alignment is the overgrown strip in the center of the photograph.**

Other Early Anglo-American Enterprises

The influx of Anglo-American settlers into Tucson following the Gadsden Purchase brought with it an influx of capital that made possible a variety of economic pursuits previously unknown in southern Arizona. In this section, we look at three such pursuits that had a significant presence in the Paseo de las Iglesias study area: milling, brick making, and entertainment. None of these industries came to dominate the Tucson economy, but all three had an impact on the landscape along the Santa Cruz River, and remnants of all three are preserved today in the study area as archaeological sites, albeit poorly documented and badly disturbed sites. We also briefly consider two other economic pursuits that had a limited presence in the study area: brewing and quarrying.

Milling

Prior to the Gadsden Purchase, the residents of Tucson and its vicinity ground their wheat into flour at the household level, or they purchased flour that had been imported from Sonora and elsewhere. After Tucson became U.S. territory, many people undoubtedly continued their same practices, but commercial grist mills soon sprang up along the Santa Cruz River, taking advantage of the river's potential for water power. Several milling operations were begun and abandoned within the study area in the second half of the nineteenth century, before the entrenchment of the Santa Cruz River in the 1890s made water-powered mills unfeasible.

Water-powered milling in the study area can be summarized with reference to two locations: the successive milling operations of William and Alfred Rowlett, William S. Grant, and James Lee at Silver Lake, just south of modern Silverlake Road, and the operation of Solomon Warner, downstream at the northeastern foot of Sentinel Peak.

Milling at Silver Lake

In 1856, William and Alfred Rowlett, who had recently arrived in Tucson from the east, decided to build a water-powered grist mill along the Santa Cruz. They began by building a small earthen dam down-stream from a spring-fed *cienega* just south of Sentinel Peak, along what would become the west bank of the Santa Cruz as it became entrenched during the last decades of the nineteenth century. Construction of the dam resulted in the formation of a pond, eventually named Silver Lake, but only long after the Rowletts had moved on to other things. The following year, the Rowletts built their mill, which was fed by a race that drew from three separate ditches originating at springs a mile or more upstream. From the mill, the water flowed by a second race into the pond, from which water was let into ditches leading to agricultural fields downstream, to the east and north of Sentinel Peak (the same area depicted in the 1862 Fergusson map; see Figure 8). The purpose of the Rowletts' dam and pond, rather than to impound water to drive the mill, was to allow the mill to use the flow of the springs without having to coordinate such use with the irrigation schedule in place for the fields (Betancourt 1990:52). The Rowlett Mill was "strongly but roughly built of cottonwood logs," and the brothers had installed "the most improved machinery, including milling stones and equipment for bolting" (cited in Pedersen 1975:130).

In 1860, only a few years after its construction, the Rowletts sold their mill to William S. Grant, another recent arrival from the east (Cosulich 1953:273). Grant expanded the mill and built a second one nearby. The new mill could grind 10 bushels of wheat per hour and was kept in constant operation to supply the three U.S. forts (Forts Buchanan and Breckenridge in Arizona, and Fort Fillmore in New Mexico) that had contracted Grant's services (Cosulich 1953:273; Pedersen 1975:129–132). In addition to the new mill, and at the same site, Grant built a large (60-by-40-foot) storehouse of adobe and timber, a blacksmith shop, a dwelling for employees, and a stock corral made of 7-foot-high upright tree trunks (Pedersen 1975:130, 132). In July 1861, both of Grant's Mills and all of the accompanying buildings were burned by the Union army as it abandoned Tucson, bent on destroying anything that might be of use to the Confederate force that was about to occupy the town. Grant also lost many tons of food and other supplies to the same logic, all of which he had freighted to Tucson to sell to the Union forts. He never returned to Tucson (Cosulich 1953:274; Pedersen 1975:135–136).

One of Grant's Mills was partially repaired in 1862 by members of the California Volunteers, the Union force that reoccupied Tucson after the Confederates abandoned it (Cosulich 1953:274). This was the extent of water-powered milling in Tucson until 1864, when an Irish immigrant named James Lee began running the mill with a partner, W. F. Scott. Cosulich surmised that Lee and Scott refurbished the newer of Grant's Mills, leaving the original Rowlett Mill in disrepair (1953:275). Six years later, the two men constructed a new mill in downtown Tucson, near the intersection of Broadway and Main. This was the Eagle Steam Flour Mill, a large steam-powered operation with a capacity of 7,000 pounds of grain per day. Four years later, they dissolved their partnership and sold the Eagle to E. N. (Edward Nye) Fish and Company (*The Citizen,* 4 July 1874). The Eagle had several different owners during the remainder of its existence and was eventually moved from Main Street to Toole Avenue (*Arizona Daily Star,* 16 March 1924).

After selling the Eagle, Lee continued to run the mill on the Santa Cruz, which came to be known as the Pioneer Mill. He also lived on land he owned near the mill pond, which people referred to as Lee's

117

Pond. It is unclear when Lee gained official title to his land. The GLO records show that he purchased the quarter section encompassing the pond (Township 14 South, Range 13 East, Section 23, SW $\frac{1}{4}$) from the federal government in 1884, the same year that he died (see Figure 11 and Table 1). However, around 1880, he reportedly leased 20 acres on the north shore of the pond to J. O. Bailey and J. F. Rickey, who then built and operated the Silver Lake Resort (see below). This was presumably when Lee's Pond was renamed Silver Lake. When Lee died, his heirs sold the mill and the rest of the property at Silver Lake (Cosulich 1953:280–281), and by 1893, the mill had ceased to operate. A newspaper article from that year reported, "The turbine wheel of the Old Jimmy Lee mill at Silver Lake has been purchased by Eugene Middleton. Mr. Middleton will move it to Dudleyville where he will run several arrastres by the water power it will utilize. He has a fine gold property there" (*Arizona Daily Star,* 24 January 1893).

Silver Lake is depicted on the 1893 Roskruge map of Pima County (see Figure 12), just south of what became Silverlake Road and straddling the course of the Santa Cruz River. The only known remnants of the mills at Silver Lake are masonry footings preserved at AZ BB:13:109, on the west bank of the Santa Cruz, just south of Silverlake Road. The footings probably represent the mill operated by Lee beginning in 1864, which was first built by Grant in 1860 (see the site description in the appendix).

Warner's Mill

Solomon Warner was one of Tucson's earliest and most enterprising Anglo-American entrepreneurs. He first arrived in Arizona in February or March of 1856 and established the first Anglo-American general store in downtown Tucson. The store was located just outside the walls of the old presidio, near the current corner of Alameda and Main Streets. It was the first store in Tucson to be stocked entirely with goods made in the United States (Cosulich 1953:102; Lockwood 1953:50–51).

Warner's store thrived, despite Apache and other depredations along his supply routes. He quickly became a well-regarded member of the community and began to acquire parcels of land in and around the small settlement. His luck changed in 1862 with the arrival of Capt. Sherod Hunter and his troop of Texas Confederate Cavalry (Cosulich 1953:108). After confiscating Warner's entire stock in the name of the Confederacy, Hunter reputedly confronted Warner and gave him the option of taking up arms with the Confederacy or leaving town. Warner departed for Santa Cruz, Sonora.

Warner's business acumen served him even better in Sonora than it had in Tucson. His wealth and reputation grew quickly, and the local inhabitants soon began referring to him as "Don Solomon." During his time in Santa Cruz, he acquired "a farm with many head of cattle, began a freight line from Guaymas to Hermosillo, established a 'flouring mill,' and married a prosperous Sonora woman with a lovely daughter named Eulalia" (Cosulich 1953:108).

For uncertain reasons, Warner returned to Tucson following the end of the Civil War, leaving his Mexican bride behind. He rebuilt and restocked his store and resumed the business relationships he had established prior to his departure (this included supplying the same Arizona forts once supplied by Grant). He prospered, and though he maintained a residence downtown, he began purchasing land and obtaining water rights to lands on the west bank of the Santa Cruz, along the eastern foot of Sentinel Peak. Warner hoped to build a grist mill there, and he began to acquire the necessary water rights and ROWs as early as 1872. In 1874, Warner managed to negotiate with Bishop Salpointe, trustee of the Catholic Church, to construct a series of races across the grounds of Mission San Agustín (Betancourt 1978b:71; Cosulich 1953:111). In striking this deal, Warner agreed to grind 40 *fanegas* of wheat flour annually for the church at a cost of 75 cents per *fanega.* This was a savings to the church of 25 cents per *fanega,* as his advertised price in 1878 was one dollar per *fanega* (*Arizona Weekly Star,* 28 February 1878).

Negotiating the right to run his races across mission grounds was apparently Warner's final obstacle, and construction of his mill was completed by 1875. An account of the new facility featured prominently in the local newspaper:

Mr. Solomon Warner possesses preeminently that element of success known as perseverance. Many long weary months ago and even years, he determined to have a gristmill and he has plodded along the way steadily and cheerfully, against enfeebled health, considerable obstacles, disadvantage of position and poor work well paid for, until there stands to-day, owned and built by Mr. Warner, just west of the old mission of Tucson, the best grist-mill in Arizona, and similar to the best in California, running with entire success, and built at an expense of between $15,000 and $16,000. Selecting for his site, the old building which used to stand at the foot of the cone shaped hill west of town, Mr. Warner has built thereon a substantial mill building about 51 × 30 feet in size, of two stories, the lower story having solid stone walls of great depth, while the upper walls are adobe, and the building contains eight good sized rooms.

. . . The first room on the ground floor is the grinding room, 30 × 18 feet in dimensions; in this are two run of 3½ feet French Burr stones of the most superior mechanical construction, the upper stones weighing 1900 pounds each, and styled old quarry, as being superior to new quarry. There is at hand an apparatus for lifting and moving these stones with the greatest ease, and the curbs covering the burrs are made of California redwood, inlaid and finished to a high degree. The second room on this floor is the packing room, 18 × 20 feet, with flour chest, etc. Adjoining this is the smut room, furnished with one of the Eureka No. 2 smutters, capacity sixty bushels an hour. . . . The grain is passed through this machine once and is then apparently clean enough for any ordinary purpose, but it is then wet and allowed to stand for twelve hours when it is again put through the machine and the last vestige of dirt is gone. There is another room on this floor for general purposes.

The first room upstairs is the bolting room, fitted up with superior apparatus and all the work finished in the finest style. . . . Back of this room is the large storage room 34-x-30 feet in size. The mill wheel is a twenty-five inch American turbine, producing a 9-horse power which will make a grind of about eight bushels an hour. The driving force is some six hundred cubic feet of water with an average fall of eleven and a half feet. To get this force Mr. Warner had to construct a ditch around the base of the cone hill, seven-eighths of a mile long to the head gates, and which is quite a piece of engineering, but as Mr. Warner says, the only badly constructed thing about the mill. This ditch has cost him already some $3500, and may cost more yet, but he will keep it until he remedies the faults in the original construction.

. . . Mr. Warner proposes to build an addition to the mill about 50 × 40 feet in size, for a grain-room, fitted up with separate bins for the use of customers, each one having a bin exclusively to himself, and when he threshes his grain in the harvest, bring it to the mill and store it in his bin as safely and securely as he could in his own store-room if he had one. In the general absence of store-houses for grain among the farmers in this vicinity, this proposed innovation of Mr. Warner's seems to us a very kindly and good idea [*The Citizen,* 30 October 1875].

Probably constructed at the same time as the mill is a second structure associated with Warner's operation (Figure 27). Immediately north of the mill, Warner constructed an "L-shaped" adobe house, presumably intended as living quarters. Betancourt (1978b:72) described the house as having a one-room-deep layout, each room with its own door to the outside patio east of the home. The southern part

119

Figure 27. Solomon Warner's house and mill, at the base of Sentinel Peak, ca. 1900 (photograph courtesy of the Arizona Historical Society, Tucson, Accession No. 14846).

of the house was arranged in a typical center-hall plan and was likely the portion occupied by Warner and his family. The northern part was a series of rooms lacking a center hall that probably provided quarters for mill employees. The house is a good example of the flat-roofed, parapeted adobe home of Spanish-American origin.

The Solomon Warner House and Mill (AZ BB:13:57) are now listed in the NRHP. The house still stands, somewhat modified, and is used as a residence. Only the foundations of the mill survive (see Chapter 5 and the site description in the appendix).

Warner's Mill prospered during its early years of operation. The increasing demand for flour provided adequate business for all of the local millers. Like many pioneers of the period, Warner's business interests were diverse. With the success of the mill, Warner constructed a small, three-stamp ore mill in 1879 to process ore from mines he was working. This mill was powered by the same water that drove the grist mill (Betancourt 1978b:72). By May of that year, ores processed by Warner achieved 70–75 percent of the assay value (*Arizona Weekly Star,* 8 May 1879).

The ditch or race that originally supplied water to Warner's Mill is described in the newspaper article above as following "the base of the cone hill [i.e., Sentinel Peak]," and being "seven-eighths of a mile long to the head gates." The precise location of the headgates, which tapped a small pond built by Warner, and the precise alignment of the race are unknown. Both have probably been obscured by modern development, especially by improvements to Mission Road along the base of Sentinel Peak. Seven-eighths of a mile upstream from the mill places the headgates just downstream from James Lee's Mill and Pond, which is consistent with references to the pond being fed by water leaking from Lee's Pond, as discussed by Betancourt (1978b:71–72, 1990:88–89). The tail race for Warner's Mill, which carried water away from the mill, ran straight east, emptying into one of the irrigation ditches serving the fields around and north of Mission San Agustín (Betancourt 1978b:71; see Figure 8 for a map of the fields). A probable portion of this race was discovered recently in excavations at the Mission San Agustín site (AZ BB:13:6) by Desert Archaeology (see Chapter 5).

Warner's initial dam created a pond no more than a few acres in size. The pond was inadequate for his larger purposes, and by 1883, he had constructed a dam large enough to form a pond covering as many as 37 acres (*Arizona Weekly Citizen,* 17 November 1883; Wheeler n.d.). Descriptions of the location of the dam, quoted by Betancourt (1990:91–92), are difficult to interpret. It began at the base of Sentinel Peak, at the point where the original race met the hill, then ran along the side of the race for a quarter mile toward Silver Lake. This implies a north-south alignment, with the resulting lake lying to the west, or at the southern foot of Sentinel Peak. No trace of the dam or the large lake it created have been found, but both were presumably located within the NW$\frac{1}{4}$ of Section 23, Township 14 South, Range 13 East, a quarter section of land between Sentinel Peak and Silver Lake that Warner purchased from the GLO in 1876 (see Figure 11 and Table 1). Again, improvements to Mission Road have undoubtedly obscured most or all of both features.

The lake created by Warner's new dam was fed by several springs, which constituted a substantial source of water previously uncaptured by the Silver Lake dam. The new lake attracted a variety of waterfowl and was soon frequented by local hunters (Betancourt 1990:92). It was also stocked with carp, which Warner might have sold to local grocers. The lake continued to supply Tucson with carp even after Warner had sold the property. In 1890, "Chan Tin Wo took a three years' lease from Allison and Son of their large carp lake, known as Warner Lake" (Xia 2001:94). Warner also planned to develop a resort at his lake that would compete with the resort at Silver Lake, but the plan died when a company that owed him money failed.

In 1884, Warner ran into legal problems prompted by his construction of the dam. Landholders downstream, experiencing a sharp drop in available irrigation water, decided that Warner's dam had deprived them of water to which they had prior rights. The basis for their claim is hard to understand, as Warner was probably capturing more water with his dam than they might otherwise have captured with their ditches and was delivering it to them intact after it ran through his mill, but this was only one of many disputes over water that erupted in the 1880s as the flow in the Santa Cruz began to be overtaxed. In the end, Warner was obliged to open the gates of his dam. In 1886, frustrated by the lack of sufficient water to regularly operate his mill, Warner sold all of his property at Sentinel Peak, and it soon ended up in the hands of the Allison brothers (see above).

Brick Making

Prior to the development of the brick industry in Tucson, the dominant construction material was adobe. The materials for making adobes were readily available, and the techniques for constructing adobe buildings were well established. Other building materials, including wood and fired brick, were not readily available until the arrival of the railroad in 1880. By the last decade of the nineteenth century, the use of brick in building construction was being touted by city officials. An article in the *Arizona Daily Star,* likely reflecting the opinions of these officials, pronounced, "The future building materials for Tucson will be brick and stone. The adobe must go, likewise the mud roof. They belong in the past and with the past they must remain" (20 August 1892; cited in A. Diehl and M. Diehl 1996:2). Since fired bricks shared many of the beneficial insulating characteristics of adobe but were structurally more stable, their use in large buildings was viewed as vastly superior.

Tucson Pressed Brick Company

The brick industry in Tucson was first developed principally by one man, Quintus Monier. Monier was a naturalized French architect who was commissioned to construct the first large-scale brick structure in Tucson. The Catholic community in Tucson had decided, in 1897, to construct a monumental cathedral, to be called St. Augustine, reflecting the earlier patronage of that saint for the original *visita* in Tucson. Based largely on his experience with the construction of the large stone cathedral in Santa Fe, it was to Monier that the Catholic community turned for the construction of their own cathedral.

Upon completion, the cathedral was received with great acclaim (M. Diehl and A. Diehl 1996:2). Recognizing a potential market, Monier remained in Tucson following the completion of the cathedral and established a brickyard on West Congress Street (Figures 28 and 29). In 1908, Monier incorporated his business as the Tucson Pressed Brick Company. M. Diehl and A. Diehl (1996:2) described Monier's operation as follows:

> Among Tucson's high-capacity brickyards, Monier's was the longest in operation, and during the peak demand for bricks it was a highly profitable enterprise. Monier reported that with the proper machinery, the Tucson Pressed Brick Company was capable of making 20,000 pressed bricks at a profit of $800 a day. Extruded bricks could be manufactured at a daily profit of $400, sewer pipe at $660, and hollow tile at $560.

Two other companies, the DeVry Brickyard and the Grabe Brick Company, were Monier's main competition at the time (see below). With Monier's death in 1923, ownership of the Tucson Pressed Brick Company passed to Albert Steinfeld, a successful local businessman. Steinfeld used the company to manufacture bricks for numerous projects, including the 11-story Pioneer Hotel, completed in 1929. In 1935, Steinfeld's son, Harold, sold the company. Although there is no known documentation of it, the sale was likely to John S. Sundt, the next owner of record (A. Diehl and M. Diehl 1996:3). Brick-making operations continued under Sundt at the West Congress location until 1963, when all of the equipment and some of the buildings were moved to a new location at 7601 South Houghton Road. Sundt died in 1965 and ownership of the Tucson Pressed Brick Company passed to the M. M. Sundt Construction

Figure 28. North end of the Paseo de las Iglesias project area, view to the northeast, ca. 1910. The Tucson Pressed Brick Company plant is visible in the left-central portion of the photograph (photograph courtesy of the Arizona Historical Society, Tucson, Accession No. B113390).

Figure 29. Sentinel Peak ("A" Mountain) viewed from downtown Tucson, ca. 1930.
The Tucson Pressed Brick Company plant is visible at the base of the hills near the right edge of the photograph.
(photograph courtesy of the Arizona Historical Society, Tucson, Accession No. BN200403).

Company. Sundt Construction sold the company to a Phoenix interest in 1971 (M. Diehl and A. Diehl 1996:33).

The remnants of the Tucson Pressed Brick Company's original plant, located just south of Congress Street on the west bank of the Santa Cruz, are now part of the Mission San Agustín archaeological site, AZ BB:13:6. A discussion of this site as a whole is provided in Chapter 5.

DeVry Brickyard

Louis DeVry was known to the Tucson community as a brick maker as early as 1902, when he was cited in the Tucson City Directory as such (even though his name was misspelled as "De Fry"). Although De-Vry might have been making his living as a brick maker at this early date, the scale of his manufacturing operation is not known. DeVry's brickyard was located on St. Mary's Road, just north of the location of the Tucson Pressed Brick Company's facility. In addition to his own operation, DeVry might also have been involved in the operation of the Santa Cruz Brickyard (later known as Pima Brick and Tile) as early as 1915 (M. Diehl and A. Diehl 1996:36).

DeVry's brickyard does not appear on area maps until 1942, when it is included on the Sanborn Fire Insurance map for that year. DeVry apparently lived at the brickyard, using one of the rooms in his house as the office for the operation. The brickyard appears to have changed little prior to its demise sometime in the 1960s. Although the DeVry Brickyard never reached the production capacity of the Tucson Pressed Brick Company, the longevity of the business testifies to its contribution to the Tucson community.

Grabe Brick Company

Another manufacturer of bricks, W. A. Grabe, established a plant on the west bank of the Santa Cruz, not far from the DeVry Brickyard and Tucson Pressed Brick Company. Grabe is first listed in the city directory as a brick maker in 1917, and he eventually formed the Grabe Brick Company (M. Diehl and A. Diehl 1996:36). Prior to 1942, the addresses for Grabe's brickyards change frequently, although all of the brickyards were located in the general vicinity north of Congress and west of the Santa Cruz River. Grabe's operation was apparently more sophisticated than that of DeVry, and his output might have rivaled that of the Tucson Pressed Brick Company in the production of common brick (M. Diehl and A. Diehl 1996:36).

The Grabe Brickyard changed little after 1942, and manufacturing continued at the facility until 1963. A number of archaeological features associated with the plant have been recorded as AZ BB:13:646, which is discussed in the appendix.

Entertainment at Silver Lake

Lee's Pond, later named Silver Lake, was probably a destination for local bathers from the moment it came into existence, but it was apparently not considered to be more than a swimming hole until Lee leased those 20 acres of land on the north shore to Bailey and Rickey around 1880 (see above). Bailey and Rickey already operated a mile racetrack nearby (Figure 30) and soon capitalized on the popularity of the lake by building a resort. A newspaper advertisement for the resort appeared in 1880 (*Arizona Daily Star,* 9 June 1880):

Figure 30. Horse racing, ca. 1900, probably at a track on the west bank of the Santa Cruz River near Silver Lake. Today's Cottonwood Lane probably occupies the former alignment of the track. (photograph courtesy of the Arizona Historical Society, Tucson, Accession No. 18797).

SILVER LAKE
SUMMER RESORT,
Adjoining Lee's Mills,
One and a half miles South of Tucson, A. T.

This resort is finely furnished throughout; has
fine pleasure boats; bath houses; shade trees and
general improvements such as to make it truly the
only Pleasure Resort in the Territory.

A First-class Saloon is always open.
apr 10 1m [?] J. A. SMITH Proprietor

The directory for the City of Tucson for 1881 (Barter 1881:40) gives a more detailed description of the facilities at Silver Lake, under the heading "Places of Public Resort":

Silver Lake—This place is situated one and one-half miles south-west of the city, and is
a constant resort, both day and night, for the inhabitants of Tucson. The lake is caused by
a dam of masonry in the Santa Cruz River, and extends over several acres. Several boats
are available for sailing or rowing up the river beyond the lake. A row of commodious

bath-houses are constructed for the accommodation of bathers, and a stout rope extends across a portion of the lake for the convenience of persons learning to swim. The hotel, bath-houses, pavilion, lake and grove occupy a space of twenty acres, leased and controlled by J. F. Rickey and J. O. Bailey, who also serve the mile race track adjacent thereto, and where the annual races are held. This is the only race track near Tucson and the only swimming baths in Arizona.

Rickey and Bailey apparently operated the resort and its hotel for several years, although it is not known if the venture was a profitable one during their ownership. For unknown reasons, the partners sold the resort to Fred Maish and Thomas Driscoll sometime between 1881 and 1884. A short notice in the *Arizona Mining Index* (27 December 1884) alludes to the change of ownership: "Maish & Driscoll, build a large hotel at Silver Lake." It is possible that Maish and Driscoll erected a new hotel to compete with Rickey and Bailey's property, but it is more likely that they added to or replaced buildings they had bought from Rickey and Bailey. Another short notice appeared a year and a half later in the *Arizona Daily Star* (27 April 1886) indicating that "the Silver Lake hotel has been refitted, refurnished, and in every way improved. The baths are also repaired, new boats have been added for pleasure seekers on the lake. So that Silver Lake hotel is the resort of Tucson. It will be opened May 1st. Fred. Maish, Prop." The hotel is pictured on the shore of Silver Lake, next to a house probably associated with it, in an 1888 photograph (Figure 31). Since it was adjacent to Lee's Mills, the hotel was presumably on the west side of the lake, which is supported by the depiction of a structure there on the 1893 Roskruge map of Pima County (see Figure 12).

Maish and Driscoll's hotel and resort might have been intended for the general population of Tucson, but they were soon catering to a rough crowd. Cosulich (1953:281–282) wrote:

> The resort at Silver Lake had been used by Civic groups, Sunday school classes and families as a place for outings. The city fathers visualized a horse-drawn street car line being built to the lake and a new residential subdivision opening there, but the rowdy and questionable quality of the men and their "soiled doves of Gay Alley," who did patronize the resort soon prevented "respectable" people from going there. Silver Lake became Tucson's first road house and night club and wild were the parties given there. Many a beruffled entertainer was thrown into the lake, squealing and kicking, and many a drunkard was pulled out of it, mumbling protestations through chattering teeth.

As floods in the Santa Cruz increased in frequency and intensity in the 1880s, the existence of Silver Lake was threatened. The dam was damaged by floods in 1886, 1887, 1889, and 1890, and with each flood, the river became more entrenched. Eventually, the entrenchment of the river, combined with the lowering of the water table, left Silver Lake out of reach of the water in the valley. In 1890, the Silver Lake Hotel either burned down, washed away in that year's flood, or both; it was never rebuilt (Betancourt 1990:106–110; Cosulich 1953:286; Kuper 1986:54–55). Foundation remnants and historical-period trash, both likely associated with the hotel, have been recorded as AZ BB:13:94 (see the appendix).

Excelsior Brewery

The same year that Rickey and Bailey first advertised their resort at Silver Lake, Conrad Mundelius, about whom little is known, first advertised the products of his brewery at the same location.

Figure 31. Silver Lake Hotel (right) and unidentified building at Silver Lake, 1888 (photograph courtesy of the Arizona Historical Society, Tucson, Accession No. 101307).

Beer! Beer!
Excelsior Brewery.
C. MUNDELIUS, Proprietor.
The finest beer ever brewed in the Territory is that made at this Brewery which is located
near Silver Lake, one mile and a half from the city.
PRINCIPAL DEPOT—Meyer Street, nearly opposite the Palace Hotel at the Excelsior
Saloon where beer can be had by the bottle and on draught, as well as by the measure.
[*Arizona Daily Star*, 9 June 1880]

A reference to the Excelsior Brewery also appears in the 1881 Tucson City Directory in a brief
description of "industrial enterprises: "Two breweries partly supply the population with beer, which is
regarded as a healthy drink in this climate. One of these is the property of Alex[ander] Levin, and situated at the Park: the other is located in the vicinity of Silver Lake" (Barter 1881:46). Levin had been
brewing in Tucson since 1869, and by 1878 he had established a 3-acre park at his brewery on Main
Street, on the east bank of the river. He was eventually outdone by Leopoldo Carrillo, who had a larger
beer garden farther south on Main (Sonnichsen 1982:88, 105–106). The amount of business Mundelius
enjoyed relative to either Levin or Carrillo is unknown.

In 1885, Mundelius purchased 160 acres from the GLO in Township 14 South, Range 13 East, Section 22, just west of Silver Lake (see Figure 11 and Table 1). This property might have included the site
of the brewery, although we have found no other evidence for this. The fate of the Excelsior Brewery and
its latest year of operation are also unknown. Mundelius does not appear as a landholder on the 1893
Roskruge map of Pima County (see Figure 12).

Sentinel Peak Quarry

Sentinel Peak, "the cone shaped hill west of town" where Warner built his mill, is linked to Tucson's
history not simply by virtue of its proximity, but by its original name, *chuk shon*, Piman for "black hill"
(Saxton et al. 1998:138). The name of the hill was extended to the Sobaipuri settlement at its base by
Kino and his successors, then to the *visita* built to serve the settlement, then to the presidio built across
the river, and finally to the community that grew up around the presidio and became present-day Tucson
(Dobyns 1976:3–4; see also Barnes 1988:455). The "black" in the name refers to the basalt that the hill is
made of, which early in the historical period began to be used as building material, especially in house
foundations. The distinctive black basalt of Sentinel Peak, or at least a similar black basalt obtained elsewhere in the Tucson Mountains, can be seen today all around Tucson's historic neighborhoods, most
notably when an old foundation is exposed by archaeologists working in advance of a construction project.

A basalt quarry was established at Sentinel Peak sometime in the second half of the nineteenth century, but the hill might have served as a source of basalt long before then. According to a 1926 *Tucson
Citizen* article, basalt rocks were collected from the hill to make metates during the Spanish Colonial
period, which gave rise to an early name for the hill, "Picacho de Metates" (*Tucson Citizen*, 30 May
1926). We have been unable to confirm this information in any other source. We have also not found any
reference to the exact year that the quarry began, but by 1930, the approximate date of a photograph of
Sentinel Peak taken from downtown Tucson (see Figure 29), the quarry is conspicuous as a large hole on
the lower north slope of the hill. It had obviously been worked for many years by that time. In 1925, at a
hearing regarding private land claims on the hill, Herbert Drachman testified that he had been the first
person to take stone from the mountain to use in a foundation; he used the stone for a house at Congress
Street and Fifth Avenue (*Arizona Daily Star*, 9 October 1925). Drachman did not give the year he first
took stone from the mountain, but he had lived in Tucson for 49 years by 1925, which, if his claim can
be believed, would mean the quarry was first worked as early as 1876.

As a source of basalt for construction, Sentinel Peak is not unique in the Tucson Basin, as the Tucson Mountains as a whole, which include Sentinel Peak, are made up largely of basalt. In 1922, a businessman named James Dodson filed a claim for a large portion of Sentinel Peak with the GLO, stating that he would develop the area as a source of basalt for construction. The following year, his wife, Christina Dodson, filed a similar claim for another large portion of the hill. The City of Tucson, a variety of civic organizations, and many Tucson citizens feared that the Dodsons would end up destroying the hill, either by quarrying it away or by subdividing it to build housing and commercial properties, which some people suspected was their real intention. Whatever the Dodsons' plans, the city risked losing an important landmark and an area used by many people for recreation. A series of hearings on the case followed, and one point made repeatedly by testifying citizens was that Sentinel Peak would never be a profitable source of basalt because of the ubiquity of the material in the mountains nearby. The case was finally resolved in 1928, when the GLO refused the Dodsons' claims. The City of Tucson eventually became owner of the hill and later developed Sentinel Peak Park (*Arizona Daily Star,* 11 October 1923, 9 October 1925, 18 November 1928).

Another part of the case against the Dodsons was the importance that Tucson, especially the University of Arizona community, placed on a large, white "A" built on the east face of the hill in 1916 (see Figure 29). The "A," built of stone and mortar by University of Arizona students and measuring 106 feet high by 70 feet wide, celebrated consecutive victories by the university's football team over Pomona College in 1914 and 1915. It gave rise to the name used most commonly for Sentinel Peak today—"A" Mountain. The "A" is still prominent on the hill (Figure 32) and continues to be maintained by University of Arizona students (and occasionally desecrated by Arizona State University students). The City of Tucson also paints it green on St. Patrick's Day each year. Even by the 1920s, this symbol was weighty enough to warrant frequent mention in the Dodsons' land-claim hearings as one of the reasons that Sentinel Peak was "so dear to the hearts of all those connected with the university" (*Arizona Daily Star,* 18 November 1928).

The quarry on Sentinel Peak was still active in the 1930s, when it was operated by Griffith Construction. The company used dynamite in the quarry to blast loose rock, which they then processed with a mechanical crusher (Figueroa and Martínez n.d.). We have not found any information on more-recent use of the quarry.

Scientific Research

The Paseo de las Iglesias study area, because it contains some of the most important prehistoric and historical-period archaeological sites in southern Arizona, has long been the focus of professional archaeological and historical research, as we discussed in Chapter 2. As part of the Santa Cruz River valley, and thus as part of an area heavily impacted by geomorphological processes initiated in the last century and a half, the study area has also been the focus of considerable research in the geosciences (see especially Betancourt [1990]). Early in the twentieth century, part of the study area also began to serve an important role as a laboratory for research in arid-lands ecology, especially the ecology of desert plant life. The University of Arizona Desert Research Laboratory, a major research facility for paleoecology, is still located immediately adjacent to the study area. Occupying a portion of the upper ridge of Tumamoc Hill, this facility owes much of its research impetus and a substantial part of its physical plant to the ecologists who first became interested in the Santa Cruz Valley and its vicinity nearly a century ago.

Figure 32. Sentinel Peak ("A" Mountain) today, viewed from the intersection of Mission Lane and Mission Road. Part of the ruins of Solomon Warner's Mill are visible in the brush at the lower right.

Desert Botanical Laboratory

The University of Arizona Desert Research Laboratory on Tumamoc Hill first opened in 1903 as the Desert Botanical Laboratory, a research outpost of the recently founded (in 1901) Carnegie Institution of Washington. The Desert Botanical Laboratory was the inspiration of two prominent American botanists, Frederick Coville, then curator of the U.S. National Herbarium, and Daniel MacDougal, then assistant director of the New York Botanical Garden. As the two members of the Carnegie Institution's Advisory Committee on Botany, Coville and MacDougal recommended that funding be provided for the establishment of a facility dedicated to the study of plants in arid environments. The facility would be constructed at a site somewhere in the western desert. To select the site, Coville and MacDougal made a tour in early 1903 of various desert locations in west Texas, New Mexico, Arizona, California, and Sonora, finally settling on Tumamoc Hill, just west of what were then the limits of urban Tucson. The same year, a large building was erected as a laboratory, and the facility's first resident investigator was appointed: William A. Cannon, a botanist and recent Ph.D. recipient from Columbia University (Coville 1903:1–2; Wilder 1967:179–185).

The selection of Tumamoc Hill as the site of the Desert Botanical Laboratory was based on a number of factors, but the principal ones were the wide variety of desert vegetation in the area, proximity to the University of Arizona and its agricultural school, the location of Tucson along the SPRR (important for accessibility from eastern academic institutions), and, notably, a rich local history that included the prehistoric and modern indigenous practice of agriculture (Coville 1903:12–17). The Carnegie Institution supported an active research program in botanical sciences at the facility for more than three decades, funding a large number of prominent arid-lands botanists in research that was central to the development of the field in the early twentieth century (McGinnies 1981:5–14; Wilder 1967:185–194). In 1937, following financial difficulties, the institution stopped funding research and closed the facility, which was soon offered to the University of Arizona for the price of one dollar. The university declined the offer, and instead, the U.S. Forest Service bought the facility for the same price.

Tumamoc Hill was a Forest Service property for the next 20 years, serving as part of the Southwestern Forest and Range Experiment Station. The facility again hosted plant-related research, although much of the fieldwork took place away from the hill, often in scattered locations in the Coronado National Forest. In 1960, the University of Arizona finally bought the facility—for a more sizeable sum this time—and it became the home of the university's multidisciplinary program in geochronology. Since then, the University of Arizona Desert Research Laboratory has come to focus primarily on paleoecological studies of the greater Southwest and has hosted researchers in a variety of disciplines, including palynologists, paleobotanists, paleontologists, and a variety of specialists in the geosciences (Betancourt 1996; Elkins et al. 1982:1–2; McGinnies 1981:15–16; Wilder 1967:194–199).

The original 860-acre parcel of land associated with the Desert Botanical Laboratory has been designated an archaeological site (AZ AA:16:51). We describe the prehistoric component of the site in Chapter 5 and provide notes on site boundaries and size in the appendix. Because of its importance as an early research facility and its distinctive, generally well-preserved architecture, the Desert Botanical Laboratory was designated a National Historic Landmark in 1965 and then listed in the NRHP in 1975 (Figure 33). In 1976, Tumamoc Hill was designated a National Environmental Study Area, in recognition of its role in ecological research and education, and in 1981, the property was designated a State Natural Area by the Arizona State Parks Board (Ash et al. 1981:7; Elkins et al. 1982:2). A study of the standing architecture at the site appeared in 1981 (Ash et al. 1981), and an overall plan for preservation of the cultural and natural resources of the hill was developed in 1982 (Elkins et al. 1982).

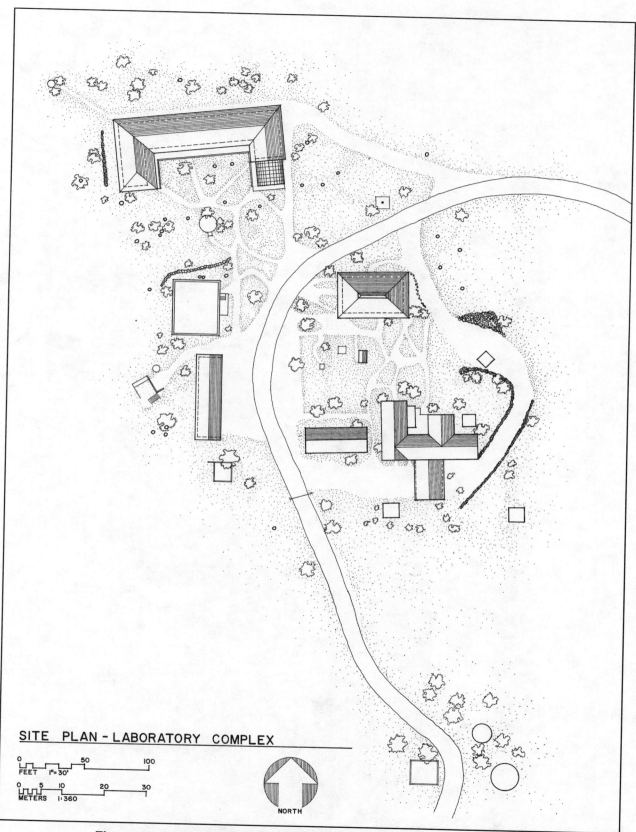

SITE PLAN - LABORATORY COMPLEX

0   50   100
FEET   1"=30'

0   5   10   20   30
METERS   1:360

NORTH

Figure 33. Site plan of the Desert Botanical Laboratory (HABS n.d.).

133

CHAPTER 5

Archaeological Sites and Survey Coverage in the Study Area

In this chapter, we summarize existing data on the nature and distribution of archaeological sites in the Paseo de las Iglesias study area and discuss the extent of previous archaeological survey coverage. We also consider in brief the archaeological potential of unsurveyed portions of the study area and identify locations of particular concern, including the presumed locations of historical-period sites known only from documentary references. We also comment on the kinds of archaeological work that will be necessary in the Paseo de las Iglesias APE before the start of construction or earthmoving.

The chapter begins with a discussion of the range of sites found in the study area, then provides detailed descriptions of 11 major sites (9 prehistoric, 2 historical-period). Basic information on the other sites in the study area is provided in Table 3, and descriptions of these sites appear in the appendix.

Previously Recorded Sites

We reviewed the archaeological site files of ASM in Tucson for the locations of archaeological sites previously recorded in the study area. This review included both the paper files kept at ASM—site cards, USGS quadrangle maps with hand-plotted site locations, and project reports—and AZSITE, the recently established on-line database for ASM archaeological site information. We transferred by hand the site plots on the ASM quadrangle maps to our own copies of the same maps. We also obtained from ASM copies of the electronic AZSITE files of digitized site locations and survey coverage, which we overlaid on digital raster graphic (DRG) images of the corresponding USGS maps. A comparison of the hand-plotted and digitized site locations showed few discrepancies, but we noted numerous discrepancies between the site plots on either set of maps and the site plots on individual site cards and in project reports. We prepared a map of the locations of previously recorded archaeological sites within or adjacent to the study area based on a combination of information from the ASM quadrangle maps, the ASM site cards, the digitized AZSITE maps, and project reports. Whenever possible, we relied on the latest available report on a site for information on site location and size. It is worth emphasizing that the locations and sizes of many sites on our map varied significantly from their depictions on the ASM maps and site cards. This is especially true for site designations that have expanded recently to encompass what were originally considered discrete sites, but sometimes the ASM site plots are simply inaccurate.

Table 3 lists the sites previously recorded in the study area and provides basic information about site temporality, function, and size. A total of 90 sites has been recorded in the study area. Of these, 38 sites date exclusively to the prehistoric period, 17 date exclusively to the historical period, and 35 have both prehistoric and historical-period components. Many sites have been characterized by their recorders as protohistoric in association. Because this characterization is often based solely on the presence of Papago wares, which may date to any part of the historical period as we define it, we count these sites as

135

ASM Site No.[a]	Site Name	Site Area[b]	...nces	NRHP Status
AA:16:3	West Branch site	398.99 acres (161.4	...l et al. 1996; Huntington 1986; ...e 1995	
AA:16:6[c]				
AA:16:7		10.38 acres (4.20 h		
AA:16:8		14.13 acres (5.71 h		
AA:16:9		16.86 acres (6.82 h	987	
AA:16:10	Mission San Xavier del Bac	3.77 acres (1.52 ha	1972, 1980; Cheek 1974; Ciolek-Torrello ...1976; Fontana 1996, 1997; Fontana et al. ...Huett & Vrettos 1998; Olsen 1974; ...on 1963	National Historic Landmark
AA:16:14[c]				
AA:16:15		65.86 acres (26.65		
AA:16:25[c]				
AA:16:26	St. Mary's Hospital site	65.89 acres (26.65	999; Ferg 1979; Hartmann & Hartmann ...acobs 1979; Jones 2000b; Miksicek 1979	
AA:16:28		0.03 acres (0.01 ha		
AA:16:33		2.33 acres (0.94 ha		
AA:16:35		< 0.01 acres (< 0.0	970; Huett & Vrettos 1998	
AA:16:36[c]				
AA:16:44	Salida del Sol site	20.30 acres (8.21 h	1997; Dart 1982; Euler 1987	
AA:16:45[c]				
AA:16:46[c]				
AA:16:47		39.68 acres (16.05	& Hewitt 1980; Kaldahl 2000	
AA:16:48[c]				
AA:16:49	Dakota Wash site	14.53 acres (5.88 h	urt 1978b; Craig 1988; Stephen & Hewitt	
AA:16:51	Desert Laboratory Tumamoc Hill site	901.73 acres (364.9	79; Fish et al. 1986; Hartmann & ...nn 1979; Huston 1986; Jones 2000b; ...1972, 1979; Masse 1979; McLean & ...1979; Wilcox 1979; Wilcox & Larson ...Vilcox et al. 1979	National Historic Landmark (Desert Laboratory)
AA:16:53[c]				
AA:16:54[c]				
AA:16:56		2.36 acres (0.95 ha		
AA:16:58	Burruel site	5.93 acres (2.40 ha	1997	
AA:16:60	Buckelew Gulch site	6.60 acres (2.67 ha	& Hewitt 1980	
AA:16:61		1.89 acres (0.76 ha	& Hewitt 1980; Williams 1982	

ASM Site No.[a]	Site Name	Site Area[b]	References[c]	NRHP Status
AA:16:62		6.55 acres (2.65 ha)	Hewitt 1980	
AA:16:67		0.62 acres (0.25 ha)		
AA:16:68	Herreras site	24.34 acres (9.85 ha)[3]		
AA:16:86		0.26 acres (0.10 ha)		
AA:16:313		0.02 acres (0.01 ha)		
AA:16:319		0.78 acres (0.31 ha)		
AA:16:320		< 0.01 acres (< 0.004		
AA:16:386		5.56 acres (2.25 ha)	t al. 1995	
AA:16:387		0.52 acres (0.21 ha)	t al. 1995	
AA:16:395		5.78 acres (2.34 ha)	95b	
AA:16:405		19.95 acres (8.07 ha)		
AA:16:411		0.60 acres (0.24 ha)	7; Wallace 1997	
AA:16:432		3.02 acres (1.22 ha)	ht & Wright 1999	
BB:13:2		6.27 acres (2.53 ha)		
BB:13:3	Martínez Hill Ruin	48.83 acres (19.76 h	7; Gabel 1931; Ravesloot, ed. 1987; 29	
BB:13:6	Clearwater site, Mission San Agustín, Tucson Pressed Brick Company	133.73 acres (54.11	001; CDA 2001; Deaver & Albright hl 1997; A. Diehl & M. Diehl 1996; & A. Diehl 1996; Doelle 1997; Dutt son & Doelle 1987a; Freeman et al. d & Doelle 1978; Mabry & Thiel ley et al. 1953; Thiel 1995b, 1995d, 8c; Williams 1986a, 1986b, 1989	determined eligible for NRHP
BB:13:7		0.45 acres (0.18 ha)		
BB:13:8		~1 acre (~0.04 ha)	t al. 1995	
BB:13:14	San Xavier Bridge site	22.89 acres (9.26 ha	; Doyel 1979; Fish & Gillespie 1987; ann 1999; Huckell 1993; Ravesloot, Ravesloot & Whittlesey 1987; 87, 1988	
BB:13:15	Valencia site	97.49 acres (39.45 h	t 1978b; Deaver & Ciolek-Torrello elle 1985; Doelle & Wallace 1984; Doelle 1986; Huckell 1993; Mayro ne 1995; Swartz 1995a; Mabry 1998	NRHP
BB:13:17	Julian Wash site	223.10 acres (90.28	t 1978; Dutt 2000a; Ezzo & y 1996; Heidke 1995; Mabry 1990, artz 1997a, 1997b; Wallace 1995; t al. 1997; Whittlesey 1999	determined eligible for NRHP
BB:13:19		3.87 acres (1.56 ha)	t 1978b; Courtwright & Wright 1999	
BB:13:20		23.95 acres (9.69 ha	t 1978b	
BB:13:21		2.89 acres (1.17 ha)	t 1978b	

Historical Period	Historical Function	References	NRHP Status
Early Statehood to present	hospital	Lindeman 1997; Stevens 1997	
protohistoric/historical, undetermined	undetermined, irrigation	Betancourt 1978b; Mabry 1990	
Territorial	townsite	Betancourt 1978b; Courtwright & Wright 1999; Hill & Garcia 1999	determined eligible for NRHP
Territorial	industrial	Wilson 1975	NRHP
protohistoric/ historical	undetermined	Betancourt 1978b	
		Betancourt 1978b; Bradley 1980; Huckell 1993; Mabry 1998	NRHP
undetermined to present	residential	Betancourt 1978b	
Territorial, Early Statehood	irrigation	Betancourt 1978b	
protohistoric/ historical	undetermined	Betancourt 1978b	
		Betancourt 1978b	
		Betancourt 1978b	
protohistoric/historical, Territorial	entertainment, undetermined	Betancourt 1978b	
protohistoric/ historical	undetermined	Betancourt 1978b	
protohistoric/ historical, Statehood	irrigation	Betancourt 1978b	
		Betancourt 1978b; Swartz 1997	
		Betancourt 1978b	
undetermined	irrigation	Betancourt 1978b	
		Betancourt 1978b	
protohistoric/historical	undetermined	Betancourt 1978b	
		Betancourt 1978b	
		Betancourt 1978b	
vity Territorial	residential	Betancourt 1978b	
		Betancourt 1978b; Courtwright & Wright 1999	
		Betancourt 1978b	
		Betancourt 1978b	

ASM Site No.[a]	Site Name	Site Area[b]	es	NRHP Status
BB:13:109	Tucson Farms Company Crosscut	0.12 acres (0.05 ha)	t 1978b	
BB:13:111	James Lee's Pioneer Mill	15.30 acres (6.19 ha	t 1978b	
BB:13:121	Timmerman site			
BB:13:129	Wrong Township Site 1	7.23 acres (2.92 ha)		
BB:13:135		6.08 acres (2.46 ha)		
BB:13:136		1.30 acres (0.52 ha)	95a	
BB:13:142		0.10 acres (0.04 ha)		
BB:13:143		0.21 acres (0.08 ha)		
BB:13:145		0.07 acres (0.03 ha)		
BB:13:154		0.39 acres (0.16 ha)	3	NRHP
BB:13:222		13.69 acres (5.54 ha		
BB:13:223		0.59 acres (0.24 ha)	993	
BB:13:323	Espinosa site	1.77 acres (0.71 ha)	90; Slawson et al. 1987	
BB:13:384		19.77 acres (8.00 ha		
BB:13:402		17.08 acres (6.91 ha	90	
BB:13:426		0.51 acres (0.20 ha)	3	
BB:13:479[c]				
BB:13:481	Acequia Madre Tercia, Acequia Madre Primera	0.08 acres (0.03 ha)	6; Thiel 1995a, 1998d	
BB:13:536		1.09 acres (0.44 ha)	Swartz 1998	
BB:13:539		2.87 acres (1.16 ha)	97	
BB:13:630		1.95 acres (0.78 ha)	ann 1999	
BB:13:646	Grabe Brick Company	3.04 acres (1.23 ha)		

[a] All site numbers preceded by "AZ." Site numbers in boldface indica
[b] Site areas are calculated from our digital plots and may differ signif
[c] Site subsumed under another site number; see the appendix.

historical-period in date. In Table 3, the historical-period component of such sites is listed as proto-historic/historical, unless other, more narrowly diagnostic artifacts are present.

The period names used for the prehistoric sites in Table 3 and the appendix generally reflect the names used by the recorders or excavators of a given site, with occasional minor changes to show a site's connection to our discussion of prehistoric culture history in Chapter 3. The period names used for historical-period sites are also those commonly used by archaeologists, but in the many cases the site recorders did not assign period names, we did. The historical periods we distinguish are Spanish Colonial (1539–1821), Mexican (1821–1854), Territorial (1854–1912), Early Statehood (1912–1945), and post–World War II (1945–present).

As the function columns in Table 3 suggest, and as is more specifically evident in the individual site descriptions in the appendix, the variety of prehistoric and historical-period sites in the study area is considerable. Among the prehistoric sites, nine large habitation sites stand out, in terms of size and complexity and in terms of the amount of research carried out at them. These sites are described in detail below. Among the historical-period sites, the two sites that define the Paseo de las Iglesias study area, San Agustín del Tucson and San Xavier del Bac, are the largest and most important sites, although neither has been subject to the degree of archaeological work seen at any of the major prehistoric sites. Both mission sites are described below, with an emphasis on historical context and degree of preservation.

Major Prehistoric Sites

West Branch Site (AZ AA:16:3)

The West Branch site is a large Hohokam village located along the West Branch of the Santa Cruz River, about midway along the Paseo de las Iglesias. The site is situated on a Pleistocene gravel terrace approximately 0.5 km from the current channel of the West Branch. Portions of what is now referred to as the West Branch site were originally recorded as several discrete sites with their own ASM registration numbers, including AZ AA:16:14, 18, 19, 20, 21, 25, 45, 46, and 48. These sites are now generally acknowledged as representing a single community that consisted of a large, central village and a series of smaller, satellite settlements and limited-activity loci (Huntington 1986:21). Data collected during excavation suggest that the large, "village" portion of the site comprised several semiautonomous "precincts," each consisting of five to seven households and their facilities. A ball court, presumed to have been encompassed by the site, is argued to have served an integrative function linking the various precincts. This model of Formative period village organization is similar to that proposed by Flannery for Formative villages in Mesoamerica (Flannery 1976). Wilcox and his colleagues applied a similar model in their analysis of village structure at the large Hohokam site of Snaketown (Wilcox et al. 1981).

Excavations have been conducted at three discrete locations at the West Branch site. The Irvington Street locus, situated at the northeastern corner of the intersection of Irvington and Mission Roads, was extensively impacted by the construction of Mission Road and several nearby businesses. Excavations were conducted in an area covering 1,600 m^2 (Huntington 1986:23). The Wyoming Street locus is situated approximately 0.5 km south of the Irvington Street locus on a remnant Pleistocene terrace, below a preserved deposit of Holocene alluvium found between two washes draining the Tucson Mountains. This locus, bisected by Mission Road, covers approximately 4,000 m^2. The third investigated area, designated the SRI locus, is at the southwestern corner of the intersection of Mission and Irvington Roads, immediately south of the Irvington Street locus.

Although there are data that suggest the presence of an Archaic period component—several Archaic period projectile points and a single house excavated at the Wyoming Street locus—the main period of occupation at the West Branch site dates to the Rincon phase of the Sedentary period (A.D. 1000–1100).

At the Wyoming Street locus, 16 features were excavated that were assigned to the early Rincon phase, including seven habitation structures and one storage structure. The locus was apparently more intensively occupied during the middle Rincon phase, with 23 habitation structures, 2 storage structures, and 13 extramural features constituting the excavated sample (Huntington 1986:46). Similar results were obtained at the SRI locus, where a total of 22 pit structures were excavated, all but three of which dated to the middle Rincon phase—a single structure was assigned to the early Rincon phase, and two were chronologically ambiguous (Altschul et al. 1996).

A significant portion of the research at the West Branch site has focused on questions of ceramic production and exchange. It has been argued that many of the West Branch villagers specialized in the production of ceramic containers that were distributed across the Tucson Basin (Heidke 1995; Wallace 1995; Wallace and Heidke 1986). This hypothesis was investigated through an analysis of the nonplastic inclusions in the clay bodies, with the assumption that potters at the West Branch site controlled a nearby, readily identifiable source of sand temper. The results indicate that pottery produced at the West Branch site was traded widely in the Tucson Basin.

Tumamoc Hill Site (AZ AA:16:51)

Tumamoc Hill is the large, basalt prominence marking the eastern edge of the Tucson Mountains and the northwest corner of the Paseo de las Iglesias study area. The summit of the hill is relatively flat, covering an area 100 by 200 m, approximately 800 feet above the floodplain of the Santa Cruz River. In 1903, the hill became the home of the Carnegie Institution's Desert Botanical Laboratory, which preserved the surrounding flanks of the hill for the study of desert plant communities. Today, the facility is a National Historic Landmark and is owned and administered by the University of Arizona (see Chapter 4). In terms of prehistoric cultural remains, Tumamoc Hill is perhaps best known for the numerous rock walls, terraces, and rooms encircling its summit, originally recorded as AZ AA:16:6. Dating to the Classic period, these features are typical of what have come to be known as *trincheras* sites; similar features have been recorded at numerous similar locations in southern Arizona and northern Mexico. The linear rock walls that typify *trincheras* sites have been interpreted variously as reflecting agricultural activities, ceremonial activities, habitations, and fortifications (Fontana et al. 1959; Masse 1979; Wilcox 1979).

The existence of rock features on Tumamoc Hill has long been known (Larson 1972:95). In part because it is part of a protected area, relatively little archaeological research has been conducted at the site. In the early 1970s, the proposed construction of an observatory by the University of Arizona prompted a detailed survey and mapping project conducted by Stephen M. Larson of the Lunar and Planetary Laboratory (Larson 1972; Wilcox and Larson 1979). With the aid of high-resolution aerial photographs, more than 1,200 linear meters of walls were identified and mapped. Also identified were several rock circles on the flat summit of the hill (Larson 1972:97–99) and remnants of a system of trails on and around the hill (Hartmann and Hartmann 1979). Finally, numerous petroglyphs were identified on the hill slopes, with concentrations observed along the northwest and southeast sides. A single Tanque Verde Red-on-brown sherd was found during the mapping project, reinforcing the hypothesis that the *trincheras* features date to the Classic period.

In the mid-1980s, ASM archaeologists conducted excavations at Tumamoc Hill as a means of providing comparative information for work carried out at Los Morteros, another *trincheras* site, located in the northern portion of the Tucson Basin (Fish et al. 1986:564). During these investigations, a trench was cut perpendicular to one of the terrace walls on the eastern edge of the summit of the hill. These excavations revealed significantly greater time depth at the site than was previously believed to be present. Several Late Archaic period projectile points were recovered from within the trench and the general vicinity (Fish et al. 1986:565). The lower stratigraphic levels contained no evidence of the later Hohokam occupation, suggesting that the mixing apparent in the upper stratigraphic levels did not extend to the earlier occupational strata at the site. Maize recovered from these lower strata was radiocarbon dated using the tandem accelerator mass spectrometry (TAMS) technique, returning dates with range midpoints of 520 B.C., A.D. 320, and A.D. 620, providing further evidence of preceramic period maize cultivation (Fish et al. 1986:569).

In 2000, an archaeological survey of state trust lands west of Tumamoc Hill expanded the boundaries of site AZ AA:16:51 to include the entire 860-acre parcel corresponding to the original Desert Botanical Laboratory (Jones 2000b). This site now subsumes all of AZ AA:16:6, previously limited to the *trincheras* features near the hill's summit, and a portion of the adjacent St. Mary's Hospital site (AZ AA:16:26). Our own calculation of the area of AZ AA:16:51, based on the boundaries specified by Jones, is somewhat larger than his figure: about 902 acres.

St. Mary's Hospital Site (AZ AA:16:26)

The St. Mary's Hospital site is a large Hohokam village located just north of the northern toe of Tumamoc Hill, on either side of a small wash draining the western slopes of the hill, approximately 1.6 km west of the current channel of the Santa Cruz River (Jacobs 1979:120). The site lies in a heavily developed area and has suffered both from considerable pothunting activity and from construction projects, including the construction of St. Mary's Hospital and Anklam Road. Although the site has been known for decades—Byron Cummings excavated portions of the site between 1920 and 1930—the site was not formally recorded until 1961.

In spite of its large size, the site has received little formal archaeological attention and virtually no study of subsurface deposits since Cummings's investigations in the 1920s and 1930s. During the winter of 1974–1975, members of the Arizona Archaeological and Historical Society organized an extensive surface reconnaissance of the site (Jacobs 1979). The project had three goals: first, to determine the size and boundaries of the site; second, to assess the temporal components represented by the site; and third, to identify and document intrasite variability as reflected in artifact and feature distribution (Jacobs 1979:120). Through an examination of both aerial photographs and surface indicators, the boundaries of the site were placed at West St. Mary's Road on the north, West Anklam Road on the south, North Silverbell on the east, and approximately St. Mary's Wash to the west. An analysis of temporally diagnostic ceramic artifacts observed on the surface indicated occupation from the Pioneer through the Sedentary periods. Relative ceramic frequencies suggest that the main occupation at the site was during the Rillito and Rincon phases; the presence of a small number of polychrome sherds suggested a Classic period component as well. The pattern of surface artifacts and features, primarily trash mounds, suggested internal differentiation, although the data preclude an accurate assessment of the nature of this differentiation.

We consider AZ AA:16:36, originally recorded as a separate site, to be part of the St. Mary's site, because it falls in the northeast corner of the latter. This area as originally recorded included basically the same range of ceramic types as the larger site, plus Jeddito Black-on-yellow, suggesting a Tucson phase component.

Dakota Wash Site (AZ AA:16:49)

The Dakota Wash site is a large, multicomponent Hohokam village situated on an alluvial fan immediately west of the West Branch of the Santa Cruz River, approximately 0.5 km south of the West Branch site. Initial survey data suggested that the site was occupied from the Pioneer through the Classic periods of the Hohokam cultural sequence. The site was first recorded by ASM archaeologists during the survey carried out for the proposed Santa Cruz Riverpark (Betancourt 1978b). The site was revisited in 1980 by archaeologists from Pima Community College during the Midvale Park survey (Stephen and Hewitt

1980). During this survey, two cremation burials found eroding out of the banks of Dakota Wash were excavated. This work was followed by limited testing in 1983, also by Pima Community College archaeologists, in a 20-m-wide corridor along Dakota Wash. Mechanical and hand excavations showed that subsurface cultural deposits at the site were largely intact and confirmed earlier assessments that the occupation dated from the Pioneer through the early Classic periods (Craig 1988:4).

A program of bank stabilization along Dakota Wash by the Pima County Department of Transportation in 1984 prompted another round of archaeological testing and data recovery. During this work, a 4,500-m^2 area was mechanically stripped, and several backhoe trenches and test pits were excavated. Eighteen pit houses, 31 cremation burials, and a small ball court were identified (Craig 1988:5). Contrary to expectations, these excavations revealed little subsurface evidence of a Sedentary or Classic period occupation. All of the excavated pit houses dated to either the Pioneer or the Colonial period. A cursory examination of ceramics from the surface of the site revealed moderate numbers of Classic period Tanque Verde Red-on-brown sherds, with Sedentary period materials virtually absent. These data were explained as reflecting an occupational hiatus at the site during the Sedentary period (Craig 1988). The apparent hiatus led investigators to consider the possibility that the Dakota Wash site represented part of a larger community with shifting foci of occupation. Subsequent work at the various loci of the West Branch site provided data in support of this hypothesis, indicating that during the Sedentary period, settlement shifted northward from the Dakota Wash site to center on the West Branch site 0.5 km to the north (Doelle and Huntington 1986:21). Together, these two sites are now generally referred to as the West Branch Community.

In May 1988, the Institute for American Research (now Desert Archaeology) returned to the Dakota Wash site for archaeological testing on a 10-acre parcel owned by the Estes Company (Craig 1988). Approximately 1,000 linear meters of backhoe trenches were excavated, exposing 115 subsurface features that included 75 pit houses, 23 extramural pits, 6 roasting pits, 4 burials, and 3 discrete trash mounds. Extrapolating from these data, it was estimated that up to 700 pit houses could be present in the tested portion of the site. Based on an analysis of the surface ceramics, most of the architectural features appeared to date to the Colonial period.

Martínez Hill Ruin (AZ BB:13:3)

Martínez Hill Ruin is located on the southeastern flank of Martínez Hill, approximately 0.8 km east of the Santa Cruz River. The site consists of a collection of noncontiguous room blocks dating to the Tanque Verde and Tucson phases of the Classic period. It was originally recorded in the 1920s by students from the University of Arizona under the direction of Byron Cummings. A second site, AZ BB:13:2, occupying the summit of Martínez Hill, is a Classic period *trincheras* site and is probably associated with occupation of AZ BB:13:3. Together, the two sites are sometimes referred to as the Martínez Hill site complex.

Excavations at AZ BB:13:3 were conducted intermittently in 1929 and 1930 under the direction of Cummings. This work is largely unpublished, but the excavations did lead to a University of Arizona master's thesis by Norman Gabel (1931). Although the site was occupied throughout the Classic period (Ravesloot 1987c:16), the excavations reported by Gabel were restricted to the Tucson phase component. This component is represented by seven adobe-walled room blocks, courtyards, and a platform mound with adobe rooms on top. The various structures are spread out over a quarter-mile-square area, all surrounded by a massive adobe wall (Gabel 1931:10). Twenty-four rooms were excavated in three of the seven Tucson phase room blocks, two of which were completely excavated (Gabel 1931:11). These excavations yielded a variety of both local and intrusive ceramic types, including Tanque Verde Red-on-brown, Tucson Polychrome, Gila Polychrome, Pinedale Polychrome, and White Mountain Red Ware, as well as corrugated red wares. Because the excavations focused on the readily visible architectural features, little is known about the distribution of nonarchitectural and other extramural features at the site. An exception is three inhumation burials recovered from wall fall in one of the room blocks. Spicer (1929) suggested that these burials represent a post–A.D. 1300 use of the site, perhaps reflecting a Sobaipuri or O'odham component.

Flooding by the Santa Cruz River appears to have played a significant role in the occupational history of Martínez Hill Ruin. Gabel noted that most of the excavated rooms were filled with flood debris and that flowing water had obscured many architectural features (Gabel 1931:17). In his field notes, Cummings commented on the depth of features buried below the alluvium, with similar water-washed sediments observed above and below the various occupational components. It is likely that periodic flooding played a significant role in the shifting location of settlement that characterizes the Martínez Hill complex and the nearby San Xavier Bridge site (AZ BB:13:14).

Clearwater Site (AZ BB:13:6)

As a means of distinguishing the prehistoric occupation from the later historical-period components, the prehistoric deposits at the Mission San Agustín site have been named the Clearwater site (Freeman et al. 1996:6). As with the later historical-period remains, the prehistoric component has been the subject of sporadic investigation over the last several decades (Doelle 1997:xiii). During their assessment of cultural remains at AZ BB:13:6 in advance of work along Mission Road, Desert Archaeology, then the Institute for American Research, identified 41 features, including 15 pit houses, that were dated to the Archaic period (Elson and Doelle 1987a). Radiocarbon dates of maize kernels obtained from pit house contexts returned dates between 765 and 358 B.C., providing further evidence of the cultivation of maize in the late preceramic periods (Freeman et al. 1996:6). Additional pit houses and extramural features were found by Desert Archaeology during testing and data recovery in 1995 and 1996 along Spruce Street south of Congress Street (Diehl 1997).

In August 2001, Desert Archaeology completed yet another data recovery project within the defined boundaries of the Clearwater site as part of ongoing research associated with the Río Nuevo project. At the time that this was written, documentation of these operations was limited to the official Río Nuevo Web site (CDA 2001). This phase of the investigation exposed portions of the foundation of the compound wall of the mission as well as several Early Agricultural period houses and pits approximately 2 feet (0.6 m) below the foundation of the mission. In all, 30 Early Agricultural period houses were identified, and portions of 20 were sampled. Based on the relative depths of the structures, two discrete Early Agricultural period occupations have been proposed. There is further evidence that a flood episode destroyed a significant portion of the later occupation. In addition to the Early Agricultural period remains, the prehistoric sample included a Formative period Hohokam canal crossing the site from the southeast to northwest (CDA 2001). With the exception of the canal, little evidence of a Hohokam occupation was observed at the Clearwater site.

San Xavier Bridge Site (AZ BB:13:14)

The San Xavier Bridge site is located immediately west of the current channel of the Santa Cruz River across from Martínez Hill (Ravesloot 1987c:15). The site is situated in the floodplain and has been heavily impacted by agricultural activities, arroyo cutting, and meanderings of the channel of the Santa Cruz River—an unknown portion of the site has undoubtedly been eroded away by the river. The site was first recorded by William Wasley in 1955, when an urn cremation was found eroding out of the bank of the river (Ravesloot 1987c:11). An examination of surface artifacts carried out in conjunction with the removal of the cremation burial suggested the existence of Rincon and Tanque Verde phase components in addition to later historical-period Tohono O'odham and Anglo occupations. Given its proximity to the complex of sites at Martínez Hill, it is likely that the cultural deposits at the San Xavier Bridge and Martínez Hill locations represent a single, disperse community whose primary occupational loci shifted through time.

In addition to the initial investigations conducted by Wasley, much of what we know about the settlement history of the San Xavier Bridge site came from two data recovery operations conducted for ADOT. In 1979, ASM archaeologists conducted salvage operations in preparation for stabilization along the eroding bank of the river (Doyel 1979:4). Excavation was limited to those features eroding out of the riverbank and included several inhumation burials, rock-filled pits, and a single architectural feature that, based on two temporally diagnostic reconstructible vessels recovered from the floor, dated to the Tanque Verde phase (Doyel 1979:9). Many of the features were deeply buried: the floor of the architectural feature was approximately 2 m below the modern ground surface. An absence of architectural stone and the relatively small postholes associated with the feature suggested that it was likely a *ramada* or another limited-use structure (Doyel 1979:9). Ceramic data from three excavated inhumation burials indicated that they dated to the Rincon and Tanque Verde phases (A.D. 900–1300). The absence of more-formal architectural features led Doyel to suggest that this area of the site served a more specialized function, perhaps related to mortuary activities (Doyel 1979:4).

The second of the two ADOT-sponsored projects was more extensive. These excavations were carried out in advance of construction activities on the San Xavier Bridge and the Interstate 19 off-ramp, which were damaged during extensive flooding of the Santa Cruz River in October 1983 (Ravesloot 1987c). Subsurface testing and feature excavations were carried out in an area measuring approximately 400 by 100 m along the west bank of the current river channel, centered on San Xavier Road (Ravesloot 1987a:Figure 2.2). A total of 113 features was documented within the project ROW. The feature inventory included 5 architectural features, 13 cremation burials, 17 inhumation burials, and a variety of extramural pits, hearths, and trash deposits. Also identified were two canal segments that were attributed to the historical-period José María Martínez land grant (Ravesloot 1987b:162).

Although considerable time depth is reflected at the San Xavier Bridge, with archaeological remains dating from Late Archaic to post-Classic times, the Tanque Verde phase occupation seems to have been the most substantial and has yielded the most data (Ravesloot 1987a:149). This phase is underrepresented at Martínez Hill, suggesting that the main locus of habitation at the larger community shifted over time. Unfortunately, few architectural features were excavated at the San Xavier Bridge site, and their formal properties are atypical of other Tanque Verde phase houses. Structures at the San Xavier Bridge site are subrectangular houses-in-pits that generally lack formal entryways, plastered floors, and floor assemblages. Based on these characteristics, the structures are thought to have functioned as field houses rather than habitation structures (Ravesloot 1987b:155). The predominant identifiable decorated ceramics at the San Xavier Bridge site are Tanque Verde phase ceramics (37 percent), further reinforcing the notion of an intense Tanque Verde phase occupation. The post–Tanque Verde phase occupation of the San Xavier Bridge site is referred to as post-Classic rather than protohistoric, because the features and artifacts stratigraphically overlying the Tanque Verde materials did not demonstrate a strong association with Sobaipuri or other protohistoric manifestations. Architectural features were distinct from Sobaipuri houses, and no Whetstone plain ware was recovered (Ravesloot and Whittlesey 1987:91).

Valencia Site (AZ BB:13:15)

The Valencia site is a large multicomponent site containing occupational components from the Paleoindian through the Formative periods. The site is located in the western Tucson Basin east of the current channel of the Santa Cruz River and extends over the two lower terraces. The site has been categorized as one of 19 "primary villages" within the Tucson Basin (Doelle and Wallace 1984). These villages, characterized by their large size, their often significant temporal depth, and the presence of "public" features such as ball courts, are assumed to have played an integrative role for a series of smaller, satellite villages and hamlets.

Prehistoric settlement at the site is believed to have been concentrated in three separate loci that have received different levels of archaeological scrutiny. Archaeological testing at Locus 1, situated on the older, upper terrace, identified a Sedentary period component represented by 12 pit houses, dated by the associated ceramics to the middle portion of the Rincon phase, and several extramural features (Huckell 1993:82:Table 3.1). Locus 2 is the largest, and apparently the earliest, of the three loci. Located on the younger, lower terrace, Locus 2 has been estimated to contain from 80 to 100 pit houses—subsurface testing in the area identified up to 38 houses (Huckell 1993:67). Ceramic and architectural data from Locus 2 indicated a substantial occupation dating to the period referred to as the Early Formative (Deaver and Ciolek-Torrello 1995) or, alternatively, the Early Ceramic period (Huckell 1993, 1995). This remains the largest single Early Formative period site in the Tucson Basin. Locus 3, separated from Locus 1 by a small tributary stream of the Santa Cruz River, has been ceramically dated to the middle Rincon phase. Like Locus 1, Locus 3 is situated on the older, upper terrace.

In 1982, Desert Archaeology, then the Institute for American Research, conducted data recovery operations for the City of Tucson along Calle Santa Cruz (Doelle 1985). This project was conducted for the City of Tucson in advance of the construction of Calle Santa Cruz between Valencia and Drexel Roads along the east bank of the Santa Cruz River. This represented a narrow corridor through the western portion of the site. Although spatially limited in their sample, the excavations along Calle Santa Cruz provided important additional information on the spatial organization of the settlement. The excavated sample included 21 pit houses dating from the Rillito phase through the late Rincon phase and 3 pit houses assigned to the Archaic period (Doelle 1985:35). In addition to the habitation structures, 53 extramural features were identified in the project ROW. Although representing only a small sample of the total site, the investigated features appeared to cluster by relative age, although the authors cautioned that it was unlikely that the sample represented the complete temporal range present at the site (Doelle 1985: 36).

The Institute for American Research continued its study of the Valencia site in the summer of 1986 with funding from the City of Tucson and the Arizona State Historic Preservation Office. Major goals of this project were to define the southern boundary of the site, until then placed arbitrarily at Valencia Road, and to obtain additional data on its occupational history and its structure (Elson and Doelle 1986:1). The project entailed both intensive surface artifact collection and the excavation of a limited number of backhoe tenches spaced at 50-m intervals. A total of 26 subsurface features was identified during trenching, of which 20 were interpreted as pit houses. These investigations also determined that the southern boundary of the site as indicated in the NRHP listing was accurate, and although prehistoric features were identified beyond the boundaries, no change to the boundaries was recommended (Elson and Doelle 1986:97). Finally, an analysis of temporally diagnostic ceramics from several trash mounds revealed that, despite an apparent shift in the intensity of occupation over time, the overall site structure remained stable, with most of the mounds containing the full range of ceramic types identified at the site (Elson and Doelle 1986:102).

In 1997, Desert Archaeology returned to the Valencia site for additional data recovery in response to the proposed expansion of the Desert Vista campus of Pima Community College. The project focused on the Early Ceramic/Early Formative period occupation of the site. The report on these excavations is still forthcoming, but in a postexcavation tour of the site, the archaeologists in charge of the investigation noted that several pit houses—some arranged around a central plaza area—tentatively dated to the Tortolita phase.

Julian Wash Site (AZ BB:13:17)

The Julian Wash site is a large, multicomponent Hohokam village that was occupied from the Pioneer through the Sedentary periods. The site is located east of the Santa Cruz River near the junction of Interstates 10 and 19, on the floodplain and first terrace of the river. The site is bisected by Julian Wash, which was channelized and redirected in the 1970s. The site has been heavily impacted by highway construction and other development projects. Because of the modern disturbances, there is some disagreement concerning the size of the site. Ezzo and Whittlesey (1996) placed the maximum dimensions of the site at 1,400 m northeast-southwest by 500 m northwest-southeast. Mabry (1996) estimated the site at 400 m east-west by 535 m north-south.

As with many of the larger prehistoric settlements in the Tucson Basin, the Julian Wash site has a long history of archaeological investigations of varying intensity. The site was first recorded in 1958 with the designation AZ BB:13:17, which was assigned to the southern portion of the site near 12th Avenue and 40th Street (Swartz 1997:3). The site was revisited in the mid-1970s, resulting in the assignment of a second number, AZ BB:13:69, to the site. Following this survey, the site was described as a Hohokam village with a dense artifact scatter, several possible trash mounds, and a single cremation (Swartz 1997:3). At about this same time, archaeologists from Pima Community College visited the site as part of a cultural resource assessment for the proposed Santa Cruz Riverpark. As part of his report on the cultural resources within the proposed Santa Cruz Riverpark district prepared for the City of Tucson, Betancourt (1978b:84) noted the substantial modern disturbances to the site, suggesting that the likelihood of buried cultural deposits at the site was low and that additional preservation efforts at the site were not warranted. A third site number, AZ BB:13:98, was assigned to the northwest portion of the site at this time. This area was described as a sherd and lithic scatter eroding from the alluvial fan onto the floodplain. All of the temporally diagnostic ceramic sherds found in this area of the site were assigned to the Rincon phase (Betancourt 1978b:87). By 1988, the three discrete segments of the site described above were combined under the AZ BB:13:17 designation (Swartz 1997:4). Additional survey and surface collections were carried out by Desert Archaeology, then the Institute for American Research, at a small (100-m²) area along Interstate 19, north of the 40th Street overpass. Temporally diagnostic sherds recovered during this project were dated to the Snaketown through late Rincon phases (Mabry 1996:4).

Subsurface investigations at Julian Wash began in 1990 with testing by Desert Archaeology for the planned Tucson Water Plant 1 Replacement Reservoir (Mabry 1990), located approximately 400 m west of the 12th Avenue Interstate 19 overpass. Testing was limited to surface collection and the excavation of five backhoe trenches that exposed two historical-period canals, a possible secondary cremation, and two shallow features of indeterminate function. Both early and middle Rincon phase sherds were recovered but were interpreted as being secondarily deposited by erosional processes from the alluvial terrace east of the site (Mabry 1990:4). With the exception of the area around the possible cremation, clearance was recommended. In 1992, Desert Archaeology returned to the area for further testing within the ROW of a proposed access road to the water plant (Castalia 1992). Two backhoe trenches excavated along the length of the ROW revealed eight subsurface cultural features: four possible pit houses, three extramural pits, and an extramural trash deposit (Mabry 1996:4). Subsequent data recovery operations identified 36 features, of which 33—including 5 pit houses, 6 extramural roasting features, 1 extramural hearth, and several postholes interpreted as having held the posts of a *ramada*—were excavated. Ceramic, radiocarbon, and archaeomagnetic data all indicated that the cultural remains in this area of the Julian Wash site dated to the transitional period between the middle and late portions of the Rincon phase (Mabry 1996:4–5).

In 1996, two more extensive data recovery projects were carried out at the Julian Wash site. SRI, under contract with the Los Angeles District of the U.S. Army Corps of Engineers and the Pima County Department of Transportation and Flood Control District, conducted data recovery along a narrow corridor through the site along the channelized portion of Julian Wash between 12th Avenue and the current

147

channel of the Santa Cruz River (Whittlesey 1999). Despite disturbances to the site related to the channelization of the wash, significant subsurface cultural remains were identified. The investigations conducted by SRI included two phases of testing, in which the extent of the subsurface cultural remains within the project ROW were identified, and one phase of data recovery. Data recovery efforts focused on the investigation of architectural features, with 42 houses excavated. This represents an 82 percent sample of the architectural features that were identified. In addition to the architectural features, SRI excavated 66 extramural features, representing approximately half of the extramural features that were identified. The extramural features included one primary inhumation and five secondary cremation burials.

Although limited to a narrow corridor through the site, the excavated sample provided important data on village structure and the occupational history of the site. The segment of the site investigated by SRI was dominated by structures occupied during the Cañada del Oro and Rillito phases of the Colonial period. A relatively small number of early Rincon phase structures also were excavated. The excavation of broad areal exposures also allowed for the investigation of domestic organization and village structure. The arrangement of architectural features adhered to the typical "Hohokam" pattern, with multiple structures arranged around exterior courtyards. SRI archaeologists noted that extramural spaces appeared to have been maintained through time, suggesting that a system of land tenure was in place during the Colonial period.

In February 1996, Desert Archaeology began a program of archaeological testing and data recovery for ADOT on a segment of the Julian Wash site north of Interstate 19 and west of 12th Avenue (Swartz 1997). The testing phase of the project involved both surface artifact collection and the excavation of a series of backhoe trenches placed at 20-m intervals. Analysis of the temporally diagnostic ceramics identified sherds dating from the Pioneer through Sedentary periods, with the largest number (30 percent) identified as middle Rincon Red-on-brown (Wallace et al. 1997:Table 3.1). Among the buff wares identified, Colonial period sherds were slightly more abundant than those assigned to the Sedentary period. A small number of historical-period Papago red ware sherds were also identified.

Subsurface investigations during testing discovered a total of 271 features grouped into 10 loci. These features included 94 pit structures, 37 possible structures, 105 extramural features, and an assortment of cremations, trash deposits, and other features (Swartz 1997:1). Based largely on an analysis of the collected ceramic sherds, Desert Archaeology archaeologists reconstructed an occupational history of the site characterized by shifting settlement location and density. Several structures identified near the edge of the first terrace above the Santa Cruz River floodplain were assigned to the Cienega phase. This assessment was based on the absence of ceramics, the relative small size of the features, and their depth below the modern ground surface (Swartz 1997:62–63). Pioneer period remains dominated in Locus J, located in the southwestern portion of the tested area. The remaining loci of the site contained Colonial and Sedentary period ceramics, representing the primary occupation of the site.

Major Historical-Period Sites

Mission San Agustín del Tucson (AZ BB:13:6)

As discussed by Doelle (1997), the ASM designation AZ BB:13:6 refers to a complex of prehistoric and historical-period sites documented over the last half century in a large area immediately northeast of Sentinel Peak. Consistent with Doelle's discussion, AZ BB:13:6 is considered here to be bounded on the north by Congress Street, on the east by the Santa Cruz River, on the west by the base of Sentinel Peak, and on the south by a former City of Tucson landfill located just south of Mission Lane. The use of this area in prehistoric times, beginning at least as early as the Early Agricultural (or Late Archaic) period, is discussed above in the description of the Clearwater site (also AZ BB:13:6). The current discussion is

148

limited to the historical-period component of the site, which centers on the Spanish Colonial *visita* (dependent mission settlement) of San Agustín del Tucson, first erected in the late eighteenth century and abandoned by 1870. Also discussed here are other aspects of the historical-period component, notably the remains of the Tucson Pressed Brick Company, which began operation on the former grounds of the mission as early as 1895.

The history of archaeological investigation at AZ BB:13:6 is discussed in detail by Hard and Doelle (1978) and Elson and Doelle (1987a). The first of these reports was prepared in anticipation of a municipal sewer line project that would affect the eastern portion of the site. The second was prompted by a proposed realignment of Mission Road, which passes along the site's western limit. The current discussion relies heavily on both reports, supplemented by the discussions of Doelle (1997), Freeman et al. (1996), Thiel (1995b, 1995d, 1997), and Williams (1986a).

Early documentary references to the small Sobaipuri settlement of San Cosme del Tucson, which probably fell at least partly within AZ BB:13:6, are summarized in Chapter 4. The same chapter discusses the place of the mission and its vicinity in the wider context of historical-period occupation of the Paseo de las Iglesias study area. At least as early as 1701, when the first resident priest was installed at San Xavier del Bac, San Cosme del Tucson was considered a *visita* of that *misión cabecera,* a settlement that would have received regular visits by the mission priest but without a resident priest of its own. As it happened, the priest at San Xavier del Bac abandoned his post within a year and was not replaced until 1732. There is no record that San Cosme del Tucson was visited by a Jesuit or any other European during the intervening 30 years. After 1732 and until the 1750s, San Xavier del Bac had a resident priest only intermittently, and San Cosme del Tucson was probably paid only occasional visits by Jesuits. Certainly, nothing was built at the site by or on behalf of the Jesuits during this period.

Following the Pima revolt of 1751, San Xavier del Bac and the other missions along the Santa Cruz River were effectively abandoned for a few years. When a Jesuit was once again installed at San Xavier in 1756, another Jesuit, Bernhard Middendorff, became the first to attempt permanent residence north of the mission. Middendorff apparently settled at San Agustín del Oiaur, several miles downstream from San Cosme del Tucson, on the east bank of the river. San Agustín del Oiaur was a settlement comparable in size to San Xavier, making it a logical choice over San Cosme, but Middendorff lasted only four months before being driven out by unfriendly Sobaipuri. His description of how the people at San Agustín del Oiaur lived—"scattered in the brush and hills" (Dobyns 1976:18)—undoubtedly also applies to the settlement pattern at San Cosme del Tucson at that time.

In 1762, the population of San Cosme del Tucson increased by at least 250 (perhaps double the original population) when a group of Sobaipuri from the San Pedro River valley were resettled there by Spanish order in an attempt to strengthen the line of defense against the Apache at the Santa Cruz River. The resettlement was accompanied by a change in the Spanish name for the settlement to San José del Tucson, but there was still no significant physical Spanish presence at the site. After the Jesuits were expelled from the Spanish colonies in 1767, Franciscans assumed responsibility for the missions along the Santa Cruz. In 1768, Francisco Garcés, the first Franciscan to reside at San Xavier del Bac, reported that the residents of Tucson had built him a tiny brush hut and that the settlement as a whole lacked even mud-walled structures (Hard and Doelle 1978:8). The first more-enduring structures at the site came a few years later, when the resettled Sobaipuri threatened to abandon the area for the Gila River because of Apache attacks. Fearing that the departure of the friendly Sobaipuri would badly compromise the Spanish presence at Tucson, Juan Bautista de Anza, commander of the presidio at Tubac, persuaded them to stay by promising to help build fortifications and a church. A large earthen breastwork, a mission residence, and a church, soon dedicated by Garcés to San Agustín, were completed by the residents of Tucson by 1773. The precise locations of the three structures are unknown, but all were built within or adjacent to the settlement at the foot of Sentinel Peak.

In 1775, the presidio at Tubac was moved to a new location immediately across the Santa Cruz from San Agustín del Tucson. The new presidio was also named San Agustín del Tucson and became the center of the small Hispanic community that eventually gave rise to modern Tucson. San Agustín del Tucson on the west bank of the Santa Cruz remained a predominantly Native American settlement, with no further architectural developments until the very end of the eighteenth century. Sometime between 1797 and 1810, the church dedicated by Garcés in 1772 was replaced by a new, more elaborate church, as well as a large, two-story mission residence (or *convento*) and other buildings. This complex of buildings served as a religious and administrative center for the *visita,* where Native American converts learned and practiced the Catholic faith, Hispanic agricultural methods, and associated crafts. By the end of the eighteenth century, the settlement consisted primarily of Tohono O'odham enticed by the Franciscans out of the western desert to replace a badly thinned Sobaipuri population. The original Sobaipuri of Tucson, along with those resettled there in 1762, had largely disappeared through disease, deliberate abandonment of the mission life, and absorption into the Tohono O'odham population. According to documents cited by Elson and Doelle (1987a:12), the O'odham lived primarily to the south of the mission, in either adobe houses or brush huts with earthen roofs. There are no known traces of O'odham houses dating to this period in the area. Also resident near the O'odham village were the *apaches mansos,* Apaches whom the Spanish military had convinced, beginning in 1793, to stop their attacks on O'odham and Spanish villages and to settle near the Tucson presidio in exchange for rations. These people settled just downstream from the presidio on the east side of the river and apparently had little to do with the O'odham community. No trace of their settlement is known to survive (Dobyns 1976:98–102).

Following Mexican independence from Spain in 1821, the *visita* at San Agustín suffered the same instability and decline suffered by all of the Santa Cruz missions, as Native American populations continued to dwindle and financial and practical support from the former center of New Spain became increasingly unreliable. Mission lands were secularized by the Republic of Mexico in 1828, which led to the departure of the last resident Franciscan from San Xavier del Bac in 1831. By 1843, still 11 years before Tucson would become a part of the United States, the mission complex was largely abandoned and its buildings had begun to deteriorate.

The nature of the mission complex at San Agustín is known through scattered documentary references from the eighteenth and nineteenth centuries, early photographs of the ruins of the mission, and the fairly limited amount of archaeological work at the site. A plan of the buildings and other features in the complex is included on an 1862 map of irrigated fields in the vicinity of the mission (Figure 34; see Williams [1986a:122] for an interpretation of the plan). Features on the map include the *convento,* the chapel, a granary, the mission gardens surrounded by a wall, and several smaller buildings. A number of acequias, forming parts of the larger irrigation system documented by the map, pass immediately adjacent to (or even through) some of the mission buildings, but it is not clear if these irrigation features were a part of the functioning mission complex. Recent, as-yet-unpublished excavations by Desert Archaeology have identified, among other features, portions of the stone foundation of a wall that once surrounded the main compound of the complex (Bawaya 2001; CDA 2001). This feature is not depicted on the 1862 map, although it was undoubtedly in evidence at the time. A sketch map of the site in 1937, included in Historic American Building Survey (HABS) documentation filed in 1939, indicated that the surviving portions of the wall were of adobe.

The church at San Agustín collapsed by 1858, but the *convento,* despite complete neglect, remained standing well into the twentieth century (see CDA [2001] for a series of historical photographs documenting the deterioration of the *convento*). By the end of the nineteenth century, its roof had collapsed entirely and the walls of its upper story were crumbling, but the *convento* remained a prominent feature on the landscape (Figure 35). Through the first half of the twentieth century, the mission grounds and the *convento* were subject to impacts from a variety of activities, including plowing for agriculture, salvage of building materials for nearby construction projects, and pothunting. One of the largest impacts began around 1900 with the establishment of the Tucson Pressed Brick Company on the former mission grounds. By 1936, the date of the earliest aerial photographs of the area, the brick-making operation had

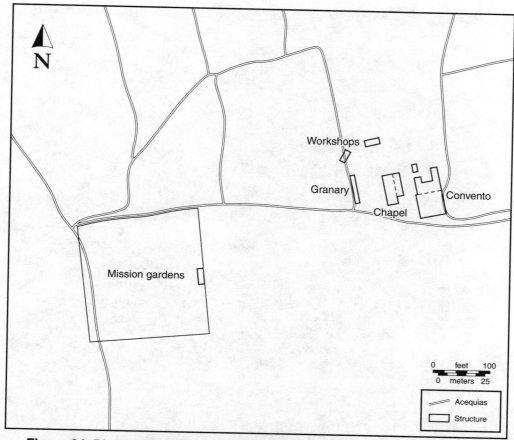

Figure 34. Plan of features at Mission San Agustín del Tucson (based on Fergusson 1862). See Williams (1986a) for identifications of buildings.

begun mining clay just east of the *convento,* and by the 1950s, it had disturbed a large portion of the former mission grounds. Nonetheless, there was apparently a deliberate effort to avoid the visible ruins of the mission, especially the *convento.* Also by the 1950s, a City of Tucson landfill had significantly impacted the area immediately south of the mission, the location of the associated Native American village. Then, in 1956, another City of Tucson landfill project knocked down the last standing remnant of the *convento* and stripped away all but the western third of the site (Elson and Doelle 1987a:16–17).

Clay mining by the Tucson Pressed Brick Company led to the first significant archaeological discoveries at San Agustín. In 1949, the company began stripping clay from an area just north of the mission complex and struck a large concentration of human burials, now interpreted as a protohistoric or early historical-period Pima (i.e., Sobaipuri) cemetery. Some 50 burials were destroyed before work was stopped; five burials were subsequently recovered by Terah Smiley, a staff member of the University of Arizona Laboratory of Tree-Ring Research (Smiley et al. 1953). Numerous burials were excavated the same year at a second location, to the south of the brickyard excavations, by Bertram Kraus, a physical anthropologist at the University of Arizona. The new location was designated Burial Area A and is now thought to have lain within the walls of the mission compound. The work by Kraus, who relied on student help and was interested primarily in obtaining classroom specimens, is not well documented. Later the same year, a University of Arizona graduate student named Wesley Bliss, using volunteer help, excavated in Burial Area B, immediately adjacent to Kraus's excavations, and also at Burial Area C, immediately west of the mission church. Bliss recovered 44 burials from Area B and 14 from Area C. Bliss drew

151

Figure 35. Ruins of Mission San Agustín del Tucson, view to the west from the east bank of the Santa Cruz River, ca. 1900 (photograph courtesy of the Arizona Historical Society, Tucson, Accession No. B113636). Note unpaved Mission Lane at far left.

a map of his excavations, but the skeletal and other materials went largely unstudied. In 1950, Smiley returned to excavate in Burial Areas A and B and recovered numerous additional burials (Hard and Doelle 1978:15).

Based on the limited documentation of the work in 1949–1950, it is likely that Burial Areas A and B represented a cemetery used during the occupation of the mission. Unlike the tightly flexed skeletons found by Smiley in the brickyard excavations, the burials in Areas A and B were fully extended, generally with the head to the east, and were accompanied by medallions, crucifixes, and other artifacts suggesting participation in the Catholic tradition. The skeletons and artifacts have gone unstudied (Hard and Doelle 1978:18–19). The last work by Smiley also discovered a layer with prehistoric materials dating to the San Pedro phase of what is now known as the Early Agricultural period. This discovery anticipated the recent work by Desert Archaeology for the Río Nuevo project, which has documented a substantial Early Agricultural component at AZ BB:13:6.

The demise of the last remnants of the *convento* in 1956 also prompted limited archaeological excavations at the site. William Wasley, an ASM archaeologist, learned of new earthmoving at the site after it had already begun, but he was able to spend several weekends working with a crew of volunteers and prison laborers to record several architectural features, including the foundations of the church, *convento*, and compound wall. He made a map of the features and took a few pages of notes. The artifacts he recovered, as well as several excavated skeletons, were never analyzed. His map, which does not include a fixed datum, is difficult to tie to extant features at the site, but it provides accurate relative locations. The notes provide several valuable details on construction methods and materials (Hard and Doelle 1978: 19–20).

Subsequent archaeological work at San Agustín has included backhoe trenching in the mid-1960s in the vicinity of the mission granary (never published; see Elson and Doelle [1987a:15]), further backhoe trenching in the 1970s along the largely disturbed east side of the site (Hard and Doelle 1978), limited hand excavations in an area just south of the church and *convento* in 1986 (Williams 1986b), further limited hand excavations within the mission gardens (Williams 1989), backhoe trenching immediately southeast of the presumed limit of the mission compound (Deaver and Albright 1992), and a variety of other, more recent surveys and test excavations carried out near the mission by Desert Archaeology (Diehl 1997; A. Diehl and M. Diehl 1996; M. Diehl and A. Diehl 1996; Freeman et al. 1996; Mabry and Thiel 1995; Thiel 1995b, 1995d, 1997, 1998c).

All of this work has served to confirm that, although much of the mission complex has been destroyed, small but significant parts remain intact, especially in the western portion of the site. Also, other significant historical-period archaeological features survive in the large area now encompassed by the AZ BB:13:6 site designation, including segments of an extensive irrigation system built at least as early as the Mexican period and used well into the U.S. period, a house foundation and other features associated with use of the area by Chinese gardeners, and the remains of the Tucson Pressed Brick Company, the business responsible for much of the destruction of the mission complex. These additional historical-period components of AZ BB:13:6 are discussed briefly below. As already noted, Desert Archaeology has recently undertaken study of the mission complex itself as a part of the City of Tucson's Río Nuevo project. Excavations completed in February 2001 showed that most of the area within the former mission compound was completely destroyed by the clay mining and landfill activities of the late 1950s. The investigators did find intact portions of the foundations of the mission compound's west wall and the granary; part of a stone-lined canal probably representing the tail race for Warner's Mill, built just west of the mission in the latter half of the nineteenth century; a former well filled with trash derived from use of the area by Chinese farmers in the late nineteenth or early twentieth century; and a variety of prehistoric features (Bawaya 2001; CDA 2001). The results of this project will be published in the near future.

The irrigation features documented at AZ BB:13:6 include several segments of the historical-period canal system represented on the 1862 map noted above, as well as several segments of probable prehistoric canals. Consistent with ASM guidelines, these scattered linear features have been assigned their own site designation, AZ BB:13:481, even though all fall within the limits of AZ BB:13:6. A discussion of the history of irrigation in the Paseo de las Iglesias study area is provided in Chapter 4.

The Tucson Pressed Brick Company, operating from a plant just west of the Santa Cruz River and just south of Congress Street, was incorporated in 1908 with Quintus Monier as owner and president. Monier was a French immigrant who had designed and built the cathedral in Santa Fe, New Mexico, prior to settling in Tucson. In 1897, he began construction of the new San Agustín Cathedral, also of his design, on Stone Avenue east of the river, then went on to design and build several other notable buildings in Tucson. He was operating a brickyard at the site of the Tucson Pressed Brick Company perhaps as early as 1895, the year he arrived in Tucson. Thus, in all likelihood, the bricks of the new San Agustín Cathedral were made from clay mined in the immediate vicinity of the old Mission San Agustín. Following Monier's death in 1923, ownership of the Tucson Pressed Brick Company changed hands several times before the company moved to a new location southeast of downtown in 1963. In 1995, as part of archaeological mitigation for a proposed storm drain project extending from Sentinel Peak to the Santa Cruz River, Desert Archaeology excavated a series of features related to the operation of the company, including part of the base of a large circular downdraft kiln (A. Diehl and M. Diehl 1996). Although the scope of the work was limited by the narrow project ROW, it is the only substantial archaeological investigation of an industrial site in the Tucson area. A brief discussion of brick making and other industries in the Paseo de las Iglesias study area is provided in Chapter 4.

As part of the same storm drain project, Desert Archaeology excavated the remains of a late-nineteenth-century Chinese gardener's household near the northeastern base of Sentinel Peak, in the northwestern corner of AZ BB:13:6 (Thiel 1997). As discussed in Chapter 4 of the current report, the coming of the SPRR to Tucson in 1880 resulted in the formation of a small Chinese enclave near downtown, as Chinese railroad workers opted to settle down and pursue other economic opportunities. Some of the Tucson Chinese established gardens on the west side of the river and became a significant presence there, growing produce for sale in the wider community and competing for irrigation water with Mexican-Americans farming in the same area. The excavations by Desert Archaeology uncovered a house compound probably first built by a Mexican-American family around 1880 but subsequently occupied by Chinese, either a family or one or more individuals. The excavated features included the stone foundation of the house compound, postholes, and trash pits containing a high percentage of Chinese-associated artifacts, such as distinctive Chinese ceramic types (e.g., soy sauce jars). In its recent excavations at the Mission San Agustín site, Desert Archaeology recorded a large pit feature containing similarly distinctive Chinese artifacts, also associated with the occupation of the area by Chinese gardeners in the late nineteenth or early twentieth century (Bawaya 2001; CDA 2001).

Another important component of AZ BB:13:6 is associated with the nineteenth-century Mexican occupation of the area. This component is poorly documented in archaeological terms, but Mexicans were undoubtedly the dominant presence in the immediate vicinity of the site until perhaps the last decade of the nineteenth century. The abundance of Hispanic names on the 1862 map of irrigated fields in the vicinity of Mission San Agustín (see Figure 8) indicates that the Gadsden Purchase was slow to affect Mexican land use and ownership in this area. Among the few recorded archaeological remains probably dating to the Mexican occupation are the house compound noted above that was later reused by Chinese people and the floor of a small structure, possibly an outbuilding associated with a larger residence, recorded just west of the mission compound by Elson and Doelle (1987a:43–46).

Mission San Xavier del Bac (AZ AA:16:10)

In contrast with AZ BB:13:6, the large, multicomponent site centered on San Agustín del Tucson, AZ AA:16:10 corresponds more or less neatly with the original extent of San Xavier del Bac as it was constructed in the late eighteenth century. This is partly because the immediate vicinity of San Xavier has not been subject to the same degree of archaeological investigation as the vicinity of San Agustín, which is attributable to the largely intact condition of the original architectural complex and to the continuing status of San Xavier del Bac as an active Catholic parish. San Xavier is still the focus of religious life for the San Xavier District of the Tohono O'odham Nation, and it has also become, especially after being designated a National Historic Landmark in 1963, a focus of tourism in the Tucson area. The range of prehistoric and historical-period components recorded at San Agustín may well characterize the area surrounding San Xavier—archaeological sites recorded nearby certainly suggest this—but it is unlikely that the intensive subsurface archaeology carried out on parts of AZ BB:13:6 will be carried out soon at intact San Xavier.

If anything, San Xavier is potentially a much richer archaeological site than San Agustín, especially in terms of the evidence of early Spanish–Native American interaction it may preserve. San Xavier was arguably the most important locus of that interaction along the Santa Cruz River, outlasting both Guevavi and Soamca, the other two *misiones cabeceras* founded along the Santa Cruz at the same time, and significantly older than Guevavi's replacement, Tumacácori. The discussion that follows summarizes the history of San Xavier del Bac, based especially on the work of Fontana (1996) but relying also on Bolton (1984), Cheek (1974), Dobyns (1976), Kessell (1970, 1976), Officer (1987), Spicer (1962), and Wagoner (1975). The focus is on the Spanish architectural presence at the site and the limited archaeological work that has been performed there.

Kino first visited the village of Bac (Piman *wahk*, "standing water") (Saxton et al. 1998:135), which he renamed San Xavier del Bac, in 1692. He came at the invitation of certain residents who had earlier visited him in Sonora and thus was well received. He preached briefly at Bac, encouraged everyone to take up the Christian life already adopted by their Pima cousins to the south, and baptized a few infants. By his report, San Xavier had 800 residents, all of whom were apparently ready to become Christians. He probably passed through San Xavier again in 1694 on his way to the Gila River and certainly stopped there in 1697, when he delivered cattle, sheep, goats, and mares to the village. Again, he was well received, and again, he performed baptisms. Later the same year, he returned to San Xavier to discover that the natives had already adopted a degree of Christianity, greeting his party with arches and crosses and supplying them with livestock and wheat bread. The residents, in anticipation of the resident priest Kino had promised them, had erected a small adobe building to house him, the first Spanish-prompted architecture at the site. Needless to say, no trace of this structure is known today.

Kino made several more visits to San Xavier in 1699 and 1700, each time more impressed by the apparent number of conversions there and the bounty of the Santa Cruz Valley. He was confident that the settlement could support a large mission and asked his superior if he could be transferred there himself from his mission at Dolores in Sonora. This never came to pass, but during one visit in 1700 Kino directed the residents of San Xavier in construction of the foundations for a church. This project apparently never got very far and is never mentioned again in the journals of Kino or his companions; the precise location of the foundations is unknown. Kino was able to assign a resident priest to San Xavier in 1701, the same year he assigned one to Guevavi, but the priest abandoned the settlement in 1702, either because of conflicts with the residents or because of illness. Kino made his last visit to San Xavier in 1702 but was never able to assign another priest to the settlement. He died in 1711, well before the first permanent mission was established along the Santa Cruz.

After Kino's last visit, San Xavier was visited sporadically over the next three decades by Jesuits based in Sonora, and some of its inhabitants remained at least nominally Christian. The next resident priest did not arrive until 1732, the same year priests were also installed at Guevavi and Soamca. The priest at Bac left after a year, and the next two decades were marked by a succession of failed attempts to make San Xavier the *misión cabecera* it was intended to be. For much of this period, it was essentially a *visita* of Guevavi, receiving occasional visits from the Guevavi priest and still lacking anything in the way of permanent mission architecture.

Things changed significantly at San Xavier following the Pima revolt of 1751. The revolt resulted in the complete elimination of "all signs of Spanish presence" (Fontana 1996:11) at San Xavier, but it also resulted in the establishment of the presidio at Tubac, which meant increased (albeit still limited) protection for the missions along the Santa Cruz. By 1756, San Xavier once again had a resident Jesuit, Alonso Espinosa, who, despite a series of conflicts with the people of San Xavier and repeated difficulties with Apaches, managed to stay nine years and build the first real church. Fontana (1996:14) described Espinosa's church as "a substantial, flat-roofed, hall-shaped structure of sun-dried adobe blocks," built with its long axis oriented north-south, on a spot just west of the extant church. The walls were a foot and a half thick and were laid directly on the ground without a stone foundation. The entrance was at the south end of the hall, just as the entrance of the extant church is on the south. A row of four columns ran down the center of the church, supporting a system of beams and rafters and a mud roof.

Espinosa left San Xavier in 1765 when he was withdrawn by his superiors because of his failing health. His replacement, José Neve, ministered at San Xavier and the *visita* of San Agustín del Tucson until July 1767, when the Jesuit order was expelled from the Spanish colonies. A year later, Francisco Hermenegildo Garcés, the first Franciscan to be assigned to San Xavier, took up residence. He remained the resident priest of San Xavier until around 1779, although much of his tenure was marked by his absence during the many journeys for which he is now well known, including the famous California expeditions of Juan Bautista de Anza, *comandante* of the Tubac presidio. Despite his frequent absences and continuing problems with Apache, San Xavier saw a period of relative stability and success, thanks in part to the efforts of Anza and the presidio. Toward the end of Garcés's tenure, another Franciscan, Juan Bautista de Velderrain, arrived at San Xavier to serve as his assistant. Velderrain eventually took Garcés's place as the head of the mission and supervised construction of a second, much more elaborate church, the one that stands at San Xavier today.

Construction of the church began around 1783 and ended around 1797. Velderrain died in 1790, but the project was already well along, and his successor, Juan Bautista Llorens, was able to concentrate on finishing the interior of the structure. Labor for the project, including for the elaborate interior decorations, was supplied almost entirely by the O'odham residents of San Xavier, trained and supervised by Spanish craftsmen. Built of fired brick and plaster, the church was, and is, a beautiful and impressive building (Figure 36). It is cruciform in plan, with a central nave measuring 99 feet long by 22 feet wide, and a 66-foot-wide transept formed by two small chapels (Figure 37). A shortage of funds in the last stages of construction kept the eastern of the two bell towers flanking the entrance to the church from being completed; it remains uncompleted today.

San Xavier enjoyed several more years of relative stability following completion of the church. Llorens concentrated on expanding the mission population by encouraging Tohono O'odham from the regions north and west of the mission to settle at San Xavier and San Agustín. This was in response to the drastic decline in the original Sobaipuri population at the mission. After Mexican independence in 1821, the Franciscans at San Xavier saw the financial and military support they had previously relied on wane rapidly, culminating in the expulsion of all Spanish-born people—and hence many Franciscans—from Mexico in 1827. San Xavier was briefly abandoned by its Spanish-born friars in 1828, only to come under Franciscan care once again later that year when the Mexican government reconsidered its actions. But the Franciscan era was drawing to a close as the northern frontier of Mexico became increasingly unstable and subject to more-frequent and more-fierce Apache raiding. The last resident Franciscan at San Xavier left in 1837.

The church at San Xavier was largely neglected following the departure of the Franciscans, and by the late 1840s, it was in serious decline. Despite official neglect, Tohono O'odham living at the mission continued to use it—or at least revere it—as a place of worship. Other parts of the mission complex that were in existence by this period were an 11-room *convento,* or living quarters, built with adobes from Espinosa's church and extending as a wing from the east side of the extant church; a mortuary chapel to the west of the extant church; and an atrium wall enclosing an area on the south side of these buildings.

Figure 36. Mission San Xavier del Bac, view to the northwest. Photograph by Leo Goldschmidt, 1887. Reproduced from Goldschmidt (1887) with the permission of the Arizona Historical Society, Tucson.

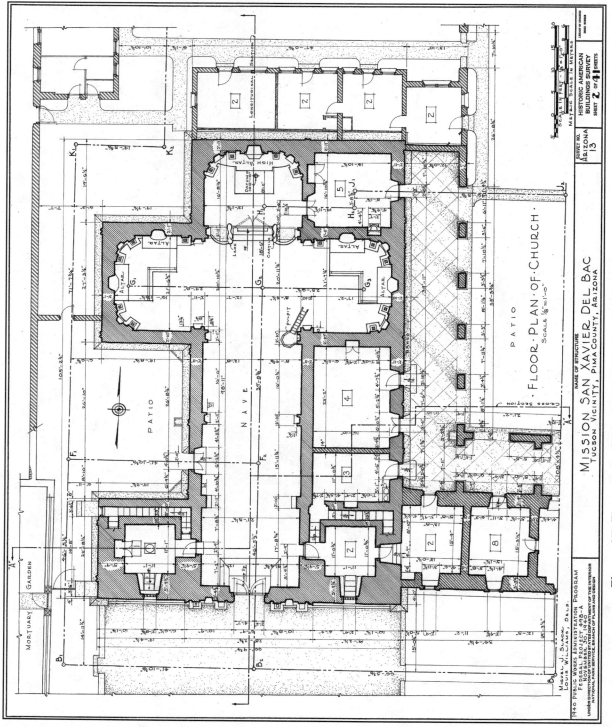

Figure 37. Floor plan of Mission San Xavier del Bac Church (HABS 1940).

It was not until 1858, four years after the Gadsden Purchase, that the Catholic Church once again became actively interested in San Xavier as a part of its presence in the region. In that year, the lands within the Gadsden Purchase became a part of the Diocese of Santa Fe under Bishop Jean Baptiste Lamy. A year earlier, in 1857, the U.S. Department of Indian Affairs had appointed the first Indian agent to the O'odham. These two events initiated a series of efforts by both the Catholic Church and the federal government to provide aid to the Tohono O'odham living at San Xavier and in the surrounding region, including intermittent attempts to restore the declining church. The most important step by the government in the latter half of the nineteenth century was the creation of the first Papago Indian Reservation by executive order in 1874. The reservation consisted of 69,200 acres surrounding the Mission San Xavier complex, which was recognized as integral to the lives of the Tohono O'odham living in the area. The Catholic presence at San Xavier in the same half century focused on schooling for O'odham children and—especially after a major earthquake destroyed parts of the complex in 1887—repairs to the church. At the end of the nineteenth century, new schoolrooms were added to the east side of the complex as a north-south wing; this wing is still in use today.

The first major changes at San Xavier in the twentieth century were a series of repairs and additions made to the mission complex by Henry Granjon, bishop of Tucson, in the period 1905–1908. Fontana (1996:49) credited Granjon with saving San Xavier from irreversible deterioration and promoting general recognition of its architectural and historical importance, a recognition that has increased steadily to today. There were two other events of importance in the early twentieth century. First, in 1910, the federal government granted title to the 14-acre parcel occupied by the mission to the Bureau of Catholic Missions, an unusual grant given that it was entirely surrounded by Indian reservation lands. The deed was eventually transferred to the Diocese of Tucson, which still owns the mission. Second, in 1913, the Franciscans returned to San Xavier as its clergy and caretakers. The Saint Barbara Province of the Order of Friars Minor, headquartered in Oakland, California, continues to administer the mission today (Fontana 1996:52).

In 1940, the architectural and historical significance of San Xavier del Bac was recognized at the federal level with the preparation of detailed HABS documentation, an effort sponsored by the Public Works Administration. This work included large-scale photographs and detailed plan and elevation drawings of the church and associated buildings (see Figure 37). In 1963, the mission was designated a National Historic Landmark. A series of minor renovations and improvements to the complex took place during the next decade and a half. Then, in 1978, a volunteer organization called the Patronato San Xavier was organized for the purpose of raising money for and coordinating restoration efforts. A significant accomplishment of the Patronato has been to gather an international team of conservators to diagnose and solve problems with the structure and ornamentation of the church. The conservators have also trained Tohono O'odham craftsmen in appropriate conservation techniques, an important step to ensure that the Tohono O'odham community plays an active role in the maintenance of the mission. As a result of this effort, the mission recently underwent extensive cleaning and restoration of its elaborately decorated interior (Fontana 1997).

San Xavier del Bac has been subject to surprisingly little archaeological work. Graduate students from the University of Arizona Department of Anthropology began excavations there in 1958, continuing casually until 1963 (Robinson 1963; see also Robinson 1976:135–136). Simultaneously, the same students carried out an ethnographic and technical study of the modern Tohono O'odham pottery tradition, which at that time still had a significant number of practitioners (Fontana et al. 1962). A primary purpose of the excavations was to establish a chronological sequence for historical-period Tohono O'odham pottery, but little in the way of relevant stratigraphy was found. The excavations did uncover a series of contiguous rooms initially interpreted as workshops associated with construction of the extant church. Based on largely unpublished records of excavations by Fontana in the 1970s, it is now evident that these rooms represent the church built by Alonso Espinosa in the period 1756–1765 (Cheek 1974: 179–183; Fontana 1996:14; see also Majewski and Ayres 1997:72).

Other than analyses of artifacts from Fontana's excavations in the 1970s (Barnes 1972, 1980; Cheek 1974; Olsen 1974), San Xavier del Bac has seen little archaeological study. The only other excavations within the immediate vicinity of the mission were carried out by Ciolek-Torrello and Brew (1976) for a proposed plaza construction just south of the church. This work consisted of a 30-m backhoe trench and a series of 2-by-2-m test units. The excavations uncovered a historical-period occupational surface, probably the former location of a large *ramada*, accompanied by artifacts primarily from the late nineteenth and early twentieth centuries. The area around the mission complex today is characterized by a typically dispersed Tohono O'odham settlement pattern, which has probably been the case since at least as early as the seventeenth century. This is strongly suggested by the results of archaeological survey in limited portions of the area, which shows a wide distribution of sites with historical-period Tohono O'odham components (AZ AA:16:7, 8, 9, 35, 386, and 395). Except for AZ AA:16:35, a single Tohono O'odham burial accompanied by a Hopi bowl dating to around 1700 (Ayres 1970), these sites have not been excavated and are known strictly from surface artifact scatters.

Designated Historic Sites and Districts in the Study Area

Considering the importance of the study area in the prehistory and history of the Tucson Basin, it is surprising that it contains only a small number of designated historic sites and districts. The seven sites and districts with official status are depicted in Figure 38 and listed and described in Table 4. In addition to these sites and districts with official status, three archaeological sites in the study area have been determined eligible for listing in the NRHP: AZ BB:13:6, the multicomponent site centered on the Mission San Agustín; AZ BB:13:17, the Julian Wash site; and AZ BB:13:56, the Los Reales townsite.

Archaeological Survey Coverage in the Study Area

Previous archaeological surveys have covered somewhat more than half of the Paseo de las Iglesias study area and perhaps 90 percent of the APE. We prepared a map of survey coverage based on the AZSITE file provided to us by ASM. The map included any survey having any portion of its coverage within the study area, but to simplify the depiction, we did not include small negative surveys that fell entirely within the bounds of a larger survey. Table 5 provides the report references corresponding to each survey and notes on the scope of coverage.

Of the 26 surveys represented in Table 5, by far the largest and most important was the earliest, that of Betancourt (Betancourt 1978a, 1978b), carried out as a part of planning for the City of Tucson's Santa Cruz Riverpark. The total coverage of the survey was 3,250 acres (1,316 ha), about half of which falls within the limits of the Paseo de las Iglesias study area. Betancourt recorded 31 of the 90 known archaeological sites in the study area and also performed basic background research on several important historical-period sites. His research into the history of water-control and irrigation features along the Santa Cruz later served as the partial basis of his dissertation (Betancourt 1990).

The next-largest block survey in the study area was that of Courtwright and Wright (1999), which covered 345 acres adjacent to Interstate 19 and about a mile north of Martínez Hill. The survey was prompted by an expansion of a large gravel quarry on both sides of the Santa Cruz River. Of the 345 acres covered in the survey, all but 6.9 acres were unsurveyable because of prior disturbance by quarrying.

With one exception, the rest of the surveys in the study area have been of relatively small parcels or of narrow, linear corridors. The exception is a survey carried out around 1980 in anticipation of construction for Midvale Park, a large housing development bounded on the north by Irvington Road, on the

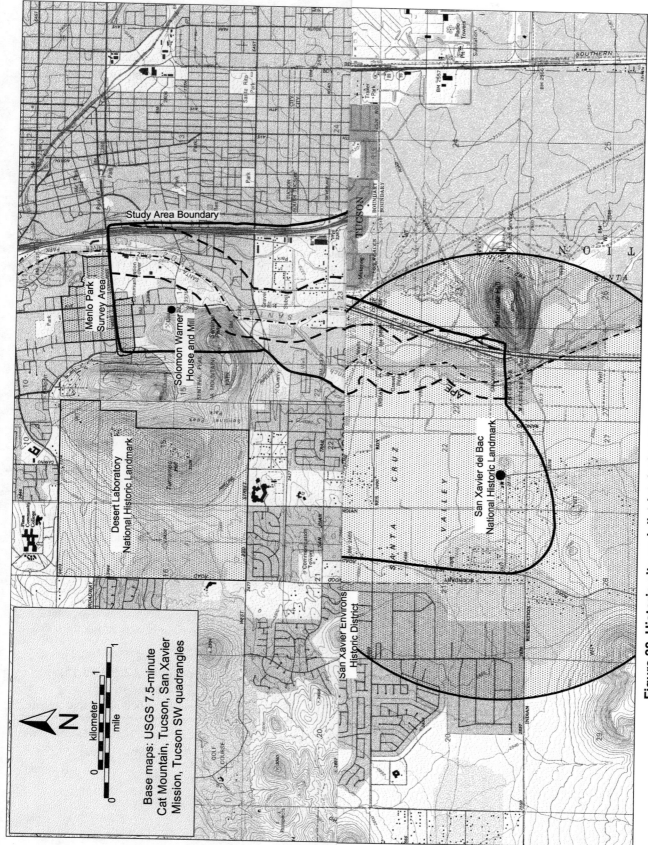

Figure 38. Historic site and district designations in the Paseo de las Iglesias study area.

Study Area Boundary

Menlo Park
Survey Area

Solomon Warner
House and Mill

Desert Laboratory
National Historic Landmark

San Xavier del Bac
National Historic Landmark

San Xavier Environs
Historic District

Base maps: USGS 7.5-minute
Cat Mountain, Tucson, San Xavier
Mission, Tucson SW quadrangles

kilometer

mile

N

Table 4. Designated Historic Sites and Districts in the Paseo de las Iglesias Study Area

Name	Type and Year of Designation	Comments
Desert Laboratory National Historic Landmark	NHL 1976 NRHP 1965 SRHP 1965	The NHL designation refers to the extant structures of the Desert Botanical Laboratory as originally built (three buildings, two reservoirs) and the original 860-acre tract of land. HABS documentation of the building complex was prepared in 1981. The University of Arizona currently owns the buildings and 340 acres; it leases the other 520 acres from the Arizona State Land Department.
Juan Bautista de Anza National Historic Trail	NHT 1990 NMT 1999	Both designations apply to a route from near Nogales, Arizona, to San Francisco, California, corresponding to the Anza expedition of 1775–1776 (see Chapter 4). In the Tucson area, the route is the same as the Santa Cruz River corridor, but no part of the trail has been recorded in the field. Six locations within Pima County were used by the expedition for overnight stays. The third such location was San Xavier del Bac, the only one within the Paseo de las Iglesias study area. The designation notes Mission San Agustín del Tucson and Presidio San Agustín del Tucson as two potential interpretive sites (NPS 2001).
Menlo Park Survey Area	NRHP 1992	This multiple-resource area is a neighborhood on Tucson's west side, at the northwest corner of the Paseo de las Iglesias study area. The area is not itself a historic district, but to date, six houses in it have been listed as NRHP individual properties. None of the six houses falls within the Paseo de las Iglesias study area.
San Xavier del Bac National Historic Landmark	NHL 1963	The NHL designation refers to the extant architecture of the mission complex. HABS documentation of the complex was prepared in 1940.
San Xavier Environs Historic District	PCHD 1972	The designation comprises an area extending 1.5 miles in all directions from Mission San Xavier del Bac. The purpose of the designation is to conserve the heritage value of the area around the mission by regulating housing density, lighting, screening, and building height.
Solomon Warner House and Mill	NRHP 1976 SRHP 1976	The NRHP designation refers to the extant Solomon Warner house, still used as a residence, the foundations of the mill, and an unspecified area encompassing them.
Valencia site (AZ BB:13:15 and AZ BB:13:74)	NRHP 1984	Our plot of this site includes the bounds of AZ BB:13:15, as currently understood, and the small, noncontiguous site, AZ BB:13:74, which has since been described as a separate site.

Key: HABS = Historic American Buildings Survey; NHL = National Historic Landmark; NHT = National Historic Trail; NMT = National Millennium Trail; NRHP = National Register of Historic Places individual property; PCHD = Pima County Historic District; SRHP = Arizona State Register of Historic Places individual property

Table 5. Archaeological Surveys in the Paseo de las Iglesias Study Area, by ASM Project Number

ASM Project No.	Reference	Comments
1979-38	Betancourt 1978b	for Santa Cruz Riverpark; 3,250 acres, about half within study area
1980-114		no report prepared
1982-5		no report prepared
1983-200	Dart 1984	clearance for repair of San Xavier Mission Road bridge
1985-184	Swidler 1985	survey of culverts along Interstate 19 from Interstate 19/ Interstate 10 interchange to Valencia Road
1987-140	Euler 1987	survey of 9 house lots, San Xavier District, Tohono O'odham Nation
1987-222	O'Brien et al. 1987	survey of fiber-optic route from California to Texas along Interstate 10 corridor
1989-192	Roth 1990	survey along Silverlake Road prior to road widening
1990-76	Mabry 1990	survey of TCE extraction well and treatment facility sites
1993-87	Goetze 1993	survey of intersection of Drexel and Midvale Park Roads
1993-213	Slawson 1993	survey of linear parks along Julian and Rodeo Washes
1995-4	Lenhart 1995	survey of 3 areas along Indian Agency Road
1995-324	Swartz 1995a	survey of proposed parking lot, south side of Irvington Road
1995-401	Stone 1995	survey of the Interstate 19/Valencia Road interchange
1996-315	Kwiatkowski 1996	survey of 2 bridge areas along Interstate 19
1996-423	Tompkins 1996	survey of 26 acres within the West Branch site (AZ AA:16:3)
1997-31	Eppley 1997	survey for Fire Station 18 near Drexel and Mission Roads
1998-36	Sliva 1998	1-acre linear survey along Silverlake Road between Mission Road and Interstate 10
1998-135	Thiel 1998	survey of the continuation of Brickyard Lane to Congress Street
1998-204	Huett and Vrettos 1998	14-acre survey of the San Xavier Mission plaza
1998-312	Diehl 1998	0.25-acre survey of the intersection of Drexel and Oaktree Roads
1999-208	Hill and Avann 1999	265-acre linear survey along Interstate 19 from Pima Mine Road to Valencia Road
1999-362	Hill and Garcia 1999	35-acre survey in 3 areas along Interstate 10 and Interstate 19
1999-450	Courtwright and Wright 1999	for expansion of materials pit; project area totaled 384 acres, of which 6.9 acres were surveyable
2000-412	Dutt 2000b	survey of 4 proposed well locations
2000-418	Tucker 2000	survey at northeast corner of Headley and Valencia Roads

south by Valencia Road, on the west by Mission Road, and on the east by the Santa Cruz River. Although a report on sites recorded in the survey is available (Stephen and Hewitt 1980), a report on the survey itself was apparently never prepared, and the project has never been filed with ASM. Lacking precise information on the limits of the survey, we do not include it in Table 5. If this survey covered the entire Midvale Park development, it would be second only to the Betancourt survey in areal coverage within the study area.

Unrecorded Historical-Period Features

In this section, we provide general comments on the range of as-yet-unrecorded historical-period features likely to exist in the study area. We also discuss documentary references to specific historical-period features in the study area that have not been recorded in the field.

Irrigation Features

Irrigation features, especially segments of canals, are the most commonly recorded historical-period features in the study area, and it is likely that numerous unrecorded irrigation features are still preserved within its limits. A sense of the original number and variety of such features can be had by looking at the early maps reproduced in Chapter 4, beginning with the 1862 Fergusson map of cultivated lands west of downtown Tucson (see Figure 8). The Fergusson map depicts three canals running south to north through a patchwork of agricultural parcels, each canal serving as a property boundary for multiple parcels. Portions of two of these canals, the Acequia Madre Primera and the Acequia Madre Tercia, were found during excavation and recorded as AZ BB:13:481 (see the site description in the appendix). Portions of the third canal, the Acequia Madre Segunda, also may be preserved in the study area. Just as important, any number of the smaller canals or laterals that undoubtedly served individual parcels also may be preserved in undisturbed areas. The fact that the three *acequias madres* all mark property boundaries suggests that the many other property boundaries on the map correspond to lateral alignments, which means that the map can potentially serve as a guide to discovering such features. The same may be said of the 1876 GLO map of the southern portion of the same area (see Figure 10), on which property lines probably also correspond with canal or lateral alignments.

South of the area covered by the Fergusson map, a similar patchwork of agricultural plots and irrigation canals may have characterized at least part of the study area during the 1860s and 1870s, as is suggested by research with pre-GLO land claims currently being carried out by Desert Archaeology as a part of the Río Nuevo project (Homer Thiel, personal communication 2001). However, the general impression is that this area was much less intensively used in the first two decades after the Gadsden Purchase than the area immediately adjacent to Sentinel Peak. When GLO claims began to be filed in the mid-1870s, virtually all of the area south of Sentinel Peak was apparently still up for grabs, and the parcels bought or claimed from the GLO were mostly 160-acre quarter sections, much larger than the average parcel depicted on the Fergusson map (see Chapter 4). This suggests that any earlier claims made in the area (either honored or ignored by the GLO) were of similar size, reflecting a much lower number of landholders in the area and less intensive use of the area for agriculture.

Nonetheless, the portion of the study area from Sentinel Peak south to San Xavier was eminently suitable for agriculture, and it is likely that irrigation features did exist there in the last quarter of the nineteenth century, especially before the entrenchment of the river that took place from about 1890

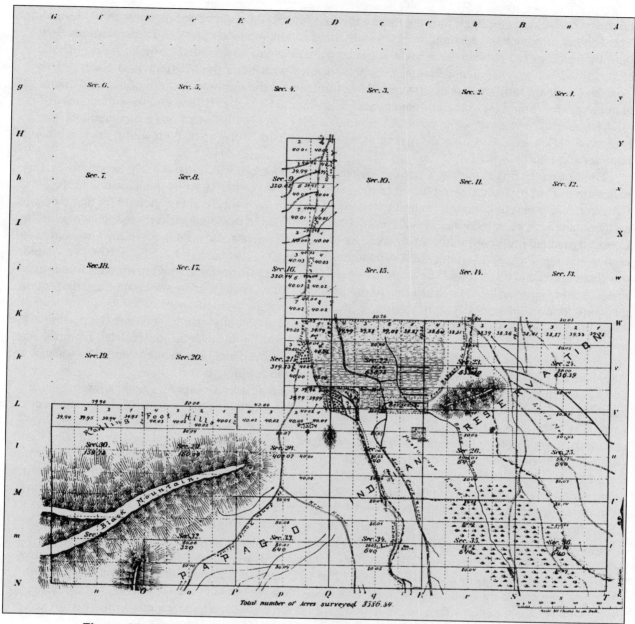

Figure 39. 1888 GLO survey plat of portion of Papago Indian Reservation within Township 15 South, Range 13 East.

onward (see Chapter 4). Actual evidence of such features in the last quarter of the century is limited largely to the portion of the area within the Papago Indian Reservation, which was established in 1874 (see Chapter 3). The 1888 GLO survey plat of Township 15 South, Range 13 East, which includes the northern portion of the reservation (Figure 39), shows a large cultivated area immediately northeast of Mission San Xavier, including a series of irrigation ditches extending from the east bank of the Spring Branch of the Santa Cruz (which later became the main branch of the river) and a ditch connecting the Spring Branch with the then-main branch (now called the West Branch). The same features are also visible on the 1891 survey plat of the Rancho de Martínez land claim (see Figure 9). This area became

165

the focus of Tohono O'odham farming during the first few decades after establishment of the reservation. The Tohono O'odham used irrigation extensively here and maintained canals and other features first built by Martínez but outside the bounds of the land claim eventually confirmed by his heirs (Effland et al. 1989:26–27). A segment of unlined canal associated with either the Martínez land claim or later Tohono O'odham farming was discovered in test trenching at the northwest corner of the land claim, about a quarter mile west of the current channel of the Santa Cruz, by Effland and his colleagues (1989: 60–61; the feature was not assigned an ASM number). It is highly likely that other such features are preserved in this area, as well as elsewhere along the west bank of the river, both within the reservation boundary and north of it.

The Tucson Farms Company Crosscut, discussed in Chapter 4, was a major early-twentieth-century irrigation project in the northern portion of the study area. Two of the 19 wells associated with the Crosscut, a segment of concrete conduit that once connected the wells, and the anchors for an associated earthen dam have been recorded as AZ BB:13:109. It is probable that other features associated with the Crosscut are also preserved in the study area. As noted in Chapter 4, the alignment of the Crosscut is still obvious on the Tucson 7.5-minute USGS quadrangle, extending due east of AZ BB:13:109. We visited this location recently and found the alignment to consist of a shallow ditch, overgrown with weeds and trees, running east from Santa Cruz Lane to the Interstate 10 ROW (a narrow street running adjacent on the south to the alignment has signs saying "26th Street," but some recent maps of the area still label this street Flowing Wells Crosscut Road). A close look at the Crosscut alignment, including the portion close to the river (to which we did not have access), may reveal additional wells or other related features. The area originally designated AZ BB:13:109 should also be surveyed and documented carefully, because the ASM site card and Betancourt's description (1978b) provide few details.

About 3 miles upstream from the Crosscut, the Tucson Irrigation Company owned a large tract of irrigated land that eventually became Midvale Farms, situated between the West Branch and the Santa Cruz. The 1920 map of these holdings (see Figure 25) shows a main canal, numerous laterals, and several wells, serving a total of about 1,300 acres. Much of this land was later developed as Midvale Park (Blanton and Cole 1957; HUD 1980), which has undoubtedly destroyed most of the irrigation features in the area, but some features may still be preserved near either river channel. The number and distribution of irrigation features depicted on the map is probably also a good indication of how many other features from the same era once existed in other parts of the study area.

By the early twentieth century, wells were a major source of irrigation water in the study area. The total number of wells dug there during the historical period is uncertain, but it was likely very high, and future archaeological surveys should be careful to record wells as archaeological features—even active wells, given that early wells may still be in use. The 1915 map of the lands of the Tucson Farms Company (see Figure 24) shows the locations of 17 wells within the limits of the study area, not including the 19 wells of the Crosscut. There were undoubtedly more wells on adjacent lands with other owners.

Other Features

Silver Lake, which once occupied roughly the center of the south half of Section 23, Township 14 South, Range 13 East (on both sides of the current channel of the Santa Cruz), was the site of a considerable amount of building during the period 1856–1890, including the dam that created the lake, at least two grist mills, a hotel and resort, and a variety of other structures. William S. Grant, builder of the second mill at the lake in 1860–1861, is known to have built a large adobe-and-timber warehouse, a blacksmith shop, at least one dwelling, and other structures near his mill (see Chapter 4). Although all of these structures were destroyed by fire in 1861, they may be represented by unrecorded archaeological features in the area. The same goes for the many later structures near the lake, particularly on its west and north sides, including the Silver Lake Hotel and Tucson's first 1-mile racetrack, which followed the current alignment of Cottonwood Lane (see Chapter 4). Betancourt (1978b) recorded two sites in this area, AZ BB:13:94 and AZ BB:13:111, both with features tentatively associated with Silver Lake businesses. These sites need to be revisited and re-recorded and the area around them intensively surveyed for other features. As in much of the study area, this task is complicated by recent impacts from development.

As discussed above in the description of the Mission San Xavier site (AZ AA:16:10), the current church at the site had two substantial predecessors. One, a large adobe structure completed in the 1760s under the direction of the Jesuit Alonso Espinosa, stood near the site of the current church and was partly incorporated into its construction. The other, a church started by Kino himself in 1700, presumably never rose higher than its foundations, and its precise location is unknown. Stoner (1937), based partly on the oral testimony of Tohono O'odham living at San Xavier in the late nineteenth century, hypothesized that Kino's church was in fact finished but that it was located on the floodplain of the Santa Cruz some 2 miles north of the current site. It is hard to say if his claim that the ruins of Kino's church survived into the nineteenth century should be taken seriously (Fontana [1996] did not even mention Stoner), but he cited enough evidence to suggest that some kind of large, old adobe structure once stood 2 miles north of the current church. This location falls just north of Valencia Road, just east of the reservation panhandle and the West Branch.

The early GLO survey plats of the study area, referred to above for the irrigation features they depict, also depict other kinds of features that may be preserved archaeologically in the study area. The 1871 plat of Township 15 South, Range 13 East (see Figure 15), depicts five individual houses in the area just east of the Papago Indian Reservation panhandle. At least one of these, located in the SW ¼ of Section 10, may correspond with a house foundation recorded as a part of AZ AA:16:61 (see the site description in the appendix); this site falls within the APE. Another house, just southeast of the first and just outside the APE, has never been recorded. The other three houses all fall close to the current west bank of the Santa Cruz, on the line between Sections 10 and 11. None of these houses has been recorded as an archaeological site; all three might have been destroyed by realignments of the channel of the Santa Cruz. Finally, a lime kiln is depicted in the NW ¼ of Section 10, on the boundary of the reservation panhandle. A large house foundation was recorded in this area as AZ AA:16:62, perhaps dating somewhat later than the plat, but no lime kiln was noted. This site falls within the APE along the West Branch.

The 1888 plat of the same township (see Figure 39), which depicts only the lands within the Papago Indian Reservation, is most notable for its depiction of a portion of a settlement labeled "Upper Reales," at the northeastern corner of the reservation panhandle. This settlement, represented by seven houses just within the reservation boundary, was known in its entirety as Los Reales and undoubtedly extended eastward from the reservation, as we discuss in the site descriptions for AZ AA:16:61 and AZ BB:13:56. The same plat also depicts two dense collections of houses within the study area, adjacent to and just northwest of Mission San Xavier, both of which are labeled "Papago Village." The southern of these villages undoubtedly corresponds to a series of historical-period Tohono O'odham sites recorded near the mission in the 1960s (AZ AA:16:7, 8, and 9), and both represent the kinds of settlements that may be represented archaeologically elsewhere within the reservation portion of the study area.

One feature on the 1891 plat of the Rancho de Martínez land claim (see Figure 9) deserves mention here. At the northern edge of the SE ¼ of the SW ¼ of Section 22, two small squares are labeled "Ruins." This is about a quarter mile east-northeast of Mission San Xavier. Effland et al. (1989) researched the history of land use in this area as part of their study of changes in the Santa Cruz floodplain north of the mission, but they were apparently unable to identify these features, and it is unclear whether the features are still visible in the field.

A final map depiction of historical-period features can be mentioned. Among the papers of the Allison family preserved at the AHS is an undated, hand-drawn sketch map of features in portions of Sections 34 and 35, Township 14 South, Range 13 East (Figure 40). The map probably dates to the last decade of the nineteenth century or the first decade of the twentieth, a period when the Allison brothers were busy buying land and developing irrigation works along the Santa Cruz (see Chapter 4). The

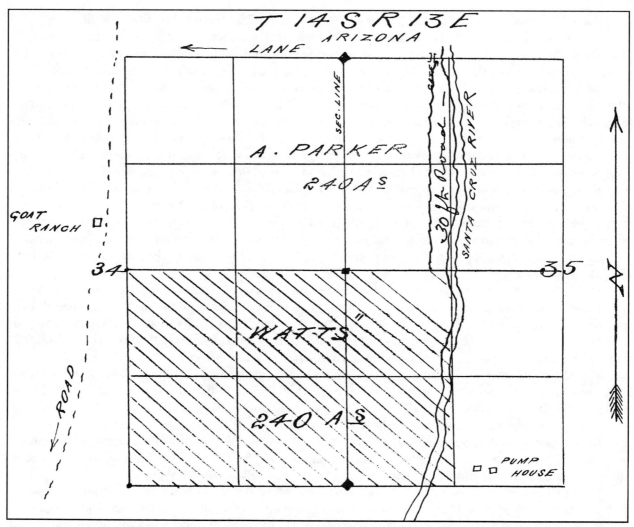

Figure 40. Undated sketch map of features in Township 14 South, Range 13 East, portions of Sections 34 and 35 (AHS n.d.d).

purpose of the map is unknown, but it depicts a "goat ranch" in the SE ¼ of the NW ¼ of Section 34, and a "pump house" (actually, two small structures) in the SE ¼ of the SW ¼ of Section 35. The goat ranch falls within the bounds of the West Branch site, but nothing corresponding to it has been recorded there. The pump house, on the other hand, falls close to the Espinosa site (AZ BB:13:323), first recorded by Slawson et al. (1987). As they recorded it, the site consists of a building foundation and three trash features, none of which has an obvious association with the depicted pump house (see also the site description in the appendix). However, in a later survey, Mabry (1990) noted the presence of two historical-period canal segments in the vicinity of the Espinosa site that were not included in the original recording. He also noted the presence of a concrete house foundation just southeast of the site and north of Irvington Road. Mabry did not suggest a specific date for either the canal segments or the foundation, but both may relate to the Allison brothers' interest in this area. The house foundation in particular seems to correspond closely with the location of the pump house indicated on the Allison map. A revisit to AZ BB:13:323 should record the canal segments and the foundation as part of the site and evaluate their possible association with each other. It is also worth noting that Alexander Davidson, a Tucson farmer, rancher, and businessman more closely associated with the early history of the Rillito Valley, stated in his reminiscences that, "My last real enterprise was a large goat ranch out near Mission Road, west of the Santa Cruz River. This I sold in 1924" (Davidson 1930–1936:27). The goat ranch on the Allison map is probably Davidson's.

Recommendations for Archaeological Survey and Testing

The Santa Cruz Valley in the vicinity of Tucson has been a continuous focus of human settlement for at least three millennia, perhaps much longer. Its importance as a place where people have lived and made their living through time is especially evident along the 8-mile stretch of the valley now designated the Paseo de las Iglesias. The density of archaeological sites already recorded in the area strongly suggests that the archaeological potential of the Paseo de las Iglesias APE is uniformly high. We recommend that, unless there is specific evidence to the contrary, all of the Paseo de las Iglesias APE be considered of high archaeological sensitivity. Sites yet to be discovered or fully documented may include both prehistoric and historical-period sites.

Prior to the impacts of nineteenth- and twentieth-century land use in the Santa Cruz Valley, the density of prehistoric archaeological sites along the Paseo de las Iglesias was undoubtedly even higher than the recorded number of sites suggests. The valley was never a static, unchanging environment even in the prehistoric period, but the variety and scale of changes increased sharply after 1854, when the Gadsden Purchase made southern Arizona a part of the United States. The arrival of Anglo-American settlers and the incorporation of southern Arizona into the U.S. economy brought a host of new impacts to the valley in the vicinity of Tucson, including water-powered flour mills, irrigation works, roads, quarries, residential development, and industry, along with related efforts to manipulate the river's flow and to protect land and other resources from flooding (see Chapter 4). All of these activities have had substantial, sometimes devastating impacts on prehistoric archaeological resources in the Paseo de las Iglesias study area, although significant portions of known major prehistoric sites are still preserved there. Ironically, many of the historical-period activities that have destroyed or obscured prehistoric archaeological sites along the Paseo de las Iglesias have themselves left behind features and deposits that now constitute significant archaeological sites. This archaeological palimpsest, common to many urbanized areas, is best exemplified in the Paseo de las Iglesias APE by AZ BB:13:6, which comprises the important prehistoric Clearwater site, the Spanish Colonial site of Mission San Agustín, a set of irrigation features from the Mexican period, and various twentieth-century features, including a brick-making plant. Virtually the entire Paseo de las Iglesias APE has a similarly complicated (if less documented) settlement and land-use history, in which the processes that have impacted prehistoric sites have themselves created potentially significant archaeological remains.

As noted earlier in the chapter, about 10 percent of the Paseo de las Iglesias APE has not been surveyed for archaeological sites. We recommend that all previously unsurveyed areas be surveyed prior to the start of the project, with particular attention to subsurface archaeological potential. Thirty-six previously recorded sites fall within or immediately adjacent to the APE, including six of the nine major prehistoric sites discussed earlier, and the multicomponent Mission San Agustín site (see Table 3). Most of these sites were originally recorded in the Santa Cruz Riverpark survey of the late 1970s (Betancourt 1978b) and have never been revisited, although all of the major sites have seen more recent work, including testing or partial data-recovery. Most of these sites, regardless of the survey that recorded them, have been documented only to a limited degree, often only on an early version of the ASM site card, and their present condition is unknown. We recommend that all sites falling within the APE (see Table 3) be revisited and re-recorded to ASM standards prior to the start of the project, with particular attention to the impacts suffered since the original recording and the potential for buried deposits. At the major prehistoric sites within the APE, the revisit and re-recording can be limited to the portion of each site actually falling within the APE. Parts of the Mission San Agustín site (AZ BB:13:6) have recently been the subject of intensive study by Desert Archaeology, and thus re-recording is probably not necessary, but the subsurface potential of the site within the APE should still be assessed.

The decision to test a site within the APE should be based both on the information gathered in survey regarding subsurface potential and on the specific kind of impact that the project will have on the site. For sites with subsurface potential that will not be impacted by earthmoving, testing may be limited to defining the horizontal extent of each site, to ensure that it is not impacted by the proposed construction.

Archaeological Site Descriptions

The 90 archaeological sites recorded to date in the Paseo de las Iglesias study area are listed or described below. The 11 major sites discussed in Chapter 5 are only minimally discussed here. The descriptions are based on the corresponding ASM site cards, supplemented with information from associated survey and excavation reports. To the extent possible, we have provided the most current available information for every site, which occasionally contradicts the information on the site cards. For many sites, the ASM site card is the only source of information, and many site cards, especially for sites recorded decades ago, provide only limited information.

AZ AA:16:3 (ASM): West Branch site
Prehistoric periods: undifferentiated Archaic, Sedentary (Rincon phase)
Prehistoric function: habitation
Historical period: protohistoric/historical
Historical function: undetermined

The historical-period component is limited to a few Papago sherds, originally recorded as AZ AA:16:53, and two metal artifacts (a .44-caliber ammunition casing and a spoon), originally recorded as AZ AA:16:54. The following sites have been subsumed under AZ AA:16:3 and are not discussed elsewhere in this report: AZ AA:16:14, 18, 19, 20, 21, 25, 45, 46, 48, 53, and 54. The reader is referred to Chapter 5 for a discussion of the prehistoric component of this site.

AZ AA:16:6 (ASM)
This site was subsumed under AZ AA:16:51.

AZ AA:16:7 (ASM)
Prehistoric period: Classic (Tanque Verde phase)
Prehistoric function: habitation
Historical periods: protohistoric/historical, Early Statehood
Historical function: undetermined

The prehistoric component of this site consists of Tanque Verde Red-on-brown ceramics and perhaps some plain wares, possible arrow shaft straighteners, mano fragments, and shell, intermixed with modern and historical-period trash. The site card mentions exposed "house floors." The temporal associations of these features are not discussed, but they are implied to be prehistoric. The historical-period component consists of twentieth-century trash (plastic, rubber, metal, ceramics) mixed with red-on-brown pottery from the underlying prehistoric component. Some Papago red and glazed wares are noted, which may be associated with the twentieth-century materials.

AZ AA:16:8 (ASM)
Prehistoric periods: Early Formative/Pioneer, Colonial (Cañada del Oro phase), Classic (Tanque Verde
    phase)
Prehistoric function: habitation
Historical period: protohistoric/historical
Historical function: undetermined

The prehistoric component consists of an artifact scatter that includes several ceramic types (Tanque
Verde Red-on-brown, Sells Red, Salado red ware [and corrugated?], Cañada del Oro, and Sweetwater),
which suggests considerable time depth. Other artifacts include mano fragments, shell, flaked stone,
hand stones, and metates. The Tanque Verde phase materials are more concentrated in the eastern portion
of the site. Some indications of cremations are present. The habitation function was inferred from artifact
diversity and the evidence for cremations. The historical-period component consists of Papago red and
plain ware sherds mixed with the more abundant prehistoric materials. When recorded in 1957, part of
the site held the melted remains of recent Tohono O'odham adobe houses.

AZ AA:16:9 (ASM)
Prehistoric period: Classic (Tanque Verde phase)
Prehistoric function: habitation
Historical period: protohistoric/historical
Historical function: undetermined

This site consists of historical-period Papago houses and associated artifacts (primarily Papago pottery
sherds, but also some metal artifacts). There is also a minor prehistoric component, restricted to Tanque
Verde Red-on-brown ceramics found around the edges of the site.

AZ AA:16:10 (ASM): Mission San Xavier del Bac
Historical periods: protohistoric to present
Historical functions: religious, residential

The reader is referred to Chapter 5 for a description of this site.

AZ AA:16:14 (ASM)
This site was subsumed under AZ AA:16:3.

AZ AA:16:15 (ASM)
Prehistoric period: Classic (Tanque Verde phase)
Prehistoric function: limited activity

The ASM site card is the only documentation, and it provides little information. Artifacts include Tanque
Verde Red-on-brown and Sells Red ceramics, a mano, and shell. The site is called a surface scatter, but
the diversity of artifacts may indicate a habitation function.

AZ AA:16:18 (ASM)
This site was subsumed under AZ AA:16:3.

AZ AA:16:25 (ASM)
This site was subsumed under AZ AA:16:3.

AZ AA:16:26 (ASM): St. Mary's Hospital site
Prehistoric periods: Early Formative/Pioneer, Colonial (Cañada del Oro phase), Sedentary (Rincon phase), Classic (Tucson phase)
Prehistoric function: habitation
Historical period: undetermined
Historical function: undetermined

A small portion (the portion south of Anklam Road) of this site as originally recorded is now subsumed under AZ AA:16:51. This site itself subsumes AZ AA:16:36, which falls in its northeast corner. The historical-period component is limited to the portion of the site recorded as AZ AA:16:36, which had a layer of "historic to modern trash" overlying the prehistoric component. The reader is referred to Chapter 5 for a description of the prehistoric component.

AZ AA:16:28 (ASM)
Historical period: Territorial
Historical function: residential

This site consists of the remains of a group of three Papago houses or possibly three trash mounds. Based on makers' marks on non-Papago pottery at the site, it was occupied as early as the 1870s and abandoned around 1900. Artifacts include Papago red and plain wares, porcelain and other non-Papago pottery, bits of iron and other metal artifacts, and glass.

AZ AA:16:33 (ASM)
Prehistoric period: Classic (Tanque Verde phase)
Prehistoric function: cemetery

This site consists of two cremations and their associated Gila Plain and Tanque Verde Red-on-brown mortuary vessels. Two manos were also found near the trench where the burials were exposed. The site card does not include any information about the remainder of the site, which was described as being at least 100 by 100 feet in size.

AZ AA:16:35 (ASM)
Historical period: protohistoric/historical
Historical function: burial

The locational information for this site is not precise, and the plot of the site on the corresponding ASM quadrangle is much larger than the site as recorded. Our plot of the site reflects the actual size of the site, but the location is still only approximate. The site consists of a protohistoric or early-historical-period burial found in 1970 in a modern Tohono O'odham house lot south of Mission San Xavier del Bac. A Hopi bowl found with the burial dates to ca. 1700.

AZ AA:16:36 (ASM)
This site was subsumed under AZ AA:16:26.

AZ AA:16:44 (ASM): Salida del Sol site
Prehistoric period: Classic (Tanque Verde phase)
Prehistoric function: habitation

This site is a prehistoric artifact scatter with two trash mounds and several discrete artifact concentrations. Artifacts include ceramics (Tanque Verde Red-on-brown, sand-tempered plain wares), shell, hammer stones, and flaked stone.

AZ AA:16:45 (ASM)
This site was subsumed under AZ AA:16:3.

AZ AA:16:46 (ASM)
This site was subsumed under AZ AA:16:3.

AZ AA:16:47 (ASM)
Prehistoric period: Classic (Tanque Verde phase)
Prehistoric function: limited activity
Historical period: protohistoric/historical
Historical function: undetermined

This site is a disturbed artifact scatter that includes Tanque Verde Red-on-brown and Papago red wares, flaked stone, and shell. The surface gave no indication of buried features.

AZ AA:16:48 (ASM)
This site was subsumed under AZ AA:16:3.

AZ AA:16:49 (ASM): Dakota Wash site
Prehistoric periods: Early Formative/Pioneer (Snaketown phase), Colonial (Rillito phase), Sedentary, Classic (Tanque Verde phase)
Prehistoric function: habitation

The reader is referred to Chapter 5 for a description of this site.

AZ AA:16:51 (ASM): Tumamoc Hill site
Prehistoric periods: Late Archaic, Classic (Tanque Verde phase)
Prehistoric functions: *trincheras,* rock art
Historical period: Territorial to present
Historical functions: research and undetermined

The limits of this site were recently redefined by Jones (2000) to correspond with the original tract of land granted to the Carnegie Institution for its Desert Botanical Laboratory. Our plot of the site follows this redefinition. Jones gives 870 acres as the size of the original tract of land, but the National Historic Landmark designation for the Desert Botanical Laboratory gives 860 acres. The National Historic Landmark boundaries also differ slightly from those given by Jones. AZ AA:16:51 now subsumes all of AZ AA:16:6 (formerly designating the *trincheras* and other prehistoric features on Tumamoc Hill) and the portion of the St. Mary's Hospital site (AZ AA:16:26) south of Anklam Road. The reader is referred to Chapter 5 for a discussion of the prehistoric component of this site. A discussion of the history of the Desert Botanical Laboratory is provided in Chapter 4.

AZ AA:16:53 (ASM)
The site is subsumed under AZ AA:16:3.

AZ AA:16:54 (ASM)
The site is subsumed under AZ AA:16:3.

AZ AA:16:56 (ASM)
Prehistoric period: undifferentiated Hohokam
Prehistoric function: limited activity
Historical period: protohistoric/historical
Historical function: undetermined

This site consists of an extensive, primarily prehistoric artifact scatter. The site is poorly described on the ASM site card, its only documentation. Prehistoric artifacts include red-on-buff, red ware, and plain ware sherds, flaked stone, and two pieces of ground stone. The historical-period component is limited to an unspecified number of Papago sherds.

AZ AA:16:58 (ASM): Burruel site
Prehistoric period: Classic (Tanque Verde phase)
Prehistoric function: habitation

This site is described as a prehistoric village with several deflated trash mounds and at least one cremation area. In addition to Tanque Verde Red-on-brown ceramics, several obliterated corrugated sherds were noted, as was a single Gila Butte Red-on-buff sherd. Also noted were ground stone and shell, including a single shell ring fragment.

AZ AA:16:60 (ASM): Buckelew Gulch site

Prehistoric periods: Colonial (Rillito phase), Sedentary (Rincon phase), and Classic (Tanque Verde phase)
Prehistoric function: undetermined
Historical period: protohistoric/historical
Historical function: undetermined

The prehistoric component of this heavily eroded site is represented by a surface scatter of ceramic and lithic artifacts. Temporally diagnostic ceramic artifacts observed on the surface include sherds of Rillito Red-on-brown, Rincon Red-on-brown, Tanque Verde Red-on-brown, and Tanque Verde Red-on-brown (white slipped variant). The historical-period component is limited to unspecified amounts of Papago sherds and other historical-period trash (glass, cans, and plastic).

AZ AA:16:61 (ASM)

Prehistoric period: undifferentiated Hohokam
Prehistoric function: undetermined
Historical period: Territorial
Historical functions: residential, ranching/farming

The prehistoric component of this site consists of a surface scatter of ceramic and lithic artifacts. The prehistoric ceramics were identified only as Hohokam plain wares. No finer-grained temporal data were provided. The historical-period component consists of a small, well-preserved, L-shaped stone foundation, a small depression (possibly a well or privy pit), a possible stock tank, a possible fire pit represented by a scatter of stones, and a 3-acre scatter of artifacts. The artifacts date to approximately 1870–1920. Williams (1982; Cohen-Williams and Williams 1982) interpreted these features as the remains of the residence of Jesús María Elías, based primarily on an 1874 map of the proposed Papago Indian Reservation, which depicts private landholdings adjacent to the proposed reservation. We have been unable to locate the 1874 map to confirm this interpretation (the original once kept in the ASM archive is missing), but based on our GLO research, Jesús María Elías did purchase a 160-acre parcel from the government in 1874, in the same location indicated by Williams (see Chapter 4). The 1893 map of Pima County (Roskruge 1893) also depicts a house in the same approximate location, labeled "J. M. Elias." This does not mean, of course, that Elías was occupying the same land before he purchased it. McGuire (1979, 1983) has given convincing evidence that Elías, along with his brother Juan, lived in separate residences at Rancho Punta de Agua (AZ BB:13:18), some 5 miles to the south of AZ AA:16:61, from about 1868 until about 1874. The establishment of the reservation in the latter year required many Mexicans and others living on reservation lands to relocate, which would explain the purchase of 160 acres by Jesús María Elías in 1874. Williams (1982) excavated the house foundation at AZ AA:16:61 in 1981–1982 and found artifacts suggesting an occupation from the 1850s to around 1900, but his specific claim that Jesús Elías occupied the site prior to 1874 is difficult to evaluate. Whoever its occupants were, the site was part of a dispersed settlement by Mexicans of the area immediately east of the panhandle of the Papago Indian Reservation that took shape after establishment of the reservation. This settlement was called Los Reales, a name that by the end of the nineteenth century was applied to a more narrowly delimited site to the east of AZ AA:16:61, on the banks of the Santa Cruz River (see the description of AZ BB:13:56 below). The GLO survey plat of Township 15 South, Range 13 East, dated 1888, depicts a line of houses along the eastern edge of the panhandle of the reservation, in the NE ¼ of Section 9, labeled "Upper Reales." An arrow accompanying the label indicates that it also applies to an area just outside the reservation boundary (see Figure 39).

AZ AA:16:62 (ASM)
Historical periods: protohistoric/historical, Territorial, Early Statehood
Historical functions: residential, ranching/farming

This site consists of a large (6-by-12-m) stone foundation with adobe remnants, accompanied by a large artifact scatter that includes Papago red ware, ironstone ceramics, a variety of glass (including sun-colored amethyst [SCA] glass), a solder-top can fragment, harness and wagon hardware, ammunition casings, and a variety of other domestic items. The site card notes that this site may be the same as one depicted in the same approximate location on a 1931 Soil Conservation Service map of the area. The artifacts suggest a late-nineteenth- or early-twentieth-century date.

AZ AA:16:67 (ASM)
Prehistoric period: undifferentiated Hohokam
Prehistoric function: limited activity

This site consists of a light scatter of plain ware sherds, flaked stone, and ground stone in a cultivated area immediately north of Valencia Road. The site has been badly disturbed by cultivation, the construction of modern irrigation canals, and the construction of Valencia and Indian Agency Roads, which cross through the site. No evidence of buried features was noted.

AZ AA:16:68 (ASM): Herreras Farmstead site
Historical period: Territorial
Historical function: residential

This site was originally recorded in 1980 by Darrell Creel, who provided the site boundary as currently defined. The ASM site card prepared by Creel describes the site as the remains of a two-room adobe building with associated trash mounds, amid an extensive scatter of historical-period artifacts, including ceramics, glass, brick, metal, and leather. The ceramics include Papago wares, Mexican glazed wares, and porcelain. The glass artifacts include SCA glass and a variety of colors. The metal items include some hand-forged pieces. The site extends east-west along both sides of Valencia Road, crossing both the eastern boundary of the San Xavier reservation and the channel of the West Branch of the Santa Cruz River. The remains of the adobe building are located just east of the West Branch and south of Valencia Road. In 1982, a portion of the site was excavated by Pima Community College, but the excavations went unreported until only recently. A site card update from 1982 by Douglas Craig mentions the excavations and depicts a much smaller site area, corresponding to the remains of the adobe building and associated trash mounds. The site has been badly disturbed by construction of Valencia Road and by flooding in the West Branch, which may have shifted course after the site was abandoned. Creel interpreted the site as an early-twentieth-century Tohono O'odham residence, but Craig called it the "Herreras site," which suggests that he associated it with an 1874 GLO land claim by José Herreras for the quarter section that the site falls in (Township 15 South, Range 13 East, Section 15, NW ¼; see Chapter 4). Old Pueblo Archaeology of Tucson has recently undertaken, on behalf of Pima County, a write-up of the 1982 excavations. The full report (Jones 2003) is still being reviewed by Pima County and is not available in its entirety, but Old Pueblo provided us with a draft chapter on the history of the Herreras family and their connection to the site (Jones and Brown 2003). It is clear from the draft chapter that the site saw a complicated sequence of occupation. A member of the Herreras family was living on the property as early as 1872, but it changed hands numerous times over the next 50 years. The full report by Old Pueblo, when it becomes available, will undoubtedly shed much new light on the site.

AZ AA:16:86 (ASM)
Prehistoric period: undifferentiated Hohokam
Prehistoric function: limited activity

This site consists of a small, sparse scatter of plain ware sherds. The site has been badly disturbed by various construction projects and may once have covered a larger area.

AZ AA:16:313 (ASM)
Prehistoric periods: Sedentary (Rincon phase), Classic (Tanque Verde phase)
Prehistoric function: limited activity

The site is characterized as a small, medium-density scatter of sherds, lithics, and fire-cracked rock. Diagnostic ceramics include Rincon and Tanque Verde Red-on-brown. Students from the University of Arizona Department of Anthropology excavated at the site in July 1986. Apparently, no report of these excavations exists beyond a note on the ASM site card that indicates "cultural materials are being found at a depth of 1 meter."

AZ AA:16:319 (ASM)
Prehistoric period: Sedentary (Rincon phase)
Prehistoric function: limited activity

This site consists of a scatter of sherds, flaked stone, and ground stone. Temporal assignment is based on a single sherd classified as "Rillito or Early Rincon Red-on-brown." Buried features are noted as possible at the site, but the soil is shallow and the modern surface is near bedrock. Parts of the site have been bladed away.

AZ AA:16:320 (ASM)
Prehistoric period: undetermined
Prehistoric function: limited activity

This site consists of a single isolated cluster of cobbles, some of which have been fire affected. The feature is interpreted as a roasting pit. There are no associated artifacts.

AZ AA:16:386 (ASM)
Prehistoric period: undifferentiated Hohokam
Prehistoric function: limited activity
Historical period: protohistoric/historical
Historical function: undetermined

This site consists of a scatter of primarily historical-period artifacts, including Papago plain and red wares, SCA glass, whiteware, porcelain, and a shell button. Prehistoric artifacts are limited to a rhyolite mano fragment and a plain ware sherd.

AZ AA:16:387 (ASM)
Prehistoric periods: Sedentary (Rincon phase), Classic (Tanque Verde phase)
Prehistoric function: habitation

This site is described as an artifact scatter with a possible trash mound. Artifacts include flaked stone, ground stone, and ceramics. Diagnostic ceramics include Tanque Verde Red-on-brown and Rincon Red-on-brown. The Rincon Red-on-brown is present in low frequency, representing about 1 percent of the sherd collection. The habitation function was inferred from artifact density and diversity and the presence of the possible trash mound. One rock ring was also recorded, but its temporal affiliation is unknown. The site has been disturbed by development.

AZ AA:16:395 (ASM)
Historical period: Territorial to present
Historical function: residential

This site consists of seven historical-period artifact concentrations associated with the current and previous occupations of several houses by the Estrada family. Artifacts include Papago ceramics, glass, Euroamerican ceramics, food cans, bone, and other metal items. The earliest concentration with diagnostic artifacts dates to the period 1881–1917.

AZ AA:16:405 (ASM)
Prehistoric periods: Colonial (Rillito phase), Sedentary (Rincon phase), Classic (Tanque Verde phase)
Prehistoric function: habitation
Historical period: protohistoric/historical
Historical function: undetermined

This site is characterized as a Hohokam village, with a small historical-period Papago component. Ceramics indicate that the site was occupied from the Colonial through the Classic periods. There is a high probability of buried structures. Some calcined bone is visible on the surface, suggesting one or more cemetery areas. In addition to the decorated ceramics, artifacts include plain wares, lithics, and shell. The historical-period component is limited to an unspecified number of historical-period Papago sherds. The site has been badly disturbed, with several modern borrow pits and pothunting holes. Our plot of the site is based on that of Dart (1988), who noted that an earlier survey also found materials to the east of Mission Road. Dart did not visit that portion of the site, and the unpublished report he cited was unavailable to us.

AZ AA:16:411 (ASM)
Prehistoric period: Classic (Tanque Verde phase)
Prehistoric function: habitation
Historical period: protohistoric/historical
Historical function: undetermined

This site is a moderate-density sherd and flaked stone scatter. The site's full extent was not determined during the original survey, and it is likely much larger in area. The habitation function is based on observations on the ASM site card, which suggest the possibility of buried features. One feature, a mound, is noted as present. In addition to the prehistoric artifacts, some glass and metal artifacts were observed.

AZ AA:16:432 (ASM)
Prehistoric period: undifferentiated Hohokam
Prehistoric function: limited activity

This site consists of a low-density artifact scatter, primarily of ceramics. Flaked stone is present in low frequency, as is ground stone and fire-cracked rock. A single buff ware sherd was observed, suggesting a pre-Classic date. Buried features are possible but, none was noted during the survey. The site is also larger than depicted on the site card, extending to the west of the current boundaries and probably extending to the east before construction of a modern materials pit.

AZ BB:13:2 (ASM)
Prehistoric periods: Late Archaic, Sedentary (Rincon phase)
Prehistoric function: habitation

This is the prehistoric site on the summit of Martínez Hill. The hill in its entirety is designated AZ BB:13:34, a designation that refers to the historical-period association of the hill with José María Martínez. Despite the breaking of the ASM rule that no nonlinear site can fall within the bounds of another nonlinear site, the two designations still stand. No ceramics were noted on the surface of the site, although a hammer stone and an undescribed projectile point were collected. The assumption is that these remains are associated with the occupation of the Martínez Hill Ruin (AZ BB:13:3). The reader is referred to Chapter 5 for a description of the latter site.

AZ BB:13:3 (ASM): Martínez Hill Ruin
Prehistoric period: Classic (Tanque Verde and Tucson phases)
Prehistoric function: habitation

The reader is referred to Chapter 5 for a description of this site.

AZ BB:13:6 (ASM): Clearwater site, Mission San Agustín del Tucson, and the Tucson Pressed Brick Company
Prehistoric periods: Middle Archaic, Late Archaic (Cienega phase)
Prehistoric function: habitation
Historical period: Spanish Colonial through post–World War II
Historical functions: religious and industrial

The reader is referred to Chapter 5 for separate descriptions of this site's prehistoric and historical-period components.

AZ BB:13:7 (ASM)
Prehistoric periods: Early Formative/Pioneer (Snaketown phase), Colonial (Cañada del Oro and Rillito phases)
Prehistoric function: habitation

This site is poorly described on the ASM site card. The card mentions a trash mound and a ball court. Wilcox and Sternberg mentioned two ball courts at the site flanking a large open area devoid of surface features (1983:122–123). Wallace revisited the site in 1981 and observed that the smaller of the two ball courts had been cut by the Indian Health Center Road. The temporal assignment of the site was inferred from the mention of ceramics dating to the Sweetwater, Snaketown, and Cañada del Oro phases. Santa Cruz Red-on-buff sherds were also identified. The Colonial period occupation seems to have been the most substantial. This site may represent an early component of the Martínez Hill Ruin community. Wallace (1981) visited the site briefly and noted a second possible ball court, cut by the Indian Health Center Road.

AZ BB:13:8 (ASM)
Prehistoric periods: Colonial (Cañada del Oro and Rillito phases), Sedentary (Rincon phase), Classic (Tanque Verde and Tucson phases)
Prehistoric function: habitation
Historical period: protohistoric/historical
Historical function: undetermined

This site subsumes AZ BB:13:479, a designation used by Lascaux et al. (1995). The current description includes information recorded under that designation. The ASM plot for AZ BB:13:8 is much larger than the "acre or so" estimated in the original recording, which implies that the ASM plot is only an approximation. We used the plot of Lascaux et al. (1995) for AZ BB:13:479 on our map. As originally recorded, AZ BB:13:8 consisted of a house compound and trash mounds. Two trash mounds showed rows of stones probably representing room walls. The ceramics were poorly described, but the architecture suggested a Classic period occupation. Ceramics noted by Lascaux et al. indicate a Cañada del Oro through Tucson phase occupation. Wallace (1981) visited the site briefly and noted that "several very large mounds are present, one is the largest I've seen in the Tucson Basin." A historical-period component documented by Lascaux et al. (1995) and alluded to on the ASM site card consists of Papago plain and decorated wares, numerous glass sherds and metal fragments, wire, bricks, machinery parts, plastic, and a circular arrangement of brick and concrete with a metal dome cover, probably a well (the interior is filled with trash).

AZ BB:13:14 (ASM): San Xavier Bridge site
Prehistoric periods: Late Archaic, Colonial, Sedentary (Rincon phase), Classic (Tanque Verde phase)
Prehistoric function: habitation
Historical period: Territorial
Historical functions: irrigation, residential

The historical-period component is limited to two canal segments attributed to the José María Martínez land grant (Ravesloot 1987:162). The site map (Ravesloot 1987:Figure 11.1) also depicts two "Papago" house foundations near one of the canal segments, but no discussion of these features is provided. The reader is referred to Chapter 5 for a description of the prehistoric component of this site.

AZ BB:13:15 (ASM): Valencia site
Prehistoric periods: Paleoindian, Late Archaic (Cienega phase), Colonial (Rillito phase), Sedentary (Rincon phase), Classic (Tanque Verde phase)
Prehistoric function: habitation

The reader is referred to Chapter 5 for a description of this site.

AZ BB:13:17 (ASM): Julian Wash site

Prehistoric periods: Late Archaic (Cienega phase), Early Formative/Pioneer (Snaketown phase), Colonial (Cañada del Oro phase), Sedentary (Rincon phase)
Prehistoric function: habitation

The reader is referred to Chapter 5 for a description of this site.

AZ BB:13:19 (ASM)

Prehistoric periods: Early Formative/Pioneer (Snaketown phase), Colonial (Cañada del Oro and Rillito phases)
Prehistoric function: limited activity
Historical period: protohistoric/historical to post–World War II
Historical functions: irrigation, undetermined

There is some confusion about the location and nature of this site. An initial survey found a prehistoric artifact scatter and a historical-period canal; a second survey found historical-period ceramics (Papago red ware, Mexican glazed ware); a third survey confirmed the results of the first survey. A fourth survey (Courtwright and Wright 1999) has apparently resolved the problem, and the location of the site given there is used here (the current ASM plot of this site does not reflect the Courtwright and Wright resurvey). The prehistoric component is a sherd and lithic scatter with Rillito and Cañada del Oro Red-on-brown and Snaketown Red-on-brown. There is no evidence of buried features, and the limited diversity of artifact types suggests a limited function. The historical-period component documented in 1999 consists of a sparse scatter of artifacts (SCA and other glass, probable Papago ceramics, insulator fragments, crown caps, a 1946 penny, machine parts, and concrete fragments) and several irrigation features, including a segment of an old-looking concrete-lined ditch with a gated culvert. Also within the site boundary are two modern canal segments that have not been recorded as features.

AZ BB:13:20 (ASM)

Prehistoric periods: Colonial (Rillito phase), Sedentary (Rincon phase), Classic (Tanque Verde phase)
Prehistoric function: limited activity
Historical period: protohistoric/historical
Historical function: undetermined

The prehistoric component of this site consists of a large sherd and lithic scatter disturbed by erosion and agriculture. No features have been recorded, but there is the possibility of buried features. The site was probably much larger prior to disturbance. The Tanque Verde sherds were noted on a later site visit. The historical-period component of the site consists of unspecified numbers of Papago red-on-brown sherds.

AZ BB:13:21 (ASM)

Prehistoric period: undifferentiated Hohokam
Prehistoric function: undetermined

This site consists of a scatter of plain ware sherds. Since its original recording, the site has been largely destroyed or buried by construction. It has either been silted over or has been destroyed by construction of a transmission line ROW.

AZ BB:13:22 (ASM)
Prehistoric period: Classic (Tanque Verde phase)
Prehistoric function: habitation

This site consists of a large sherd scatter with a few flaked stone tools. Diagnostic ceramics include Tanque Verde Red-on-brown, Rillito Red-on-brown, obliterated corrugated, and San Carlos Brown ware. Based on the Rillito sherds, the site may have a pre-Classic component.

AZ BB:13:34 (ASM): Martínez Hill
Historical periods: Early Statehood to present
Historical function: hospital

This site consists of the entirety of Martínez Hill and fully encompasses AZ BB:13:2, a discrete prehistoric site on the summit of the hill (see the site description above for AZ BB:13:2). Martínez Hill was designated AZ BB:13:34 in 1961 solely on the basis of its association with the José María Martínez land grant, which is located between the hill and Mission San Xavier del Bac (see Chapter 4). The site is not known to include any features associated with the land grant, and the only historical-period component at the site is the Indian Health Service hospital compound located on the lower east slope of the hill. The original construction of the hospital compound took place in 1931–1933, and it is still an active facility (Lindeman 1997).

AZ BB:13:35 (ASM)
This site is subsumed under AZ BB:13:56.

AZ BB:13:48 (ASM)
Prehistoric period: Classic (Tanque Verde phase)
Prehistoric function: habitation

This site is characterized as a possible village. No artifacts other than ceramics are noted, but these include Tanque Verde Red-on-brown, plain wares, polished red wares, and one Reserve or Tularosa sherd. Determination of site function is difficult because of recent alluvium in the site area.

AZ BB:13:49 (ASM)
This site is subsumed under AZ BB:13:56.

AZ BB:13:55 (ASM)
Prehistoric period: Sedentary (Rincon phase)
Prehistoric function: limited activity
Historical periods: protohistoric/historical and undetermined
Historical functions: irrigation and undetermined

The prehistoric component of this site consists of a low-density sherd scatter. The temporal assignment was based on a single Rincon Red-on-brown sherd. Recent alluvium may have buried other artifacts. The historical-period component as described on the ASM site card is limited to five Papago red ware sherds and one Mexican green glazed ware sherd. However, on a map of the vicinity of this site prepared during the recording of nearby AZ BB:13:402, a historical-period canal is indicated as passing immediately adjacent to the eastern limit of this site (Mabry 1990). No discussion of the feature is provided in the accompanying report.

AZ BB:13:56 (ASM): Los Reales

Prehistoric periods: Early Archaic, Colonial (Rillito phase), Sedentary (Rincon phase), Classic (Tanque Verde phase)
Prehistoric function: undetermined
Historical period: Territorial
Historical function: townsite

The prehistoric occupation of the site includes an Archaic period component, reflected in a Cochise-style projectile point, and a surface scatter of ceramic and lithic artifacts (Hill and Garcia 1999:39). Temporally diagnostic ceramic artifacts observed at the site include sherds dated to the Rillito through Tanque Verde phases. No evidence of the existence of subsurface cultural deposits was observed. The historical-period component consists of the remains of an adobe building originally believed to be associated with a Mexican or Anglo-American ranching operation dating to around 1900. The building remains are accompanied by glass and stoneware sherds, cartridge casings, and other artifacts. Betancourt (1978b:94) has suggested that AZ BB:13:56 is a part of the late-nineteenth-century Mexican community of Los Reales, known from map depictions and documentary references. The site of the community was designated AZ BB:13:35 in 1961, but that designation was based solely on documentary references; the plot for the site on the corresponding ASM quadrangle is only an approximate one. The site card for AZ BB:13:35 originally described the site as located at the west end of Los Reales Road, "where it runs into the Santa Cruz River." Based on the location of Los Reales on the 1893 map of Pima County (Roskruge 1893), it is probable that AZ BB:13:56 does, in fact, represent a part of Los Reales. Therefore, we have not plotted AZ BB:13:35, nor do we consider it a separate site.

AZ BB:13:57 (ASM): Warner's Mill

Historical period: Territorial
Historical function: industrial

This site consists of the remains of a flour mill and house built by Solomon Warner in 1875 at the eastern foot of Sentinel Peak. The mill was originally a two-story building with a foundation and first-floor walls of basalt; the upper story was of adobe. Only portions of the basalt foundation survive. The house, an L-shaped single-story adobe on a basalt foundation, is mostly intact today, although it has been modified by the current owners. A discussion of Warner and his milling operation is provided in Chapter 4. The only archaeological work that has been carried out in relation to the site has been the excavation of small segments of what was probably the mill race, leading from the mill back to the Santa Cruz River. A probable segment crossing the Mission San Agustín gardens was excavated by Williams (1989). More recently, another probable segment was excavated just south of the site of Mission San Agustín, to the south of Mission Lane (CDA 2001).

AZ BB:13:65 (ASM)
Prehistoric periods: Colonial (Rillito phase), Sedentary (Rincon phase)
Prehistoric function: limited activity
Historical period: protohistoric/historical
Historical function: undetermined

This site is a highly disturbed, dispersed scatter of prehistoric and historical-period artifacts. The prehistoric artifacts consist of flaked stone and ceramics, including Santa Cruz–Sacaton Red-on-buff and Gila Plain wares. The historical-period component, probably the primary component at the site, consists of Papago ware, Mexican glazed ware, SCA glass, and solder-top cans. Despite the disturbance to the site, the potential for buried features still exists.

AZ BB:13:74 (ASM)
Prehistoric periods: Late Archaic (Cienega phase), Sedentary (Rincon phase), Classic (Tanque Verde phase)
Prehistoric function: habitation

This site was originally recorded as a part of the Valencia site (AZ BB:13:15), but it is now considered a separate site (apparently it remains a part of the Valencia site as listed in the NRHP). The site is described as a low- to moderate-density artifact scatter, with two areas of artifact concentration that appear to be low mounds. Diagnostic ceramics include Rincon Red-on-brown, Tanque Verde Red-on-brown, and Gila Plain. The Cienega phase component, discovered in later excavation, was documented by Bradley (1980).

AZ BB:13:89 (ASM)
Historical period: undetermined to present
Historical function: residential

This site consists of a concrete building foundation and a cistern, with standing (occupied) adobe buildings nearby. The foundation and standing adobes may have originally formed a complex of buildings. Sherds of SCA glass were noted on the site surface, but no other artifacts are indicated.

AZ BB:13:90 (ASM)
Prehistoric periods: Sedentary (Rincon phase), Classic (Tanque Verde phase)
Prehistoric function: cemetery
Historical period: Territorial and Early Statehood
Historical function: irrigation

The prehistoric component of this site consists of a cremation area eroding out of a modern borrow pit and dump area. In addition to probable human bone, ceramics have been exposed by the erosion, including Tanque Verde Red-on-brown and Rincon Red-on-brown bowls and jars. The historical-period component of this site is limited to a canal segment discovered in test trenching at the site in 1978. The segment may represent one of several canals known to have been constructed across the vicinity of the site in the period 1870–1920, although the most likely candidate is the Farmer's Ditch, one of four canals in use in the area in the early 1900s (Betancourt 1978b:76–79).

AZ BB:13:91 (ASM)
Prehistoric periods: Sedentary (Rincon phase), Classic (Tanque Verde phase)
Prehistoric function: habitation
Historical period: protohistoric/historical
Historical function: undetermined

This site is a dense sherd and lithic scatter with clusters of fire-affected rock. Ceramics include both prehistoric diagnostics (Rincon and Tanque Verde Red-on-brown) and historical-period Papago red ware. The site appears to have a high potential for buried features.

AZ BB:13:92 (ASM)
Prehistoric periods: Colonial (Rillito phase), Sedentary (Rincon phase), Classic (Tanque Verde phase)
Prehistoric function: habitation

This site is characterized as a small village. Probable buried pit houses and a few charcoal lenses were observed along a natural-gas line that runs through the site. In addition to the types used to assign phase designations, red and plain wares were also noted, as were several pieces of flaked stone. There has been some disturbance to the site surface, but this has probably not impacted buried features.

AZ BB:13:93 (ASM)
Prehistoric periods: Sedentary (Rincon phase), Classic (Tanque Verde phase)
Prehistoric function: habitation

This site, a sherd and lithic scatter located at the confluence of the West Branch and the Santa Cruz River, is characterized as a possible habitation site. Rincon and Tanque Verde Red-on-brown sherds are the only diagnostic ceramics noted. The flaked stone materials reflect a variety of different raw materials. The site has been disturbed both by development and by erosion from the West Branch.

AZ BB:13:94 (ASM): Silver Lake Hotel
Prehistoric periods: Sedentary (Rincon phase), Classic (Tanque Verde phase)
Prehistoric function: limited activity
Historical period: protohistoric/historical, Territorial
Historical function: undetermined and entertainment

This site consists primarily of a dense artifact scatter of large but indeterminate area, covered in places by a landfill. Prehistoric artifacts include Rincon and Tanque Verde Red-on-brown ceramics and flaked stone. Historical-period artifacts, which appear to be more numerous than prehistoric ones, include unspecified numbers of Papago red ware and porcelain sherds, possibly derived in part from the landfill. The historical-period component also includes structural foundations of basalt boulders and associated trash, including many square nails. Betancourt (1978b:85) noted, based partly on the testimony of a longtime resident of the area, that the foundations may be the remains of the Silver Lake Hotel, located on the western shore of Silver Lake (see Chapter 4). This is supported by the depiction of Silver Lake on the 1893 map of Pima County (Roskruge 1893) and by Betancourt's field observation of low, wide benches on either side of the Santa Cruz River at this point. Subsequent entrenchment of the river, combined with landfilling on both banks, has probably obscured most of the former lake.

AZ BB:13:95 (ASM)
Prehistoric periods: Colonial (Rillito phase), Sedentary (Rincon phase), Classic (Tanque Verde phase)
Prehistoric function: limited activity
Historical period: protohistoric/historical
Historical function: undetermined

The prehistoric component at this site consists of a sparse sherd and lithic scatter, with considerable depth indicated by several hearths eroding from the adjacent river bank. Diagnostic ceramics include Rillito, Rincon, and Tanque Verde Red-on-brown, but the relative frequencies of these types are not provided. A historical-period component is represented by an unspecified number of Papago red ware sherds and SCA glass shards.

AZ BB:13:96 (ASM)
Prehistoric periods: Colonial (Rillito phase), Sedentary (Rincon phase), Classic (Tanque Verde phase)
Prehistoric function: habitation
Historical periods: protohistoric/historical and Early Statehood
Historical function: irrigation

The prehistoric component is described as a dense sherd and lithic scatter possibly representing a village. Diagnostic ceramics include Rincon, Rillito, and Tanque Verde Red-on-brown, and Rincon Red ware. Flaked stone, ground stone, and a single projectile point were also noted. The relative frequencies of the diagnostic ceramics are not provided. The historical-period component consists of a few Papago red ware sherds, a historical-period canal, and a 1930s-era concrete slab foundation.

AZ BB:13:97 (ASM)
Prehistoric periods: protohistoric/historical and Sedentary (Rincon phase)
Prehistoric function: limited activity

This site is described as a sparse sherd and lithic scatter. In addition to Rincon Red-on-brown, an unidentified Hohokam buff ware was also noted at the site. Subsurface testing near the site in 1997 exposed no subsurface features; a small number of historical-period aboriginal ceramics were noted, along with historical-period glass dating to the early 1900s (Swartz 1997:5).

AZ BB:13:99 (ASM)
Prehistoric periods: Colonial (Rillito phase), Sedentary (Rincon phase)
Prehistoric function: limited activity

This site consists of a low-density sherd and flaked stone scatter. Diagnostic ceramics include Rillito and Rincon Red-on-brown sherds. The artifacts appeared to be in secondary contexts, but the subsurface may be undisturbed.

AZ BB:13:100 (ASM)
Prehistoric periods: Colonial (Rillito phase), Sedentary (Rincon phase)
Prehistoric function: limited activity
Historical period: undetermined
Historical function: irrigation

This site is a sherd and lithic scatter possibly associated with the Valencia site (AZ BB:13:15), which is located immediately to the east, on the opposite bank of the Santa Cruz River. Diagnostic ceramics include Rillito and Rincon Red-on-brown sherds. The western limit of this site was not determined. The site has been heavily disturbed by agriculture and power-line construction. The site map on the ASM site card indicates a "historic canal" running southeast to northwest across the length of the site, but no discussion of this feature is provided.

AZ BB:13:101 (ASM)
Prehistoric period: undifferentiated Hohokam
Prehistoric functions: agricultural and habitation

This site consists of a low-density sherd and lithic scatter containing Hohokam buff wares, Tucson Basin plain wares, and siliceous limestone flakes. The site is impacted by erosion of the Santa Cruz River. Site function is not clear from the surface materials, but the location suggests the site was either a farming area or a small village.

AZ BB:13:102 (ASM)
Historical period: protohistoric/historical
Historical function: undetermined

This site consists of a small scatter of Papago red ware sherds and SCA glass shards, plus large fragments of concrete, possibly from a foundation. The surface artifacts, many derived from a recent rodent burrow, may derive from buried features.

AZ BB:13:103 (ASM)
Prehistoric periods: Colonial (Rillito phase), Sedentary (Rincon phase), Classic (Tanque Verde phase)
Prehistoric function: habitation

This site consists of a sherd and flaked stone scatter eroding from road cuts and erosional features. Diagnostic ceramics include Rillito, Rincon, and Tanque Verde Red-on-brown, and Rincon red ware. Flaked stone artifacts include a bifacial core and several retouched flakes of chert and rhyolite.

AZ BB:13:104 (ASM)
Prehistoric periods: undifferentiated Hohokam and Classic (Tanque Verde phase)
Prehistoric functions: habitation and agricultural

This site, a sherd and lithic scatter, is characterized as a small village and is located immediately south and west of Airport Wash and east of the Santa Cruz River. Ceramics include Tanque Verde Red-on-brown and Hohokam buff wares. The latter suggest the possibility of a pre-Classic occupation. The site is described as being in excellent condition, and only one pothunter's hole was noted.

AZ BB:13:105 (ASM)
Prehistoric period: Sedentary (Rincon phase)
Prehistoric functions: habitation and limited activity
Historical period: Territorial
Historical function: residential

This site consists of three scatters of brick, two associated with distinct building outlines. A basalt boulder foundation also was noted. Artifacts include Papago red and plain ware sherds and glass shards. The site is thought to date to the early 1900s. The prehistoric component is ephemeral and consists only of a few Sacaton Red-on-buff sherds.

AZ BB:13:106 (ASM)
Prehistoric periods: Sedentary (Rincon phase), Classic (Tanque Verde phase)
Prehistoric functions: agricultural and habitation

This site is described as a sherd and lithic scatter, with hearths eroding from the surface and from small gullies that cross the site. The artifact scatter includes Rincon Red-on-brown, Rincon Red, and Sells Red sherds, as well as flaked stone. The Tanque Verde phase assignation is based solely on the presence of Sells Red. The site may be associated with the prehistoric component of nearby AZ BB:13:56.

AZ BB:13:107 (ASM)
Prehistoric period: undifferentiated Archaic
Prehistoric function: resource procurement/processing

This site is a flaked stone scatter observed in a small arroyo in a heavily dissected area of the Santa Cruz River floodplain. When recorded in 1978, the site was threatened by gravel quarrying. The site may have a Middle Archaic or even an Early Archaic association.

AZ BB:13:108 (ASM)
Prehistoric period: undifferentiated Archaic
Prehistoric function: resource procurement/processing

This site is a flaked stone scatter eroding from the bank of Airport Wash. The temporal assignment is apparently not based on diagnostic artifacts. There is a discrepancy between the ASM site card, which calls the site a possible San Pedro phase site, and the text of the associated report (Betancourt 1978:98), which says that it is possibly a Chiricahua or even Sulphur Spring phase site. The report also mentions that the remains of a hearth were found eroding from the wash bank.

AZ BB:13:109 (ASM): Tucson Farms Company Crosscut (Pima Land and Water Company Crosscut)
Historical periods: Early Statehood
Historical function: irrigation

This site consists of two wells, a section of large concrete conduit, and two earthen mounds, possibly the anchors of an earthen dam. The two mounds are located on either side of the Santa Cruz River, immediately below its current confluence with the West Branch, suggesting that a dam once extended across the river between them. Both mounds are neatly cut on their river side by later entrenchment of the river. The east mound has a series of wooden and concrete steps leading to its top. The ASM site card, prepared by Julio Betancourt and others following the Santa Cruz Riverpark survey (1978b), states that the two mounds once formed part of the Silver Lake Dam, in existence from 1857 to around 1900; this, however, is not consistent with Betancourt's discussion of AZ BB:13:109 in the survey report (1978b:80–81) or with other information about the location of Silver Lake, which was almost certainly located a quarter mile to the south, just south of modern Silver Lake Road (see Chapter 4 and the description of AZ BB:13:111 below). Betancourt (1978b:80) stated that the two wells and concrete conduit were parts of the Pima Land and Water Company Crosscut, later called the Tucson Farms Company Crosscut, built around 1912 (see Chapter 4). According to a local resident consulted by Betancourt, the earthen mounds were also associated with the Crosscut, but Betancourt hesitates to affirm that connection.

Based on the location of AZ BB:13:109 and on the description of the Crosscut by Hinderlider (1913; also consulted by Betancourt), it is highly probable that the wells, the conduit, and the earthen mounds are all remnants of the Crosscut. Hinderlider (1913:200) included an earthen dam in his description of the features of the Crosscut, although he was not specific about its function. The two wells and the segment of conduit are undoubtedly parts of the Crosscut's line of 19 wells, connected by a buried horizontal concrete conduit, that crossed the Santa Cruz and West Branch at this location. A plan of the Crosscut included by Hinderlider (see Figure 21 of the current report) depicts an earthen dam immediately upstream of the line of wells on the West Branch (note that the confluence of the Santa Cruz and West Branch was then about a quarter mile below the current confluence). Unfortunately, Betancourt did not provide any information about the relative locations of the wells, conduit, and mounds in the survey report, or any description of the wells and conduit. The ASM site card does not even mention the wells and conduit, but it does provide a small sketch map showing the locations of the two mounds. The map does not have a scale, so it is difficult to judge how closely the two mounds correspond to the earthen dam depicted in Hinderlider's plan, but the west mound seems to be at just the right location. The east mound may be a related (or possibly later) feature not depicted on the 1913 plan. It is clear from the sketch map that the two mounds are in an almost direct line with the north side of 26th Street, which extends eastward from Santa Cruz Lane, the north-south street running just east of the site. As noted in Chapter 5, the former alignment of the Crosscut is still evident on the most recent Tucson 7.5-minute USGS quadrangle in just this location, and it is also still visible in the field along the north side of 26th Street, which is also known as Flowing Wells Crosscut Road along this stretch. The ASM site card depicts a linear berm running from the east bank of the Santa Cruz to Santa Cruz Lane, parallel and immediately south of the east mound. The berm is labeled "raised area where buried gas line is," but this may also be part of the original Crosscut alignment, used later as a gas line corridor.

AZ BB:13:111 (ASM): James Lee's Pioneer Mill
Prehistoric period: undifferentiated Hohokam
Prehistoric function: resource procurement/processing
Historical period: Territorial
Historical function: industrial

This site is located 15 m south of Silverlake Road, just west of the Santa Cruz River. The prehistoric component is described as "an extensive Hohokam sherd scatter," but no other information is provided. The historical-period component consists of large masonry footings of limestone, identified by Betancourt (1978b) as the remains of James Lee's Pioneer Mill, a grist mill operating at this location as early as 1864 and abandoned by 1893. Lee probably used a mill built by William S. Grant in 1860, so the stone footings probably predate Lee's operation. Grant himself operated both a mill he had built and an existing mill built in 1857 by the Rowlett brothers (see Chapter 4). The footings may be associated with either mill. Both the survey report and the ASM site card lack any information about the dimensions of the footings themselves, although the site card indicates site size as 15 by 20 m. The survey report notes that "turn-of-the-century trash is scattered about the area, with no definable concentration" (Betancourt 1978b:81). When the site was recorded in 1978, the footings had been badly damaged by the recent digging of two drainage ditches; the current condition of the stone footings observed by Betancourt is unknown.

AZ BB:13:121 (ASM): Timmerman Site
Prehistoric period: undifferentiated Hohokam
Prehistoric functions: resource procurement/processing and rock art

This site, located on the lower northeast slope of Tumamoc Hill, consists of a 50-m-long rock wall, several bedrock mortar holes, a concentration of petroglyphs, and a large metate. No other artifacts are noted.

AZ BB:13:129 (ASM): Wrong Township Site 1
Prehistoric period: undetermined
Prehistoric function: limited activity
Historical period: undetermined
Historical function: undetermined

This site consists of a scatter of prehistoric plain ware sherds and historical-period glazed sherds. No information is provided regarding the number or density of sherds of either kind. The site is located in a plowed field immediately west of the Santa Cruz River.

AZ BB:13:135 (ASM)
Prehistoric period: Classic (Tanque Verde phase)
Prehistoric functions: rock art and resource procurement/processing
Historical period: undetermined
Historical function: undetermined

The prehistoric component of this site consists of a low-density sherd and lithic scatter accompanied by 30 bedrock mortars, 50 small bedrock "cupules," and a series of petroglyphs. The site is adjacent on the south to Warner's Mill, extending up the lower 40 m of Sentinel Peak. The temporal assignment is based on a single Tanque Verde Red-on-brown sherd; an earlier component is likely. The historical-period component consists of an overlying trash layer (cans and bottles) of unspecified age.

AZ BB:13:136 (ASM)
Prehistoric period: undifferentiated Hohokam
Prehistoric function: limited activity
Historical period: protohistoric/historical
Historical function: undetermined

The prehistoric component of this site is limited to unspecified numbers of lithic and shell artifacts, which are not otherwise described. The historical-period component consists of a light scatter of Papago ware, glazed ware, and glass, as well as modern trash. The entire site has been disturbed by agriculture and road construction.

AZ BB:13:142 (ASM)
Historical periods: Territorial and Early Statehood
Historical function: public works

This site represent the remains of Tucson Water Pumping Plant No. 2 and consists of a large cistern (18 feet 7 inches in diameter and 60 feet deep), a large (about 20-by-60-foot) concrete foundation representing the pumping plant, and a 25-foot-long tunnel connecting the plant and cistern. The plant was constructed ca. 1905 and abandoned ca. 1945. These features have since been destroyed by construction of a bridge for Irvington Road over the Santa Cruz River.

AZ BB:13:143 (ASM)
Prehistoric period: Sedentary (Rincon phase)
Prehistoric function: resource procurement/processing

This site, a sherd scatter, is characterized as a "food preparation area" based on the presence of burned, weathered sherds in ashy soil. In addition to Rincon Red-on-brown sherds, red ware and "Pimería brown ware" sherds were noted. No other artifacts or features are discussed. Limited test excavations were carried out at the time of recording.

AZ BB:13:145 (ASM)
Prehistoric period: Sedentary (Rincon phase)
Prehistoric function: limited activity

This site is a small sherd and lithic scatter with Rincon Red-on-brown sherds, "Pimería brown wares," flaked stone, and half of a mano. The site has been disturbed by blading and collecting.

AZ BB:13:154 (ASM)
Prehistoric period: undifferentiated Hohokam
Prehistoric functions: resource procurement/processing and rock art
Historical period: protohistoric/historical
Historical function: undetermined

This site consists of five bedrock mortars, two smaller bedrock depressions, and isolated petroglyphs. No diagnostic artifacts were noted, but a few plain ware sherds were recorded. The historical-period component of this site is limited to an unspecified number of glass shards.

AZ BB:13:222 (ASM)
Prehistoric period: Sedentary (Rincon phase)
Prehistoric function: limited activity

This site is a light sherd and lithic scatter with only a small number of sherds. Buried features are unlikely, given the apparently shallow soil. The temporal assignation is based on a single Rincon Red-on-brown sherd. In addition to this sherd, plain wares, flaked stone, mano fragments, and one metate fragment were noted.

AZ BB:13:223 (ASM)
Prehistoric periods: Sedentary (Rincon phase), Classic (Tanque Verde phase)
Prehistoric function: habitation

This site consists of a light sherd and lithic scatter. Ceramics include possible Rincon Red-on-brown, Tanque Verde Red-on-brown, possible Gila Red, and plain wares. Other artifacts include flaked stone and a one-hand mano. Testing of the site revealed an unburned pit house and another possible feature. The presence of these features was used to infer site function, although the site might simply be a field house and an associated pit.

AZ BB:13:323 (ASM): Espinosa site
Prehistoric period: Sedentary (Rincon phase)
Prehistoric function: habitation
Historical period: Territorial
Historical functions: irrigation and ranching/farming

The prehistoric component is a large, dense artifact scatter of plain ware, Rincon Red-on-brown, flaked stone, ground stone fragments, and calcined bone. The historical-period component of this site consists of a building foundation and three trash features. Historical-period artifacts at the site include Papago wares, Mexican glazed ware, other ceramics, glass, and metal. In 1986, Slawson et al. (1987) excavated two of the trash features. The foundation and the third trash feature were destroyed before they could be recorded. The excavators noted that the historical-period features may be associated with a homestead patent at the same location issued in 1883 to Román Espinosa, hence the site name. SRI has found an undated map of the area (see Figure 40) that shows a pump house in the vicinity of the foundation. The map probably relates to use of the area by the Allison brothers for irrigated agriculture around 1900. Both the homestead and the later irrigation component may be represented at the site.

AZ BB:13:384 (ASM)
Prehistoric period: undifferentiated Archaic
Prehistoric function: limited activity

This site consists of a lithic scatter with unifacial and bifacial tools. All of the tools were patinated to some extent, but no diagnostics were noted. In addition to flake tools, ovate bifacial tools and choppers were noted. No evidence of features was noted.

AZ BB:13:402 (ASM)
Prehistoric periods: Colonial (Cañada del Oro and Rillito phases), Sedentary (Rincon phase)
Prehistoric function: limited activity
Historical periods: protohistoric/historical and undetermined
Historical functions: undetermined and irrigation

The prehistoric component of this site consists of an artifact scatter with flaked stone, ground stone, and decorated ceramics. Recognizable ceramic types are Cañada del Oro Red-on-brown (n = 1), Gila Butte Red-on-buff (n = 1), Rillito/Early Rincon Red-on-brown (n = 2), Rincon Red-on-brown (n = 2), Rincon Red (n = 2), and a possible protohistoric red ware sherd. In addition, several indeterminate red-on-brown sherds were noted. The historical-period component of this site as described on the ASM site card is limited to several Papago red ware sherds. However, the site map shows a historical-period canal running approximately north-south through the western portion of the site for several hundred meters. No discussion of this feature is provided on the site card or in the associated report (Mabry 1990).

AZ BB:13:426 (ASM)
Historical period: Early Statehood
Historical function: undetermined

This site consists of a light scatter of historical-period trash, including hard-paste earthenwares, Japanese and Chinese porcelain, SCA glass, cans, shell buttons, and Papago pottery.

AZ BB:13:479 (ASM)
This site was subsumed under AZ BB:13:8.

AZ BB:13:481 (ASM): Acequia Madre Tercia, Acequia Madre Primera
Historical period: Territorial
Historical function: irrigation

This site consists of various segments of a historical-period canal system depicted on an early map of the area west of the Santa Cruz River, north and east of Sentinel Peak (Fergusson 1862; see Figure 8). Among the archaeologically documented segments are the Acequia Madre Tercia, first recorded in 1995 (Thiel 1995a), and the Acequia Madre Primera, discovered during recent (2001) excavations by Desert Archaeology for the City of Tucson's Río Nuevo development project. One segment of the system, discovered below Spruce Street at the northern end of the project area, shows evidence of having been re-worked, probably by the Allison brothers in the 1880s as a part of their expansion of irrigation along this stretch of the Santa Cruz (Thiel 1995b). Readers are referred to Chapter 4 for a discussion of historical-period irrigation in the project area.

AZ BB:13:536 (ASM)
Prehistoric periods: Sedentary (Rincon phase), Classic (Tanque Verde phase)
Prehistoric functions: habitation and agricultural

This site consists of a ceramic, ground stone, and fire-cracked rock scatter associated with an undated pit house, and a possible canal segment. The temporal assignation for the site is tentative and is based on a single plain ware sherd identified as "West Branch" variety.

AZ BB:13:539 (ASM)
Historical period: Early Statehood
Historical function: irrigation

This site consists of an aboveground concrete irrigation pipe (1½ feet in diameter) with turnout structures, probably dating to the 1930s. The pipe is at least 0.3 miles long, but the end points of the feature were not established.

AZ BB:13:630 (ASM)
Historical period: protohistoric/historical
Historical function: undetermined

This site is a small, low-density scatter of about 60 sherds, primarily Papago red wares.

AZ BB:13:646 (ASM): Grabe Brick Company
Historical periods: Early Statehood and post–World War ll
Historical function: industrial

This site consists of three features associated with the Grabe Brick Company plant, which began operation at least as early as 1917 and closed in 1963. The site is completely covered by a modern landfill. The three features were discovered during monitoring of construction. Other buried features may be present at the site.

Ahlstrom, Richard V. N., and Mark C. Slaughter
  1996   Site Chronology and Dating Methods. In *Excavation of the Gibbon Springs Site: A Classic Period Village in the Northeastern Tucson Basin,* edited by Mark C. Slaughter and Heidi Roberts, pp. 481–489. Archaeological Report No. 94-87. SWCA, Tucson.

Allison, Warren
  1938   Pioneer Days in Tucson as Told by Mr. Warren Allison. Manuscript 13, Allison Family Papers, series 4, folder 30. On file, Arizona Historical Society, Tucson.

Altschul, Jeffrey H., Trixi Bubemyre, Kellie M. Cairns, William L. Deaver, Anthony Della Croce, Suzanne K. Fish, Lee Fratt, Karen G. Harry, James Holmlund, Gary Huckleberry, Charles H. Miksicek, Arthur W. Vokes, Stephanie M. Whittlesey, Maria Nieves Zedeño, and Lara F. Ziady
  1996   *Archaeological Investigations at the SRI Locus, West Branch Site (AZ AA:16:3 [ASM]): A Rincon Phase Village in the Tucson Basin.* Draft. Statistical Research, Tucson. Submitted to the Pima County Department of Transportation and Flood Control District, Tucson.

Altschul, Jeffrey H., and Edgar K. Huber
  1995   *Archaeological Testing Report and Treatment Plan for the Dairy Site (AZ AA:12:285 [ASM]).* Technical Report 95-8. Statistical Research, Tucson.

Anderson, Adrienne
  1968   The Archaeology of Mass-Produced Footwear. *Historical Archaeology* 2:56–65.

  1970   From Family Home to Slum Apartment: Archaeological Analysis within the Urban Renewal Area, Tucson, Arizona. Unpublished Master's thesis, Department of Anthropology, University of Arizona, Tucson.

Antone, Geri
  1997   *A Cultural Resources Survey of a Half Acre House Lot: Allotment 56, San Xavier District, Tohono O'odham Nation.* Archaeological Report No. 97-128. SWCA, Tucson.

Arizona Daily Star (ADS) [Tucson]
  1880   "Advertisement for Silver Lake Resort and Excelsior Brewery." 9 June:1. Tucson.

  1886   "Announcement for Silver Lake Resort placed by Fred Maish, proprietor." 27 April:4. Tucson.

  1892   Nogales News. 13 August. Tucson.

  1892   The Tucson and Nogales Road. General Allen Replies with Facts and Figures. 14 September. Tucson.

1893 "Small announcement on sale of Jimmy Lee Mill turbine wheel." 24 January:4. Tucson.

1917 Professional Opinion. 11 May. Tucson.

1923 Sentinel Peak Hearing Is Continued until Tuesday, 'A' Cost $6,000, Revealed. 11 October. Tucson.

1924 Eagle Milling Company: One of Oldest Industries, Showing Big Growth. 16 March:6. Tucson.

1925 Old Residents Tell of Uses of Sentinel Peak during Old Days Here. 9 October. Tucson.

1928 Sentinel Peak Now Tucson's, Every Dodson Claim Denied. 18 November. Tucson.

Arizona Department of Transportation (ADOT)
1977 *Historical Notes: Existing Road System and Current Regulations of Highway Transport in Arizona.* Transportation Planning Division, Arizona Department of Transportation, Phoenix.

Arizona Highway Department
1952 *Arizona State Highway System: 1952, An Economic Study.* Division of Economics and Statistics, Arizona Highway Department, Phoenix, in cooperation with U.S. Department of Commerce Bureau of Public Roads. On file, Government Documents, Arizona State University, Phoenix.

Arizona Historical Society (AHS)
n.d.a The Tribulations and Deaths in the Marinez [sic] Family. Unpublished transcription by Carl Hayden of an early newspaper account. Hayden file, José María Martínez items, Arizona Historical Society, Tucson.

n.d.b Biographical note on the Roy Probasco family. On file, Probasco collection, Arizona Historical Society, Tucson.

n.d.c Undated sketch map of features in Township 14 South, Range 13 East, Section 14. Manuscript 13, Allison family papers, series 6, folder 32. On file, Arizona Historical Society, Tucson.

n.d.d Undated sketch map of features in Township 14 South, Range 13 East, portions of Sections 34 and 35. On file (Ms.13, Allison family papers, series 6, folder 32), Arizona Historical Society, Tucson.

Arizona Mining Index
1884 "Small announcement in 'Year in Review' section." 27 December:3. Tucson.

Arizona State Engineer
1918 *Third Biennial Report of the State Engineer to the Governor and the Commission of State Institutions and to the Boards of Supervisors of the Several Counties for the Period July 1, 1916, to June 30, 1918.* On file, Research Department, Arizona Department of Library, Archives, and Public Records, Phoenix.

1920　*Fourth Biennial Report of the State Engineer to the Governor of the State of Arizona for the Period July 1, 1918, to December 31, 1920.* On file, Research Department, Arizona Department of Library, Archives, and Public Records, Phoenix.

1922　*Fifth Biennial Report of the State Engineer to the Governor of the State of Arizona for the Period July 1, 1920, to June 30, 1922.* On file, Research Department, Arizona Department of Library, Archives, and Public Records, Phoenix.

1924　*Sixth Biennial Report of the State Engineer to the Governor of the State of Arizona, for the Period July 1, 1922, to June 30, 1924.* On file, Research Department, Arizona Department of Library, Archives, and Public Records, Phoenix.

Arizona Weekly Star
1878　"Short notice of milling services at Warner's Mill." 28 February:3. Tucson.

1879　"Short notice announcing M. Thomas Gilmore as miller and assayer at Warner's Mill." 8 May:3. Tucson.

Ash, Charles W., Scott L. Battles, John A. Black, Joel M. Byko, Ignacio A. Coppola, J. Donald Couvillion, Ernest Federico, Peter Hosmer, Edward T. Marley, Joanna L. Meitz, Jorge Pierson, Lisa Ann Smith, Scott C. Smith, Thomas B. Todd, and Lawrence R. Wilson
1981　Desert Botanical Laboratory, Tumamoc Hill, Tucson, Arizona: Historical Report. Manuscript on file, Special Collections, University of Arizona Library, Tucson.

Atondo Rodríguez, Ana María, and Martha Ortega Soto
1985　Entrada de colonos españoles en Sonora durante el siglo XVII. In *Historia general de Sonora,* vol. 2, edited by Sergio Ortega Noriega and Ignacio del Río, pp. 77–110. Gobierno del Estado de Sonora, Hermosillo, Mexico.

Ayres, James E.
1968　Urban Renewal Salvage Archaeology in Tucson, Arizona. Paper presented at the 33rd Annual Meeting of the Society for American Archaeology, Santa Fe. Manuscript on file, Arizona State Museum Library, University of Arizona, Tucson.

1969　Innovations in the Use of Ceramics: A Case from Historical Archaeology. Paper presented at the 12th Annual Ceramic Conference, Flagstaff, Arizona. Manuscript on file, Arizona State Museum Library, University of Arizona, Tucson.

1970a　An Early Historic Burial from the Village of Bac. *The Kiva* 36(2):44–48.

1970b　Problem-Oriented Historical Archaeology in Tucson, Arizona. Paper presented at the 35th Annual Meeting of the Society for American Archaeology, Mexico City. Manuscript on file, Arizona State Museum Library, University of Arizona, Tucson.

1971　Buildings and Bottles. *Southern Arizona Genealogical Society Bulletin* 6(3):48–51.

1978　Archaeological Report: Preliminary Report of Excavations at TUR 1:6 (The Cordova House). In *The Restoration of the La Casa Cordova,* compiled and edited by J. B. Hunt, pp. 13–17. Junior League of Tucson, Tucson.

1979   Archaeological Excavations in the Art Center Block: A Brief Summary. In *Master Plan for the Tucson Museum of Art,* Appendix 2. James Gresham and Associates, Tucson.

1980   Analysis of Historic Artifacts from Tucson, Arizona's Urban Renewal Area. Manuscript on file, Arizona State Museum Library, University of Arizona, Tucson. Final report submitted to the National Endowment for the Humanities, Grant RO-21419-75-217.

1984a   *Rosemont: The History and Archaeology of Post-1880 Sites in the Rosemont Area, Santa Rita Mountains, Arizona.* Archaeological Series No. 147, vol. 3. Cultural Resource Management Division, Arizona State Museum, University of Arizona, Tucson.

1984b   The Anglo Period in Archaeological and Historical Perspective. *The Kiva* 49:225–232.

1990   *Historic Archaeology at the Tucson Community Center.* Arizona State Museum Archaeological Series No. 181. University of Arizona, Tucson.

1991   Historical Archaeology in Arizona and New Mexico. *Historical Archaeology* 25(3):18–23.

Ayres, James E., and Lyle M. Stone
1983   Historic Period Cultural Resources. In *An Archaeological Assessment of the Middle Santa Cruz River Basin, Rillito to Green Valley, Arizona, for the Proposed Tucson Aqueduct, Phase B, Central Arizona Project,* by Jon S. Czaplicki and J. D. Mayberry, pp. 63–77. Archaeological Series No. 164. Cultural Resource Management Division, Arizona State Museum, University of Arizona, Tucson.

Baar, Sam
1996   *Interstate 10 Frontage Road Project: Results of Archaeological Testing, South of Speedway Parcel.* Technical Report No. 96-11. Center for Desert Archaeology, Tucson.

Bahr, Donald
1971   Who Were the Hohokam? The Evidence from Pima-Papago Myths. *Ethnohistory* 18:245–266.

1975   *Pima and Papago Ritual Oratory: A Study of Three Texts.* Indian Historian Press, San Francisco.

Bahr, Donald, Juan Gregorio, David I. Lopez, and Albert Alvarez
1974   *Piman Shamanism and Staying Sickness (Ká:cim Múmkidag).* University of Arizona Press, Tucson.

Bahr, Donald, Lloyd Paul, and Vincent Joseph
1997   *Ants and Orioles: Showing the Art of Pima Poetry.* University of Utah Press, Salt Lake City.

Bahr, Donald, Juan Smith, William Smith Allison, and Julian Hayden
1994   *The Short, Swift Time of Gods on Earth: The Hohokam Chronicles.* University of California Press, Berkeley.

Bahre, Conrad Joseph
1991   *A Legacy of Change: Historic Human Impact on Vegetation in the Arizona Borderlands.*
        University of Arizona Press, Tucson.

Bancroft, Hubert H.
1889   *History of Arizona and New Mexico, 1530–1888.* The History Company, San Francisco.

Bandelier, Adolph F.
1890   *Final Report of Investigations among the Indians of the Southwestern United States Carried
        on Mainly in the Years 1880–1885,* pt. 2. Papers of the Archaeological Institute of America,
        American Series No. 4. John Wilson and Son and Cambridge University Press, Cambridge.

Bannon, John Francis
1955   *The Mission Frontier in Sonora, 1620–1687.* United States Catholic Historical Society, New
        York.

1964   Introduction. In *Bolton and the Spanish Borderlands*, edited by J. F. Bannon, pp. 3–19.
        University of Oklahoma Press, Norman.

1970   *The Spanish Borderlands Frontier, 1513–1821.* Holt, Rinehart and Winston, New York.

1978   *Herbert Eugene Bolton: The Historian and the Man.* University of Arizona Press, Tucson.

Barnes, Mark R.
1972   Majolica of the Santa Cruz Valley. In *Mexican Majolica in Northern New Spain*, by Mark R.
        Barnes and R. V. May, pp. 1–23. Occasional Paper No. 2. Pacific Coast Archaeological
        Society, Ramona, California.

1980   Mexican Lead-Glazed Earthenwares. In *Spanish Colonial Frontier Research,* edited by
        Henry F. Dobyns, pp. 91–110. Center for Anthropological Studies, Albuquerque.

1983   Tucson: Development of a Community. Unpublished Ph.D. dissertation, School of Arts and
        Sciences, Catholic University of America, Washington, D.C.

1984   Hispanic Period Archaeology in the Tucson Basin: An Overview. *The Kiva* 49:213–223

Barnes, Thomas C., Thomas N. Naylor, and Charles W. Polzer
1981   *Northern New Spain: A Research Guide.* University of Arizona Press, Tucson.

Barnes, Will C.
1988   *Arizona Place Names.* University of Arizona Press, Tucson.

Barter, G. W. (compiler)
1881   *Directory of the City of Tucson for the Year 1881.* G. W. Barter, Tucson.

Barton, C. Michael, Kay Simpson, and Lee Fratt
1981   *Tumacacori Excavations, 1979/1980: Historical Archeology at Tumacacori National
        Monument, Arizona.* Publications in Anthropology No. 17. Western Archeological and
        Conservation Center, USDI National Park Service, Tucson.

Basso, Keith H.

   1969   *Western Apache Witchcraft.* Anthropological Papers No. 15. University of Arizona, Tucson.

   1970   *The Cibicue Apache.* Holt, Rinehart and Winston, New York.

   1983   Western Apache. In *Southwest,* edited by Alfonso Ortiz, pp. 462–488. Handbook of North American Indians, vol. 10, William C. Sturtevant, general editor, Smithsonian Institution, Washington, D.C.

   1996   *Wisdom Sits in Places: Landscape and Language among the Western Apache.* University of New Mexico Press, Albuquerque.

Bawaya, Michael

   2001   A City Searches for Its Roots. *American Archaeology* 5(2):24–30.

Beals, Ralph L.

   1943   *The Aboriginal Culture of the Cáhita Indians.* Ibero-Americana No. 19. University of California Press, Berkeley.

   1945   *The Contemporary Culture of the Cáhita Indians.* Bulletin No. 142. Bureau of American Ethnology, Smithsonian Institution, Washington, D.C.

Bean, Lowell J., and William M. Mason

   1962   *Diaries and Accounts of the Romero Expeditions in Arizona and California, 1823–1826.* Ward Ritchie, Los Angeles.

Beaubien, Paul

   1937   *Excavations at Tumacacori, 1934.* Southwestern Monuments Special Report 15. USDI National Park Service, Washington, D.C.

Berge, Dale L.

   1968   Historical Archaeology in the American Southwest. Unpublished Ph.D. dissertation, Department of Anthropology, University of Arizona, Tucson.

Betancourt, Julio

   1978a *An Archaeological Synthesis of the Tucson Basin: Focus on the Santa Cruz and Its Riverpark.* Archaeological Series No. 116. Cultural Resource Management Division, Arizona State Museum, University of Arizona, Tucson.

   1978b *Cultural Resources within the Proposed Santa Cruz Riverpark Archaeological District: With Recommendations and a Management Summary.* Archaeological Series No. 125. Cultural Resource Management Division, Arizona State Museum, University of Arizona, Tucson.

   1990   Tucson's Santa Cruz River and the Arroyo Legacy. Unpublished Ph.D. dissertation, Department of Geosciences, University of Arizona, Tucson.

   1996   *The Desert Laboratory on Tumamoc Hill: Past and Present.* University of Arizona Geosciences Newsletter, Fall 1996. Department of Geosciences, University of Arizona, Tucson.

Bieber, Ralph P.
   1937   *Southern Trails to California in 1849.* Arthur H. Clark, Glendale, California.

   1938   *Exploring Southwestern Trails: 1846–1854, by Philip St. George Cooke, William Henry Chase Whiting, Francois Xavier Aubry.* Arthur H. Clark, Glendale, California.

Blaine, Peter, Sr. (with Michael S. Adams)
   1981   *Papagos and Politics.* Arizona Historical Society, Tucson.

Blanton and Cole
   1957   *A Master Plan and Planning Objectives for the Development of Midvale Farm Lands, Tucson, Arizona.* Prepared for the Charles Deere Wiman Estate, Moline, Illinois. Blanton and Cole, Tucson, Arizona. On file, Arizona Historical Society Library, Tucson.

Bolton, Herbert E.
   1930   *Font's Complete Diary of the Second Anza Expedition.* Anza's California Expeditions, vol. 4. University of California Press, Berkeley.

   1948   *Kino's Historical Memoir of Pimeria Alta.* University of California Press, Berkeley.

   1964   The Mission as a Frontier Institution in the Spanish American Colonies. In *Bolton and the Spanish Borderlands,* edited by John F. Bannon, pp. 187–211. Reprinted. University of Oklahoma Press, Norman. Originally published 1917, University of Oklahoma Press, Norman.

   1984   *Rim of Christendom: A Biography of Eusebio Francisco Kino, Pacific Coast Pioneer.* Reprinted. University of Arizona Press, Tucson. Originally published 1936, Macmillan, New York.

   1990   *Coronado: Knight of Pueblos and Plains.* University of New Mexico Press, Albuquerque. Originally published 1949.

Bradley, Bruce A.
   1980   *Excavations at Arizona BB:13:74, Santa Cruz Industrial Park, Tucson, Arizona.* CASA Papers No. 1. Complete Archaeological Service Associates, Oracle, Arizona.

Brew, Susan A., and Bruce B. Huckell
   1987   A Protohistoric Piman Burial and a Consideration of Piman Burial Practices. *The Kiva* 52:163–191.

Bronitsky, Gordon R., and James D. Merritt
   1986   *The Archaeology of Southeast Arizona: A Class I Cultural Resources Inventory.* Cultural Resource Series No. 2. Arizona State Office, USDI Bureau of Land Management, Phoenix.

Bryan, Kirk
   1922   Routes to Desert Watering Places in the Papago Country, Arizona. Water Supply Paper No. 490-D. USDI U.S. Geological Survey. U.S. Government Printing Office, Washington, D.C.

Burrus, Ernest J.
   1971   *Kino and Manje: Explorers of Sonora and Arizona.* Jesuit Historical Institute, Rome, Italy,
           and St. Louis, Missouri.

Burton, Jeffery F.
   1992a   *San Miguel de Guevavi: The Archaeology of an Eighteenth Century Jesuit Mission on the
           Rim of Christendom.* Publications in Anthropology No. 57. Western Archeological and
           Conservation Center, USDI National Park Service, Tucson.

   1992b   *Remnants of Adobe and Stone: The Surface Archaeology of the Guevavi and Calabazas
           Units, Tumacacori National Historical Park, Arizona.* Publications in Anthropology No. 59.
           Western Archeological and Conservation Center, USDI National Park Service, Tucson.

Byars, Charles
   1966   The First Map of Tucson. *Journal of Arizona History* 7:188–195.

Castalia, Patricia
   1992   *Archaeological Testing of the Access Easement to the Water Plant No. 1 Replacement
           Reservoir Site.* Letter Report No. 92-112. Center for Desert Archaeology, Tucson.

Castetter, Edward F., and Willis H. Bell
   1942   *Pima and Papago Indian Agriculture.* University of New Mexico Press, Albuquerque.

Castetter, Edward F., and Ruth M. Underhill
   1935   *The Ethnobiology of the Papago Indians.* Ethnobiological Studies in the American South-
           west II. University of New Mexico Bulletin, Biological Series, vol. 4, no. 3. University of
           New Mexico, Albuquerque.

Center for Desert Archaeology
   2001   Tucson Origins: Archaeology and History for the Río Nuevo Project. Electronic document,
           http://www.rio-nuevo.org/rionuevo/index.html, accessed November 1, 2001.

Chamber of Commerce
   1936   Points of Interest of Tucson and Vicinity. Chamber of Commerce, Tucson, and Tucson
           Sunshine Club, Tucson. Map on file, Arizona Historical Society, Tucson.

Chambers, George W.
   1955   The Old Presidio of Tucson. *The Kiva* 20(2–3):15–16.

Chavarria, Sara P.
   1996   *Archaeological Investigations at the Summit at Alvernon Site, AZ BB:9:280 (ASM): Archaic,
           Hohokam, Protohistoric, and Historical Use of an Upper Bajada Environment in the Tucson
           Basin.* Archaeology Report No. 4. Old Pueblo Archaeology Center, Tucson.

Cheek, Annetta L.
   1974   The Evidence for Acculturation in Artifacts: Indians and Non-Indians at San Xavier del Bac,
           Arizona. Unpublished Ph.D. dissertation, Department of Anthropology, University of Ari-
           zona, Tucson.

Ciolek-Torrello, Richard S.
1995   The Houghton Road Site, the Agua Caliente Phase, and the Early Formative Period in the Tucson Basin. *Kiva* 60:531–574.

Ciolek-Torrello, Richard S. (editor)
1998   *Early Farmers of the Sonoran Desert: Archaeological Investigations at the Houghton Road Site, Tucson, Arizona.* Technical Series 72. Statistical Research, Tucson.

Ciolek-Torrello, Richard S., and Susan A. Brew
1976   *Archaeological Test Excavations at the San Xavier Bicentennial Plaza Site.* Archaeological Series No. 102. Cultural Resource Management Division, Arizona State Museum, University of Arizona, Tucson.

Ciolek-Torrello, Richard S., and Mark T. Swanson (editors)
1997   *Pit House, Presidio, and Privy: 1,400 Years of Archaeology and History on Block 180, Tucson, Arizona.* Technical Series 63. Statistical Research, Tucson.

The Citizen [Tucson]
1874   "Short announcement under 'Local Matters' regarding E. N. Fish and Co." 4 July. Tucson.

1875   The Mission Flour Mills. 30 October. Tucson.

City of Tucson
1996   *Celebrating Tucson's Heritage.* City of Tucson and the Tucson–Pima County Historical Commission, Tucson.

Clemensen, Berle
1987   *Cattle, Copper, and Cactus: The History of Saguaro National Monument, Arizona.* USDI National Park Service, Denver.

Clonts, John
1983   Some Long Overdue Thoughts on Faunal Analysis. In *Forgotten Places and Things: Archaeological Perspectives on American History,* edited by A. E. Ward, pp. 349–354. Contributions to Anthropological Studies No. 3. Center for Anthropological Studies, Albuquerque, New Mexico.

Coggin, H. Mason
1987   A History of Placer Mining in Arizona. In *History of Mining in Arizona,* edited by J. Michael Canty and Michael N. Greeley, pp. 177–190. Mining Club of the Southwest Foundation, American Institute of Mining Engineers Tucson Section, Tucson, and Southwestern Minerals Exploration Association, Tucson.

Cohen-Williams, Anita, and Jack S. Williams
1982   Los Reales Viejo. Paper presented at the Tucson Basin Conference, Tucson. On file, Arizona Historical Society, Tucson.

Collins, William
2001   Cattle Ranching in Arizona, 1540–1950. Draft National Register of Historic Places Multiple Property Documentation Form. On file, USDI National Park Service, Washington, D.C.

Colton, Harold S., and Lyndon L. Hargrave
  1937   *Handbook of Northern Arizona Pottery Wares.* Bulletin No. 11. Museum of Northern Arizona, Flagstaff.

Conkling, Roscoe B., and Margaret B. Conkling
  1947   *The Butterfield Overland Mail, 1857–1869.* 3 vols. Arthur H. Clark, Glendale, California.

Cooke, Ronald U., and Richard W. Reeves
  1976   *Arroyos and Environmental Change in the American South-West.* Clarendon, Oxford.

Cosulich, Bernice
  1953   *Tucson.* Arizona Silhouettes, Tucson.

Courtwright, J. Scott, and Thomas E. Wright
  1999   *Cultural Resources Survey of Ca. 45 Acres of Private Land for United Metro Aggregate Materials Plant # 221 (#CM0068), Tucson, Pima County, Arizona.* Project Report No. 99-78. Archaeological Research Services, Tempe, Arizona.

Coville, Frederick Vernon
  1903   *Desert Botanical Laboratory of the Carnegie Institution.* Publication No. 6. Carnegie Institution of Washington, Washington, D.C.

Cowdery, Richard B.
  1948   The Planning of a Transcontinental Railroad through Southern Arizona, 1832–1870. Unpublished Master's thesis, Departments of History and of Political Science, University of Arizona, Tucson.

Craig, Douglas B.
  1988   *Archaeological Investigations at AZ AA:16:49 (ASM): The Dakota Wash Mitigation.* Anthropology Series Archaeological Report No. 14. Pima Community College, Tucson.

Craig, Douglas B., and Henry D. Wallace
  1987   *Prehistoric Settlement in the Cañada del Oro Valley, Arizona: The Rancho Vistoso Survey Project.* Anthropological Papers No. 8. Institute for American Research, Tucson.

Crosby, Alfred
  1972   *The Columbian Exchange: Biological Consequences of 1492.* Greenwood, Westport, Connecticut.

Curriden, Nancy T.
  1981   *The Lewis-Weber Site: A Tucson Homestead.* Publications in Anthropology No. 14. Western Archeological Center, USDI National Park Service, Tucson.

Danson, Edward B.
  1946   An Archaeological Survey of the Santa Cruz River from Its Headwaters to the Town of Tubac in Arizona. Unpublished Master's thesis, Department of Anthropology, University of Arizona, Tucson.

Dart, Allen

1982   Archaeological Testing at AZ AA:16:44, the Salida del Sol Hohokam Site. In *Archaeological Test Excavations in Southern Arizona,* edited by Susan A. Brew, pp. 19–36. Archaeological Series No. 152. Cultural Resource Management Division, Arizona State Museum, University of Arizona, Tucson.

1984   *An Archaeological Clearance Survey for Arizona Department of Transportation Project ER-19-1 (97): San Xavier Mission Road Bridge Repairs on the Santa Cruz River, Pima County, Arizona.* Arizona State Museum, Tucson.

1988   *An Archaeological Survey of the Francisco Allotment near Mission and Drexel Roads, San Xavier Indian Reservation, Arizona.* Technical Report No. 88-1. Institute for American Research, Tucson.

1989   *The Gunsight Mountain Archaeological Survey: Archaeological Sites in the Northern Sierrita Mountains near the Junction of the Altar and Avra Valleys Southwest of Tucson, Arizona.* Technical Report No. 89-1. Center for Desert Archaeology, Tucson.

Davidson, Alexander J.

1930–1936   Reminiscences of Alexander J. Davidson as Told to Mrs. George F. Kitt, 1930–1936. Manuscript 208, Alexander J. Davidson Papers, 1931 [*sic*]–1936. On file, Arizona Historical Society, Tucson.

Deaver, William L.

1989   Pottery and Other Ceramic Artifacts. In *The 1979–1983 Testing at Los Morteros (AZ AA:12:57 ASM), a Large Hohokam Village Site in the Tucson Basin,* by Richard C. Lange and William L. Deaver, pp. 27–81. Archaeological Series No. 177. Cultural Resource Management Division, Arizona State Museum, University of Arizona, Tucson.

Deaver, William, and Eric H. Albright

1992   *Archaeological Testing along the Santa Cruz River Park South of Mission Lane near the Historic Mission San Agustín del Tucsón (AZ BB:13:6 [ASM]).* Submitted to the Pima County Department of Transportation and Flood Control District, Tucson. Statistical Research, Tucson.

Deaver, William L., and Richard S. Ciolek-Torrello

1995   Early Formative Period Chronology for the Tucson Basin. *Kiva* 60:481–529.

DeJong, David H.

1992   "See the New Country": The Removal Controversy and Pima-Maricopa Water Rights, 1869–1879. *Journal of Arizona History* 33:367–396.

Diehl, Allison C.

1998   *An Archaeological Survey of the Intersection of Drexel Road and Oaktree Road, Tucson, Arizona.* Letter Report No. 98-203. Desert Archaeology, Tucson.

1999   *An Archaeological Survey of St. Mary's Road between Silverbell Road and Camino Santiago, Tucson, Arizona.* Letter Report No. 99-115. Desert Archaeology, Tucson.

Diehl, Allison C., and Michael W. Diehl

    1996   Building Tucson in the Nineteenth and Twentieth Centuries. *Archaeology in Tucson* 10(3):1–5.

Diehl, Allison Cohen, Timothy W. Jones, and J. Homer Thiel

    1996   *Archaeological Investigations at El Dumpé, a Mid-Twentieth-Century Dump, and the Embankment Site, Tucson, Arizona.* Technical Report No. 96-19. Center for Desert Archaeology, Tucson.

Diehl, Michael W.

    1996   *Further Archaeological Investigations of the Rio Nuevo South Property, City of Tucson, Arizona.* Technical Report No. 96-5. Center for Desert Archaeology, Tucson.

    1997   *Archaeological Investigations of the Early Agricultural Period Settlement at the Base of A-Mountain, Tucson, Arizona.* Technical Report No. 96-21. Center for Desert Archaeology, Tucson.

Diehl, Michael W., and Allison C. Diehl

    1996   *Archaeological Investigations of the Tucson Pressed Brick Company, Tucson, Arizona.* Technical Report No. 96-13. Center for Desert Archaeology, Tucson.

Di Peso, Charles C.

    1948   Preliminary Report of a Babocomari Indian Village. *The Kiva* 14:10–14.

    1951   *The Babocomari Village Site on the Babocomari River, Southeastern Arizona.* Amerind Foundation Publication No. 5. Amerind Foundation, Dragoon, Arizona.

    1953   *The Sobaipuri Indians of the Upper San Pedro River Valley, Southeastern Arizona.* Publication No. 6. Amerind Foundation, Dragoon, Arizona.

    1956   *The Upper Pima of San Cayetano del Tumacacori.* Publication No. 7. Amerind Foundation, Dragoon, Arizona.

    1967   *The Amerind Foundation.* Amerind Foundation, Dragoon, Arizona.

Doak, David P., Elizabeth Noll, James E. Ayres, and Thomas N. Motsinger

    1995   *Archaeological Report for the Tucson, Arizona, Area Nexrad: Data Recovery at AZ EE:2:167 (ASM) and Recording and Evaluation of Two Additional Sites in the Empire Mountains, Pima County, Arizona.* Archaeological Report No. 95-78. SWCA, Tucson.

Dobyns, Henry F.

    1959   Tubac through Four Centuries: A Historical Resume and Analysis. 3 vols. Commissioned by the Arizona State Parks Board. Manuscript on file, Arizona State Museum Library, University of Arizona, Tucson.

    1974   The Kohatk: Oasis and Akchin Horticulturalists. *Ethnohistory* 21:317–327.

    1976   *Spanish Colonial Tucson: A Demographic History.* University of Arizona Press, Tucson.

1981   *From Fire to Flood: Historic Human Destruction of Sonoran Desert Riverine Oases.* Ballena Press, Socorro, New Mexico.

Doelle, William H.
1984   The Tucson Basin during the Protohistoric Period. *The Kiva* 49:195–211.

1985   *Excavations at the Valencia Site: A Preclassic Hohokam Village in the Southern Tucson Basin.* Anthropological Papers No. 3. Institute for American Research, Tucson.

1997   Preface. In *Archaeological Investigations of a Chinese Gardener's Household, Tucson, Arizona,* by J. Homer Thiel, pp. ix–xxiii. Technical Report No. 96-22. Center for Desert Archaeology, Tucson.

Doelle, William H., and Frederick W. Huntington
1986   Site Description. In *Archaeological Investigations at the West Branch Site: Early and Middle Rincon Occupation in the Southern Tucson Basin,* by Frederick W. Huntington, pp. 17–24. Anthropological Papers No. 5. Institute for American Research, Tucson.

Doelle, William H., Frederick W. Huntington, and Henry D. Wallace
1987   Rincon Phase Reorganization in the Tucson Basin. In *The Hohokam Village: Site Structure and Organization,* edited by David E. Doyel, pp. 71–96. Southwestern and Rocky Mountain Division, American Association for the Advancement of Science, Glenwood Springs, Colorado.

Doelle, William H., and Henry D. Wallace
1984   *Hohokam Settlement Patterns in the San Xavier Project Area.* Technical Report No. 84-10. Institute for American Research, Tucson.

1986   *Hohokam Settlement Patterns in the San Xavier Project Area, Southern Tucson Basin.* Technical Report No. 84-6. Institute for American Research, Tucson.

Dowell, Shelton G.
1933   The Big Business of Road Building: New Highways Being Constructed to Serve Very Definite Needs of Traffic. *Arizona Highways.* 9(9):4–5.

Downum, Christian E.
1993   *Between Desert and River: Hohokam Settlement and Land Use in the Los Robles Community.* Anthropological Papers No. 57. University of Arizona Press, Tucson.

Doyel, David E.
1977   *Excavations in the Middle Santa Cruz River Valley, Southeastern Arizona.* Contribution to Highway Salvage Archaeology No. 44. Arizona State Museum, University of Arizona, Tucson.

1979   *Archaeological Investigation at AZ BB:13:14 (ASM) in the Tucson Basin, Arizona.* Contribution to Highway Archaeology No. 58. Arizona State Museum, University of Arizona, Tucson.

Dutt, Andrew

    1999   *Results of Archaeological Monitoring at Rio Nuevo Center, Tucson, Arizona.* Project Report No. 99-163. Desert Archaeology, Tucson.

    2000a *Cultural Resources Survey and Phased Data Recovery Plan for the Santa Cruz Bike Path between Silverlake and Ajo Roads, Tucson, Pima County, Arizona.* Letter Report No. 98-120. Desert Archaeology, Tucson.

    2000b *An Archaeological Survey of Four Proposed Well Locations in Tucson, Pima County, Arizona.* Project Report No. 00-116. Desert Archaeology, Tucson.

Dutt, Andrew, and J. Homer Thiel

    1999   *Results of a Testing Program and a Plan for Archaeological Data Recovery of a Portion of Block 136, Tucson, Arizona.* Technical Report No. 99-8. Desert Archaeology, Tucson.

Effland, Richard W., Jr., Adrianne Rankin, Jannette Schuster, and Michael Waters

    1989   *Tohono O'odham Nation Papago Water Supply Project: Cultural Resources Investigations for the San Xavier Farm Rehabilitation Project.* Archaeological Consulting Services, Tempe. Submitted to U.S. Bureau of Reclamation, Lower Colorado Region.

Elkins, Rosemary, Gayle H. Hartmann, Robert C. Johnson, Thomas Saarinen, Terah L. Smiley, Brock Tunnicliff, and Stanley K. Brickler

    1982   Tumamoc Hill Policy Plan. Submitted to the Tumamoc Hill Advisory Committee. Manuscript on file, Special Collections, University of Arizona Library, Tucson.

Elson, Mark D.

    1986   *Archaeological Investigations at the Tanque Verde Wash Site, a Middle Rincon Settlement in the Eastern Tucson Basin.* Anthropological Papers No. 7. Institute for American Research, Tucson.

    1997   *An Archaeological Survey of a Proposed Power Line, Water Line, and Water Storage Tank South of Martinez Hill in the San Xavier District of the Tohono O'odham Reservation.* Letter Report No. 97-121. Desert Archaeology, Tucson

Elson, Mark D., and William H. Doelle

    1986   *The Valencia Site Testing Project: Mapping, Intensive Surface Collecting, and Limited Trenching of a Hohokam Ballcourt Village in the Southern Tucson Basin.* Technical Report No. 86-6. Institute for American Research, Tucson.

    1987a *Archaeological Assessment of the Mission Road Extension: Testing at AZ BB:13:6 (ASM).* Technical Report No. 87-6. Institute for American Research, Tucson.

    1987b *Archaeological Survey in Catalina State Park with a Focus on Romero Ruin.* Technical Report No. 87-4. Institute for American Research, Tucson.

Eppley, Lisa

    1997   *An Archaeological Survey for Fire Station 18 near Drexel Road and Mission Road in Tucson, Arizona.* Letter Report No. 97-108. Desert Archaeology, Tucson.

Eppley, Lisa G., and Jonathan Mabry
  1991   *Archaeological Testing and Mitigation Plan for the Hotel Catalina Site, AZ BB:13:405 (ASM).* Technical Report No. 91-4. Center for Desert Archaeology, Tucson.

Erickson, Winston P.
  1994   *Sharing the Desert: The Tohono O'odham in History.* University of Arizona Press, Tucson

Erskine, Michael
  1859   *The Diary of Michael Erskine Describing His Cattle Drive from Texas to California Together with Correspondence from the Gold Fields 1854–1859.* Nita Stewart Haley Memorial Library, Midland, Texas.

Etter, Patricia A.
  1995   To California on the Southern Route—1849. *Overland Journal* 13(3).

Euler, R. Thomas
  1987   *Archaeological Clearance Surveys (T:87:02) of Nine House Lots for the Papago Housing Authority, San Xavier District, Tohono O'odham Nation, Pima County, Arizona.* Tohono O'odham Nation, Arizona.

Ewing, Russell Charles
  1945   The Pima Uprising of 1751: A Study of Spanish-Indian Relations on the Frontier of New Spain. In *Greater America: Essays in Honor of Herbert Eugene Bolton,* pp. 259–280. University of California Press, Berkeley.

Ezell, Paul H.
  1961   *The Hispanic Acculturation of the Gila River Pima.* American Anthropological Association, Menasha, Wisconsin.

  1983   History of the Pima. In *Southwest,* edited by Alfonso Ortiz, pp. 149–160. Handbook of North American Indians, vol. 10, William C. Sturtevant, general editor, Smithsonian Institution, Washington, D.C.

Ezzo, Joseph A., and William L. Deaver
  1998   *Watering the Desert: Late Archaic Farming at the Costello-King Site.* Technical Series 68. Statistical Research, Tucson.

Ezzo, Joseph A., and Stephanie M. Whittlesey
  1996   *The Julian Wash Site (AZ BB:13:17): Results of Testing between Tenth Avenue and the Santa Cruz River, Tucson, Arizona.* Draft. Submitted to the U.S. Army Corps of Engineers, Los Angeles District. Statistical Research, Tucson.

Fansett, George R.
  1952   Small Scale Gold Placering. In *Arizona Gold Placers and Placering,* 5th rev. ed., pp. 87–119. Arizona Bureau of Mines, University of Arizona, Tucson.

Farish, Thomas Edwin
  1915–1918 *History of Arizona.* 8 vols. Filmer Brothers Electrotype, San Francisco.

Farrell, Mary
    1993   Kentucky Camp: Big Dreams, Small Prospects. *Archaeology in Tucson* 7(2):1–4.

    1995   *Tearing Up the Ground with Splendid Results: Historic Mining on the Coronado National Forest.* USDA Forest Service, Southwest Region, Albuquerque, New Mexico.

Faught, Michael K.
    1995a   *Archaeological Testing, Limited Data Recovery, and an In-Place Archaeological Site Preservation Plan for the Madera Reserve Property Development in Green Valley, Pima County, Arizona.* Archaeology Report No. 94-2. Old Pueblo Archaeology Center, Tucson.

    1995b   *Archaeological Monitoring of Water and Sewer Pipeline Installations in the Village of San Xavier del Bac (W:ak), Tohono O'odham Nation.* Letter Report No. 95-139. Desert Archaeology, Tucson.

Faulk, Odie B.
    1969   *The Geronimo Campaign.* Oxford University Press, New York.

Ferg, Alan
    1979   The Petroglyphs of Tumamoc Hill. *The Kiva* 45:95–118.

Fergusson, David
    1862   Map No. 1 of the Cultivated Fields in and about Tucson A.T. Surveyed by order of Major D. Fergusson, 1st Cavalry Cal[ifornia] Vol[unteer]s. J. B. Mills, surveyor. On file, Arizona Historical Society, Tucson.

Figueroa, Gabriel, and Ricky Martínez
    n.d.   Looking into the Westside: Untold Stories of the People, 1900–1997: The People's Mountain. Electronic document, http://dizzy.library.arizona.edu/westside/062101 _peoples.html, accessed July 12, 2004.

Figueroa, Paul
    1938   Letter from Paul Figueroa to Mrs. Harold H. Royaltey, March 11, 1938. On file, Arizona Historical Society, Tucson.

Fish, Paul R., Suzanne K. Fish, Austin Long, and Charles Miksicek
    1986   Early Corn Remains from Tumamoc Hill, Southern Arizona. *American Antiquity* 51:563–572.

Fish, Suzanne K., Paul R. Fish, and John H. Madsen
    1992   Evolution and Structure of the Classic Period Marana Community. In *The Marana Coummunity in the Hohokam World,* edited by Suzanne K. Fish, Paul R. Fish, and John H. Madsen, pp. 20–40. Anthropological Papers No. 56. University of Arizona Press, Tucson.

Fish, Suzanne K., Paul R. Fish, and John Madsen (editors)
    1992   *The Marana Community in the Hohokam World.* Anthropological Papers No. 56. University of Arizona Press, Tucson.

Fish, Suzanne K., and William B. Gillespie
    1987   Prehistoric Use of Riparian Resources at the San Xavier Bridge Site. In *The Archaeology of the San Xavier Bridge Site (AZ BB:13:14), Tucson Basin, Southern Arizona,* edited by John C. Ravesloot, pp. 71–80. Archaeological Series No. 171. Cultural Resource Management Division, Arizona State Museum, University of Arizona, Tucson.

Flannery, Kent V. (editor)
    1976   *The Early Mesoamerican Village.* Academic Press, New York.

Fontana, Bernard L.
    1960   Assimiliative Change: A Papago Indian Case Study. Unpublished Ph.D. dissertation, Department of Anthropology, University of Arizona, Tucson.

    1965   *An Archaeological Survey of the Cabeza Prieta Game Range, Arizona.* Manuscript on file, Arizona State Museum Library, University of Arizona, Tucson.

    1971   Calabazas of the Rio Rico. *The Smoke Signal* 24:66–88.

    1983a   Pima and Papago: An Introduction. In *Southwest,* edited by Alfonso Ortiz, pp. 125–136. Handbook of North American Indians, vol. 10, William C. Sturtevant, general editor. Smithsonian Institution, Washington, D.C.

    1983b   History of the Papago. In *Southwest,* edited by Alfonso Ortiz, pp. 137–148. Handbook of North American Indians, vol. 10, William C. Sturtevant, general editor, Smithsonian Institution, Washington, D.C.

    1987   Santa Ana de Cuiquiburitac: Pimería Alta's Northernmost Mission. *Journal of the Southwest* 29:133–159.

    1989   *Of Earth and Little Rain: The Papago Indians.* University of Arizona Press, Tucson.

    1994   *Entrada: The Legacy of Spain and Mexico in the United States.* Southwest Parks and Monuments Association, Tucson.

    1996   Biography of a Desert Church: The Story of Mission San Xavier del Bac. *The Smoke Signal* 3 (rev. ed.).

    1997   Mission San Xavier del Bac: A Model for Conservation. *CRM* 11:30–31.

Fontana, Bernard L., and J. Cameron Greenleaf
    1962   Johnny Ward's Ranch. *The Kiva* 28(1–2).

Fontana, Bernard L., J. Cameron Greenleaf, and Donnely D. Cassidy
    1959   A Fortified Arizona Mountain. *Kiva* 25(2):41–52.

Fontana, Bernard L., and Daniel S. Matson
    1987   Santa Ana de Cuiquiburitac: Pimería Alta's Northernmost Mission. *Journal of the Southwest* 29:133–159.

Fontana, Bernard L., William J. Robinson, Charles W. Cormack, and Ernest E. Leavitt, Jr.
 1962 *Papago Indian Pottery.* University of Washington Press, Seattle.

Fortier, Edward M.
 1980 *Archaeological Excavations at the Stevens House, Tucson, Pima County, Arizona.* Submitted to the Tucson Museum of Art, Arizona.

Fratt, Lee
 1981 *Tumacacori Plaza Excavation, 1979: Historical Archeology at Tumacacori National Monument, Arizona.* Publications in Anthropology No. 16. Western Archeological and Conservation Center, USDI National Park Service, Tucson.

Freeman, Andrea K. L., William H. Doelle, Mark D. Elson, and Allison Cohen Diehl
 1996 *Archaeological Investigations for the Menlo Park Storm Drain Project: Prehistoric and Historic Canal Systems at the Base of A-Mountain.* Technical Report No. 96-14. Desert Archaeology, Tucson.

Frick, Paul
 1954 An Archaeological Survey in the Santa Cruz Valley, Southern Arizona. Unpublished Master's thesis, Department of Anthropology, University of Arizona, Tucson.

Fulton, William S.
 1940 Observations. In *An Archaeological Site near Gleeson, Arizona,* by William S. Fulton and C. Tuthill, pp. 63–64. Papers No. 1. Amerind Foundation, Dragoon, Arizona.

Fulton, William S., and Carl Tuthill
 1940 *An Archaeological Site near Gleeson, Arizona.* Papers No. 1. Amerind Foundation, Dragoon, Arizona.

Gabel, Norman E.
 1931 Martinez Hill Ruins: An Example of Prehistoric Culture of the Middle Gila. Unpublished Master's thesis, Department of Anthropology, University of Arizona, Tucson.

General Land Office (GLO)
 1921 Map of Township 15 South, Range 13 East, Gila and Salt River Base and Meridian, Arizona. General Land Office, Washington, D.C. On file, Arizona State Office, USDI Bureau of Land Management, Phoenix.

Gerhard, Peter
 1993 *The North Frontier of New Spain.* Rev. ed. University of Oklahoma Press, Norman and London.

Gilman, Catherine
 1997 *Archaeological Monitoring of the NDC/Tucson Lightwave Fiber Optic Network Installation Project.* Technical Report No. 97-6. Center for Desert Archaeology, Tucson.

Gilman, Catherine, and Deborah L. Swartz
   1998   *Archaeological Testing and Monitoring of the Speedway to Ajo Reclaimed Pipeline Project (Phase I)*. Technical Report 98-2. Desert Archaeology, Tucson.

Gladwin, Harold S., Emil W. Haury, E. B. Sayles, and Nora Gladwin
   1937   *Excavations at Snaketown: Material Culture*. Medallion Papers No. 25. Gila Pueblo, Globe, Arizona.

Gobierno del Estado de Sonora
   1997   *Historia general de Sonora*. 6 vols. 2nd ed. Gobierno del Estado de Sonora, Hermosillo, Sonora, Mexico.

Goetz, William C.
   1918   Road map issued by the Chamber of Commerce, Tucson, Arizona: showing roads leading out of Tucson. On file, Arizona Historical Society, Tucson.

Goldschmidt, Leo
   1887   Photograph of Mission San Xavier del Bac by Leo Goldschmidt. Downloaded from Historic American Buildings Survey/Historic American Engineering Record Web site, http://memory.loc.gov/.

Goodwin, Grenville
   1939   *Myths and Tales of the White Mountain Apache*. Memoirs No. 33. American Folklore Society, New York.

   1969   *The Social Organization of the Western Apache*. Reprinted. University of Arizona Press, Tucson. Originally published 1942, University of Chicago Press, Chicago.

Grady, Mark A.
   1975   *The Tucson Sewage Project: An Archaeological Survey and Consideration of the Southwest Interceptor Alignment*. Archaeological Series No. 80. Cultural Resource Management Division, Arizona State Museum, University of Arizona, Tucson.

Graeme, R. W.
   1987   Bisbee, Arizona's Dowager Queen of Mining Camps: A Look at Her First 50 Years. In *History of Mining in Arizona,* edited by J. Michael Canty and Michael N. Greeley, pp. 51–76. Mining Club of the Southwest Foundation, American Institute of Mining Engineers Tucson Section, and Southwestern Minerals Exploration Association, Tucson.

Greenleaf, J. Cameron
   1975   *Excavations at Punta de Agua in the Santa Cruz River Basin, Southeastern Arizona*. Anthropological Paper No. 26. University of Arizona Press, Tucson.

Gregonis, Linda M., and Lisa W. Huckell
   1979   *The Tucson Urban Study*. Archaeological Series No. 138. Arizona State Museum, University of Arizona, Tucson.

Gregory, David A.
1999   *Excavations in the Santa Cruz River Floodplain: The Middle Archaic Component at Los Pozos.* Anthropological Papers No. 20. Center for Desert Archaeology, Tucson.

Griffith, James S.
1973   The Catholic Religious Architecture of the Papago Reservation, Arizona. Unpublished Ph.D. dissertation, Department of Anthropology, University of Arizona, Tucson.

1992   *Beliefs and Holy Places: A Spiritual Geography of the Pimería Alta.* University of Arizona Press, Tucson.

Guy, Donna J., and Thomas E. Sheridan (editors)
1998   *Contested Ground: Comparative Frontiers on the Northern and Southern Edges of the Spanish Empire.* University of Arizona Press, Tucson.

Hackenberg, Robert A.
1974   Aboriginal Land Use and Occupancy. In *Papago Indians I,* edited by D. A. Horr, pp. 23–308. Garland, New York.

Hadley, Diana, Thomas H. Naylor, and Mardith K. Schuetz-Miller (editors)
1997   *The Central Corridor and the Texas Corridor, 1700–1765.* The Presidio and Militia on the Northern Frontier of New Spain, vol. 2, pt. 2. University of Arizona Press, Tucson.

Hadley, Diana, and Thomas E. Sheridan
1995   *Land Use History of the San Rafael Valley, Arizona (1540–1960).* USDA Rocky Mountain Forest and Range Experiment Station, Fort Collins, Colorado.

Halbirt, Carl D., and T. Kathleen Henderson (editors)
1993   *Archaic Occupation of the Santa Cruz Flats: The Tator Hills Archaeological Project.* Northland Research, Flagstaff.

Hammack, Nancy S., and Bruce Bradley
1979   Test Excavations at AZ BB:13:15 and AZ BB:13:74, Santa Cruz Industrial Park, Tucson, Arizona. Manuscript on file, Arizona State Museum, Tucson.

Hard, Robert J., and William H. Doelle
1978   *The San Augustín Mission Site, Tucson, Arizona.* Archaeological Series No. 118. Cultural Resource Management Division, Arizona State Museum, University of Arizona, Tucson.

Harry, Karen G., and Richard S. Ciolek-Torrello
1992   *Farming the Floodplain: A Look at Prehistoric and Historic Land-Use along the Rillito: Test Excavations and National Register Evaluations of Eight Prehistoric and Historic Sites along the Rillito River, Pima County, Arizona.* Technical Series 35. Statistical Research, Tucson.

Hartmann, Gayle Harrison, and William K. Hartmann
1979   Prehistoric Trail Systems and Related Features on the Slopes of Tumamoc Hill. *The Kiva* 45(1–2):39–70.

Hartmann, William K.
  1989   *Desert Heart: Chronicles of the Sonoran Desert.* Fisher Books, Tucson.

Hastings, James Rodney, and Raymond M. Turner
  1965   *The Changing Mile: An Ecological Study of Vegetation Change with Time in the Lower Mile of an Arid and Semiarid Region.* University of Arizona Press, Tucson.

Hatcher, H. C.
  1931   What is the Seven Per Cent System? *Arizona Highways.* 7(8):7–8, 12.

Haury, Emil W.
  1932   *Roosevelt 9:6: A Hohokam Site of the Colonial Period.* Medallion Papers No. 11. Gila Pueblo, Globe, Arizona.

  1945   *The Excavation of Los Muertos and Neighboring Ruins in the Salt River Valley, Southern Arizona.* Papers of the Peabody Museum of American Archaeology and Ethnology Vol. 24, No. 1. Harvard University, Cambridge.

  1953   Discovery of the Naco Mammoth and the Associated Projectile Points. *American Antiquity* 19:1–14.

Haury, Emil W., and Isabel Fathauer
  1974   *Tucson from Pithouse to Skyscraper.* Tucson Historical Committee, Tucson.

Haury, Emil W., E. B. Sayles, and William W. Wasley
  1959   The Lehner Mammoth Site, Southeastern Arizona. *American Antiquity* 25:2–42.

Hayden, Julian D.
  1957   *Excavations, 1940 at University Indian Ruin, Tucson, Arizona.* Technical Series No. 5. Southwest Monuments Association, Tucson, and Gila Pueblo, Globe, Arizona.

Haynes, C. Vance, and Bruce B. Huckell
  1986   Sedimentary Successions of the Prehistoric Santa Cruz River, Tucson, Arizona. Manuscript on file, Arizona Bureau of Geology and Mineral Technology Geological Survey Branch, Tucson.

Heidke, James
  1995   Production and Distribution of Rincon Phase Pottery: Evidence from the Julian Wash Site. In *A Rincon Phase Occupation of the Julian Wash Site, AZ BB:13:17 (ASM),* by Jonathon B. Mabry. Technical Report No. 94-1. Center for Desert Archaeology, Tucson.

Helen, George
  1900   *Map of the City of Tucson, Pima County, Arizona, with the Several Additions and Adjacent Territory.* On file, Arizona Historical Society, Tucson.

Heuett, Mary Lou, and Sandra J. Vrettos
  1998   *A Cultural Resource Inventory of the San Xavier Mission Plaza (Redevelopment Plan B) for the San Xavier District of the Tohono O'odham Nation, Pima County, Arizona.* Cultural and Environmental Systems, Tucson.

Hill, Matthew E., Jr., and Douglas Avann
  1999   *Cultural Resources Survey for the Interstate-19, Pima Mine Road to Valencia Road, Pavement Preservation Project, Pima County, Arizona.* Dames and Moore, Phoenix.

Hill, Matthew E., and Daniel Garcia
  1999   *Cultural Resources Inventory Report and Discovery/Monitoring Plan for Phase I of the Tucson Freeway Management System along Portions of Interstates 10, 19, and B-19, Pima County, Arizona.* Dames and Moore, Phoenix.

Hinderlider, M. C.
  1913   Irrigation of Santa Cruz Valley—Parts 1 and II. *Engineering Record* 68(8):200–201, 242–244.

Historic American Buildings Survey (HABS)
  n.d.   Site plan of the Desert Botanical Laboratory Complex, Tumamoc Hill, Tucson. HABS No. AZ-138. Electronic document, http://memory.loc.gov/, accessed November 1, 2001. Historic American Buildings Survey/Historic American Engineering Record Web site.

  1940   Floor plan of Mission San Xavier del Bac Church, Tucson, Arizona. HABS No. AZ-13. Electronic document, http://memory.loc.gov/, accessed November 1, 2001. Historic American Buildings Survey/Historic American Engineering Record Web site.

Housing and Urban Development (HUD)
  1980   *Final Environmental Impact Statement, Midvale Park.* Department of Housing and Urban Development, Los Angeles.

Huckell, Bruce B.
  1982   *The Distribution of Fluted Points in Arizona: A Review and an Update.* Archaeological Series No. 145. Cultural Resource Management Division, Arizona State Museum, University of Arizona, Tucson.

  1984a   Sobaipuri Sites in the Rosemont Area. In *Miscellaneous Archaeological Studies in the ANAMAX-Rosemont Land Exchange Area,* by Martyn D. Tagg, R. G. Ervin, and Bruce B. Huckell, pp. 107–146. Archaeological Series No. 147, pt. 4. Cultural Resource Management Division, Arizona State Museum, University of Arizona, Tucson.

  1984b   The Paleoindian and Archaic Occupation of the Tucson Basin: An Overview. *The Kiva* 49:133–145.

  1984c   *The Archaic Occupation of the Rosemont Area, Northern Santa Rita Mountains, Southeastern Arizona.* Archaeological Series No. 147. Arizona State Museum, University of Arizona, Tucson.

  1987   Summary and Conclusions. In *The Corona de Tucson Project: Prehistoric Use of a Bajada Environment,* by Bruce B. Huckell, Martyn D. Tagg, and Lisa W. Huckell, pp. 261–296. Archaeological Series No. 147. Cultural Resource Management Division, Arizona State Museum, University of Arizona, Tucson.

1993   *Archaeological Testing of the Pima Community College Desert Vista Campus Property: The Valencia North Project.* Technical Report No. 92-13. Center for Desert Archaeology, Tucson.

1995   *Of Marshes and Maize: Prehistoric Agricultural Settlements in the Cienega Valley, South-eastern Arizona.* Anthropological Paper No. 59. University of Arizona Press, Tucson.

Huckell, Bruce B., and Lisa W. Huckell
1982   Archaeological Test Excavations at Tubac State Park. In *Archaeological Test Excavations in Southern Arizona,* compiled by S. A. Brew, pp. 63–102. Archaeological Series No. 152. Arizona State Museum, University of Arizona, Tucson.

Hughes, John Taylor
1850   *A New Map of Mexico, California, and Oregon.* J. A. and U. P. James, Cincinnati.

Huntington, Frederick W.
1986   *Archaeological Investigations at the West Branch Site: Early and Middle Rincon Occupation in the Southern Tucson Basin.* Anthropological Papers No. 5. Institute for American Research, Tucson.

Huston, Ann
1986   National Register of Historic Places Inventory-Nomination Form for the Desert Laboratory of the Carnegie Institution, Tucson, Arizona. On file, Arizona State Museum, University of Arizona, Tucson.

Hyde, Charles K.
1998   *Copper for America: The United States Copper Industry from Colonial Times to the 1990s.* University of Arizona Press, Tucson.

Irvin, G. W.
1987   A Sequential History of Arizona Railroad and Mining Development, 1864–1920. In *History of Mining in Arizona,* edited by J. Michael Canty and Michael N. Greeley, pp. 253–278. Mining Club of the Southwest Foundation, American Institute of Mining Engineers Tucson Section, Tucson, and Southwestern Minerals Exploration Association, Tucson.

Jackson, Robert H.
1994   *Indian Population Decline: The Missions of Northwestern New Spain, 1687–1840.* University of New Mexico Press, Albuquerque.

1998   Northwestern New Spain: The Pimería Alta and the Californias. In *New Views of Borderlands History,* edited by Robert H. Jackson, pp. 73–97. University of New Mexico Press, Albuquerque.

Jacobs, Mike
1979   The St. Mary's Hospital Site. *The Kiva* 45:119–130.

Janus Associates, Inc.

1989   *Transcontinental Railroading in Arizona, 1878–1940: A Component of the Arizona Historic Preservation Plan.* Submitted to the State Historic Preservation Office, Arizona State Parks Board, Phoenix. Janus Associates, Phoenix.

1993   *Historic Trails in Arizona From Coronado to 1940: A Component of the Arizona Historic Preservation Plan.* Submitted to the State Historic Preservation Office, Arizona State Parks Board, Phoenix. Janus Associates, Phoenix.

Johnson, Alfred E.

1960   Archaeological Investigations at Fort Lowell. Manuscript on file, Arizona State Museum Library, University of Arizona, Tucson.

Jones, Jeffery T.

1995a   *Archaeological Test Excavations at AZ EE:1:194 (ASM) and Surface Mapping of Nearby Archaeological Sites for the Santa Rita Springs Property Development in Green Valley, Pima County, Arizona.* Archaeology Report No. 94-3. Old Pueblo Archaeology Center, Tucson.

1995b   *Archaeological Test Excavations at the Green Valley Electrical Substation Portion of AZ EE:1:32 (ASM) for Tucson Electric Power Company in Green Valley, Pima County, Arizona.* Archaeology Report No. 95-3. Old Pueblo Archaeology Center, Tucson.

1996   *Removal of a Possibly Protohistoric O'odham Human Burial from a Gravel Pit along Indian Agency Road in Tucson, Arizona.* Letter Report No. 95-12. Old Pueblo Archaeology Center, Tucson.

1997   *Archaeological Excavations at the Continental Site in Green Valley, Pima County, Arizona, in 1995: An Investigation of the Portion of Site AZ EE:1:32 (ASM) within Tucson Electric Power Company's Substation Expansion Zone.* Archaeology Report No. 9. Old Pueblo Archaeology Center, Tucson.

1998   Hohokam of the Southern Frontier: Excavations at the Continental Site, a Classic Period Village South of Tucson, Arizona. *Kiva* 63:197–216.

1999   *Archaeological Test Excavations for the Genesee Company along Silverbell Road North of Grant Road in Tucson, Arizona.* Technical Report No. 99-2. Old Pueblo Archaeology Center, Tucson.

2000a   *Archaeological Inspection of an Existing Utility Trench and Disturbed Area at the Recorded Location of Site AZ AA:16:67 (ASM) within the Northern Valencia Road Right-of-Way in Tucson, Arizona (Pima County W.O. 4VRMRI).* Letter Report No. 2000.039. Old Pueblo Archaeology Center, Tucson.

2000b   *Cultural Resources Survey of 145 Acres of State Trust Land West of Tumamoc Hill in Tucson, Arizona.* Letter Report No. 2000.049. Old Pueblo Archaeology Center, Tucson.

2001   *An Archaeological Investigation at the Bojórquez Ranch, an 1870s Mexican Homestead in the Northern Tucson Basin.* Archaeology Report No. 20. Old Pueblo Archaeology Center, Tucson.

2003   *Pima Community College's 1982 Archaeological Excavations at the Herreras Farmstead Site, AZ AA:16:68 (ASM): A Pima County–Funded Report for the Valencia Road Widening Project in Tucson (Pima County W.O.4VRMRI).* Draft report submitted to Pima County, February 2003. Archaeology Report No. 27. Old Pueblo Archaeology Center, Tucson.

Jones, Jeffrey T., and Linda Brown
2003   History of the Herreras Family and the Herreras Farmstead. In *Pima Community College's 1982 Archaeological Excavations at the Herreras Farmstead Site, AZ AA:16:68 (ASM): A Pima County–Funded Report for the Valencia Road Widening Project in Tucson (Pima County W.O.4VRMRI)*, by Jeffrey T. Jones. Draft report submitted to Pima County, February 2003. Archaeology Report No. 27. Old Pueblo Archaeology Center, Tucson.

Jones, Jeffery T., and Allen Dart
1997   *Prehistoric and Historical Sites on the Community Civano Development Property in Tucson, Arizona.* Archaeology Report No. 16. Old Pueblo Archaeology Center, Tucson.

Jones, Oakah L.
1979   *Los Paisanos: Spanish Settlers on the Northern Frontier of New Spain.* University of Oklahoma Press, Norman.

Kaldahl, Eric J.
1999   *Archaeological Test Excavations at AZ BB 13:124 (ASM) near the Los Reales and Wilmot Roads Intersection in Tucson, Arizona.* Technical Report 99-6. Old Pueblo Archaeology Center, Tucson.

2000   *Cultural Resources Survey for Guadalajara Wash Sewer Protection Project in Tucson, Arizona. (Pima County W.O. HYX-566).* Letter Report 2000.027. Old Pueblo Archaeology Center, Tucson.

Kaut, Charles R.
1957   *The Western Apache Clan System: Its Origin and Development.* Publications in Anthropology No. 9. University of New Mexico, Albuquerque.

Keane, Melissa, and Allen E. Rogge
1992   *Gold and Silver Mining in Arizona, 1848–1945: A Context for Historic Preservation Planning.* Research Paper No. 6. Dames and Moore, Phoenix.

Keith, Stanton B.
1974   *Index of Mining Properties in Pima County, Arizona.* Bulletin No. 189. Arizona Bureau of Mines, University of Arizona, Tucson.

Kelly, Isabel T.
1978   *The Hodges Ruin: A Hohokam Community in the Tucson Basin.* Anthropological Paper No. 30. University of Arizona Press, Tucson.

Kelly, William H.
    1953   *Indians of the Southwest: A Survey of Indian Tribes and Indian Administration in Arizona.* First Annual Report of the Bureau of Ethnic Research, University of Arizona, Tucson.

Kessell, John L.
    1970   *Mission of Sorrows: Jesuit Guevavi and the Pimas, 1691–1767.* University of Arizona Press, Tucson.

    1976   *Friars, Soldiers, and Reformers: Hispanic Arizona and the Sonora Mission Frontier, 1769–1856.* University of Arizona Press, Tucson.

King, Thomas F., Patricia P. Hickman, and Gary Berg
    1977   *Anthropology in Historic Preservation: Caring for Culture's Clutter.* Academic Press, New York.

Kozak, David L., and David I. Lopez
    1999   *Devil Sickness and Devil Songs: Tohono O'odham Poetics.* Smithsonian Institution Press, Washington, D.C.

Kuper, Douglas E.
    1986   Diversity through Adversity: Tucson Basin Water Control Since 1854. Unpublished Master's thesis, Department of History, University of Arizona, Tucson.

Kwiatkowski, Scott
    1996   *A Cultural Resources Survey in the Vicinity of Arizona Department of Transportation Bridges 1247 and 1248 along Interstate 19, Tucson, Pima County, Arizona.* Project No. 96-73. Archaeological Research Services, Tempe, Arizona.

Lacy, John C.
    1987   Early History of Mining in Arizona: Acquisition of Mineral Rights, 1539–1866. In *History of Mining in Arizona,* edited by J. Michael Canty and Michael N. Greeley, pp. 1–12. Mining Club of the Southwest Foundation, American Institute of Mining Engineers Tucson Section, Tucson, and Southwestern Minerals Exploration Association, Tucson.

Lamar, Howard
    1966   *The Far Southwest, 1846–1912: A Territorial History.* Yale University Press, New Haven, Connecticut.

Larson, Stephen M.
    1972   The Tumamoc Hill Site near Tucson, Arizona. *The Kiva* 38:95–102.

    1979   The Material Culture Distribution on the Tumamoc Hill Summit. *The Kiva* 45:71–82

Lascaux, Annick, Geri Antone, and Heidi Roberts
    1995   *Archaeological Survey of 139 House Lots Located in 40 Communities on the Tohono O'odham Nation, Maricopa, Pima, and Pinal Counties, Arizona.* Archaeological Report No. 95-20. SWCA, Tucson.

Layhe, Robert W. (editor)

1986   *The 1985 Excavations at the Hodges Site, Pima County, Arizona.* Archaeological Series No. 172. Cultural Resource Management Division, Arizona State Museum, University of Arizona, Tucson.

Lenhart, Austin B.

1995   *Results of Archaeological Subsurface Testing at Three Areas of the Indian Agency Road Property in Section 15, T15S, R13E, G& SRB&M, in Tucson, Arizona.* Letter Report No. 95-1. Old Pueblo Archaeology Center, Tucson.

Levi, Laura J.

1996   *Archaeological Monitoring in the Barrio Libre, Tucson, Arizona.* Technical Report No. 96-9. Center for Desert Archaeology, Tucson.

Limerick, Patricia Nelson

1987   *The Legacy of Conquest: The Unbroken Past of the American West.* W. W. Norton and Co., New York.

Limerick, Patricia Nelson, Clyde A. Milner, and Charles E. Rankin (editors)

1991   *Trails: Toward a New Western History.* University Press of Kansas, Lawrence.

Lindeman, Mike

1997   *An Archaeological Survey of the Indian Health Service Hospital Compounds in Sells and San Xavier on the Tohono O'odham Reservation, Pima County, Arizona.* Letter Report 97-130 (rev. ed.). Desert Archaeology, Tucson.

Lister, Florence C., and Robert H. Lister

1989   *The Chinese of Early Tucson: Historic Archaeology from the Tucson Urban Renewal Project.* University of Arizona Press, Tucson.

Lockwood, Frank C.

1953   *Life in Old Tucson.* Ward Ritchie, Los Angeles.

Logan, Michael F.

2002   *The Lessening Stream: An Environmental History of the Santa Cruz River.* University of Arizona Press, Tucson.

Mabry, Jonathan

1990   *Archaeological Survey of City of Tucson TCE Extraction Well and Treatment Facility Sites.* Letter Report No. 90-114. Desert Archaeology, Tucson.

1991   The History of Cattle Ranching in the Cañada del Oro Valley. In *Archaeological Testing at the Romero Ruin,* by Deborah L. Swartz, pp. 57–78. Technical Report No. 91-2. Center for Desert Archaeology, Tucson.

1996   *A Rincon Phase Occupation at the Julian Wash Site, AZ BB:13:17 (ASM).* Technical Report No. 96-7. Center for Desert Archaeology, Tucson.

Mabry, Jonathan B. (editor)
    1998   *Archaeological Investigations of Early Village Sites in the Middle Santa Cruz Valley: Analysis and Synthesis.* Anthropological Papers No. 19. Center for Desert Archaeology, Tucson.

Mabry, Jonathan B., James E. Ayres, and Regina L. Chapin-Pyritz
    1994   *Tucson at the Turn of the Century: The Archaeology of Block 83.* Technical Report No. 92-10. Center for Desert Archaeology, Tucson.

Mabry, Jonathan B., and Jeffery J. Clark
    1994   Early Village Life on the Santa Cruz River. *Archaeology in Tucson* 8(1)1–5.

Mabry, Jonathan B., Deborah L. Swartz, Helga Wöcherl, Jeffrey J. Clark, Gavin H. Archer, and Michael W. Lindeman
    1997   *Archaeological Investigations of Early Village Sites in the Middle Santa Cruz Valley: Descriptions of the Santa Cruz Bend, Square Hearth, Stone Pipe, and Canal Sites.* Anthropological Papers No. 18. Center for Desert Archaeology, Tucson.

Mabry, Jonathan B., and J. Homer Thiel
    1995   A Thousand Years of Irrigation in Tucson. *Archaeology in Tucson* 9(4):1–6.

MacTavish, Caton
    1924   The Story of the Canoa Ranch and Scotch Farms—Tucson, Arizona. In *The Pure-Bred Herefords of the Canoa Ranch and Scotch Farms, Tucson, Arizona.* Young and McCallister, Los Angeles. Promotional brochure on file at University of Arizona Library Special Collections.

Majewski, Teresita
    1998   Historical Profiles of the Apache and Yavapai Reservations in Arizona. In *Overview, Synthesis, and Conclusions,* edited by Stephanie M. Whittlesey, Richard Ciolek-Torrello, and Jeffrey H. Altschul, pp. 319–336. Vanishing River: Landscapes and Lives of the Lower Verde Valley: The Lower Verde Archaeological Project. SRI Press, Tucson.

Majewski, Teresita, and James E. Ayres
    1997   Toward an Archaeology of Colonialism in the Greater Southwest. *Revista de arqueología americana* 12:55–86.

Manje, Juan M.
    1954   *Unknown Arizona and Sonora 1693–1721.* Translated by Harry J. Karns and Associates. Arizona Silhouettes, Tucson.

Masse, W. Bruce
    1979   An Intensive Survey of Prehistoric Dry Farming Systems near Tumamoc Hill in Tucson, Arizona. *The Kiva* 45:141–186.

    1981   A Reappraisal of the Protohistoric Sobaipuri Indians of Southeastern Arizona. In *The Protohistoric Period in the North American Southwest, A.D. 1450–1700,* edited by David R. Wilcox and W. Bruce Masse, pp. 28–56. Anthropological Research Paper No. 24. Arizona State University, Tempe.

1985   The Peppersauce Wash Project: Excavations at Three Multicomponent Sites in the Lower
        San Pedro Valley, Arizona. Manuscript on file, Arizona State Museum Library, University
        of Arizona, Tucson.

Mattison, Ray H.
    1946   Early Spanish and Mexican Settlements in Arizona. *New Mexico Historical Review*
            21:273–327.

Mayro, Linda
    1987   *Archaeological Record Check and Survey of the Valencia Road Bridge Area, W.O. 4BVLSC
            (FC-87-53).* Institute for American Research, Tucson.

    1999   *Ranching in Pima County, Arizona: A Conservation Objective of the Sonoran Desert
            Conservation Plan.* Pima County Board of Supervisors, Tucson.

Mazany, Terry
    1981   *Archaeological Test Excavations at the Lee Site, Downtown, Tucson.* Manuscript on file,
            Arizona State Museum Library, University of Arizona, Tucson.

McCarty, Kieran R., O.F.M.
    1976   *Desert Documentary: The Spanish Years, 1767–1821.* Monograph No. 4. Arizona Historical
            Society, Tucson.

    1981   *A Spanish Frontier in the Enlightened Age: Franciscan Beginnings in Sonora and Arizona,
            1767–1770.* Academy of American Franciscan History, Washington, D.C.

    1996   Jesuits and Franciscans. In *The Pimería Alta: Missions and More,* edited by James E.
            Officer, Mardith Schuetz-Miller, and Bernard L. Fontana, pp. 35–45. Southwestern Mission
            Research Center, Tucson.

McDonald, James A., William B. Gillespie, and Mary M. Farrell
    1995   Kentucky Camp. In *Tearing Up the Ground with Splendid Results: Historic Mining on the
            Coronado National Forest,* pp. 49–66. Heritage Resources Management Report No. 15.
            Southwestern Region, USDA Forest Service, Albuquerque.

McGinnies, William G.
    1981   *Discovering the Desert: Legacy of the Carnegie Desert Botanical Laboratory.* University of
            Arizona Press, Tucson.

McGuire, Randall H.
    1979   *Rancho Punta de Agua: Excavations at a Historic Ranch near Tucson, Arizona.* Contribution
            to Highway Salvage Archaeology in Arizona No. 57. Arizona State Museum, University of
            Arizona, Tucson.

    1983   Ethnic Group Status and Material Culture at the Rancho Punta de Agua. In *Forgotten Places
            and Things: Archaeological Perspectives on American History,* edited by Albert E. Ward,
            pp. 193–203. Contributions to Anthropological Studies No. 3. Center for Anthropological
            Studies, Albuquerque.

McGuire, Thomas R.
  1986   *Politics and Ethnicity on the Río Yaqui: Potam Revisited.* University of Arizona Press, Tucson.

McLean, David R., and Stephen M. Larson
  1979   Inferences from the Distribution of Plainware Sherd Attributes on Tumamoc Hill. *The Kiva* 45:83–94.

Mehren, John
  1993   *An Archaeological Survey of Airport Wash.* Letter Report No. 93-135. Desert Archaeology, Tucson.

Meyer, Michael C.
  1996   *Water in the Hispanic Southwest: A Social and Legal History, 1550–1850.* University of Arizona Press, Tucson.

Miksicek, Charles H.
  1979   From Parking Lots to Museum Basements: The Archaeobotany of the St. Mary's Site. *The Kiva* 45:131–140.

Moisés, Rosalio, Jane H. Kelley, and William Curry Holden
  1971   *A Yaqui Life: The Personal Chronicle of a Yaqui Indian.* University of Nebraska Press, Lincoln.

Myrick, David F.
  1975   *The Southern Roads.* Railroads of Arizona, vol. 1. Howell-North, Berkeley.

Nabhan, Gary P.
  1982   *The Desert Smells Like Rain: A Naturalist in Papago Indian Country.* North Point, New York.

  1983   Papago Fields: Arid Lands Ethnobotany and Agricultural Ecology. Unpublished Ph.D. dissertation, Department of Arid Lands Resource Sciences, University of Arizona, Tucson.

  1985   *Gathering the Desert.* University of Arizona Press, Tucson.

National Park Service (NPS)
  2001   Juan Bautista de Anza National Historic Trail. Electronic document, http://www.nps.gov/juba/, accessed July 12, 2004.

Naylor, Thomas H., and Charles W. Polzer (editors)
  1986   *The Presidio and Militia on the Northern Frontier of New Spain: A Documentary History, Vol. 1: 1570–1700.* University of Arizona Press, Tucson.

Noll, Elizabeth, and R. Thomas Euler
  1996   *Presidio Cultural Resource Monitoring and Evaluation of Parking Facilities.* SWCA Archaeological Report No. 96-107. SWCA, Tucson.

O'Brien, Patrick M., J. Simon Bruder, David A. Gregory, A. E. Rogge, and Deborah A. Hull
1987 *Cultural Resource Technical Report for the U.S. Telecom Fiber Optic Cable Project from San Timoteo, CA, to Socono, TX: The Arizona Segment.* Project No. 14865-001-050. Dames and Moore, n.l.

Officer, James E.
1987 *Hispanic Arizona, 1536–1856.* University of Arizona Press, Tucson.

1991 Mining in Hispanic Arizona: Myth and Reality. In *History of Mining in Arizona,* vol. 2, edited by J. Michael Canty and Michael N. Greeley, pp. 1–26. Mining Club of the Southwest Foundation, Tucson, and the American Institute of Mining Engineers Tucson Section, Tucson.

Olsen, John W.
1978 A Study of Chinese Ceramics Excavated in Tucson. *The Kiva* 44:1–50.

1983 An Analysis of East Asian Coins Excavated in Tucson, Arizona. *Historical Archaeology* 17(2):41–55.

Olsen, Stanley
1974 The Domestic Animals of San Xavier del Bac. *The Kiva* 39:253–257.

Olson, Alan P.
1985 Archaeology at the Presidio of Tucson. *The Kiva* 50:251–270.

Opler, Morris E.
1937 An Outline of Chiricahua Apache Social Organization. In *Social Anthropology of North Amercian Tribes,* edited by Fred Eggan, pp. 171–239. University of Chicago Press, Chicago.

1941 *An Apache Life-Way: The Economic, Social, and Religious Institutions of the Chiricahua Indians.* University of Chicago Press, Chicago.

1942 *Myths and Tales of the Chiricahua Apache Indians.* Memoirs of the American Folklore Society 37. Menasha, Wisconsin.

1983 Chiricahua Apache. In *Southwest,* edited by Alfonso Ortiz, pp. 401–418. Handbook of North American Indians, vol. 10, William C. Sturtevant, general editor, Smithsonian Institution, Washington, D.C.

Orrell, F. L.
1998 Kentucky Camp and the Santa Rita Water and Mining Company. In *History of Mining in Arizona,* vol. 3, edited by J. Michael Canty, H. Mason Coggin, and Michael N. Greeley, pp. 113–132. Mining Foundation of the Southwest, Tucson.

Ortega Noriega, Sergio
1985a El sistema de misiones jesuíticas: 1591–1699. In *Historia general de Sonora,* vol. 2, edited by Sergio Ortega Noriega and Ignacio del Río, pp.35–75. Gobierno del Estado de Sonora, Hermosillo.

1985b   Crecimiento y crisis del sistema misional: 1686–1767. In *Historia general de Sonora,* vol. 2, edited by Sergio Ortega Noriega and Ignacio del Río, pp. 111–150. Gobierno del Estado de Sonora, Hermosillo.

Pedersen, Gilbert J.
1975   A Yankee in Arizona: The Misfortunes of William S. Grant, 1860–1861. *Journal of Arizona History* 16:127–144.

Pfefferkorn, Ignaz
1989   *Sonora: A Description of the Province.* Translated and annotated by Theodore E. Treutlein. Reprinted. University of Arizona Press, Tucson. Originally published 1949, University of New Mexico Press, Albuquerque.

Phoenix Gazette [Phoenix]
1971   Tucson-Nogales Highway More Than Half Completed. 6 April. Phoenix.

Pilles, Peter J., Jr.
1981   A Review of Yavapai Archaeology. In *The Protohistoric Period in the North American Southwest, A.D. 1450–1700*, edited by David R. Wilcox and W. Bruce Masse, pp. 163–182. Anthropological Research Papers No. 24. Arizona State University, Tempe.

Pima County
1922   Official relief map of Pima County including Santa Cruz County, Arizona. Compiled by the Pima County Highway Department. On file, Arizona Historical Society, Tucson.

1932   Map of Pima County including Santa Cruz County, Arizona. Compiled by the Pima County Highway Department. On file, Arizona Historical Society, Tucson.

Pinkley, Frank
1936   Repair and Restoration of Tumacacori, 1921. *Southwestern Monuments Special Report* 10:261–284. USDI National Park Service, Washington, D.C.

Polzer, Charles W.
1968   Legends of Lost Missions and Mines. *The Smoke Signal* 18:170–183.

1976   *Rules and Precepts of the Jesuit Missions of Northwestern New Spain.* University of Arizona Press, Tucson.

1998   *Kino: His Life, His Works, His Missions, His Monuments.* Jesuit Fathers of Southern Arizona, Tucson.

Polzer, Charles W., and Thomas E. Sheridan
1997   *The Californias and Sinaloa-Sonora, 1700–1765.* The Presidio and Militia on the Northern Frontier of New Spain, vol. 2, pt. 1. University of Arizona Press, Tucson.

Radding, Cynthia
1997   *Wandering Peoples: Colonialism, Ethnic Spaces, and Ecological Frontiers in Northwestern Mexico, 1700–1850.* Duke University Press, Durham, North Carolina.

Ravesloot, John C.

1987a   Chronological Relationships of Features. In *The Archaeology of the San Xavier Bridge Site (AZ BB:13:14), Tucson Basin, Southern Arizona,* edited by John C. Ravesloot, pp. 61–69. Archaeological Series No. 171. Cultural Resource Management Division, Arizona State Museum, University of Arizona, Tucson.

1987b   Results of Excavations: Feature Descriptions. In *The Archaeology of the San Xavier Bridge Site (AZ BB:13:14), Tucson Basin, Southern Arizona,* edited by John C. Ravesloot, pp. 155–179. Archaeological Series No. 171. Cultural Resource Management Division, Arizona State Museum, University of Arizona, Tucson.

Ravesloot, John C. (editor)

1987   *The Archaeology of the San Xavier Bridge Site (AZ BB:13:14), Tucson Basin, Southern Arizona.* Archaeological Series No. 171. Cultural Resource Management Division, Arizona State Museum, University of Arizona, Tucson.

Ravesloot, John C., and Stephanie M. Whittlesey

1987   Interpreting the Protohistoric Period in Southern Arizona. In *The Archaeology of the San Xavier Bridge Site (AZ BB:13:14), Tucson Basin, Southern Arizona,* pts. 1 and 2. Archaeological Series 171. Cultural Resource Management Division, Arizona State Museum, University of Arizona, Tucson.

Rea, Amadeo M.

1997   *At the Desert's Green Edge: An Ethnobotany of the Gila River Pima.* University of Arizona Press, Tucson.

1998   *Folk Mammalogy of the Northern Pimans.* University of Arizona Press, Tucson.

Reff, Daniel T.

1990   *Disease, Depopulation, and Culture Change in Northwestern New Spain, 1518–1764.* University of Utah Press, Salt Lake City.

1998   The Jesuit Mission Frontier in Comparative Perspective: The Reductions of the Río de la Plata and the Missions of Northwestern Mexico, 1588–1700. In *Contested Ground: Comparative Frontiers on the Northern and Southern Edges of the Spanish Frontier,* edited by Donna J. Guy and Thomas E. Sheridan, pp. 16–31. University of Arizona Press, Tucson.

Reid, Jefferson, and Stephanie Whittlesey

1997   *The Archaeology of Ancient Arizona.* University of Arizona Press, Tucson.

Renk, Thomas

1969   A Guide to Recording Structural Details of Historic Buildings. *Historical Archaeology* 3:34–48.

Riley, Carrol L.

1975   The Road to Hawikuh: Trade and Trade Routes to Zuñi-Cíbola during Late Prehistoric and Early Historic Times. *The Kiva* 41:137–159.

1976   *Sixteenth-Century Trade in the Greater Southwest.* Mesoamerican Studies No. 10. University Museum, Southern Illinois University, Carbondale.

1985   The Location of Chichilticalle. In *Southwestern Culture History: Collected Papers in Honor of Albert H. Schroeder*, edited by C. H. Lange, pp. 153–163. Papers of the Archaeological Society of New Mexico No. 10. Ancient City Press, Santa Fe.

1987   *The Frontier People: The Greater Southwest in the Protohistoric Period.* University of New Mexico Press, Albuquerque.

Robinson, William J.
1963   Excavations at San Xavier del Bac, 1958. *The Kiva* 29:35–57.

1976   Mission Guevavi: Excavations in the Convento. *The Kiva* 42:135–175.

Rogers, Malcolm J.
1939   *Early Lithic Industries of the Lower Basin of the Colorado River and Adjacent Desert Areas.* Museum Papers No. 3. San Diego Museum of Man, San Diego.

Roskruge, George J.
1893   *Official Map of Pima County, Arizona.* Pima County Board of Supervisors, Tucson.

Roth, Barbara J.
1990   *City of Tucson Silverlake Road Survey.* Project No. L:89:10. Cultural Resource Management Division, Arizona State Museum, University of Arizona, Tucson.

Roubicek, Dennis
1969   The Historical Archaeology of the Jacobs Mansion, Tucson, Arizona. Unpublished Honors thesis, College of Liberal Arts, University of Arizona, Tucson.

Roubicek, Dennis, Ellen Cummings, and Gayle Hartmann
1973   A Reconnaissance and Preliminary Evaluation of the Archaeology of Rancho Romero. Manuscript on file, Arizona State Museum Library, University of Arizona, Tucson.

Russell, Frank
1908   The Pima Indians. In *Twenty-Sixth Annual Report of the Bureau of American Ethnology to the Secretary of the Smithsonian Institution 1904–1905*, pp. 3–389. Bureau of American Ethnology, Smithsonian Institution, Washington, D.C.

Santiago, Mark
1998   *Massacre at the Yuma Crossing: Spanish Relations with the Quechans, 1779–1782.* University of Arizona Press, Tucson.

Saxton, Dean, Lucille Saxton, and Susie Enos
1998   *Tohono O'odham/Pima to English, English to Tohono O'odham/Pima Dictionary.* 2nd ed. University of Arizona Press, Tucson.

Sayles, E. B.

    1941   Archaeology of the Cochise Culture. In *The Cochise Culture,* by E. B. Sayles and Ernst Antevs, pp. 1–30. Medallion Papers No. 29. Gila Pueblo, Globe, Arizona.

    1983   *The Cochise Cultural Sequence in Southeastern Arizona.* Anthropological Paper No. 42. University of Arizona Press, Tucson.

Sayles, E. B., and Ernst Antevs

    1941   *The Cochise Culture.* Medallion Papers No. 29. Gila Pueblo, Globe, Arizona.

Schillingberg, William B.

    1999   *Tombstone, A.T.: A History of Early Mining, Milling, and Mayhem.* Arthur H. Clark, Spokane, Washington.

Schmitt, Martin F. (editor)

    1960   *General George Crook: His Autobiography.* University of Oklahoma Press, Norman.

Schott, George C.

    1978   Drexel Road Archaeological Investigation. Manuscript on file, City of Tucson.

Schroeder, Albert H.

    1974a   A Study of the Apache Indians, Part V: "Tonto" and Western Apaches. In *Apache Indians IV*, edited by D. A. Horr, pp. 327–645. Garland, New York.

    1974b   A Study of Yavapai History. In *Yavapai Indians*, by A. H. Schroeder and A. B. Thomas, pp. 23–354. Garland American Indian Ethnohistory Series, D. A. Horr, general editor. Garland, New York.

Schuetz-Miller, Mardith, and Bernard L. Fontana

    1996   Mission Churches of Northern Sonora. In *The Pimería Alta: Missions and More,* edited by James E. Officer, Mardith Schuetz-Miller, and Bernard L. Fontana, pp. 61–95. Southwestern Mission Research Center, Tucson.

Seymour, Deni J.

    1989   The Dynamics of Sobaipuri Settlement in the Eastern Pimeria Alta. *Journal of the Southwest* 31:205–222.

Seymour, Deni J., Robert P. Jones, Robin Stipe-Davis, Kerry Nichols, and Laura L. Paskus

    1997   *Archaeological Survey of 1,755 Acres for Vail Valley Ranch Development, Pima County, Arizona.* Report No. 124. Lone Mountain Archaeological Service, Albuquerque.

Shenk, Lynette O.

    1976   *San José de Tumacácori: An Archaeological Synthesis and Research Design.* Archaeological Series No. 94. Arizona State Museum, University of Arizona, Tucson.

Shenk, Lynette O., and George A. Teague

    1975   *Excavations at the Tubac Presidio.* Archaeological Series No. 85. Arizona State Museum, University of Arizona, Tucson.

Sheridan, Thomas E.

1986   *Los Tucsonenses: The Mexican Community in Tucson, 1854–1941.* University of Arizona Press, Tucson.

1988   Kino's Unforeseen Legacy: The Material Consequences of Missionization. *The Smoke Signal* 49–50:151–167.

1992   The Limits of Power: The Political Ecology of the Spanish Empire in the Greater Southwest. *Antiquity* 66:153–171.

1995   *Arizona: A History.* University of Arizona Press, Tucson.

2000   Human Ecology of the Sonoran Desert. In *A Natural History of the Sonoran Desert,* edited by Steven J. Phillips and Patricia W. Comus, pp. 105–118. Arizona-Sonora Desert Museum Press, Tucson, and University of California Press, Berkeley.

Sheridan, Thomas E., Charles W. Polzer, Thomas H. Naylor, and Diana W. Hadley (editors)

1991   *The Franciscan Missions of Northern Mexico.* Garland, New York.

Sherman, James E., and Edward F. Ronstadt

1975   Wagon Making in Southern Arizona. *The Smoke Signal* 31:2–20.

Simpson, Kay, and Susan J. Wells

1983   *Archaeological Survey in the Eastern Tucson Basin, Saguaro National Monument, Rincon Mountain Unit, Cactus Forest Area.* Publication in Anthropology 22(1). Western Archeological and Conservation Center, USDI National Park Service, Tucson.

1984   *Archaeological Survey in the Eastern Tucson Basin, Saguaro National Monument, Rincon Mountain Unit, Tanque Verde Ridge, Rincon Creek, Mica Mountain Areas.* Publication in Anthropology 22(3). Western Archeological and Conservation Center, USDI National Park Service, Tucson.

Sires, Earl W., Jr.

1987   Hohokam Architectural Variability and Site Structure during the Sedentary-Classic Transition. In *The Hohokam Village: Site Structure and Organization,* edited by David E. Doyel, pp. 171–182. Southwestern and Rocky Mountain Division, American Association for the Advancement of Science, Glenwood Springs, Colorado.

Slaughter, Mark C.

1996   Architectural Features. In *Excavation of the Gibbon Springs Site, a Classic Period Village in the Northeastern Tucson Basin,* edited by Mark C. Slaughter and Heidi Roberts, pp. 69–140. Archaeological Report No. 94-87. SWCA, Tucson.

Slaughter, Mark C., Susan B. Bierer, and Linda M. Gregonis

1995   *Archaeological Monitoring of Tree Holes at the Roy P. Drachman Agua Caliente Park: The Whiptail Site and Agua Caliente Ranch Site, Pima, County, Arizona.* Archaeological Report No. 95-46. SWCA, Tucson.

Slaughter, Mark C., Susan B. Bierer, and David A. Phillips, Jr.
  1993   *Archaeological Test Excavations at AZ BB:9:242 (ASM), the Sabino Springs Project, Pima County, Arizona.* Archaeological Report No. 93-89. SWCA, Tucson.

Slawson, Laurie V.
  1990   *The Terminal Classic Period in the Tucson Basin: Rabid Ruin, a Late Tucson Phase Hohokam Settlement.* Southwest Cultural Series No. 10. Cultural and Environmental Systems, Tucson.

  1993   *A Class III Archaeological Survey for the Julian and Rodeo Wash Linear Parks in Tucson, Arizona.* Cultural and Environmental Systems, Tucson. Submitted to the Pima County Department of Transportation and Flood Control District, Tucson.

Slawson, Laurie V., and James E. Ayres
  1992   *Copper Mining, Railroading, and the Hellhole of Arizona: Archaeological Investigations in the Silver Bell Mining District.* Southwest Cultural Series No. 12. Cultural and Environmental Systems, Tucson.

  1993   *Archaeological Investigations at Vulcan Camp: Historic Mining on the Vulcan and Prince Rupert Claims in the Pima Mining District.* Southwest Cultural Series No. 13. Cultural and Environmental Systems, Tucson.

  1994   *Archaic Hunter-Gatherers to Historic Mining: Prehistoric and Historic Utilization of the Silver Bell Mining District.* Southwest Cultural Series No. 16. Cultural and Environmental Systems, Tucson.

Slawson, Laurie V., David C. Hanna, Skip Miller, and Ronald P. Maldonado
  1987   *The Espinosa Site: An Example of Prehistoric and Historic Utilization of the Santa Cruz River.* Southwest Cultural Series No. 8. Cultural and Environmental Systems, Tucson.

Sliva, Jane
  1998   *Archaeological Survey of Silverlake Road between Mission Road and Interstate 10, Tucson, Arizona.* Letter Report No. 98-113. Desert Archaeology, Tucson.

Smiley, Terah, Henry F. Dobyns, Bonnie Jones, and James T. Barter
  1953   *San José de Tucson, Its History and Archaeological Exploration.* Manuscript on file, Arizona State Museum Library, University of Arizona, Tucson.

Sonnichsen, C. L.
  1982   *Tucson: The Life and Times of an American City.* University of Oklahoma Press, Norman.

Sonnichsen, C. L. (editor)
  1986   *Geronimo and the End of the Apache Wars.* University of Nebraska Press, Lincoln.

Southwestern Mission Research Center
  1986   *Tucson: A Short History.* Southwestern Mission Research Center, Tucson.

Spicer, Edward H.
    1929   Five Skulls from the Hohokam Region. Cummings Field Notes 1929, File 41. Manuscript on file, Arizona Historical Society, Tucson.

    1940   *Pascua: A Yaqui Village in Arizona.* University of Chicago Press, Chicago.

    1954   *Potam: A Yaqui Village in Sonora.* Memoirs of the American Anthropological Association 77. Menasha, Wisconsin.

    1962   *Cycles of Conquest: The Impacts of Spain, Mexico, and the United States on the Indians of the Southwest, 1533–1960.* University of Arizona Press, Tucson.

    1980   *The Yaquis: A Cultural History.* University of Arizona Press, Tucson.

    1983   Yaqui. In *Southwest,* edited by Alfonso Ortiz, pp. 250–263. Handbook of North American Indians, vol. 10, William C. Sturtevant, general editor, Smithsonian Institution, Washington, D.C.

Stein, Pat H.
    1990   *Homesteading in Arizona, 1862–1940: A Guide to Studying, Evaluating,and Preserving Historic Homesteads.* Arizona State Historic Preservation Office, Phoenix.

    1993   Historical Resources of the Northern Tucson Basin. In *The Northern Tucson Basin Survey: Research Directions and Background Studies,* edited by John H. Madsen, Paul R. Fish, and Suzanne K. Fish, pp. 85–122. Archaeological Series No. 182. Arizona State Museum, University of Arizona, Tucson.

    1994   *Historic Trails in Arizona from Coronado to 1940: A Component of the Arizona Historic Preservation Plan.* Report No. 94-72. SWCA, Flagstaff.

Stephen, David V. M., and James M. Hewitt
    1980   *Archaeological Resources of the Midvale Park Property, Tucson, Arizona.* Submitted to Dooley-Jones and Associates, n.l. Pima Community College, Tucson. On file, Arizona State Museum Library, University of Arizona, Tucson.

Sterner, Matthew A.
    1996   *Schroeder's Well and the Davidson Flume: A Glimpse into Tucson's Mormon Culture.* Technical Report 96-5. Statistical Research, Tucson.

    1999   Historical-Period Resources at Sunset Mesa Ruin. In *Investigations at Sunset Mesa Ruin: Archaeology at the Confluence of the Santa Cruz and Rillito Rivers, Tucson, Arizona,* edited by R. Ciolek-Torrello, E. K. Huber, and R. B. Neily, pp. 193–202. Technical Series 66. Statistical Research, Tucson.

Sterner, Matthew A., and Teresita Majewski
    1998   *Homesteading and Ranching on Fort Huachuca's East Range: National Register of Historic Places Evaluations of the Slash Z Ranch Site (AZ EE:7:84 [ASM]) and Three Associated Sites (AZ EE:7:194 [ASM], AZ EE:7:196 [ASM], and AZ EE:7:201 [ASM]).* Technical Report 98-22. Statistical Research, Tucson.

Stevens, Michelle N.
1997   *An Archaeological Survey of a Proposed Access Road South of Martinez Hill in the San Xavier District of the Tohono O'odham Reservation.* Letter Report. No. 97-145. Desert Archaeology, Tucson.

Stone, Bradford W.
1995   *Cultural Resources Survey of the Interstate-19/Valencia Road Traffic Interchange in South Tucson, Northeastern Pima County, Arizona.* Letter Report No. 95-19. Archaeological Research Services, Tempe.

Stone, Lyle M.
1979   *Archaeological Research, Site Stabilization, and Interpretive Development Planning at Calabazas, an Historic Spanish Visita in Santa Cruz, County, Arizona.* Archaeological Research Services, Tempe.

Stoner, Victor R.
1937   Original Sites of the Spanish Missions of the Santa Cruz Valley. *The Kiva* 2(7–8):25–32.

Sugnet, C. L., and J. Jefferson Reid (editors)
1994   *The Surface of Presidio Santa Cruz de Terrenate.* Bureau of Land Management, Tucson.

Swanson, Earl H., Jr.
1951   An Archaeological Survey of the Empire Valley. Unpublished Master's thesis, Department of Anthropology, University of Arizona, Tucson.

Swartz, Deborah L.
1991   *Archaeological Testing at the Romero Ruin.* Technical Report No. 91-2. Center for Desert Archaeology, Tucson.

1993   *Archaeological Testing at the Romero Ruin: Part 2.* Technical Report No. 93-8. Center for Desert Archaeology, Tucson.

1995a   *An Archaeological Survey along Valencia Road.* Letter Report No. 95-137. Desert Archaeology, Tucson.

1995b   *An Archaeological Survey of a Proposed Parking Lot on Irvington Road.* Letter Report No. 95-143. Desert Archaeology, Tucson.

1997   *Archaeological Testing in the Santa Cruz River Floodplain within and near the Julian Wash Site, AZ BB:13:17 (ASM).* Technical Report No. 97-9. Center for Desert Archaeology, Tucson.

1999   *Archaeological Investigations for the I-10/I-19 Interchange Focused on the Julian Wash Site, AZ BB:13:17 (ASM).* Technical Report No. 99-8. Desert Archaeology, Tucson.

Swidler, Nina B.
1985   Archaeological Investigations of Project I-19-1-401, Tucson, Arizona. Manuscript on file, Arizona State Museum, University of Arizona, Tucson.

Teague, George A.
  1980 *Reward Mine and Associated Sites: Historical Archeology on the Papago Reservation.* Publication in Anthropology No. 11. USDI National Park Service, Western Archeological and Conservation Center, Tucson.

Thiel, J. Homer
  1993 *Archaeological Investigations of Tucson Block 94: The Boarding House Residents of the Hotel Catalina Site.* Technical Report No. 93-5. Center for Desert Archaeology, Tucson.

  1995a *Archaeological Testing along the A-Mountain Drainage System.* Technical Report No. 95-6. Center for Desert Archaeology, Tucson.

  1995b *Archaeological Testing on the Rio Nuevo South Property, Tucson, Arizona.* Technical Report No. 95-11. Center for Desert Archaeology, Tucson.

  1995c *Archaeological Testing of the Proposed Evo A. DeConcini Federal Building and United States Courthouse Property.* Technical Report No. 95-12. Center for Desert Archaeology, Tucson.

  1995d *Archaeological Test Excavations in Sunset Park, Tucson, Arizona.* Technical Report No. 95-15. Center for Desert Archaeology, Tucson.

  1996 *A Summary of Archaeological Investigations in Sunset Park, Tucson, Arizona.* Technical Report 96-10. Center for Desert Archaeology, Tucson.

  1997 *Archaeological Investigations of a Chinese Gardener's Household, Tucson, Arizona.* Technical Report 96-22. Center for Desert Archaeology, Tucson.

  1998a *Uncovering Tucson's Past: Test Excavations in Search of the Presidio Wall.* Technical Report No. 98-1. Center for Desert Archaeology, Tucson.

  1998b In Search of El Presidio de Tucson. *Archaeology in Tucson* 12(3):1–4.

  1998c Uncovering the Story of Tucson's Chinese Gardeners. *Archaeology in Tucson* 12(2):1–5.

  1998d *Archaeological Testing Beneath the Duffield Addition to the Fish-Stevens-Duffield House, AZ BB:13:24 (ASM), Tucson, Arizona.* Technical Report 98-14. Center for Desert Archaeology, Tucson.

Thiel, J. Homer, and Danielle Desruisseaux
  1993 *Archaeological Test Excavations for the Water Plant No. 1 Expansion, Historic Block 138, City of Tucson.* Technical Report No. 93-12. Center for Desert Archaeology, Tucson.

Thiel, J. Homer, Michael K. Faught, and James M. Bayman
  1993 Archaeology in the Heart of Downtown Tucson. *Archaeology in Tucson* 7(3):1–5.

  1995 *Beneath the Streets: Prehistoric, Spanish, and American Period Archaeology in Downtown Tucson.* Technical Report No. 94-11. Center for Desert Archaeology, Tucson.

Thrapp, Dan L.
1967   *The Conquest of Apacheria.* University of Oklahoma Press, Norman.

Tompkins, Charles Nichols
1996   *An Archaeological Survey of a 26-Acre Portion of the West Branch Site in Tucson Arizona.* Technical Report No. 96-24. Tierra Archaeological and Environmental Consultants, Tucson.

Tuck, Frank J.
1963   *History of Mining in Arizona.* 2nd rev. ed. State of Arizona Department of Mineral Resources, Phoenix.

Tucker, David B.
1997   *Data Recovery at Site AZ AA:12:311 (ASM) and Archaeological Monitoring for the Coventry Homes Pipeline Project.* Archaeological Report No. 97-177. SWCA, Tucson.

2000   *A Cultural Resource Survey at the Northeast Corner of Headley and Valencia Roads, Tucson, Arizona.* Cultural Resource Report No. 00-513. SWCA, Tucson.

Tucson Citizen (TC) [Tucson]
1922   The Miles of No. 1 Paving Included in Improvement. 15 January. Tucson.

1926   Sentinel Peak: The Pioneer Path of the Sentinels. 30 May. Tucson. On file, Arizona Historical Society, Tucson.

1959   In Old Tucson: 45 Years Ago (1914). On file, Arizona Historical Society, Tucson, Arizona.

Tucson Farms Company
1915   Map of Land Owned by Tucson Farms Company, Tucson, Arizona, and First National Bank Building, Chicago, Illinois. Globe E. and E. Company, Chicago. On file, Arizona Historical Society, Tucson.

Tucson Irrigation Company
1920   Map of Tucson Irrigation Company, Midvale Farm Tract. On file, Arizona Historical Society, Tucson.

Underhill, Ruth M.
1938   *Singing for Power: The Song Magic of the Papago Indians of Southern Arizona.* University of California Press, Berkeley.

1939   *The Social Organization of the Papago Indians.* Contributions to Anthropology No. 30. Columbia University, New York.

1946   *Papago Indian Religion.* Contributions to Anthropology No. 33. Columbia University, New York.

Underhill, Ruth M., Donald M. Bahr, Baptisto Lopez, Jose Pancho, and David Lopez
1979   *Rainhouse and Ocean: Speeches for the Papago Year.* University of Arizona Press, Tucson.

Vanderpot, Rein, Stephanie M. Whittlesey, and Susan A. Martin
  1993 *Archaeological Investigations at AZ AA:12:57/377: a Butterfield Stage Stop, the Ruelas Ranch, and a Hohokam Village (Los Morteros) near Point of the Mountain, Pima County, Arizona.* Technical Report 93-1. Statistical Research, Tucson.

Van Willigen, John
  1971 The Role of the Community Level Worker in Papago Indian Development. Unpublished Ph.D. dissertation, Department of Anthropology, University of Arizona, Tucson.

Wagoner, Jay J.
  1952 *History of the Cattle Industry in Southern Arizona, 1540–1940.* University of Arizona Bulletin 23(2). Social Science Bulletin No. 20. University of Arizona, Tucson.

  1970 *Arizona Territory, 1863–1912: A Political History.* University of Arizona Press, Tucson.

  1975 *Early Arizona: Prehistory to Civil War.* University of Arizona Press, Tucson.

Walker, Henry P.
  1973 Wagon Freighting in Arizona. *The Smoke Signal* 28:182–204.

Wallace, Henry D.
  1981 Observations from the Field Notes of Henry Wallace on a Continuing Education Class Field Trip to the Martinez Hill Ruin (AZ BB:13:7). Manuscript on file, Site Files Office, Arizona State Museum, University of Arizona, Tucson.

  1995 *Rincon Phase Decorated Ceramics in the Tucson Basin: A Focus on the West Branch Site.* Anthropological Papers No. 1. Institute for American Research, Tucson.

  1996 *Documentation of a Platform Mound Compound and Monitoring of the Excavation of a Septic System Leach Field within AZ BB:13:8, San Xavier District, Tohono O'odham Reservation.* Letter Report No. 96-128. Desert Archaeology, Tucson.

  1997 *Archaeological Survey for Water and Sewer Lines along Little Nogales Road, Walk Lane, and in the Two Hills Development, San Xavier District of the Tohono O'odham Nation.* Letter Report No. 97-124. Desert Archaeology, Tucson.

  1998 *A Research Design for the Dove Mountain Project: The Archaeology and History of the Northern Tucson Basin.* Technical Report 98-9. Center for Desert Archaeology, Tucson.

  2003 *Roots of Sedentism: Archaeological Excavations at Valencia Vieja, a Founding Village in the Tucson Basin of Southern Arizona.* Anthropological Papers No. 29. Center for Desert Archaeology, Tucson.

Wallace, Henry D., and James Heidke
  1986 Ceramic Production and Exchange. In *Archaeological Investigations at the Tanque Verde Wash Site: A Middle Rincon Settlement in the Eastern Tucson Basin,* edited by Mark Elson, pp. 233–270. Anthropological Papers No. 7. Institute for American Research, Tucson.

Wallace, Henry D., James M. Heidke, and Michael K. Wiley
    1997   Julian Wash Ceramic Studies. In *Archaeological Investigations for the I-10/I-19 Interchange Focused on the Julian Wash Site, AZ BB:13:17 (ASM),* by Deborah L. Swartz, pp. 34–57. Draft. Technical Report No. 97-8. Center for Desert Archaeology, Tucson.

Wasley, William W.
    1956   *History and Archaeology in Tucson.* Manuscript A-767. On file, Arizona State Museum Archives, University of Arizona, Tucson.

    1957   Highway Salvage in Arizona. *The Kiva* 23:4–7.

Waters, Michael R.
    1987   Holocene Alluvial Geology and Geoarchaeology of AZ BB:13:14 and the San Xavier Reach of the Santa Cruz. In *The Archaeology of the San Xavier Bridge Site (AZ BB:13:14), Tucson Basin, Southern Arizona,* edited by John C. Ravesloot, pp. 39–60. Archaeological Series No. 171. Arizona State Museum, Cultural Resource Management Division, University of Arizona, Tucson.

    1988   Holocene Alluvial Geology and Geoarchaeology of the San Xavier Reach of the Santa Cruz River, Arizona. *Geological Society of America Bulletin* 100:479–491.

Waugh, Rebecca J.
    1995   Plainware Ceramics from the Midden at Presidio Santa Cruz de Terrenate, Arizona. Unpublished Master's thesis, Department of Anthropology, University of Arizona, Tucson.

Weber, David J.
    1979   *New Spain's Far Northern Frontier: Essays on Spain in the American West.* University of New Mexico Press, Albuquerque.

    1982   *The Mexican Frontier, 1821–1846: The American Southwest Under Mexico.* University of New Mexico Press, Albuquerque.

    1988a   Turner, the Boltonians, and the Spanish Borderlands. In *Myth and the History of the Hispanic Southwest,* by D. J. Weber, pp. 33–54. University of New Mexico Press, Albuquerque.

    1988b   John Francis Bannon and the Historiography of the Spanish Borderlands: Retrospect and Prospect. In *Myth and the History of the Hispanic Southwest,* by D. J. Weber, pp. 55–88. University of New Mexico Press, Albuquerque.

    1988c   *Myth and the History of the Hispanic Southwest.* University of New Mexico Press, Albuquerque.

    1991   Introduction. In *The Idea of Spanish Borderlands,* edited by D. J. Weber, pp. xiii–xxxviii. Garland, New York.

    1992   *The Spanish Frontier in North America.* Yale University Press, New Haven, Connecticut.

Weekly Arizonan [Tubac, Arizona]
1859   Route to Sonora. 4 April. Tubac, Arizona.

Wellman, Kevin D.
1994   *Archeological Survey of Saguaro National Monument, 1994: The Saguaro Land Acquisition and Trails Inventory.* Publications in Anthropology No. 65. Western Archeological and Conservation Center, USDI National Park Service, Tucson.

Wellman, Kevin D., and Mark C. Slaughter
2001   *Archaeological Investigations at Roy P. Drachman Agua Caliente Park: The Whiptail Site and Agua Caliente Ranch.* Cultural Resources Report No. 00-03. SWCA, Tucson.

Wells, Susan J., and Stacie A. Reutter
1997   *Cultural Resources of the Tucson Mountain District, Saguaro National Park.* Publications in Anthropology No. 69. Western Archeological and Conservation Center, USDI National Park Service, Tucson.

West, Robert C.
1993   *Sonora: Its Geographical Personality.* University of Texas Press, Austin.

Whalen, Norman M.
1971   Cochise Culture Sites in the Central San Pedro Drainage, Arizona. Unpublished Ph.D. dissertation, Department of Anthropology, University of Arizona, Tucson.

Wheeler, C. C.
n.d.   History and Facts Concerning Warner and Silver Lake and the Santa Cruz River. Manuscript 853. On file, Arizona Historical Society, Tucson.

White, Richard
1991   *"It's Your Misfortune and None of My Own": A History of the American West.* University of Oklahoma Press, Norman.

Whittemore, Isaac T.
1893   The Pima Indians, Their Manners and Customs. In *Among the Pimas; or the Mission to the Pima and Maricopa Indians,* edited by C. H. Cook, pp. 51–96. Printed for the Ladies' Union Mission School Association, Albany, New York.

Whittlesey, Stephanie M.
1986   Restorable and Partial Vessels. In *Archaeological Investigations at AZ U:14:75 (ASM): A Turn-of-the-Century Pima Homestead,* edited by R. W. Layhe, pp. 74–102. Archaeological Series No. 172. Arizona State Museum, University of Arizona, Tucson.

1994   Three Centuries of Pottery in the Pimería Alta. Paper presented at the Prehistoric and Historic Archaeology of the Borderlands Symposium. Arizona Archaeological Council Spring Meeting, Tucson.

1995   Mogollon, Hohokam, and Ootam: Rethinking the Early Formative Period in Southern Arizona. *The Kiva* 60:465–480.

1997   Culture History: Prehistoric Narratives for Southern Arizona. In *Background and Research Design for Archaeological Resources,* by Carla R. Van West and Stephanie M. Whittlesey, pp. 45–80. Cultural Resource Management Plan for the Fairfield Canoa Ranch Property, vol. 1. Draft. Statistical Research, Tucson.

1998   The Vanished River: Historical-Period Impacts to Desert Landscapes and Archaeological Implications. In *Overview, Synthesis, and Conclusions,* edited by Stephanie M. Whittlesey, Richard Ciolek-Torrello, and Jeffrey H. Altschul, pp. 29–57. Vanishing River: Landscapes and Lives of the Lower Verde Valley: The Lower Verde Archaeological Project. SRI Press, Tucson.

1999   *Introduction and Results of Fieldwork.* Draft. Archaeological Investigations at the Julian Wash Site (AZ BB:13:17 ASM), Pima County, Arizona, vol. 1. Technical Report 99-27. Statistical Research, Tucson.

Whittlesey, Stephanie M., and Su Benaron
1998   Yavapai and Western Apache Ethnohistory and Material Culture. In *Overview, Synthesis, and Conclusions,* edited by S. M. Whittlesey, R. Ciolek-Torrello, and J. H. Altschul, pp. 143–183. Vanishing River: Landscapes and Lives of the Lower Verde Valley: The Lower Verde Archaeological Project. SRI Press, Tucson.

Whittlesey, Stephanie M., Richard S. Ciolek-Torello, and Matthew A. Sterner
1994   *Southern Arizona the Last 12,000 Years: A Cultural-Historic Overview for the Western Army National Guard Aviation Training Site.* Technical Series 48. Statistical Research, Tucson.

Wilcox, David R.
1979   Warfare Implications of Dry-Laid Masonry Walls on Tumamoc Hill. *The Kiva* 45:15–38.

1987   New Models of Social Structure at the Paloparado Site. In *The Hohokam Village: Site Structure and Organization,* edited by David E. Doyel, pp. 223–248. Southwestern and Rocky Mountain Division, American Association for the Advancement of Science, Glenwood Springs, Colorado.

Wilcox, David R., and Stephen M. Larson
1979   Introduction to the Tumamoc Hill Survey. *The Kiva* 45:1–14.

Wilcox, David R., Stephen Larson, W. Bruce Masse, Gayle H. Hartmann, and Alan Ferg
1979   A Summary of Conclusions and Recommendations of the Tumamoc Hill Survey. *The Kiva* 45:187–195.

Wilcox, David R., Thomas R. McGuire, and Charles Sternberg
1981   *Snaketown Revisited.* Archaeological Series No. 155. Cultural Resource Management Division, Arizona State Museum, University of Arizona, Tucson.

Wilder, Judith C.
1967   The Years of a Desert Laboratory. *Journal of Arizona History* 8:179–199.

Williams, Jack S.

    1982   The Casa de Elías: A Case Study in the Implications of Archaeological Remain [*sic*] for Ethnicity and Economics. 3 vols. Manuscript on file, Arizona Historical Society, Tucson.

    1986a San Agustín del Tucsón: A Vanished Mission Community of the Pimería Alta. *The Smoke Signal* 47–48:112–128.

    1986b A Plan for Mission Visita of San Agustín del Tucson City Historic Park. Manuscript on file, Statistical Research, Tucson. Submitted to the City of Tucson.

    1986c The Presidio of Santa Cruz de Terrenate: A Forgotten Fortress of Southern Arizona. *The Smoke Signal* 47–48:129–148.

    1988   Fortress Tucson: Architecture and the Art of War (1775–1856). *The Smoke Signal* 49–50:168–188.

    1989   *In the Shadow of Sentinel Peak: An Archaeological and Historical Survey.* On file, Arizona Historical Society, Tucson. Submitted to the Tucson–Pima County Historical Commission.

    1992   *Archaeological Investigations at the Captains' House at the Presidio of Tubac 1992.* Center for Spanish Colonial Archaeology, Mesa, Arizona.

Wilson, Eldred D.

    1949   *History of Mining in Pima County, Arizona.* 5th rev. ed. Tucson Chamber of Commerce, Tucson.

    1952   Arizona Gold Placers. In *Arizona Gold Placers and Placering,* 5th rev. ed., pp. 11–86. General Technology Series No. 45. Bulletin No. 160. Arizona Bureau of Mines, University of Arizona, Tucson.

Wilson, John P.

    1995   The Mining Frontier. In *Tearing Up the Ground with Splendid Results: Historic Mining on the Coronado National Forest,* by Mary M. Farrell, William B. Gillespie, James A. McDonald, Patricia M. Spoerl, and John P. Wilson, pp. 2–26. Heritage Resources Management Report No. 15. Southwestern Region, USDA Forest Service, Albuquerque.

Wilson, Marjorie

    1975   National Register of Historic Places Inventory-Nomination Form for the Solomon Warner House and Mill, Tucson, Arizona. On file, Arizona State Museum, University of Arizona, Tucson.

Wright, Barton A., and Rex E. Gerald

    1950   The Zanardelli Site: AZ BB:13:12. *The Kiva* 16:8–15.

Wyllys, Rufus K.

    1931   Padre Luís Velarde's Relación of Pimería Alta. 1716. *New Mexico Historical Review* 6(2):111–157.

Xia, Jingfeng
  2001   Foodways and Their Significance to Ethnic Integration: An Ethnoarchaeogical and Historical
          Archaeological Survey of the Chinese in Tucson. Unpublished Ph.D. dissertation, Depart-
          ment of Anthropology, University of Arizona, Tucson.

Yoder, Thomas D., Richard G. Holloway, Laural Myers, and Mark Slaughter
  1996   *Archaeological Testing Report for the Proposed Kino Stadium Pima County, Arizona.*
          Archaeological Report No. 96-170. SWCA, Tucson.

Yoder, Thomas D., Laural Myers, and Mark C. Slaughter
  1996   *Archaeological Testing Report for the Proposed Juvenile Courts, Pima County, Arizona.*
          Archaeological Report No. 96-171. SWCA, Tucson.

STATISTICAL RESEARCH, Inc., is committed to distributing the results of cultural resource management studies to a wide audience. Toward this goal, we maintain three publication series, designed to achieve different objectives and reach different readers.

SRI Press produces broad-interest volumes in archaeology, anthropology, history, and ethnography. These studies will appeal to professional archaeologists, avocational archaeologists, and general readers. Titles include:

- *Rivers of Rock: Stories from a Stone-Dry Land,* by Stephanie Whittlesey. 2003.

- *Islanders and Mainlanders: Prehistoric Context for the Southern California Bight,* edited by Jeffrey H. Altschul and Donn R. Grenda. 2002.

- *Sixty Years of Mogollon Archaeology: Papers from the Ninth Mogollon Conference, Silver City, New Mexico, 1996,* edited by Stephanie M. Whittlesey. 1999.

- *Vanishing River: Landscapes and Lives of the Lower Verde Valley.* CD (3 volumes) and book. 1998.

The SRI Technical Series presents the results of our most significant cultural resource management projects and is aimed toward a professional audience. A limited number of these reports are offset printed and perfect bound. Out-of-print volumes can be photocopied as requested. Readers of *San Xavier to San Agustín* will find the following studies of special interest:

- *Of Stones and Spirits: Pursuing the Past of Antelope Hill,* edited by Joan S. Schneider and Jeffrey H. Altschul (Technical Series 76, 2000). The results of nearly 10 years of research into the archaeology, ethnography, and history of a major milling implement quarry, rock-art complex, and sacred site in the lower Gila River valley.

- *El Macayo: A Prehistoric Settlement in the Upper Santa Cruz Valley,* edited by William L. Deaver and Carla Van West (Technical Series 74, 2001). The results of data recovery in a section of a prehistoric village located on the periphery of the Hohokam and Trincheras cultures.

- *From the Desert to the Mountains: Archaeology of the Transition Zone: The State Route 87–Sycamore Creek Project,* Vol. 1: *Prehistoric Sites,* edited by Rein Vanderpot, Eric Eugene Klucas, and Richard Ciolek-Torrello (Technical Series 73, 1999), and Vol. 2: *Analyses of Prehistoric Remains,* edited by Eric Eugene Klucas, Richard Ciolek-Torrello, and Rein Vanderpot (Technical Series 73, 2003).The results of archaeological investigations at 29 prehistoric sites in the Sycamore Creek valley and Mazatzal Mountains of central Arizona.

- *Pit House, Presidio, and Privy: 1,400 Years of Archaeology and History on Block 180, Tucson, Arizona,* edited by Richard Ciolek-Torrello and Mark T. Swanson (Technical Series 63, 1997). The results of intensive archaeological and historical research focused on a part of the original townsite of Tucson.

- *Investigations at Sunset Mesa Ruin: Archaeology at the Confluence of the Santa Cruz and Rillito Rivers, Tucson, Arizona,* edited by Richard Ciolek-Torrello, Edgar K. Huber, and Robert B. Neily (Technical Series 66, 1999). The results of excavations at a Hohokam settlement and late-nineteenth- century Mexican-American homestead at the confluence of the two major streams of the Tucson Basin.

- *The Forgotten Soldiers: Historical and Archaeological Investigations of the Apache Scouts at Fort Huachuca, Arizona,* by Rein Vanderpot and Teresita Majewski (Technical Series 71, 1998). The results of archival, oral-historical, and archaeological research into the lives of the Apache men who served with the U.S. Army in southeastern Arizona.

- *Prehistoric Painted Pottery of Southeastern Arizona,* by Robert A. Heckman, Barbara K. Montgomery, and Stephanie M. Whittlesey (Technical Series 77, 2000). An illustrated guide to the prehistoric ceramics of one of the most culturally diverse areas in the U.S. Southwest.

SRI's Technical Report series provides an outlet for all cultural resource management reports conducted under contract. These compliance reports can be photocopied as needed. The titles listed above, along with selected others, can be obtained from the University of Arizona Press at 355 S. Euclid, Suite 103, Tucson, AZ 85719, or (800) 426-3797 (outside Arizona) or (520) 621-5813. For a complete list of the three series, write to SRI at P.O. Box 31865, Tucson, AZ 85751-1865.